# ABLE
# SEAMEN

# ABLE
# SEAMEN

## The Lower Deck of the Royal Navy
## 1850–1939

### BRIAN LAVERY

WITHDRAWN

CONWAY

A Conway book

© Brian Lavery, 2011

First published in Great Britain
in 2011 by Conway,
an imprint of Anova Books Company Limited,
10 Southcombe Street,
London W14 0RA
www.anovabooks.com
www.conwaymaritime.com

British Library Cataloguing in Publication Data:
A catalogue record for this book is available from the British Library

ISBN 9781844861408

Anova Books Company Ltd is committed to respecting the intellectual
property rights of others. We have made all reasonable efforts to ensure
that the reproduction of all content on these pages is included with the
full consent of the copyright owners. If you are aware of any unintentional
omissions please contact the company directly so that any necessary
corrections may be made for future editions. Full details of all the books
can be found in the Bibliography.

Editing and design by DAG Publications Ltd
Printed by T. J. International Ltd., Cornwall

To receive regular email updates on forthcoming Conway titles,
email conway@anovabooks.com with Conway Update
in the subject field.

# CONTENTS

# MAPS AND DIAGRAMS
## IN THE TEXT

# INTRODUCTION

The lower deck seaman, the ordinary sailor of the Royal Navy, has not had his share of attention over the years. Governments have often taken his loyalty for granted, and his pay and conditions have tended to lag behind. Social historians have devoted far more attention to the working class ashore. Traditional naval history has tended to ignore the 'common seaman' unless there is a serious problem with mutiny, indiscipline or recruitment. There have been some important works covering the ordinary sailor in the first half of the twentieth century, notably *The Lower Deck of the Royal Navy* by Anthony Carew and *Sober Men and True* by Christopher McKee. But much of the period from 1850 to the present is a clean sheet as far as the historian is concerned – much more so than the period before 1815, when the works of historians such as Nicholas Rodger, for example, have said a great deal about the lower deck.

It has been said that 'Nine English traditions out of ten date from the latter half of the nineteenth century.'[1] This is as true of the navy as anything else. Lower deck uniform is the most obvious: it was established in 1857 and its essential features – square collar and bell bottoms – are still used today in most of the world's navies, a legacy of British sea power. It was only in 1864 that the white ensign became the established flag of the Royal Navy, and it was during the reign of Queen Victoria that it became common for women to launch ships. It was during this period that sails were abandoned and sailors got used to living in iron and steel ships. For the lower deck, the idea of 'continuous service' (rather than being recruited to a ship for a single voyage) became standard in 1853. The well-known ratings of chief petty officer and leading seaman were established at the same time, and the skilled technician, the artificer, came in a few years later. The lower deck has seen many changes since then, but its traditions and its basic rating structure remain the same.

This is the second part of a three-volume work. I have tried to make it unnecessary to read the first volume, *Royal Tars*, to follow this one, though anyone seeking further information might do so. The definition of the lower deck that I used then was 'a group of men (and later women) who perform the essential tasks of any navy with little expectation of promotion to the higher ranks. This does not exclude the possibility of a minority of its members rising to officer status, but it does not include cadets and midshipmen, who are recruited in the belief that they will eventually be commissioned.' There is no reason to change this, except that the expectations of a commission from the lower deck have greatly improved in the last few decades. It is no longer true that the ordinary sailors live on a different deck from the officers, but the term 'lower deck' is still used and is still valid – it is the 'Collective term for all non-commissioned members of the Royal Navy, i.e., everyone who is not actually commissioned as an officer.'[2]

As I said in the previous work, 'The concept of the lower deck demands several preconditions'. A permanent navy offering more or less permanent employment can be taken for granted today. Specialised warships are certainly the norm, so large-scale state funding is needed to create and maintain them rather than hire or requisition them in an emergency (even if merchant ships were still needed in warfare as recently as the Falklands and Gulf Wars). And the concept requires a degree of distinction (not necessary by class), in which the officers are segregated from the men – which is true in practically all armed forces in the world, even revolutionary ones. Of course, the distinction is far less today than it was in Victorian times – future officers and future ratings might well go to school together, and promotion prospects to commissioned rank are good. One can still speculate about the future, whether electronics will ever 'take over all the tasks that do not need decision making at officer level and the lower deck will become obsolete – though so far developments in electronics have not nearly gone far enough for that. Until that happens, every navy needs its lower deck.' But in fact the trend seems to be going in the opposite direction. Conflicts against organised naval powers could perhaps be fought by radar, sonar, computers and guided missiles. Campaigns against terrorism and piracy are likely to rely more on human vigilance, cunning and bravery.

Officers (and some historians) have often assumed that sailors fight well because of loyalty to their leaders. Of course, there is much truth in this, and they will certainly be inspired by good leadership. But it is not the whole story. Sailors have at least as much loyalty to their messmates, their ship, the navy as a whole and their country. They do not necessarily cheer on their side at a football match, for example, because they love their officers. Likewise, in battle their courage is inspired by patriotism or group loyalty, or by the respect of the population.

As in the previous volume, I have not dealt with the Royal Marines in any detail, but only as they affect the rest of the lower deck. I have been rather cursory in the story of the Women's Royal Naval Service, as its members were not truly of the lower deck, for reasons of class and service, until near the end of the twentieth century.

I acknowledge the help of numerous friends and colleagues (often unwittingly) over the years. These include the late David Lyon, David Syrett, Dave Topliss, Alan Pearsall and Colin White. Former colleagues include Roger Knight, Robert Blyth, Simon Stephens and Rina Prentice of the National Maritime Museum; Jenny Wraight and Iain Mackenzie of the Naval Historical Library, and Campbell MacMurray of the Royal Naval Museum. Academics include Eric Grove of Salford, Nicholas Rodger of All Souls Oxford, Andrew Lambert of King's College London, Pat Crimmin of Royal Holloway College and many more.

Former members of the lower deck I have spoken to include Rear Admiral Roy Clare, Peter Goodwin of HMS *Victory*, David Taylor of the National Maritime Museum and Len Barnett.

Most of the material in this volume is from manuscripts in the National Archives, supplemented by others in the British Library and National Maritime Museum; thanks are due to the staffs of these institutions. For printed books I have mostly used the British Library and the National Maritime Museum, and especially the London Library, with its huge range of books available for borrowing.

# I

# THE BEGINNING OF CHANGE
# 1850–1856

By the 1850s, Britain was very different from the country that had maintained a great fleet of a thousand ships and 140,000 men during almost constant wars against Revolutionary and Napoleonic France from 1793 to 1815. Famine had at last disappeared after the horrific events in Ireland in the previous decade. The growing pains of industrialisation were over, but Britain was still the only real industrial power in the world. Revolutionary ideas had declined rapidly since the defeat of the Chartist movement in 1848. Queen Victoria and her husband Albert were seen as constituting a model of family life, in contrast to the dissolute affairs of their Hanoverian predecessors. Religion was strong and not yet threatened by the ideas of Darwin. The penny post was taken for granted as a means of communication, while literacy was gradually increasing. The idea of 'progress' was beginning to take hold and offered a better future. Police forces had been set up in most parts of the country and were beginning to reduce crime, while free trade opened Britain to the rest of the world. The railway age had truly begun – the amount of mileage had quadrupled since 1840, with more than a thousand miles opened between 1848 and 1850 alone. All the major cities were now linked by rail and also by the electric telegraph, which could send a message across the country in seconds. The growing middle class was more powerful and confident, while the Great Exhibition of 1851 showed a nation and empire at the peak of its strength. On the surface at least, it was a rational, ordered world in which almost anything seemed possible.

All this was protected by the Royal Navy, which was inclined to live in its past glories as far as social affairs were concerned. In theory it still relied on barbaric practices such as the flogging round the fleet and the press gang, even if this was in abeyance since 1815. Contrary to popular myth, it was not aimed at the general population, but the crown claimed the right to force professional seamen to enter the naval service, and it had often used brutal methods to do so. In 1852 Sir Thomas Byam Martin, an admiral of the old school who had memories of the mobilisations of the 1780s and '90s, had no doubts: 'The power of impressments must unquestionably be maintained, and I fear must be resorted to in any sudden emergency.'[1] This was very different from what Captain Denman of the Royal Navy believed:

> The moment press-warrants were issued, the slumbering recollections of the last war would spring into a dangerous activity. Many still live who endured the rigour of the system; thousands, as the children and relatives of pressed men, witnessed the misery it so widely spread. The necessary difficulties created by the withdrawal of many thousand seamen from their ordinary employment would be aggravated by the horror of impressment, which has, in all times, driven away our seamen to foreign lands and into other employment, when most required, and has also prevented enterprising young landsmen from coming forward to offer their services. To become a seaman was, in fact, to forfeit all the rights of an Englishman.[2]

There were more specific naval problems too. The navy had always relied on the merchant service to train the majority of its men in seamanship, taking them in as volunteers or pressed men when there was a threat of war. The new economic ideology was based on free trade. The Navigation Acts, which demanded that British trade be carried in British ships with British crews, were finally repealed in 1849. Merchant ships were no longer obliged to take on apprentices and were able to recruit foreigners freely, so the merchant marine as a 'nursery for seamen' for the Royal Navy was likely to dry up. At the same time, many British seamen were being attracted into the American service, both the merchant marine and the United States Navy, which, it was claimed, still recruited most of its crews from Britons. Many more had been lured by the gold rushes in California and Australia, either as well-paid crew in the ships going there, or to look for gold on their own account.

There had been some moderate reforms in the navy since the end of the great wars in 1815. In 1830 the old ship of the line *Excellent* became the first real training ship, teaching the seamen the skills of gunnery, which they were not likely to learn in the merchant service. In 1835 a registry of seamen was set up with a view to replacing the press gang with a more regular system of conscription, while the five-year term was introduced instead of the single-ship commission. And the training of boys was introduced aboard old ships at Cork and Plymouth. By an act of 1847 they had to serve for at least seven years in the navy, like apprentices in civil life.

## Ships and Men

In 1850, the thirteenth year of Queen Victoria's long reign, the navy had 71 sailing ships of the line, 67 sailing frigates, 103 smaller sailing ships and 76 that were fitted with steam power to some extent, including paddle frigates and half a dozen ships of the line with the new-fangled screw propeller. All were built in wood and armed with smooth-bore, breech-loading guns firing through gunports in their sides. They were still divided into traditional categories. Ships of the line had two or three full decks of guns and were used as the main force against an enemy battlefleet. A frigate had a single deck and was used for reconnaissance, convoy escort and numerous other tasks. Smaller vessels included sloops and gunboats. The paddle frigates had very low gun-power, as their decks were interrupted by the paddles. The screw ship of the line had more or less the traditional format with the engine added below decks and reduced gun-power. Their range under steam was very short, and they were regarded mostly as coast-defence floating batteries, while the pure sailers would do the real work of seeking out and fighting an enemy fleet anywhere in the world.

The Navy was authorized to have 38,500 officers and men, but only 33,000 of these were borne on the books of ships, and less than 29,000 were actually mustered. Its senior officers included Thomas Bladen Capel, who had brought home the news of Nelson's victory at the Nile in 1798 and was now commander-in-chief at Portsmouth; and the maverick hero Thomas Cochrane, Earl of Dundonald, who had been reinstated after dismissal and imprisonment for an alleged Stock Exchange fraud and was

now in charge in the West Indies. Greenwich Hospital, on the banks of the Thames, was full of retired seamen who could earn extra money by reminiscing about the great battles of Nelson, tales that were no doubt improved and embellished with the telling.

The navy was not nearly as backward as popular legend suggests in embracing steam power, but socially it was a very conservative organization. While the middle class was rising elsewhere in society, it was being squeezed out of the navy, as the limited number of peacetime officers' appointments was increasingly reserved for aristocratic and upper middle class candidates. As a corollary, it was now practically impossible for a common seaman (known as a rating) to rise to become a commissioned officer. The best he could hope for was to become a warrant officer, a gunner, carpenter or boatswain, where he was offered secure employment but no chance to rise beyond the specialization of his craft, and no say in the higher affairs of the navy. The ratings, on the other hand, had no job security at all, in common with the great majority of merchant seamen of the day. Attempts to make them sign on for a fixed period of five years had largely failed, and a man was likely to serve in a single ship for a single commission of perhaps three years. The navy was only just beginning to train its own seamen systematically from the beginning, and most of them had learned the trade as boys in the merchant service. There was no regular uniform, though an individual captain might try to impose one on his own ship.

On board ship, the seaman slept in a hammock on the main deck or decks, often sharing the space with the big guns. At mealtimes he set up a table between a pair of guns and ate with his mess, the centre of his social life. He worked hard when climbing the rigging or exercising the guns, but there were long periods when there was very little to do. He was proud of his skills with rope and in the rigging, and of his fearless courage. His life was precarious, and he tended to live for the moment. On board, he might be promoted to petty officer, a term that tended to mean the holder of a particular office, such as boatswain's mate or quarter gunner, rather than a permanent rank. If he fell out of favour with the captain, or moved to another ship, he was likely to lose his rating and the pay that went with it. If he

committed a crime, even a minor one such as drunkenness or negligence, he was liable to be flogged at the gangway. The incidence of flogging varied very much with the policy of the captain, and it matched the style of punishment often used ashore, though civil society was moving towards imprisonment rather than physical punishment as a means of correction.

## RECRUITING

The navy had no systematic recruiting policy. It still relied largely on the old-fashioned tavern, optimistically known as a 'rendezvous' for recruiting its men. The most famous one was the pub run by Mrs Louisa Wafer on the Hard at Portsmouth. It was claimed that she 'kept a respectable house' and had recruited 26,572 men in the twelve years up to 1858. But in general the recruiting service was not popular. 'At present the officers are mixed up frequently with the worst characters in the seaport towns, and they are obliged to sit there all day endeavoring to attract men to this place by music and other means to obtain their services ...'[3] H. Y. Moffat was recruited in another traditional way, by joining an individual ship when HMS *Pembroke* visited Leith in 1857. Though he was only 12½, he forged his mother's signature and pretended to be 14:

> He took me to the Pembroke, and on arriving at the top of the gangway ladder, he said to the master-at-arms:–
>
> 'A boy come to join.'
>
> The master-at-arms took out his note-book in which he jotted down my answers to various questions he put to me, such as: what was my name and age, where did I live, and had I my parents' consent ...
>
> The master-at-arms then read out my former answers from his note-book, and the Lieutenant said, 'All right, take him down to the doctor.'
>
> I stripped, was examined and passed in a few minutes, the master-at-arms then taking me to the officer where a young clerk asked me the same questions as before. I was then enrolled as a second-class boy in the British Navy.[4]

## TRAINING SHIPS

The new training ships for boys and novices were beginning to have some success. The flagship at Portsmouth, Nelson's famous *Victory* and her

tender, the brig *Rolla*, had begun to train apprentices in 1849. Each boy stayed on the ship for about twelve months, and in an average year 195 were sent to the navy. The 98-gun *Impregnable* of 1810 was the flagship at Plymouth and was also used for boys. Those trained in this way were well regarded in the fleet. Later Boatswain William Smith reported of the boys generally,

> In the last ship I was in, the 'Superb', when she was in commission, we had boys come on board as apprentices, and they were paid off as able seamen; then they joined a sloop-of-war, with Captain Hamilton, in the 'Vestal'; he was an old shipmate of mine, and he asked me if I could recommend these ship lads for his work, and he gave them second-class petty officers' ratings, and they turned out very smart lads.[5]

By 1852 it was becoming recognized that separate training ships were needed, as the guardships and flagships had too many other things to do.

> Flag-ships are the receptacle for all deserters, stragglers, thieves, &s., in short, of men of the worst character from other ships; and the boys, with every precaution taken to prevent it, must be more or less thrown amongst them; at any rate they are aware of their presence, and by degrees become familiar with offences and language which, at their early age, must be injurious to them.[6]

The old 74-gun *Illustrious* of 1803 was set up as a static training ship for novices at Portsmouth in January 1854, with the brig *Sealark* to give more practical experience. Initially it had 150 men and 150 boys, increased to 250 each in August. It was soon sending 259 ordinary seamen second class to the navy annually, and 195 boys. A young man by the name of John Hodgkinson presented himself on board *Illustrious* in 1855, having 'devoured Robinson Crusoe and not a few books of travel and wild adventure', and eventually a lieutenant asked him if he could read.

> Most certainly I could. 'Well then, look at that,' and he handed me a bill, pasted on a board, stating the advantages of serving one's country in the Royal Navy, scale of wages, provisions, and a list of necessary clothing. I

read the bill, and gave it back, telling him I fully understood it: 'Then you'll enter for ten years' continuous service, will you?'

'Yes, sir,' I unhesitatingly answered.[7]

Not all the boys were well fed when they first arrived on board, and Captain Arthur Lowe of *Impregnable* commented, 'generally speaking, they have only been half fed up to that time, and quickly pick up weight with our regularity of meals and better quality of provisions.'[8]

For John Hodgkinson's First Instruction he had three days of learning knots and hitches – 'The knots were mostly simple and easy, but now and then I got treated as a "muff" by blundering into a difficulty were [sic] none existed.' This was followed by the Second Instruction in rowing – 'The first thing necessary was to pull together, and very trying it was for those who could do so to suffer for those who couldn't or wouldn't …' During this he was issued with his clothing, comprising a pair of blue trousers, two pairs of white duck trousers, two blue serge and two white frocks, two white jumpers, two pairs of stockings, three flannels, two caps, a knife and a type (stamp) to mark his name on them. He was offered sixpence for his old clothes, but he believed they were worth much more – he gave them away in the end. For the Third Instruction he learned cutlass and small-arms drill in a party of twenty under an old marine called John Clement. In small-arms drill, 'We were taught how to use the weapon; the platoon and various exercises, and, finally, to fire, which operation most of us liked; albeit, some made very poor marksmen, others fired with great accuracy, and a third lot were so timid that, failing to pull the trigger vigorously, the piece hung fire, and they looked sheepish …' Fourth Instruction was on the big guns, under Gunner's Mate John Carter. Like most seamen, Hodgkinson enjoyed the comradeship and effort involved in this. For the Fifth Instruction he returned to ropework but far more advanced this time, and under the boatswain, 'an officer of the old school.' They learned the Matthew Walker, the Turk's Head and numerous splices. Then, using a model, he was taught the uses of the different ropes of the ship. Finally he learned the lead-line for finding the depth of water and the points of the compass.[9]

After six months in *Illustrious* he joined the training brig *Sealark*, where he found going aloft in the rigging without shoes was 'a heavy trial'. He was not affected by seasickness like many of his fellows, who 'would lay on the deck and there remain, in spite of kicks and cuffs liberally bestowed by the boatswain's mate'. During three months on board he cruised to Cowes, Weymouth, Lyme Regis, Plymouth and across the Channel. He passed well, and at the end he was offered the choice of drafting to the 94-gun *Cressy* or the steam frigate *Highflyer*. He chose the latter.[10]

## CONTINUOUS SERVICE

In 1852 a committee of naval officers sat to consider the manning of the navy, and this recommended a radical reform of the seamen's conditions of service. It was generally agreed that the five-year term as established in 1835 was not working. With few ships in service in home waters, a ship was usually commissioned for three or three-and-a-half years abroad and then returned home. The remaining part of the man's five years was not long enough to fit in another commission, there were no real facilities for him in port except the gunnery ships, and it would be awkward to have to discharge him in foreign parts, so he was often released, just as he would have been in the old days. Naval officers lamented that so many men were lost to the service after they had reached a peak in their training. 'With such a heterogeneous crew, the first year is employed in teaching them habits of cleanliness and common decency; and it is only in the third year of their service that the ship becomes really efficient. Just as that point had been reached, all hands ... are turned off, to make room for another experiment.'[11] They were eligible to re-enter, but out of 406 petty officers and 1,335 seamen paid off during three months of 1852, only 351 did so.[12]

The committee found out various things about the seamen's attitudes to the navy. Seaman-rigger George Cavendish told them that, 'Merchant seamen think little about the navy till they are in distress, and can get nothing better; entering as a last resource.' When asked why men failed to re-enter after a voyage, he replied, 'Men like a change. They go on a trip in merchant employ to the West Indies, or somewhere, and then return to the navy; others go away altogether.'[13] This was confirmed by Captain

Denman, who wrote: 'seamen love change; and for many years, at the end of a voyage, they have always been sure of fresh employment.'[14]

Nevertheless, the committee recommended that ten years should gradually be established as the normal period for enlistment in the navy in order to give it a more permanent character, 'both as a means of increasing its efficiency and discipline, and of substantially promoting the welfare and comfort of the petty officers and seamen of the fleet'. According to the circular of June 1853, which established continuous service,

> My Lords are desirous that the change in the existing system should be accomplished wholly by voluntary means. Seamen are therefore to be permitted, as at present, to enter for the customary period of service, and for particular ships; but by the future entry of boys for longer terms of continuous and general service, and by holding out the inducement of increased pay and other advantages, to men who volunteer to serve under the new system, their Lordships contemplate that a gradual and beneficial change will be introduced in the present mode of manning Her Majesty's Ships.[15]

Boys, then were to sign on for ten years' service after the age of eighteen rather than the seven-year apprenticeship. They could buy themselves out if they did not like it, at a cost of £8 with less than three years service, £10 between three and five years, and £12 after five years. Hodgkinson did so in 1861, after much delay.

> I went away in one of the ship's boats to the dockyard, walked up to the office and presented my paper, and was told to call after ten days, when my discharge would most likely be down. So at the end of that time I went again, but nothing had come; I waited a week, and went again, but nothing had come. I waited another week, went once more to Woolwich, and was at last told the discharge had come. But as I had served only five of the ten years agreed on, I had to pay *l*21.16*s*. [£12.80] for the bit of parchment … However, with a light heart, and a pocket equally light, I stepped out of the office a free man, and no longer a servant of the Queen.[16]

The advantages of transferring to a continuous service engagement were to be explained to boys and men already in the service. New adult recruits for continuous service would enjoy increased pay and be given preference for promotion and for courses on the gunnery ships. After a slow start, these would become the standard terms of lower deck service for more than a century.

There were other changes in the order of June 1853. The old rating of Landsman, for an inexperienced adult, was considered too close to that of ordinary seaman second class, and was abolished. Seamen were to be allowed to arrange exchanges between ships, and men were to be given 'every facility' to help them get home after being paid off, though only if a ship was going that way anyway, and without any expense to the service.

## RESERVES

Continuous service and the recruitment of boys did nothing to solve the immediate problem of mobilizing a greatly expanded navy at the start of a war if the press gang were no longer practicable. The Registry of Seamen, also set up in 1835, was not working either, and Rear Admiral Berkeley testified,

> At first, I was taken in by the theory. In practice I believe it to have totally failed, and that at present it is money thrown away. There is nothing to be said in its favour. It neither detects desertion to any minute extent, nor can it be available for any practical purpose. If the holding of a ticket conferred any benefit on the man, it might, but not without difficulty, be turned to some account.[17]

The idea of selecting seamen by a 'ballot', or drawing lots, as was done for land service with the militia, was considered but dismissed most effectively by Admiral Byam Martin:

> Ballot implies a numerous class of persons, upon whom the chance of the ballot is to act; but the seamen of the country are but a small class compared with the whole population, and in time of war every seaman belonging to the nation is required, and more too, if they could be had. If, then, all the registered seamen be required, a ballot is out of the question.
>
> But suppose the scheme to be persisted in, I presume the registry, like a muster-book, records the names of the men, and probably many fanciful particulars as to where they are to be found at short notice. Well, upon the

commencement of an armament, the book is to be opened for ballot, and A.B.C. and the whole alphabet are to be called over, but scarcely any are forthcoming; they are all in the East Indies, the Pacific, at the gold-diggings, and worst of all, nearly all the ships-of-war of the United States are manned with British seamen.[18]

The 1852 report suggested the building up of three main reserves, each with its strengths and weaknesses. The Coastguard Service had many duties, including recruitment to the navy and rescue, but its main one was to aid the Customs service in preventing smuggling. Since 1845 it had been recruited from men who had completed at least seven years' service in the navy. They were liable to recall in the event of mobilization, though it was not clear if the agreement was legally binding. They lived on shore, or close to it in ex-naval guardships round the main ports, or in revenue cruisers. Most of them still spent a good deal of time afloat, and nearly half of them were trained in the great guns. When a group went on board HMS *Cyclops* in 1848, Captain Hastings found them to be very efficient and cheerful.

The Coastguard had a total of 5,691 men in 1852, including 4,208 who were under 50 years of age, and 1,522 who had agreed to recall into the navy. But they did not cover the whole country, as the east and north were largely exposed. Smuggling had declined with the coming of free trade, and the force had been cut, but now tobacco smuggling was clearly on the increase. It was decided to increase the force by up to 2,000 men to fill these gaps and at their same time strengthen their value as a naval reserve, partly by transferring control from the Customs to the Admiralty. This would encourage recruiting to the navy, as men could hope to make the transfer to the Coastguard, while married men already in the service might prefer service nearer home. It would create a reserve of experienced men, though limited in numbers. On the other hand, there was the difficulty of what would happen in wartime if so many coastguards were withdrawn and smuggling got out of hand.

The next reserve was to be found among the seamen-riggers of the Royal Dockyards, ex-naval men employed for fitting out ships for sea. Their duties were:

Fitting and refitting rigging and sails for ships and for store, examining, repairing, and relaying moorings, transporting and navigating ships, stowing and restowing mooring-chains, anchors, tanks, iron ballast &c., assisting in docking and undocking ships, and putting them in and out of the basin &c.[19]

They were a useful class of men, but their numbers were small: only 357 were enrolled out of an establishment of 475.[20]

Finally, the Royal Naval Coast Volunteers were set up by recruiting sailors who were not likely to stray too far from home, such as fishermen and ferrymen. According to regulations issued in 1856, these were aged between 18 and 35, or up to 45 if they had naval experience. Each man would be interviewed by an officer and given a ten-shilling bounty if successful. They would be called out for occasional training by means of the Coastguard. They would not be expected to serve more than 100 leagues or 600 miles from home, which made them available for service in the English Channel or North Sea but not the Mediterranean or Baltic, where major fleets often operated.[21]

Obviously a reserve force was no use without ships to put the men in, and a new 'steam ordinary' was set up, with men permanently on board each ship to ensure a degree of readiness. They were classed in four groups. A ship of the first division was constantly tested and 'kept in a state of perfect readiness for the reception of her officers and men'; a ship of the line had a crew of a master, the usual three warrant officers, two engineers, four stokers, three shipkeepers for maintenance purposes and five boys. For a ship in the second division, the masts, guns and equipment were not on board but kept ready in store. In the third division, the hulls were complete, but the rigging had not yet been cut out; in the fourth, many of the internal fittings such as coal bunker and magazines were not fully fitted to allow the air to circulate. A ship of the line in that condition had a warrant officer, an engineer, two stokers, three shipkeepers and three boys.[22]

## THE LEADING SEAMAN AND CHIEF PETTY OFFICER

The 1852 Committee also recommended two new ratings, which were to become very important in naval life. For some time there had been concern that the rating of able seamen was being diluted by men who were not properly qualified. The Committee suggested a rating of Leading Seaman, and this was confirmed by an Admiralty circular of April 1853. It was offered 'as an inducement to seamen to render themselves proficient in all branches of their duty'. The term 'leading' was used in the dictionary sense of 'a directing influence or guidance', for the leading seaman was not expected to have any authority to give orders to the crew, in the way that a petty officer did. Instead they were to be 'thorough helms-men and leads-men, able to assist in repairing sails, and who are practical riggers, capable of doing duty as such in any part of the ship'. Each candidate was to be examined by the commander of his ship, a senior lieutenant, the master and the boatswain. As a badge he was allowed the single anchor of the petty officer second class but without the crown above it, and he was given 2*d* per day extra pay, which might also be combined with gunnery pay. Each ship was allowed a certain complement of leading seamen, which perhaps undermined the aim of rewarding skills. A large first rate had 60, a frigate had 8–15 and a small sloop or gun brig had 2.[23]

At the top of the ratings' tree, the chief petty officer was added as an encouragement to experienced petty officers. Ten different types were established in 1853, but only five of them were seamen, and they were only to be found on third rates and above – the chief gunner's mate, chief boatswain's mate, chief captain of the forecastle, chief quartermaster and admiral's coxswain, who was of course only to be found in a flagship. Non-seamen were the master-at-arms, schoolmaster, steward and cook. For a badge, the chiefs used another variation of the anchor motif, a single one enclosed in a laurel wreath and surmounted by a crown. When uniform was introduced later in the decade, the seaman chief petty officer wore the standard bell-bottoms and square collar.[24]

## THE DECLINE OF THE WARRANT OFFICER

In the wars with France it had been possible, though far from common, for a lower-deck seaman to rise to commissioned rank. This route was now closed, and only an Order in Council could elevate a man in this way. As the *United Services Magazine* claimed with some exaggeration,

In the latter half of the nineteenth century, the Royal Navy of England is the only trade or profession in which a man, entering from the ranks of the people, is precluded from promotion. The son of a small farmer or tradesman can by good conduct, ability, and industry, attain the position of a bishop, or a judge, or a law lord. In the army, a man enlisting, entering the ranks as a private, may – if fortune favour him – rise to be a General Officer. But a man entering the Royal Navy, 'before the mast', is doomed to a hopeless situation. The highest rank he may reasonably look for, as the reward of long, gallant and meritorious service, with the most exemplary conduct, is that of Boatswain, alias chief flogger.[25]

This should have made the prospect of warrant rank all the more important to the lower deck, but it was far less attractive than it might have been. Originally the term had included a wide range of people and jobs, from the physician of the fleet to the cook of a sixth rate. The old wardroom warrant officers – the master, purser and surgeon – had been appointed by commission since 1843. The lower grades of warrant officers such as cooks and artisans were now regarded as ratings. This left the traditional standing officers of boatswain, gunner and carpenter as well as the new grade of engineer, but they faced threats to their status. The withdrawal of widow's pensions in 1830 was still felt very keenly and was regarded as insult to their integrity and that of their wives. Even worse, from 1844 they were under the authority of young naval cadets and they complained, 'Their present position prevents them from doing their duty with alacrity and dispatch, by the frequent interference of young and inexperienced officers, and a want of respect from petty officers and seamen.' According to William Smith,

> when as boatswain of a ship I had to attend in getting the cock-pit hammocks up, and I have been told by the young gentlemen when I have said I would lower them down if they did not get up, that they were my superior officers. I have been told so … when they have been doing duty as mates of the forecastle; if I have hailed the top or the foreyard, I have been told by the midshipman, that he was the officer of the forecastle.[26]

The warrant officers' informal leader, the highly articulate Gunner Thomas Howels, complained that the amount of work had increased with the size of ships and that he had to pay for an expensive uniform. His colleague, Boatswain Smith of Pembroke Yard, knew many men who refused to 'take the warrant', or only did so after much persuasion, such as a former petty officer in *Winchester*, who initially 'refused on account of the pay being too small'.[27] As a result, the ambitious lower-deck seaman had little to expect from naval service.

## THE HULKS

One problem with keeping a reserve of seamen in the home ports was where to accommodate them. Even after continuous service became normal, the navy built very few shore barracks for men between voyages, and the great majority lived in hulks. Rear-Admiral George Elliot was concerned about the new recruit with little or no money and testified,

> if he had a barrack on shore he could go to the pump and wash himself; and go out and come back again in an hour or two; he would have smoked his pipe and refreshed himself, and come back to his bed without trouble and without expense; but in the hulk he must go on shore, and in large ships' crews there are not the means of sending him on shore in a boat; for instance, in bad weather, it may be blowing hard and raining, and he cannot get on shore without expense, and he cannot get off at night without expense; he has no money, and therefore he must stop on shore, and that stopping on shore costs him money, and it generally ends by his selling his clothes, and getting more into debt, and the inducement to get money to go on shore leads to constant theft on board the hulk, and the hulk is not a place where thefts can be easily discovered from their constant communication [sic] with the shore and the cramped-up space.[28]

The *United Services Magazine* asked,

> Let our naval readers recal [sic] to mind their first introduction to a hulk. The black dirty decks, pitched sides, foul smells, slovenly aspect, which presented themselves on first entering. The neatness and regularity of a sea going ship strikes everyone with admiration; while the hulk bring to the recollection of everything which is sickening and disgusting.[29]

Sir Charles Napier stated with characteristic venom, 'As for the hulks, I would burn the whole of them; they are a nuisance; they fill up the harbours; they are nothing but a curse, and the men hate and detest them.'[30]

The problem had been particularly bad at Sheerness, where shore accommodation was very poor, and even civilian dockyard workers lived in hulks. The climate was very unhealthy among the marshlands, making malaria very common, and the voyage to and from ships in the exposed anchorage at the Nore was very difficult in bad weather. According to Captain Boyd,

> I have seen the men come on board in the winter through the ice drift famished with cold and wet, and with no dry clothes to shift. So often, in fact, are working parties weather-bound on shore at that port, it is customary to keep a cask of beef or pork at the yard, an order that, should the parties fail to get off at noon, there be some semblance of a meal issued to them.[31]

A storehouse was converted into a barracks, and Boyd noted the improvement:

> The men were as comfortable as need be, and the officers also. The officer has a hold over the men that he has not in a hulk. There, no shore boats come alongside after the officers are gone to their dinner to entice the men. When the work and supper are over, the liberty men are mustered and marched out of the dockyard, and you receive them in the same manner in the morning. It is not possible for the men to escape during the night, and a system of discipline is established that cannot be realized in a hulk.[32]

There were suggestions to improve the hulks in other ports. They would be far more convenient if they were tied up alongside rather than moored out in the harbour, but there was a great shortage of space in the dockyards before the expansion programme of the 1860s – in the 1850s there were only 34 acres of wet-dock space in all the British dockyards, compared with 180 acres in France.[33] Another possibility was to upgrade the facilities of the hulks, as was done with *Bellerophon* at Portsmouth in 1856.

Not everyone agreed about the alternatives. Captain Howlett claimed, 'there is a great disadvantage in putting the men in barracks. Seamen very soon get into what is called long shore habits. They put on their frock coats, and black hats, and lose the character of seamen entirely.'[34]As a result, a Royal Commission of 1858 took the easier and cheaper line: it recommended the improvement of existing hulks on the model of *Bellerophon*, and the question of building barracks was shelved for the moment.[35]

## GUNNERY

HMS *Excellent*, an old 74-gun ship, was set up as a training ship in Portsmouth Harbour in 1830 with a view to 'establishing a permanent corps of seamen to act as Captains of Guns, as well as a Depot for the instruction of the officers and seamen of His Majesty's Navy in the theory and practice of Naval Gunnery, at which a uniform system shall be observed and communicated throughout the navy'.[36] It introduced the ideas of harbour-based training, standard principles throughout the fleet, more permanent ratings who would sign on for several years and return to a depot, and increased pay for long service and skill. By 1852 *Excellent* and her tender, *Edinburgh*, were turning out around 600 petty officers and able seamen per year as seaman-gunners. Many of them came to regard *Excellent* as their 'home' in the navy, where they would return at the end of a seagoing commission, as an alternative to the degrading and aimless life in the other hulks.[37]

In 1852, a gunner first class was usually a petty officer, 'An intelligent, painstaking man, with a "very good" character, who can write and cipher well, and is thoroughly fit for an instructor'. He was expected to produce an illustrated copy-book based on the instructions to gunners. A seaman-gunner second class was similar but slightly less well qualified and suitable for a gunner's mate. The third class consisted of 'Heavy, dull men, or idlers, who are only fit for captains of guns, and not good instructors; these are not qualified for gunner's mates'.[38]

The Manning Committee of 1852 recognized that the seaman-gunner was increasingly important but found that the places in *Excellent* were not all taken up. It proposed two main classes. In the higher one the man should

29

be capable of rising to gunner's mate or gunner and would be paid 2*d* extra per day. The others would be 'required to pass through a course of instruction in training as to render them capable of teaching a gun's crew', with 1*d* per day. There were to be 25 seamen gunners in a first-rate ship of the line, down to three in a sloop and two in a gun-brig or schooner.[39] In November 1854, captains were ordered that selected men were to be 'encouraged to volunteer for this Service', and on foreign stations they were to be trained on board as acting seamen gunners until they came home to do a course in *Excellent*.[40] To increase the supply, *Cambridge* was opened as a gunnery ship at Devonport in 1856, but that was not enough, and in 1859 the extra pay of gunners first class was increased to 4*d* per day, of gunners second class to 2*d*. In 1860 the category of trained man was recognized – a man of the first class was at least an ordinary seaman and was allowed 1*d* extra per day, while gunnery instructors on board ship were to be given 6*d* per day.

## THE CRIMEAN WAR

The carefully laid plans of 1852 were interrupted by the outbreak of war two years later. The so-called 'Crimean War' was an unusual one by any standards. Practically all British wars over the centuries (apart from internal conflicts) were fought against the near neighbours of Spain, France, Germany or the Netherlands, or in the far-flung empire. This one was fought in alliance with France and against Russia. Even its name was inaccurate, for it had started over a trivial dispute about the Holy Places in Jerusalem, followed by a campaign in the Black Sea with the support of Turkey, and another in the Baltic. It was only later that attention was centred on the attack on the Crimea and the naval base at Sebastopol. Though it was a war against a European power, there was never the slightest prospect that the homeland or any British territory might be invaded. Defeat would have been humiliating for the western allies and would have increased Russian confidence in an expansion towards the Mediterranean, but it would not have been catastrophic.

All this was becoming clear as the navy mobilized for war in 1854. With no threat of invasion, it would have been even more difficult than usual to enforce the press gang, and as a matter of economy no bounties were offered to seamen. Under the Act of 1835 that would have involved giving equal money to the seamen already in the navy, which would have cost a million pounds more. Instead the Admiralty relied on patriotic feeling, which was certainly strong enough in the country at large, though not necessarily among merchant seamen.

There was already a substantial Mediterranean Fleet, which would cooperate with the French navy and the British, French and Turkish armies, but a Baltic Fleet was needed to attack Russia on another front, and it had to be built up from scratch. This was the greatest problem with manning. The Coastguard men were called up, but according to Captain Byam Martin, they were 'mostly old, worn-out men'. Later he reported, 'It is a melancholy thing to see the poor old men whom Berkeley has dragged from the coastguard stations to man the navy. They are too old to learn, and too stiff to move; sending them aloft would be murder.' But with some effort recruits could be found, as Lord Clarence Paget found:

> Sure enough there was a scarcity, indeed almost an absence of seamen. However with the assistance of several valuable officers who were appointed to the ship, and by dint of handbills and touting of all sorts, we managed to enter at the average of 200 to 230 per week, such as they were. Scarcely any of them had been in a man-of-war, and consequently they were entirely ignorant of the management of great guns and muskets; and we set to work rigging, etc in good earnest.[41]

Paget demanded experienced Coastguard men, claiming that without them his flagship 'should be taken by the first Russian frigate we fell in with'. The alarmed Admiralty sent him 200, but many of them turned out to be 'worn out and very useless folk'. Otherwise the fleet was manned by patriotic and enthusiastic landsmen, 'even to butcher's boys, navvies, cabmen, etc. – *not* men of the standard of the Guards', as Admiral Berkeley put it.[42] The 84-gun *Monarch* put to sea with only eight able seamen in a complement of 850.[43] And the seamen were not necessarily very well disciplined once they were on board. In the flagship *Duke of Wellington*,

Strong symptoms of insubordination were evinced by the crew of the whole ship this Saturday night and Sunday, when they destroyed the whole of their mess utensils, and took shot from the racks and rolled them about the decks ... numbers of men made off by scaling the walls of the yard.[44]

The First Lord of the Admiralty could only urge that the fleet should recruit as it went along:

A proportion of Swedes and Norwegians, or even of Danes, would strengthen you, for they are hardy seamen and brave; and their enmity to Russia is undoubted. The only difficulty will be with their respective Governments; but, if the men enlist freely and come to you outside the harbours I cannot see why you should be over nice and refuse to take on board good seamen without much enquiry as to the places from whence they came.[45]

Despite everything, there were enough experienced men to put on a good show as the fleet sailed out of Spithead, past the Queen in her yacht, *Fairy*. The crew of *Duke of Wellington* 'sprang up the rigging with astonishing rapidity, not stopping according to custom at the cross-trees, but mounting upwards until they had reached the very summit, for the possession of which they struggled. One daring fellow coolly seated himself upon the truck of the main-topmast, where with one hand he waved his cap in cheering, while he held the other extended, to show that he was unsupported.' Her Majesty was duly impressed by 'a splendid and never-to-be-forgotten sight' and listened to the cheers of the crews 'as I think none but British tars CAN give'.[46]

The Mediterranean Fleet, under Admiral Sir Richard Dundas, entered the Black Sea and began the attack on the Crimea that gave the war its name. When the Anglo-French force mounted an unsuccessful attack on Sebastopol in October, W. H. Hankin, coxswain of *Sans Pareil,* saw the action as captain of the tenth gun on the main deck:

Having fired between 1400 and 1500 rounds from our guns, the casualties were 11 killed (including one midshipman) 59 wounded. The vessel was struck a great number of times by shot, shell and other missiles; also a great deal of damage to spars, rigging, etc. the magazine had to be cleared for some time owing to the bends being on fire.[47]

With his naval superiority, Admiral Dundas was able to land parties of seamen and marines to support the army in the Crimea, though this tended to undermine the real functions of the ships and was looked on with great caution by the Admiralty. Another tactical development, which would have an effect on the future, was in the use of small gunboats to control the Sea of Azof to the east of the Crimean Peninsula, and to operate in the shallow waters of the Baltic. These came in four different sizes and were all designed and built very quickly. They were very successful. The captain of one of them, the screw gun vessel *Beagle* of 1854, described the actions of Seaman Joseph Trewavas of Mousehole in Cornwall:

Cut the hawsers of the floating bridge in the straits of Genitchi under a heavy fire of musketry on which occasion he was wounded. This service was performed by the crews of the captain's gig and one of the paddle-box boats of the Beagle, under heavy fire of musketry at a distance of eighty yards the beach being completely lined with troops and the adjacent holes filled with riflemen. Trewavers is especially mentioned in dispatches as having been the person who cut the hawser.[48]

## After the War

With the end of the conflict in 1856, the government rashly began to cut the navy. Continuous service men were offered the chance to get out of their engagements, and many did so, including John Trewavas of *Beagle*. Though they had all volunteered to leave, it was seen as a breach of faith by the government and undermined the whole concept of continuous service. And in the training ships, entries to *Illustrious* were stopped in January 1857. A hundred and twenty men and boys were discharged, though they were nearly ready to go to sea.

Another and more lasting result of the Crimean War was the institution of the Victoria Cross, the first real gallantry medal and one that was available to all ranks. Five petty officers, four seamen and a stoker were awarded the medal for the Russian War, though the presentation by the Queen in February 1857 had more than its share of mystery and controversy. John Trewavas had already left the service but attended as a civilian. Stoker William Johnstone, who had accompanied an officer on a cloak-and-dagger mission in the Baltic, did not attend, and the medal was posted to him. It is possible that his real name was Johanssen and that he was a Scandinavian recruited by Napier, as instructed by Graham.[49] James Gorman was one of three seamen at the land Battle of Inkermann who kept up an intensive fire to deflect a Russian attack. He was later impersonated by one John Devereaux, another of the three, who had not been awarded a medal but apparently felt he should have been.[50]

The war had exposed many faults in the naval system, but it got off lightly in the press and in history. William Howard Russell, the pioneering war correspondent of *The Times*, found enough incompetence in the army and the medical services and paid very little attention to the navy.

# 2

# THE RISE OF STEAM
## 1856–1860

### The Birth of Sea Power

As well as exposing the vulnerability of wooden ships to modern gunfire, the attack on Sebastopol showed that some kind of steam power was necessary in every warship on active service. Ships without engines had to be brought into action by tugs lashed alongside. Early in 1855 the First Lord of the Admiralty told the House of Commons, 'it is not intended by the government to send any sailing ships whatever to the Baltic. Our experience has taught us that the intermixture of screw and sailing ships is not conducive to the interests of the service. They cannot be manoeuvred together.'[1] Sir Howard Douglas, a general in the army but also a great expert on naval tactics, wrote in 1858:

> We are now at the commencement of a new era in naval warfare, in consequence of the introduction of steam as a propelling power for ships, and its application, by all the maritime powers of Europe, to vessels of war, from those of the lowest class to line-of-battle ships of the greatest magnitude. This new power will necessarily modify, and, to a great extent, overturn, the present tactics of war on the ocean.[2]

Douglas was not worried by the changes:

> Our superiority holds good also with respect to their training in the employment of steam. The machinery for the propulsion of a British steamer is the best that can be executed, and the engineers who attend it are well known to have greater skill and more experience than men of like class in other nations ...[3]

In 1858, Captain Milne was asked if seamen preferred sail to steam and replied, 'There is not much choice now, as almost all vessels have steam power.'[4] But even Sir Howard Douglas agreed that sail was still needed when not in battle:

> Even with the utmost economy in the consumption of fuel, screw steam-ships cannot in general, from a want of stowage-room for coals, continue more than a few days steaming either at full speed or expansively. Exhaustion of fuel on the eve of a battle, or during a protracted action, is a contingency which must at all events be effectually guarded against.[5]

In 1856 the Admiralty ordered that steam power was not to be used 'but in cases of necessity'.[6] This meant that experienced seamen were needed in every warship, but opinions varied on how many. Lord Paget suggested that a 90-gun ship would need 300 men aloft and 100 on deck to handle her sails, out of a complement of 860. Labour-saving devices such as patent sheaves and roller reefing were now used on merchant ships, but he rejected them for the navy –

> you have to consider what would be the effect supposing the halliards were shot away or any of the lifts were shot away. In our present mode of reefing topsails, carrying away our halliards would not prevent us reefing the sail, but in the new system, as I understand it, if the halliards were shot away you could not reef the sail.[7]

Captain B. J. Sullivan, who had served in the Baltic during the war with Russia, commented,

> I believe that our vessels must be worked as sailing ships, even in a seaway, although you may work them with reduced sail, therefore you must still have a fine body of seamen in every ship sufficient for that work ... roughly I would say that half the numerical crew of any ship should be good seamen; you would want, at least, to every gun six well trained and active men as well as good gunners.[8]

The skilled engineers were now warrant officers, with commissioned officers with titles like 'inspectors of machinery afloat' to supervise them. On the lower deck, stokers were still comparatively few in number but highly-regarded and well paid. Steam engines of the 1850s were hungry for fuel and needed up to five pounds of coal for every horsepower per hour, compared with less than two pounds by the end of the century.[9] But they were rarely used, for 121-gun ships could only steam for eight days at full power, and 90s of the *Renown* class for six.[10] Moreover they had very low power. The *Marlborough* of 121 guns had only 800 horsepower and needed a crew of 7 engineers and 26 stokers – approximately 1 stoker for every 30 horsepower. The stoker was well paid – as much as a petty officer first class – and according to Milne in 1858, 'There are plenty of volunteers for stoking. Every one goes stoking if he can.' No previous knowledge was needed: new men were given some instruction but no examination.[11] From 1856, seamen who did acting duties as stokers were given certificates entitling them to extra pay.[12] But in 1852 Robert Murray had already identified the need for more specialized stokers.

> The management of the first on board a steam vessel affects the question of economy in the consumption of coal to so great an extent, that the importance of skilful [sic] firemen cannot be too much insisted upon. It is a great mistake to suppose, as many captains and owners of steam vessels do, that any able-bodied men who can throw coals on a fire is fit for a stoker: and under this impression, sailors are frequently engaged, instead of firemen ...[13]

A good stoker would keep the fuel level inside his furnace rather than letting it pile up at one end. He would close the fire doors as much as possible to save heat; he would break up large pieces of coal, clear the bars of his furnace, re-use half-burnt cinders and make sure his fires were clean for the next watch. A reliable man would be needed to keep an eye on the water level inside the boiler – too low and some of the plates might overheat and create the danger of an explosion, too high and the water would boil over and go into the engine.

### THE INDIAN MUTINY

In 1857 the sepoys of the Indian army mutinied, partly due to a rumour that the cartridges they were expected to bite were greased with a mixture of pig and cow fat, and therefore anathema to both Hindu and Muslim. It soon developed beyond an army mutiny, though never quite into a national revolt by the Indian population. British troops and loyal sepoys set about the task of putting the insurrection down, but the army lacked heavy artillery and turned to the navy for help. Though there was no hostile naval force in the region, the Admiralty was still unhappy about withdrawing men from their normal duty and urged 'that the officers and men comprising the Naval brigades may be returned to their respective ships as soon as the exigencies of the service will admit'.[14]

Arthur O'Leary was a seaman in *Shannon* under Captain Peel, one of a party of over 400 men that went more than 500 miles up the River Ganges in hired steamboats. On the way up, some of the seamen were issued with a double rum ration by mistake, and the others 'came aft in an improper manner to demand its issue, which was refused'. Thomas Oates, captain of the maintop, was considered to be the ringleader and was disrated. After that the officers took care that the men were indoctrinated in the cause – at Calcutta the Archbishop told them the story of the massacre at Cawnpore, when soldiers and civilians were killed after being promised safe conduct. There was a further speech from Lord Elgin, and on 4 October, as the brigade mustered at Allahabad, Captain Peel formed them in a 'hollow square and told them, "one ship, one crew"'. After that they set off as part of an army formation, as described by O'Leary much later in the form of a letter to his old officer, now Admiral Sir Nowell Salmon:

> Start for the front. Our company, 53rd, 84th and 93rd Highland Foot and 4 24-pdrs; arrival at Cawnpore. The scene of the Massacre – Slaughter House and Well in the Compound History scratched on the walls by the wives and daughters of the 32nd will never be erased from my memory … march for Lucknow … driving sepoys out of the College of Martineau and across the canal. The flank movement to the right on the Goomtee; gun sunk in sand, raised by elephant; howitzer to front. Capture of Secunderabagh; breach of

the gate; charge. Advance on Char-bagh; hot fire from the Mess House; guns forward, Bengal battery on left, supported by 93rd; explosion of caisson; fire from topes; advance of 93rd. Call for naval gun; dragged up, extreme elevation; the burning huts. Daring reconnaissance by yourself, dear Admiral, from the summit of the palm tree; the breach and charge.[15]

A separate party of more than 250 men was formed from the crew of the screw corvette *Pearl*. At Ahora, Leading Seaman William Rayfield, Able Seamen John Lee and Samuel Simmonds, and Stoker Joseph Williams dashed forward with the cavalry to take an enemy gun. Jesse Ward, captain of the foretop, also captured a gun, while John Goodfellow, captain of the forecastle, proved to be an expert gunlayer who 'scarcely ever missed his object'.[16] In all the naval brigades were engaged in 26 different actions and suffered 108 casualties.[17] The revolt was eventually crushed.

## GUNNERY

There was already a feeling that gunnery was at least as important as seamanship, and Lord Clarence Paget stated in 1858, 'Seamen, as sailors only, may be procured with much greater facility than you can gunners; in fact, gunners must be taught; you can get seamen ready made, but you cannot get gunners ready made; and the most important part of our service now is the duty of the gunners.'[18] The shipowner W. S. Lindsay agreed.

Efficient gunnery has become of greater importance than able seamanship, though the necessity of preserving the latter must not be overlooked. The introduction of steam navigation, and the almost universal application of the screw propeller to vessels of war will produce an entire change in the mode of carrying on naval hostilities.[19]

Though gunnery training was vital especially in the early stages of a war when men might be brought in from the merchant service, it was much easier to learn than seamanship. According to Rear Admiral Elliot, 'It is easy to make a man a good captain of a gun, perhaps in four months, but it takes many years to make a sailor.'[20]

By this time potential warrant officers studying for the certificate of '1st Class for Gunner' were expected to undergo a rigorous academic course and be

> perfect in all the drills and details, as laid down in the Gunnery Books ... They are also required to pass the Laboratory, and to go through the course of School instruction, which comprises the Rule of Three, Vulgar and Decimal Fractions, Square Root, the use of Logarithms, and finding the distance of a ship at sea, or laying out a target by means of a quadrant. They are further expected to be superior instructors.

Those on the next level down, studying for a 1st Class certificate as gunner's mate, could miss the school course and the laboratory instruction but were also expected to be good instructors. Candidates for the 2nd Class certificate were not expected to know the whole contents of the gunnery manual, except the Great Gun Exercise, which was also issued in the form of a card, but they should be 'instructed in the Manual Exercise' and know it practically. There was also provision for acting captains of guns, who would be trained on board ship with a view to going to gunnery school when they arrived home. All seaman gunners were expected to be good shots and were tested with 120 rifle rounds, 20 from a revolver, 30 from a 6-pounder and 10 from a larger gun.[21]

On commissioning a ship it was vital to begin gunnery instruction as soon as possible, as many of the crew often had no experience of it. Captains were instructed to order the crew

> to go to general Quarters every day, and cast loose all the guns, run them in, and exercise the men in worming, sponging and loading, for twenty minutes; then run out and exercise 'both sides', pointing at objects, working coins [quoins] and handspikes for twenty minutes more; afterwards man one side, and exercise the Quarters in slow time with the guns in various positions for another twenty minutes.

Untrained men should be drilled further during their duty watch, and if there were not enough qualified gun captains (which was usually the case) the captain was to select suitable men to be trained under the gunnery officer. Gun crews took up a huge proportion of a crew in action – 866 men were allocated to the 131 guns of *Duke of Wellington* and 94 more to the shell rooms and magazines, leaving only 77 of the lower deck for other duties in the engine room, rigging and steering. A 31-gun frigate such as *Tribune* had 256 men on gunnery duties and 51 ratings and marines on other tasks.[22]

## UNIFORM

Uniform was important in Victorian times. At the beginning of the century it had virtually been confined to the army, to naval officers, mail coach guards and footmen. Over the next few years it was issued to firemen, postmen, convicts and policemen, and to large numbers of railway employees. Meanwhile, servants' dress conformed more to established patterns, and later in the century uniform was adopted by religious bodies such as the Salvation Army and youth groups such as the Boys Brigade. It would be surprising if the Royal Navy, the nation's most cherished body, was an exception to this trend.

In the past, sailors had worn their own clothes or purchased 'slops' from the purser when these wore out. There was no formal uniform, but seamen had their own distinctive style of dress with short jacket and loose trousers, at a time when men on shore usually wore long coats and breeches. A new style began to emerge in the 1820s – open-necked shirts with wide, loose collars, in contrast to the stiff and buttoned-up appearance of their officers, sometimes with stripes in various patterns, including a dark-blue collar with one or two white stripes round the edges. In the 1840s, the men in *Excellent* were wearing identical white 'frocks' with blue collars, and the sailors on the Royal Yacht *Victoria and Albert* were wearing a version with a V-neck in front and a very square shape to the rear.[23] An example that survives to this day was made for the young Prince of Wales, and Queen Victoria wrote in her diary, 'Bertie put on his sailor's dress, a new one, beautifully made by the man who makes for our men.'[24] It was also taken up by the crews of other private yachts, such as an English one that visited the Firth of Forth around this time.[25] The Prince of Wales's uniform had three stripes round the collar and cuffs, but there was no consensus about that. Many captains ordered a particular dress, which could be inconvenient for the men, who often had to change it to suit their whims. Seaman-Rigger Donnelly complained that, 'You go on board one ship, and you have blue cloth frock, or white frocks, and you have perhaps two rows of tape, one row broad and the other narrow. Perhaps that would be the uniform of the ship you had joined.' He agreed that 'it would be a popular choice among the men if there would be some particular cut to the clothes laid down as the rule of the service, so that a man's clothing would suit all ships alike, and so have one pattern throughout the navy'.[26]

From the official point of view, the biggest problem was the seaman's tendency to sell his clothing and buy cheaper and inferior articles:

> There is a system prevailing at the seaports among slop-sellers, of keeping an inferior description of clothing ready to furnish to the seamen, in exchange for the clothing with which they are supplied, and the seamen receive the difference in value as money, and these things in a very short time become quite unfit to be seen, and the ship's company becomes dirty and discreditable to the officers.[27]

The Admiralty already had this in mind by the beginning of 1856, and the Uniform Committee, of two rear admirals, a commodore, a captain and a dockyard commissioner, was ordered to 'consider the Dress of the Seamen of the Fleet with a view to the Establishment of such a degree of Uniformity as shall appear to us desirable ...' It interviewed several petty officers, and came to the conclusion that a uniform would be popular in the fleet. Proof patterns of various items were ready by the end of February and were sent out to the Port Admirals at Portsmouth and Plymouth for their consideration. They consulted their captains, and those at Plymouth spoke to the petty officers about the quality of the cloth on issue.[28]

The most controversial item was the jacket. According to the Uniform Committee it was to be 'the Established jacket of the Royal Navy', though it was 'not intended to be worn except on particular occasions, and never as a Working Dress'. Eight out of nine of the captains consulted at Portsmouth did not favour a jacket at all, but Vice Admiral Seymour suggested that as a compromise it should only be worn by petty officers, to increase their status. The officers at Plymouth wanted a blue jacket,

> No 1 cloth, double breasted, stand and fall collar, sleeves sufficiently large to go over a duck and serve frock easily. To reach the hip, with an opening at the cuffs on the seam and two covered silk buttons. One breast pocket inside left side, and seven navy pattern crown and anchor buttons (waistcoat size) on each side.

This was very similar to the pattern that was eventually adopted by the Admiralty. It was the most expensive item in the sailor's kit, costing 17s 8d (88p).

If the jacket was the most controversial, the 'frock' was to prove the most distinctive and lasting item in the sailor's kitbag. As with most items there, it was based on a traditional pattern that had developed over the decades. The officers at Portsmouth preferred two stripes round the collar, while those at Plymouth, who had far more influence on the eventual result, advocated three. According to legend, this was based on Nelson's three great victories, but there is no evidence for that. On the other hand, three was an important and almost mystical number for seamen – they were not particularly religious but they knew about the Holy Trinity; a rope was made of three strands; a sailing ship had three masts; and a large one had three decks. A traditional fleet had three squadrons, each divided into three divisions. In any case, the three stripes became characteristic of seamen's uniform, in Britain and the rest of the world.

The frock was a loose garment in white or blue according to climate and duty, with single buttons only on the cuffs. It was intended to be tucked into the waistband of the trousers, which also became iconic. No belts were allowed, so it was a slightly uncomfortable arrangement unless they fitted well, which brought the seaman's skill with needle and thread into play. According to the orders of 1857, the 'trowsers' were to be 'made of Navy Blue cloth, of the ordinary Naval Pattern, fitting tight at the waistband, with two pockets and a broad flap, and stained bone buttons'. They had already acquired their characteristic 'bell-bottoms', presumably part of the 'ordinary Naval Pattern'. Another version was available in white duck, a plain weave fabric that was suitable for tropical wear.

The seaman was to use a new-pattern round cap, 'of No 1 Cloth, and partially stiffened across the crown, similar in shape to that worn by Naval Officers, without the peak'. The crown was eight inches in diameter for boys and ten inches for men, with the ship's name on a ribbon, and a chinstrap attached for use in windy weather. But the cap was only supposed to be worn 'at night, and at sea when ordered' – the standard seaman's headgear was the wide-brimmed hat made of sennet, a naval form of straw. It might be in natural colour or painted black, according to the climate.

The issue of the Uniform Regulations was a very low-key affair, and late in 1858 the members of the Royal Commission and their witnesses seemed to know very little about it. Several of them recommended a free suit of clothes to be issued to the seamen, and even Mr Pennell, the Chief Clerk at the Admiralty and one of the organizers of the Continuous Service system, commented, 'With regard to the Continuous Service men, I have always thought that they might have some kind of uniform, however simple it might be …'[29] No one corrected him on this point, but when Boatswain Uffen commented that, 'There is a great deal of expense entailed upon the men frequently in regard to shifting their uniforms,' he was asked, 'You are aware that that has been put a stop to, and that there is now a uniform?' He answered, 'I was not aware that that had been carried out.'[30]

Uffen was probably not unusual, for the Admiralty had done very little to implement the new regulations. It was only in November 1858 that it began to make contracts with local suppliers in the main naval ports and issued detailed descriptions of the cloth to be supplied for each item. The blue cloth jacket, for example, used between 56 and 52 inches of No 1 cloth according to size. It also needed 33 inches of black shalloon for lining, a yard of white calico, 2 yards of stay tape, blue jean for pockets, 18 buttons and 5 other items.[31] It is not clear how fast progress was after that, but it seems likely that the seamen were beginning to wear their new uniforms by the end of the decade.

## THE ROYAL COMMISSION OF 1858

In 1858, in the light of the Crimean War, Parliament appointed a Royal Commission to 'inquire into the best Means of Manning the Navy, and in what Manner and under what Arrangements Seamen may be readily obtained for such Purpose, either during Peace or in case of sudden Emergency or War ...'[32] It interviewed nearly 80 witnesses, including admirals, captains, warrant officers, seaman riggers, shipping agents, coastguard officials and customs officers. Seaman-rigger John Donelly gave his views on continuous service:

> The only objection that I have ever known about it is that many men do not fancy it. Perhaps I have got into a ship where the discipline is very strict, and the consequence is I may think I have only about eighteen months to two years to run, and my ship will be paid off, and I can go and be my own master; but if I am a continuous service man I might get into trouble.[33]

Admiral Shepherd pointed out to him that on continuous service he could have earned enough extra pay by the end of his first commission to buy himself out with £3 or £4 to spare, but that failed to make any impression on the seaman, who perhaps felt that he would never be able to save any money like that.

There were many who were ready to dismiss continuous service as a failure. According to Captain Matthew Connolly,

> To suppose the mere fact of filling up a ship's complement by drafts from Tower Hill, Bristol, Liverpool &c.; the very scum and refuse of those delectable places, is manning her, is a marvelous delusion; and yet, under the Continuous Service Warrant, there are some thousands of such fellows entered in the service, and whom it will be difficult to get rid of – fellows who have never done a day's willing work in their lives, who are driven from deck to deck, turned from mess to mess, too lazy even to fetch their own victuals from the galley, who are in every page of the defaulter's book for skulking, thieving, filthy habits, throwing their dirty hammocks and clothes overboard rather than have the trouble of scrubbing them, insolence, and gross insubordination of course &c., &c., &c.[34]

But Connolly could also see a way forward:

> The entry and training of boys for the Service, I consider to be the most
> important consideration connected with the subject of Manning the Navy.
> It is on them only that we can depend for making our smart man-of-war
> sailors, and upon them only that I propose to confer the benefit to the
> Continuous Service Warrant, and not upon the class of 'sailors' on whom
> it has been thrown away ...[35]

The committee, with one exception, concluded that the system of
continuous service and boy training was working well but that the reserves
needed some attention.

## THE ROYAL NAVAL RESERVE

By 1858 opinion had turned decisively against the press gang, even since
1852, except for a few diehards. One of many witnesses to the Royal
Commission, the Registrar of Seamen asserted:

> There are many circumstances different from the state of things when
> impressments existed before that it appears to me to be quite an
> impossibility to carry it into effect .... The construction of docks has altered
> ... Formerly the ships used to be in the rivers or alongside of wharves with
> their crews on board, now the men are all ashore, and could only be taken
> by force out of the lodging houses or other habitations. Again, the Reform
> Bill made a vast difference in the constituencies of the country. Most of
> those men are the relatives of tradespeople or persons who have votes, and
> who would strongly protest and use their influence, no doubt, against
> anything of this kind .... Again the warrant must be backed by a magistrate,
> if executed on shore. In London it must be backed by the Lord Mayor, and
> there would be difficulty about that. Then I do not think that the police or
> other constables would lend their cordial assistance. Moreover there must
> be a vast number of people employed to impress, there would be
> convulsion and bloodshed, trials for murder, and convictions ... and after
> all, the pressed men would be unwilling men and untrained men, and they
> would not be available, under present circumstances, until they had gone
> through training in gunnery, let them be ever so good seamen.

The Superintendent of the P&O steamship line went even further: 'I believe that the men would die first; you would have a revolution in every sea-port town. I believe they would burn and destroy rather than submit to impressment.'[36]

As early as 1852, Quartermaster John Brophy had claimed that few young seamen understood what the press was. But in other cases memories were all too long, and six years later it was reported that in Dundee, 'Not one man in ten at this port have ever had their foot on a man-of-war's deck, and know nothing of the royal navy except traditional stories of the "press gang" and severe discipline ...' [37] But more traditional naval and political figures, such as Sir James Graham, pointed out that it might be necessary to use the press in an extreme emergency, and it was never abolished – then or later.

In the meantime, the other reserves were clearly not adequate. Little was now said about the seamen-riggers. The Royal Commission was optimistic about the Coastguard and wanted to increase the total force to 12,000 men, most of whom would be suitable for recall in an emergency, but many doubts lingered after the experience of the Crimean War, and even the expanded force would be too small in a major war. As to the Coast Volunteers, Rear Admiral Milne was hopeful in 1858:

> They are now embarked in the coast-guard ships for training. We have already enrolled 6,000 men, and they have been lately entering at the rate of 350 a month ... With regard to any emergency that may arise these coast volunteers are all trained to the great guns; and I must say that it is working in a most satisfactory manner.[38]

But Milne rejected the idea of extending the scheme to the coastal trades, which were not seasonal, like fishing, so it would be difficult to take men out for 28 days' training. The 600-mile limit was a fatal flaw in the scheme – suppose a fleet partly manned by these volunteers had to chase an enemy across an ocean, as Nelson did in 1805? The Royal Commission concluded, 'no great reliance could be placed upon them for manning the fleet in case of an emergency.'[39]

Instead the Commission proposed the formation of a new reserve, initially called the Volunteer Reserve Force and later the Royal Naval

Reserve, or RNR. It was anxious not to damage relations with the merchant service, but at the same time it believed that a strong navy was in everyone's interests as it would show foreign powers that 'our defences are impregnable'. It considered the possibility of a merchant seaman's fund, which would eventually offer him a pension while making sure that he stayed under the British flag, but had to concede that it would not in itself provide trained men for the navy and would be resented as an extra tax. Instead it proposed to raise up to 20,000 men who would train for 28 days per year. In return they would get good wages, a pension at 50–55, admission to the Coastguard and the benefits of Greenwich Hospital. Unlike the Coast Volunteers, they would be liable to serve anywhere. In the first instance, men would be selected from the short-service trades and given training in gunnery. This was important, for it was no longer common for merchant ships to be armed, except for small signaling guns. In the meantime, naval guns were becoming ever more sophisticated – at that very time the breech-loading Armstrong gun was under trial – so gunnery was becoming an increasingly important aspect of the naval seaman's training. In the long run, it was hoped, members of the RNR would be recruited as boys and perhaps even trained alongside those of the navy: this would reduce the widening gap between merchant and Royal Navy seamen that was inevitable with continuous service.

The recruitment and training of boys never happened on any great scale, but the RNR was successful in attracting adults. By 1869 it was regarded as 'an established institution of the country', and after taking part in fleet exercises it was considered to be 'a most valuable body, more than sufficient to afford, on any sudden emergency, an effective force of blue-jackets large enough to man any fleet which could possibly be got ready.'[40] But it would not be tested in action for some considerable time, as Britain was not involved in a European war for many decades.

## TYPES OF MEN

Naval officers had a good idea of what they wanted in recruits, though they did not always achieve it. In 1858 Captain Harris of *Illustrious* wrote of the great value of 'the peasantry in those country districts from which the healthiest and most desirable lads volunteer'.[41] Another officer described his policy in the following year:

> There has never been any difficulty in procuring any number of boys from the London schools, but experience has shown that they are not the best recruits for the navy, for although they possess superior intelligence, they bring many vices with them, their habits are most restless, and they do not become attached to the service, in fact, as soon as they get sufficient money, a large part of them endeavour to purchase their discharge. A limit was consequently put on the entries, and recruiting is now carried on more inland from among the country lads, who though at first less intelligent, after a time succeed as well, and are more healthy, as also become attached to the service.
>
> An impression generally prevails that we get boys from the sea coast, but the reverse is the fact, in consequence of them all being too valuable and productive to their parents. They are mostly engaged, not only in fishing, but as ropemakers, sailmakers, carpenters, and other trades connected with the repairs and furnishing of shipping generally.

There was some debate about the best age to recruit boys. Many captains believed thirteen was too young, and fourteen was generally favoured, though others thought the best boys were started at seventeen.

The navy's recruitment policy was not rigidly racist, but it did tend to bow to popular pressure. In July 1859 a party recruited at the Liverpool rendezvous included 19 'coloured' men out of 33, and the Admiralty commented that, 'so large a proportion of coloured men may be distasteful to the rest of the crew'. Until then, black seamen had featured regularly in prints and paintings of the Royal Navy, and one even appears on one of the friezes on Nelson's Column, but they are conspicuous by their absence from crew photographs of the later nineteenth century. Partly this reflected a change in naval recruiting policy, for naval ratings were no longer experienced merchant seaman from different parts of the world, but were taken on as boys. There were comparatively few non-white people resident in Britain at the time, and it is difficult to be sure what pressures stopped them from applying to join the navy, or from being accepted if they did, but in any case the issue was absent from the messdecks for a century or so.

W. S. Lindsay, in a minority report to the 1858 Commission, wanted to expand the use of marines, both ashore and on board ship. But in fact the marines still worked uneasily with the seaman at that time. The Royal Marine Artillery was useful in mortar ships, but it struggled to find a role in the fleet generally. Marine infantrymen were often trained in gunnery to a certain extent, but captains were reluctant put them in charge of guns, however well they were qualified, unless forced to do so through shortage of good seamen.[42]

Lindsay suggested perceptively that, 'The fastest ships having the heaviest guns of the longest range and fully manned with the most efficient gunners, will in all probability prevail in an action.' Furthermore, though traditional skills should not be overlooked, efficient gunnery was now considered of greater importance than able seamanship.[43] His solution was to increase the number of marines, who could do all the work of seamen except going aloft, which was less necessary in the age of steam. Captain Matthew Connolly had the same idea and wanted half the complement of every ship to be marines.[44] But others defended the role of the seaman. Marines, it was pointed out, were 'never called upon either to go above the hammock netting or do the duty in a boat; that is, not to row'. Also, it was claimed, 'There are some duties on deck which the marines could not do. For instance the marines could not pass the nippers, stoppering ropes, and the belaying ropes; and such duties as the marines are not supposed to do.'[45] The ultimate answer was to make the seaman more of a soldier and gunner than he had been in the past.

The status of the petty officer was not greatly improved. One of John Hodgkinson's reasons for leaving the service was that 'All I could hope for was a petty-officer's rating at 3l. per month, and with scarcely a privilege beyond that of an ordinary seaman.'[46] Captain Francis Liardet was ambiguous in his treatment of petty officers. It was not common for them to mess separately from the men.

Many officers are of opinion that it would be beneficial to the service if the petty officers were to mess together, and leading men were appointed to take charge of the messes. This would certainly place the petty officers in a better position for exacting attention to the immediate duties of the ship;

and I confess I had once a strong bias in its favour; but having more deeply reflected on the subject, it appears to me that if petty officers were removed from the ship's company's messes, the want of their respectability and good example would soon be felt.[47]

The petty officer still had no security in his rating, and Liardet advised how to reduce a man in rank:

When it becomes requisite to disrate a petty officer for bad conduct, it will be desirable that he should be removed from the part of the ship in which he has been accustomed to do duty; otherwise, you do not give him a fair chance of recovering his character ... When it is to be done, his badge of office ought to be taken off in the presence of the whole ship's company, at divisions or morning quarters; it should be done with the least possible annoyance, beyond the loss of rating, as an example.[48]

John Hodgkinson describes his companions in the screw frigate *Highflyer*, a mixture of old and new navy:

Fancy to yourself a lower-deck mess table! – time a quarter to eight bells in the forenoon – presently I heard the bugle playing up cheerly 'The Roast Beef of Old England', and aft to the galley rush the hands whose turn it is to do duty as cooks to draw the day's allowance of meat. It is drawn and on the table, and my messmates sit round, and are soon busily engaged in criticising. No matter for dirty hands or tangled hair: it doesn't do to be particular on board ship.

The mess was headed by a petty officer, Harry B, who was 'an open hearted, intelligent man, fond of reading, and very well informed. He is tolerably lenient and impartial in his judgement.' The next member was Mikey, 'good tempered when sober, but inclined to liquor, and when so, extremely wild and rackety'. J. W. was an old Arctic hand who had been in two expeditions to look for the Arctic explorer Franklin and told incredible tales about how he had been towed six miles underwater by a whale. He was 'light hearted and cheerful' with 'one sad failing; whenever he can he gets drunk, and firmly believes it does him good.' Bill was 'a young fellow who has served most of his time in big ships. He disliked small ones because 'they ain't half manned, and wants the work done big-ship fashion all the same'. Young Joe was 'dissipated' but had a 'redeeming blue eye, and an amiable temper'. He was 'very ignorant of books' but ready to listen to those who read them. Quimbo, a West Indian, was good natured and simple, with a quick temper. He was a dandy, and 'the general butt of the mess'. The carpenter or 'wood-spoiler' was the least popular, 'a disagreeable fellow'. John himself was quite well educated and apparently something of a misfit on the messdeck, for he was becoming 'very sick of the company I was in, and my mode of life.' He found some comfort in the friendship of his fellow reader Harry B, with whom he often had 'a romp together'. The most junior member was Dick, a representative of the new style of school-ship boy – 'a fine sprightly little fellow, with a good elementary education, with a fair stock of common sense; not a bad seaman, and one day will do some good for himself.'[49]

A survey of coastguard ships on the Irish station in 1859 showed that there was still a great deal of 'dead wood', and men who had not sought or achieved any promotion. A few men were quickly tested and made up to AB when an Admiralty circular drew attention to the issue. In the *Brunswick*, Robert Perry and Joseph Dawe refused to take the rating until ordered to do so. Others were congenitally unfit and had been recruited under the old system. Henry Edward, in the afterguard of *Orion*, was an 'imbecile – not fit for the service' and was to be discharged as soon as his debts were cleared. James Marshall of *Renown*, though entered for continuous service, had 'very weak eyesight' and could not see the compass to steer. Some were shoemakers, carpenters, flax-dressers and gardeners, who were never likely to become sailors. Many others failed in one of the vital requirements of an able seaman. Many did not know the marks on the lead line, or the points of the compass. Some could not work aloft for one reason or another, such as Thomas Bartholomew of the gunner's crew of *Brunswick*, who had served ten years in the navy but was 'unable to work aloft from giddiness'. Service in the merchant marine did not guarantee success in the Royal Navy, as it did not necessarily provide all the range of experience necessary. Samuel Hesketh of *Orion* had spent ten years in small coasters but was 'awkward aloft', presumably because his previous ships were barges with fore-and-aft rig. John Wearing of *Renown* had been brought up on canal barges, but he could not take the helm or cast the lead. Phillip Wash was 41 years old and had spent twelve years as a fisherman and more than four in the navy, but he could not heave the lead, had no desire to learn and was employed as a waister – the lowest grade of man, unable to work aloft or in more skilled jobs on the quarterdeck or forecastle, but only in the waist of the ship. But the worst of all was George Hoskins of *Brunswick*, 28 years old and still an ordinary seaman second class after four years in the navy, who was unable to go aloft and was 'useless'. It seemed that men learned more on small ships, where there was a chance for everyone to take a turn at all the tasks. The screw corvette *Raccoon*, with a crew of 85, reported only two men who had not passed for able seaman after a reasonable time, but one of these had already been invalided out. This left John Drake, a former ploughman, 28 years old and 4½ years in the navy; despite the fact that his officers had evidently done their best, 'Though constantly practiced at them as well as other points relating to his trade, he is a man of no ability ...'[50]

## LIFE AT SEA

The new steam warships were even more overcrowded than sailing ships had been. At the beginning of the decade, Captain Alexander Milne reported on the screw sloop *Plumper*. The problem was that engine room had 'taken up the largest space in the Ship, and thereby reduced the stowage and accommodation':

> She cannot berth her ship's co[mpany]. The space allotted to them is miserably small and confined. There is not room to hang up more than 56 Hammocks without using space over the Engine room and the Engine room passages for that purpose and when steam is up, it is impossible for the men to sleep there. In consequence of the confined space on the lower deck the men are obliged to sleep on the Deck or where they best can.

It was not because the crew was excessively large – 'The complement of 110 is not more than enough for the Guns. It is much too large for the accommodation and yet it is not large enough for the Masts and Yards.'[51]

At the end of the decade, a committee of officers tried hard to find room to stow the men's bags:

> Owing to causes which are well known, the classification of any number of H M ships is next to impossible. In line of battleships whose gun force is nominally the same, every variety of dimensions prevails, and in one thing only connected with this subject is there any similarity, and that is the absence of sufficient space provided for the stowage of the ship's company's bags ...
>
> It might at first be supposed that the increased dimensions given of late to our ships would have facilitated the solution of this problem, but the reverse is really the case. The vast space occupied by the Engines, Boilers and Coal, still more than keeps pace with the increased dimensions. These have in the worst cases led to an increased number of guns, to guns of a larger calibre, and consequently to increased complements of men.[52]

Boys lived among the adult seamen, as H. Y. Moffat found on joining at Leith in 1857:

> I was appointed to a mess on the lower deck. All the sailors were divided into messes of twenty to twenty-four men with one or two boys, and the mess-tables hung between each gun on the lower deck ...[53]

Captain Francis Liardet described how the boys should be trained on a seagoing ship:

> The lads and boys who do not move smartly aloft, should go over the mast-head every morning, before they dress for quarters. This will give them by degrees breath for running aloft, to hand the small sails or cross topgallants &c. Boys so exercised become after a short time, your smartest topmen for light work aloft; and if proper attention be paid to making them seamen, while going through their other exercises, you will have in them your best men-of-war sailors, clean, active, and well-disciplined from their youth; and the time has come when we must look to the seamen of our own bringing up, for the requisite qualities of good men-of-war's men.[54]

Most captains took care to train the men in gunnery. Rear Admiral George Elliot described his policy:

> I consider, from my experience, that the greatest amount of drill that is possible in a large ship to give each separate man in a week, taking them alternately, is one hour of the great gun exercise, one hour of musket drill, and one hour of cutlass drill, in a week, and the general quarter-day exercise, which is probably two hours. This drill, except the latter, is almost always in his watch on deck, in every ship; and there is not time, if the captain wished, to give a greater amount than this ...[55]

Liardet's book, published in 1858, makes no mention of steam and tends to imply that ships would get out of harbour under sail alone; presumably it deals with the experience of the early rather than the late 1850s. Hodgkinson first set sail in the screw frigate *Highflyer* in the autumn of 1856. He was entranced by the engines:

> I seemed to enjoy being in so large a steam-ship, and was fond of looking down the engine room hatchways at the ponderous but beautifully-working machinery; and long afterwards when steaming in calm nights, and everything on deck was quiet. I used to fancy the engines said, as they steadily revolved, Going ahead, sir – going ahead, sir.[56]

He was not involved in coaling, which at Rio de Janeiro was done by chained and underfed negroes – he could not make up his mind whether they were slaves or convicts.[57] He was much more occupied when the ship began to sail and the engines were turned off:

> the boatswain soon gave us work by piping, 'Up screw'; the little iron capstan was speedily rigged, and we merrily danced the screw up for the first time. 'Away aloft'; 'loose sails,' was the next order; and soon the ship was covered in a cloud of canvas ...[58]

But the experience of taking in sail in bad weather had not changed much:

> The order, 'Hands reef topsails!' is followed by a tremendous rush, each one of us striving to be in the rigging before his fellow, treading on one

another's fingers, hustling and well-nigh capsizing a shipmate out of the shrouds. Then holding on by the yard, we get out on the foot-ropes, and gather up the sail as far as the reef-band, and hold it firmly in our grasp, ready to tie the points, while the captain of the top is hauling out the weather-earring, which must be always secured first. All this time it may be raining hard, pelting into your eyes and ears, running in a merry stream down your back; and the yard strains and jerks with the furiously flopping sail till you are all but knocked off.[59]

Though the central government had done little to promote universal education, the new-style seaman was far more literate than the old, and Liardet wrote, 'The crews of ships of war now write ten or twelve letters where they formerly wrote one.'[60] Mail could be delivered even in remote stations such as China, where it was distributed by the master-at-arms:

'Hillo, Bill, what's up? You look down on your luck; didn't she write again this time?' 'Write be bothered, no; she's run away with a soger.' 'Well, if people won't write to me, I won't to them; s'pose they're getting too good.' 'John,' they used to shout to me, 'Here's a bushel basket-full for you; by Jove, you're always the one.'[61]

But in general the culture on the messdeck was far from literary:

Truly reading and writing on board ship are done under trying difficulties. On all sides, fore-and-aft, men are singing and talking, card-playing, fighting, and even drinking; for in spite of all the strict and severe rules against the smuggling of liquor into the ship, men will and do do it, heedless of consequences. Or perhaps in the mess next your own they are keeping a chum's birthday. Before them on the table is a large kettle of rum, or brandy-flip; the glass is passed repeatedly round, till the liquor beginning to take effect, they commence singing, dancing, and quarrelling, which often leads to fighting; in such cases the results are, the liquor is capsized, the combatants look nasty at one another, and knock each other about to their utmost, till the master-at-arms, attracted by the noise, comes to the scene of the conflict, collars the chief actors, and marches them on to the quarterdeck, where the first-luff [first lieutenant], making but short work of it, orders them in irons.[62]

Seamen still had no guarantee of shore leave during a commission. Hodgkinson was disappointed on his first visit to Cape Town – 'Seamen do not see much of foreign countries after all, for I was only ashore for about an hour.'[63] Liardet suggested a policy for leave, which could become important as an instrument of control. Short periods ashore were not to be encouraged, except when the ship was fitting out. 'When an opportunity offers pick out some well-behaved retiring men, and bring them forward for leave; this will show the bare-faced fellows your opinion of them ... The liberty list, if well attended to, gives the commanding officer an increase of power for the management of the ship's company.'[64]

## SCARE AND EXPANSION

Those who believed that the Crimean War was merely a diversion from the eternal struggle with France soon had their day as Emperor Napoleon III made sudden switches in foreign policy after the war was over, and the British public became extremely hostile to him. From a naval point of view, the completion of the breakwater around the great artificial harbour of Cherbourg gave the French fleet a major port in the English Channel for the first time, within 60 miles of the English coast. In the naval estimates of 1859, Sir John Pakington asked for an increase of a million pounds in the budget, from nearly £9 million to nearly £10 million, and a rise in the number of men from 64,400 to 84,100. He agreed that 'the Vote for men we are now going to propose is, I admit, of a very unusual amount. I believe it is the largest Vote of men ever proposed in this House in a time of peace.'[65] The government resorted to an ancient means of raising the men – a bounty of £10 for able seamen on enlistment, which was announced by Royal Proclamation on 30 April 1859.

There were still hopes of recruiting merchant seaman on a regular basis, and ships were sent out to the west and north in search of recruits. Captain Bedford Pim of the paddle frigate *Gorgon* made a tour of the north-east of England, which he believed had many 'first rate men' who so far had 'not contributed at all to man the fleet'. He put up posters and held a series of lively meetings in various towns. Some men complained about the end of the Navigation Acts, which had finally been repealed, and the lack of

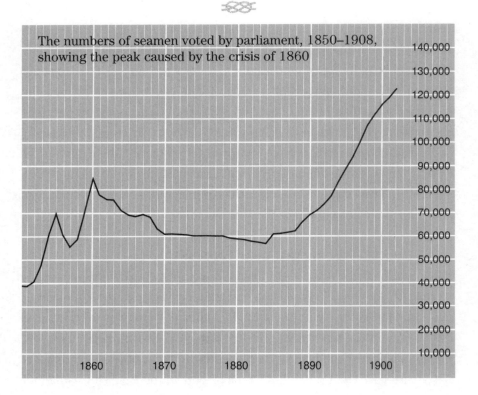

The numbers of seamen voted by parliament, 1850–1908, showing the peak caused by the crisis of 1860

protection for British seamen, but that was beyond Pim's authority. Some had read in the press about the use of the lash in the navy and were put off by that. Some were old seamen who had served in the wars and offered their reminiscences. In Sunderland, one John Robinson suggested that if the Admiralty was serious about recruiting, it would be better to 'send down something to look at, and not an old rattle-trap like the *Gorgon*'. Perhaps he had read the book by his namesake William Robinson or Jack Nastyface, whose *Nautical Economy* was a rather lurid account of life in the fleet at the time of Trafalgar, for he said that he was 'opposed to going on board a man-o'-war to be kicked about by stripling boys'. Pim then made himself unpopular by criticizing the seaman's union and was hissed by parts of the audience. He entered about twenty men after all his efforts.[66]

The Admiralty urged officers to treat merchant seamen well if they did enter, not just for their own sakes but also for the reputation of the Royal Navy and for recruitment in times to come. They were to be given a 'cordial reception', and it was be borne in mind that they would 'have to renounce many old customs and adopt others which will at first be irksome to them'. There was to be no 'harsh attempt' to impose naval discipline on them, their instructors should be 'patient and forbearing' without actually abandoning naval discipline.[67]

The navy got its recruits in the end, though it was complained that only a thousand out of 7,000 were able seamen. The *United Services Magazine* jeered that,

> The Royal Commissioners tried coaxing, extra rations of biscuit, beef, cocoa, onions and plum duff, as well as pensions seen through a hazy vista of twenty years' service. Their baits were useless. Jack declined them all, but he has bitten at £10 in a lump. The Queen's bounty goes straight to the heart of the man; while a nice balancing act of additional pay, better rations, allotments, badge-money and pensions were looked on as so much bilge-water.[68]

## NAVAL MUTINY

The expanded fleet revived the old prospect of indiscipline and mutiny. As the *United Services Magazine* commented in August 1859, 'It was hardly to be expected that the 10,000 seamen collected from the four winds of heaven to man the Navy, under the recent proclamation, should all settle down in their berths without some little outbreak.'[69] The rapid expansion caused considerable tension within the navy, and the 1850s ended with several outbreaks of mutiny that were reminiscent of the old days. The newly commissioned steam frigate *Liffey* was at Plymouth early in 1859 when she received orders to proceed on foreign service. The men were refused leave before setting off, and a disturbance took place. The Admiralty took a fair stance and allowed the men leave, but this concession looked like a sign of weakness and led to more demands. The inexperienced recruits and boys of the screw ship-of-the-line *Hero* were refused permission when the older men were given it, and took action.

The screw battleship *Princess Royal* had been a difficult ship since she was re-commissioned after the war and most of her men refused to re-enlist. It took some time to find a crew, and when she finally sailed she had a high proportion of bad characters. Captain Giffard started treating them leniently but soon turned to harsh punishments. The Admiralty noticed this from the punishment returns and replaced him with Captain Thomas Baillie, a gentle figure. But his leniency and compassion did not work, and on one occasion off Alexandria the crew took the unusual and highly dangerous step of refusing to go aloft as a gale blew up. Back in Portsmouth, it was decided to pay her off. On 12 November, Queen Victoria was in the dockyard for the launch of a ship bearing her name, and the crew asked for leave, which was not normally given to ships paying off. It was agreed to give it to one watch, but the seamen wanted to settle it amongst themselves, selecting men from both watches. The captain agreed, but then some of the crew began to demand 'leave for all or none'. The port admiral heard of this and cancelled all leave, so the crew went into open mutiny and took possession of the lower deck. Marines were brought in to restore control, and 108 men were tried by court martial and sentenced to terms of imprisonment ranging from three months to two years.

Naval officers put the wave of mutiny down to three different causes – variation in discipline between ships, excessive punishments and leave, which was unregulated and depended entirely on the whim of the captain. This was addressed by an Admiralty Circular of April 1860, with the first regulations for leave. Normally it was to be limited to 48 hours, though that might be extended to four days if the ship were under repair. If a ship was being taken out of commission, the men were to stay on board until the ship had been completely de-rigged. After that they might be allowed up to 24 days' leave at a time while waiting for the paperwork to be completed.[70]

As the decade ended, it was not clear if any of the new policies had succeeded. The *United Services Magazine* claimed that continuous service was 'a complete failure'.[71] The new uniforms had barely reached the men on the messdecks and the new Royal Naval Reserve was not yet up and running. But all of these were essentially long-term policies, which would take years to bear fruit.

# 3

# THE AGE OF IRON
# 1860–1875

In 1859 the launch of the French ironclad *Gloire* changed the naval world. She was quickly followed by the much superior British *Warrior*. This began a new revolution, and for the next 30 years ship design remained unstable, as one innovation followed another. In 1866 the Battle of Lissa between the Italians and the Austrians seemed to demonstrate the value of the ram bow, and it was adopted by *Warrior*'s successors. The naval battles of the American Civil War showed that guns could be fitted in turrets to increase their utility greatly, but that was not easy in a sailing ship. *Captain* of 1870 attempted to combine turrets with a sailing rig but was quickly lost in the Bay of Biscay. Another type was the central battery ship, in which large guns were fitted in an armoured citadel, to be moved on rails from one gun port to another. In 1871 *Devastation* went further and abandoned sail power altogether, but her reliance on engines meant that her range was short and she was largely confined to coastal defence. In view of the instability in technology and the constant threat that a new weapon might appear, doubts were raised about whether the navy was the most effective defence of the country. The army became more prominent and popular, and the Palmerston forts (or follies) were built to defend the three main naval bases.

## GREENWICH HOSPITAL

Greenwich Hospital had been founded by Queen Mary in 1694 as a refuge for retired and disabled seamen. It might affect the seaman at both ends of his career, though its importance was declining. The Royal Naval School[1] educated the sons of sailors and sent them into the navy. The Director General of the Medical Department of the Navy thought that the education in the Lower School was 'quite perfect', in contrast to the Upper School for the sons of officers, which was dominated by patronage.[2] By 1852 captains were noticing that Greenwich boys were well trained but physically inferior to the general run of recruits. Captain Thomas Maitland stated, 'I have found about one-third of them undersized, and not to be compared with the boys selected by the standard of height and weight.' And they were not suitable to be employed as servants like other boys – 'the *school* boys imbibe loftier notions than arise from emptying a bucket of slops.'[3]

Discipline in the School was tightened by Captain Charles Burney after he became headmaster in 1870, but it began to move in a different direction to become an industrial school, training boys in crafts such as tailoring, shoemaking and bricklaying. It was no longer compulsory to enter the navy, and by the late nineteenth century the Greenwich boys formed a much lower proportion of the fleet than they had previously.

The Greenwich Pensioners were at the other end of the age scale. From 1848, more than thirty years after the most recent war, it was noticed that the numbers of men applying for the Hospital were declining – by 1858 there were 900 vacancies, about a third of the full complement. Sir Charles Napier identified some of the problems:

A married man, who goes into Greenwich Hospital, gets his clothes, his victuals and his lodging; but if he has a wife, how is she to be maintained? He is obliged to take his provisions out of Greenwich Hospital, and give his wife half, and live upon the other half in the Hospital, or lodge out on the value of his provisions and tobacco money. Just suppose an old sailor, who has been accustomed to racket about in the world, shut up in Greenwich Hospital; he has a fine coat on his back to be sure, and has a comfortable cabin, and his victuals are good, but he has nothing to spend – he has nothing to go and amuse himself with – he has no garden to cultivate, and he gets tired of life.[4]

Furthermore, a man had to give up any status he had once had in the navy, unless he were made a boatswain and put in charge of the discipline of his ward. 'All distinctions of rank are effaced. Men who have attained the rank of petty, and even warrant officer are disrated and mingled indiscriminately with ordinary seamen and the refuse of the naval service.'[5] He was expected to wear an old-fashioned cocked hat, which was ridiculed by the boys of the neighbourhood. A man could not expect any rest in the Hospital:

> With regard to the discipline, I am disposed to think that it is too strong for old sailors. The old sailors imagine that they enter the hospital for the purpose of being happy after their fashion for the rest of their lives, but if they commit themselves by taking too much grog they are liable to be stopped, and are generally stopped at the gates, and afterwards sent to the council. The regulations of the council are very strict.[6]

As a result, the standard of men in the Hospital had declined, and they were now of 'a very inferior class'. There was some reform, and the pensioners' pocket money was increased, but it was a dying institution. Increased out-pensions were offered to eligible men, and the last pensioners moved out of Greenwich Hospital in October 1869. Even the seamen's graves were dug up, and the remains of 3,000 men were reburied several miles away.

## LIFE IN THE TRAINING SHIPS

The training ships for boys were well established, and very detailed regulations were drawn up in 1864 to ensure uniformity. On arrival, a boy was to be measured and weighed, and the chaplain would examine him in reading and writing. He would be questioned about his particulars in the presence of the master-at-arms, and then given a bath and a haircut. The gunner supplied him with a hammock and bedding. By 1880 it had been discovered that 'the boys are far from being sufficiently clad in cold weather, especially when wearing their night clothing', and extra underclothing was recommended, including two white woollen jerseys with a blue edge and two pairs of 'stout cotton drawers'.

His schooling began, a combination of normal education and training in seamanship. On a Monday morning, for example, the boys would get up at

5 a.m., stow their hammocks and clean the upper deck until breakfast was served at 6.30. They would then fall in to loose the ship's sails before being inspected by the instructors and ship's police – a small yard was set up just above the deck so that the younger boys could practice on it before going aloft properly. Later in the morning, some would go to gunnery or rifle drill, while others would be trained by the boatswain in handling the boats. After a hard morning's work their messes were inspected at 11.50, just before dinner. Work continued all day until the boys were ready for bed at 8.20. HMS *Impregnable* at Plymouth had a boat fitted with a wheel for steering practice, and asked for more to be fitted in 1867.[7] School work, in reading, writing and arithmetic, was not to be interrupted except on medical orders. Boys were not to be kept too long at any one subject, 'otherwise they will get tired and weary', and a 'magic lantern' was available to show slides. Backward boys had to attend evening classes in groups of about twelve or fifteen. The petty officer instructors were 'a very interesting set of men. Mostly bearded, they were men of the mast and sail era, alert and agile aloft; their mastery of the craft of seamanship inspired us boys with something akin to awe.'[8]

The regulations suggest a benevolent despotism in a classic Victorian manner. Boys could earn badges by good work, which entitled them to extra leave. Those with parents in the area were allowed home on certain weekends, and the ships closed down for Christmas and for a vacation in the summer. Each mess was in the charge of two boys, who wore anchors on their arm, and petty officer boys wore the crown and anchor. A fiddler gave the boys the opportunity of dancing and helped to 'promote cheerfulness'. The school rooms were open in the evening, and the authorities believed that 'many boys will be delighted to avail themselves of this accommodation to write letters, read books and amuse themselves with quiet games'. The ship's police were to 'check bad language and violent conduct'. Discipline was to be light and subtle – flogging was only to be used 'in cases of theft or highly immoral character', and the cane would 'rarely be required':

It has been found by experience, that where a good system has been established, and where the boys have felt that the commanding officer has an interest in their well-being, that very little punishment has been needed; and, indeed, that there has been an almost entire absence of it.[9]

It is doubtful if the boys read these regulations, and they would have been amazed if they did. Far from a life in which violence was forbidden, they were constantly harassed by the sticks and ropes wielded by petty officers, particularly the ship's police. Charles Humphreys joined HMS *Boscawen* at Portland in November 1870: 'I cannot describe those 12 months of learning discipline. We were very often short of food and many a rope's end did I feel. Our instructors were very cruel, but I suppose it was mainly because we had a very stern captain.'[10] Thomas Holman joined *St Vincent* at Portsmouth two years later and was far more positive, for it was 'my wildest dream realized'. But even he was 'accelerated at times by a sharp cut from the Corporal's cane, which sent me bounding up the ladders between the decks, three steps at a time'.[11] Sam Noble reached the same ship in 1875 after a long trip from Scotland and found that most of the warrant officers carried a 'small piece of rope known as a "Corrector." It was about eighteen inches long, ending in a wall knot and crown – and as supple as a serpent.'[12]

## THE CHARACTER OF THE SEAMAN

The way forward for the lower deck was not to increase the number of marines, as some had suggested, but to militarise the seamen. They were already wearing uniform, and they would learn to take part in landing parties, carry out drill like the army and fire small arms. In January 1860, for example, orders were given to set up a rifle range for seamen at Portsmouth.[13] Continuous service became increasingly dominant in the navy. By 1860 the CS man already formed the majority, 21,397 men out of 39,597. Numbers of non-continuous-service men had dropped to less than 4,000 by 1890, while overall numbers had risen to more than 39,000. By 1869, when Henry Capper joined, the non-CS men seemed creatures from a bygone age. They were still recruited by Mrs Wafer near the gate of Portsmouth Dockyard. They were of 'a socially inferior type' but provided many of the best seamen for working aloft. 'Tom Huntingdon was a rascal, but the finest practical sailor on board. He was rated Chief Quartermaster and must have been 70 years of age.'[14]

Promotion from ordinary to Able Seaman was far from a foregone conclusion in 1860, especially since men recruited under the old system were often unsuitable and lacked training. Twenty years later when the great majority of naval seaman had been through the training ships, such men were almost extinct. But even then, passing for Able Seaman was still a significant moment for a young seaman. As Sam Noble wrote, 'Five pence a day meant something near two pounds extra a quarter and that sum (to me) opened up great possibilities, not to mention the glory of having "A.B." on your letters from home.'[15]

The Victorian sailor had already acquired his sentimental love of animals, and any exception to this was likely to be punished. In 1863, Stoker Biddlecombe of HMS *Glasgow* was ordered to get rid of a dog brought on board by another man. He killed it in a most barbarous manner, and when he was tried by the local magistrates, the seamen and stokers of his own ship gave evidence against him: he was given three months' imprisonment and discharged from the navy.[16] In the screw gunvessel *Swallow* a few years later, the captain had a small brown spaniel, while monkey Jacko became a universal favourite. 'He slept with a different man every night; and never a word was said when he was found coiled up in a hammock. The owner knew it was his turn, and just pushed him over a bit and turned in.'[17]

Good conduct stripes, rather like NCOs' chevrons in the army, were first awarded in 1849, one each for five years' service up to a maximum of three. Using the 'carrot' rather than the 'stick', the Admiralty began to extend their use to encourage the men. In 1860 two years were knocked off the requirement for each badge, so that the first one was awarded after three years, the second after eight and the third after thirteen. It had also been noticed that petty officers were not allowed to qualify for more badges after their promotion, though they could wear the ones they already had, and this anomaly was removed.[18]

## DISCIPLINE AND PUNISHMENT

The outbreak of mutiny in 1859–60 caused the Admiralty seek a new Naval Discipline Act from Parliament and to produce the first *Queen's Regulations and Admiralty Instructions* two years later. As a result, the offence of mutiny was better defined, leave policies were liberalized and made more uniform, and there was an attempt to recruit a new type of ship's police from a 'superior class of person'. All this had some effect. There were a few sporadic outbreaks of mutiny in 1863 and 1865, and four men were tried for the offence in 1878, but the 1880s were free of courts martial for mutiny.[19]

Society at large was turning against the idea of physical punishment, and flogging became increasingly difficult to justify against Parliamentary pressure. In 1861 Commander Nicolas of HMS *Trident* was dismissed his ship with disgrace after excessive flogging of two boys. The returns given to Parliament showed a gradual decline in its use, from one in every 147 men in the Channel Fleet 1863 to one in 200 in 1864.[20] In 1871 flogging was severely restricted, though it was retained for boys; and in 1879 it was suspended in peacetime. This led to a search for other punishments, as outlined in the new *Queen's Regulations* of 1862. The authorities produced an impressive list of fifteen punishments for minor offences alone, including solitary confinement in a cell or under a canvas screen, stoppage of grog or its watering down, stoppage of leave, deductions from pay and extra drills. There was some attempt to make the punishment fit the crime: 'Persons of careless and inattentive habits, with reference to their clothes, hammock, or bag, may be made to carry them on their shoulder, but not to exceed an hour on the same day; and limited to three days.'[21]

By 1857 the Admiralty was worried about the policy of sending offenders to civil prisons. The regime there was very harsh, particularly for those sentenced to hard labour. Even worse, most prisons now enforced the 'separate system and the entire prevention of intercourse between the Prisoners'. This was very cruel to sailors, who were used to the gregarious life of the messdeck. Moreover, men were being set there for 'very trifling breaches of discipline', to serve alongside hardened civilian criminals. The Admiralty did not want to interfere in the independence of courts martial but reminded officers of the consequences of harsh sentences.[22]

This was only partly reflected in the court martial returns for November 1862 to March 1863. William Blytheway, a ship's corporal in *Indus*, probably thought he got off lightly when convicted for desertion in North

America: 'In consideration of very good character, sentenced only to be disrated to ordinary seaman, and to be imprisoned in one of Her Majesty's Gaols without hard labour for six months.' Ordinary Seaman John Moran of *Galatea* used 'insubordinate and disgusting language' to his lieutenant and was awarded 48 lashes and four years in civilian prison. Michael Cronin, another ship's corporal from *Revenge,* used 'insulting and threatening language to the Master at Arms' and struck another corporal 'in a violent manner' but got off with disrating to able seaman, reduction to the second class for conduct and dismissal from the ship. In all, fifteen men were sentenced to imprisonment during the period, ending with four men who deserted from *Fawn* at Portsmouth and were given nine to eighteen months in the naval prison at Lewes (which had been established after an Act of 1847, together with one at Bodmin).[23] In 1887, eighteen men of the 'seaman class' in home waters were sentenced to hard labour, plus five of the 'non-seaman class.' As always, the discipline problem was worse on foreign stations, where 53 men of the navy received hard labour, and 18 suffered other forms of imprisonment.

According to rules drawn up in 1862, only men who were going to stay on in the navy were to be sent to the naval prisons; those who were to be discharged at the end of their sentences went to civil ones. They were not to arrive after 6 p.m., or on a Sunday, Christmas Day or Good Friday. On arrival each man was to be placed in a reception cell, where he would be 'strictly and minutely searched, but with all possible regard to decency'. He would be deprived of all his belongings, shaved on the head and face, and issued with 'a complete prison dress, with proper marks or badges for the purpose of distinguishing the class to which each prisoner belongs'. He would normally be put into the third class on entry, working at hard labour in the daytime, and then picking oakum until eight o'clock. Every second night he would sleep fully clothed in a rough bed, 'in the same manner as a soldier on guard'. After a period, longer for repeat offenders, and having shown good conduct, he might be promoted to the second class, when the requirement to pick oakum was removed and he slept in a normal bed for two nights out of three. But still he was not allowed to communicate with other prisoners, and his spare time was to be spent in reading or instruction. Having shown 'quiet orderly habits and general good conduct', he might be promoted to the first class: his labour was slightly less hard, and after 6 p.m. and during meals, 'prisoners of this class, in an associated prison, shall be permitted to communicate with each other in an orderly manner under the general superintendence of an Officer ...' A prisoner was expected to wash and shave every day and wash his feet once a week. He was allowed a clean shirt and socks twice a week. His hair was cut very short at least once a month, though he was permitted to grow it longer in the last part of his sentence if he was in the first class. At the end of his sentence he was released at seven in the morning, but if it expired on a Sunday he would be let out the evening before. In either case, he would be escorted back to his duty on a ship or station.[24]

## The Gunnery Revolution

Gunnery training in HM ships *Excellent* and *Cambridge* became more important than ever. In 1862 both officers and men were expected to know a long catechism, with questions that must have strained the literacy of the average seamen. New types of guns were coming into use, and candidates were asked:

> Q. What advantages have elongated projectiles over spherical ones?
> A. They are superior in weight to spherical balls of the same diameter, and are of considerably less diameter, if of the same weight; they consequently lose their velocity far less rapidly ... When the head of the projectile is conical, the resistance of the air is less than with a flat head.[25]

This was only the beginning of a revolution that would transform naval gunnery. The iron plates of *Warrior* were practically immune to enemy shot, so all the major powers began to develop rifled guns that would penetrate them. Captain Cowper Coles of the Royal Navy invented a revolving turret holding a pair of guns, while in the American Civil War the success of USS *Monitor* showed what could be done with such a concept. All this had an effect on gunnery training. By 1870 the Admiralty had realized that, with most of the new turret ships having only four main guns each, accuracy of firing rather than saturation coverage was the key to success. First and second captains of guns were to be trained in aiming over a distance, and others would be trained to replace them in the event of casualties. Competitions were instituted, with prizes of up to £2 10s for the best gun crews. In each exercise, two targets were to be dropped 100–150 yards apart, and independent firing was to begin when the ship had steamed at least 600 yards from one of them. Eight rounds were fired from each gun, and officers aloft and next to the gun were to assess the effects. The captain of the gun, usually a petty officer, would be told the approximate range of his target before firing, but otherwise it was to be done by eye.[26]

Seaman gunners were established in three classes, which were largely independent of a man's 'substantive' rating as a petty officer, leading seaman and so on. By orders of 1868, an acting seaman gunner was a man who had trained on board his ship to gain 'a good knowledge of the Drills of the Great Guns mounted on board their respective ships, also of the Rifle and Cutlass Exercises'. Seaman gunners second class were trained by a course of 98 days at *Excellent* or *Cambridge*, and seaman gunners first class had deeper knowledge and some ability as instructors. Gunnery instructors

> must either be Petty Officers, Leading Seamen, or have passed for Leading Seaman ... They are required to be of 'very good' character, to have a thorough knowledge of every part of the Course of Instruction for Seaman Gunners and Instructors, with the addition of details, and to be fully capable of instructing and bringing forward classes.[27]

In practice nearly all of the gunnery instructors were petty officers first class. Despite the title, they did not necessarily do much instruction but were superior technicians.

## THE SHIP'S POLICE

The master-at-arms was the head of the ship's police, now that his older job of training the crew in small arms had become obsolete. In the 1860s he and his assistants, the ship's corporals, were given extra duties and status.

The new rating of ship's corporal second class was created, though misleadingly he was equivalent to a petty officer first class. He had to pass a stiff examination and receive a certificate from his captain stating that, 'He writes a fair legible hand, can keep Accounts correctly, and is of good character, and produces satisfactory testimonials, and I consider him an active intelligent man, fit for the Rating ...'[28] It was not a 'pushover', and in 1861 it was complained that at Portsmouth 'great numbers' had been 'rejected, either from physical defects or from inability to pass the requisite examination in arithmetic'.[29] The master-at-arms needed yet higher qualifications, and according to the Regulations,

> When first nominated, he is to undergo an examination by the Captain and Naval Instructor of the Flag Ship at Woolwich, Sheerness, Portsmouth or Devonport. To qualify a man for this rating, he must produce certificates of servitude and good conduct for three years in the Navy, Army or Police Force, or in such other service or employment as may peculiarly fit him for the duties that will devolve upon him.

He was to be 30 to 40 years old, and no 'unworthy or incompetent person' was to be selected.[30]

Most of the master-at-arms' instructions were derived directly from past ages – to patrol the decks at night and see that lights were put out (which became less important in iron and steel warships lit by electricity). He was to prevent the traffic in spirits and to report all defaulters to the captain in the morning.[31] Police duties included patrolling the ports from the local depot ships such as HMS *Victory* at Portsmouth. In 1861 Captain Byrne of that ship was generally pleased with the way things were going, though he had only ten men to patrol the area and often had to find others to draft into ships commissioning.[32] In return, the ship's police were exceptionally well paid by lower-deck standards. A corporal second class got a minimum of 2 shillings a day, equal to any other petty officer first class, but unlike them he could rise to 2s.8d per day. As a corporal first class he could reach 3s 8d per day, far more than any chief petty officer of the seaman branch. As a master-at-arms he would start on a minimum of 5 shillings per day – other chiefs were on a fixed rate of 2s.3d per day.

The police service was open to men of various branches, and this caused discontent with the seamen, who resented a landsman or stoker being put over them: 'The grievance is that for instance an A.B. who cannot get on, or a stoker, or a marine or signalman, who can't get on, may become a ship's corporal (petty officer first class), and go over the head of a petty officer of many years' standing.' Even one of the masters-at-arms agreed: 'There have been cases where the ship's corporals have been taken from the wrong class of people, such as sick-bay men, steward's assistants, sick-berth stewards, able seamen and marines.'[33] In 1879 it was stated that men often transferred to the ship's police to seek promotion, as Josephin Howard, master-at-arms of *Agincourt,* did. He was looking for 'more pay, and in order to better my position'. Boatswain's Mate John Buckley of *Arrogant* confirmed this from his experience:

> There was an able seaman at the time that I was captain of the 'Top', who could not be trusted in regard to doing any duties as a seaman; he could not be trusted even with splicing a rope, but in paying-off from the ship he happened to be turned into a guard ship and passed for a ship's corporal.[34]

Men applied from different motives, as various masters-at-arms testified in 1887. Robert Cluett of *Duke of Wellington* 'never had any particular liking for a seaman's life'. The family of Edwin Morgan of *Devastation* had a tradition of service in the civilian police force. John Williams of *Iron Duke* found that he could make 3 shillings a day as a ship's corporal. But the general view on both the quarterdeck and the lower deck was that they were 'professional failures' who could not make it in a more skilled part of the navy.[35]

The ship's police never lived up to the high hopes placed in them by the authorities. James Wood noticed their corruption from the moment he entered HMS *Impregnable* in 1878. He gave them his civilian clothes to be sent home for his brother, but they never arrived. Later he found the police acting as *agents provocateurs* and operating a 'perpetual system of espionage'. 'Why the ship's police were ever introduced into the navy I do not know; in the majority of ships they lead useless, idle lives, and seem to try to justify their existence by reporting men for petty trifles.' They demanded bribes to pass men as correctly dressed for leave and to have a man kept on in an easy billet in a depot ship. They were less oppressive at sea, and he found his master-at-arms was an excellent shipmate until they arrived back at Portsmouth, where he was engaged in 'reaping the benefits of those perquisites which were looked on at the time as belonging by right to his class'. [36]

Many officers disliked the police system for a different reason – that it encouraged the other petty officers to neglect their duties. The officers composing the Committee on Ratings of 1887 asked many of their witnesses,

> Is it not the fact that when the petty officers have finished their duty on deck with the men, they consider themselves relieved of all further responsibility as regards the men of their part, and that when on the lower deck, the men come under the supervision of the police only?[37]

The majority of witnesses agreed that this was the case, and the Committee recommended the abolition of the ship's police, which was not accepted by the Admiralty.

### STOKERS AND ARTIFICERS

High pay and a flexible recruiting and promotion policy meant that some stokers were quite well qualified in the early 1860s. By the 1862 Regulations, a stoker was paid 2 shillings a day, 3d more than a leading seaman. Captains were ordered to examine candidates with the commander and the chief engineer to see if they were 'duly qualified for the situation'. If not 'sufficiently experienced for that rating, if in every other respect desirable men for the service', they were to be entered as stokers second class.[38] They were eligible for promotion to leading stoker, which confusingly was equivalent to a petty officer in the seaman class. William Walker had already served an apprenticeship as a fitter before he was attracted by these conditions. He entered in 1859, and he was soon promoted to leading stoker.[39]

In June 1863 the Admiralty created the new rating of chief stoker, a chief petty officer who was to be paid the same as a master-at-arms. He was to be 'a skilled mechanic, capable of managing an engine and of taking the place of a junior engineer'. This would 'give an additional stimulus to the important class of stokers by holding out the prospect of promotion and of an increase in pay to those men who may qualify themselves for it – a strict examination for Chief Stoker will be imposed.' The rating was indeed created, and a few suitable men were found. William Bateman had served an apprenticeship as a turner in brass and iron with the London & North Western Railway. He worked in Sheerness Dockyard until 'family affairs induced me to leave', and he was entered as a chief stoker in 1864 at the age of 28.[40] But it seems that not many stokers of the period had the education and training to take on such a role, and the Admiralty had to look elsewhere.

The rank of chief stoker was abolished, and a new and unique rating was introduced by an Order-in-Council of March 1868. The engine room artificer was intended to replace the old assistant engineer, who had been a warrant officer and was expected to do a certain amount of skilled manual work on the repair of engines, as well as supervising their running. The new ERA was to be equivalent to a chief petty officer, the highest rating on the lower deck, and still quite rare at that time. In contrast to the mature CPOs, the ERA could be recruited at any age from 21 to 35. He would already have served an apprenticeship as an engine fitter, boilermaker, blacksmith or coppersmith. He needed a good enough education to keep a log and to learn more about engines. He would be examined by the chief engineer of a dockyard and the inspector of machinery, and if successful he would be taken on for a year's probation. By the end of that time,

> He must understand the uses and management of the various gauges – of the feed, injection, and blow-off cocks; he must know how to ascertain the density and height of the water in the boilers, and what should be done in the event of priming.
>
> He must also know how to regulate the water admitted for condensation; what should be do in the event of water passing into the cylinders; or of a bearing becoming heated; and how to act, on the occurrences of any of the ordinary casualties of an engine-room.[41]

He was also to get a certificate from his captain that he was fit to take charge of a watch in the engine room. His metalworking skills would be especially useful in a ship on an isolated station in the far-flung empire, while his education and status made him far more reliable and resourceful than a stoker to take charge of the machinery.

The original Admiralty circular had plenty of ambiguities. Potential recruits at Plymouth wanted to know if the probation clause was reciprocal – if they could leave after a year if they found the duties were not what they expected. The Admiralty ruled that continuous service meant what it said: they would have to stay on unless they purchased their discharge. It was also pointed out that the late entry at 35 would disqualify a man from a pension, as he would not have time to put in the necessary service before retirement at 45. But the most contentious issue, with far-reaching consequences, was the uniform. The sailor's uniform was still not popular, and potential entrants expressed the wish that they would not be compelled to wear the blue serge frock. Nothing was said about this in the circular, but the Admiralty agreed to a blue jacket with gilt buttons, but none on the cuff, and a peaked cap instead of the seaman's round hat. It would have a small crown-and-anchor badge, as worn by the civil branch of the navy.

An examination was held in the Keyham Steam Factory in Devonport Dockyard in May 1868. A large number of men applied, but only 35 of these passed the surgeon and 29 passed the examination. Only 9 wanted to enter under existing regulations, including 2 chief stokers who were already in the steam reserve. The rest were rated in the third class, so the scheme was slow to take off.[42] By 1876 however, it was reported that 'plenty of applications for entry at Chatham are made by boilermakers, fitters, moulders and coppersmiths'. They were 'willing to enter for [the] present rate of pay, but get discontented after'.[43]

The ERA was part of the Victorian 'aristocracy of labour' and very conscious of the fact. Though he was grounded in the trade union movement, it was in craft unions, which were more interested in preserving the privileges of a particular sector than in working-class solidarity. Even when the rest of the lower deck showed a kind of trade union militancy, the ERA stood aside. He was always very jealous of the privileges that kept him apart from other members of the crew. Indeed, he was a very different figure from the rest of the lower deck, including the seamen and stokers:

Engine Room Artificers who have served their apprenticeship as fitters or boiler makers, and have thus placed themselves in a certain position of independence, join the Naval Service at an age of between twenty and thirty, having already contracted the habits of their class on shore; they have been accustomed to regular limited hours of work, to pass their Sundays at home, and on returning from their work daily to find their meals ready, their house cleaned for them, and themselves relieved from all supervision and work other than that of their trade. On board [a] ship of war they find themselves surrounded by men who have been brought up to a different system from boyhood, and who cannot therefore understand that the habits of their own ordinary course of life may prove a hardship to others, who for many years have been accustomed to a different mode of living.[44]

Relations reached a low point in the battleship *Vanguard* when the sailors and marines 'were continually jawing at you, and pitching potatoes and bits of bread into your mess, and come and sit at the end of the table, making remarks'. James Borlase found it very difficult to read in that atmosphere: 'They want to know what book you have got, and where you have got it from; and if you tell them it is your own book, they will not believe you, but will spin a yarn about one thing or another ...'[45]

Without definite instructions from above, it was difficult to fit the ERA into the accommodation on board ship. That issue was becoming increasingly vexed in any case, as the new iron and steel ships had far more compartments but fewer enclosed spaces, with different groups competing for the best ones. James Borlase did not like messing with the seamen petty officers: they were 'not good company, if you want to become a blackguard you can mix with them'. William Barrett, on the other hand, was happy to mess with the chiefs. 'I have found the blue-jacket chief petty officers very companionable men, and men that I could agree with.' But his situation was not comfortable: he often came off watch to find that no food was laid on for him, and he had to get it in the best way he could – or do without.

The location of the mess was also important. William Walker was quite happy to eat with the schoolmaster in *Immortalité*, 'right forward on the starboard side', but the long distance from the engine room caused problems as he had to pass through other messes in his dirty overalls. The ERAs were contented in *Invincible* in 1875 because they had their own mess on the lower deck with a stoker to clean it for them. This was another issue, as ERAs were not used to such chores. James Borlase was reported by a chief boatswain's mate in the gunboat *Pigeon* for failing to keep his mess clean. They were much happier when a stoker or boy was appointed to clean it for them, a privilege normally only allowed to the master-at-arms on the lower deck. But some ERAs were not happy to mess with the master-at-arms, and they resented his status, as the only member of the lower deck in authority over them. Masters-at-arms seem to have taken great delight in exercising this power and in controlling the leave and uniform of the ERAs. William Barrett found this 'very obnoxious':

> For instance, I might be at work below, and I have been told that I might have leave when I had finished my work, well when I go to the master-at-arms, and tell him that I want leave, he would put some obstacle in the way, he must see the commanding officer, and could not do it now because the commanding officer was at dinner, that sort of thing.[46]

The ERA also resented the fact that the master-at-arms had a grander uniform, a frock coat rather than a reefer jacket, which William Barrett did not think was 'at all becoming a man'.

## THE RISE OF THE SIGNALLER

By the Regulations of 1862, a yeoman of signals was a petty officer first class, the head of the signal department in a ship of the line or a frigate. Under the yeoman were three signalmen in a ship of the line and two in a frigate, rated as petty officers second class. They were selected from the better-educated able seamen and expected to send and receive flag signals, mostly by day. They were not completely trusted, for the regulations also demanded that an officer be appointed to look out for signals from the flagship.

In the 1860s, Captain Colomb developed a system of flashing lights using Morse code. As well as making signalling by night more practicable, this demanded a new level of skill in order that Morse messages should be transmitted and received as fast as possible. In 1869 Captain Willes of *Agincourt* pointed out that a much greater signal complement was needed and suggested that they should be selected as boys, with new ratings of signalmen second and third class, equivalent to able and ordinary seamen. The senior rating in the branch should be regularized as the chief yeoman of signals. This was enforced by an Admiralty order of March 1870.[47]

The Branch soon expanded, and they were the only specialists, outside the seaman branch itself, who were entitled to take military command. But still the signallers were not happy. Though they had better promotion prospects to petty officer than the seamen, they were not entitled to non-substantive pay as gunners. Chief yeomen were only borne in a few flagships, and there were only about twenty posts in the service, and there was no warrant rank for them to be promoted to. Opportunities were very uneven, for there were no chief yeomen at all in the South America station, and only one in China – the highest rating in South America was a single petty officer second class, with 12 lower ratings. Meanwhile there were 7 chiefs in the home ports, 32 petty officers first class, 52 of the second class and 45 ratings.[48] A new rating of leading signalman was introduced, equivalent to a leading seaman. The Rating Committee of 1889 recommended that a roster be kept at each of the home ports so that advancement was spread more evenly and did not depend on the station the man was serving in. A distinguishing badge of crossed flags was introduced, and some men were to be trained in electric telegraphy for shore communication. Unlike many of the recommendations of the Committee, most of these were adopted by the Admiralty.[49]

## ACTION IN THE EMPIRE

The end of the Crimean War led into the great age of the gunboat, as imperialism became increasingly fashionable and steam power made many more things possible, while the world network of electric telegraphs allowed the authorities to communicate with distant colonies. In the five years up to 1861 there were more than a hundred requests for naval assistance from the Foreign Office, Colonial Office, consuls, groups of merchants and even from the Trustees of the British Museum, who wanted help with an archaeological expedition in Turkey. Only a few of these were refused or deferred, and British seamen found themselves serving on every continent and every ocean. In 1861 alone, they carried out 22 operations. They were sent to Newfoundland to 'preserve peace during apprehended riots', to Japan to protect British subjects, to the Bahamas to prevent wrecking, to Zanzibar against the slave trade, to Italy, to Gibraltar, to Mauritius and to the Malay coast.

Thus James Wood found himself in boats off Zanzibar chasing Arab dhows and trying to prevent the slave trade – though he had doubts when he found that the slaves actually lived a comfortable life but were subjected to hazards and hardship during and after a chase by the British navy.[50] Sam Noble patrolled off the west coast of Africa in the gunboat *Swallow* and visited both sides of the Atlantic, including Uruguay and Argentina.

The 1860s and '70s were also a golden age for large, well-armed landing parties known as naval brigades. There were about sixteen major operations, from New Zealand to Dominica, and from South Africa to Egypt. They gave the seaman experiences of many different kinds of warfare. Petty Officer William Jenkin of HMS *Shah* faced a Zulu charge in 1879:

> The enemy sighted by our scouts 6 am. Order 'man the trenches', every man in his place in three seconds. Zulus commenced fire at 6.30 pm, advancing in horseshoe formation, estimated number of Zulus 1500 to 3000. Gatlings and 6 pdrs opened with shell at 800 yards. Enemy advance courageously and ignorantly to within thirty yards of our trenches, one man throwing his assegai at a Gatling gun.[51]

Ordinary Seaman Charles Hickman of *Invincible* spent five days on police work after landing in Alexandria in 1882, 'the orders being that if any Arab is found with loot in his possession … he is to be lashed up and have six dozen with the cat'. Later he served as a fireman with the station in a disued theatre.[52]

Most sailors enjoyed the work on shore. They vied to be selected for the party and sometimes became distressed when turned down. Seaman gunners formed the bulk of most parties, and their training at *Excellent* and *Cambridge* was tailored to this kind of work. Stokers were mostly left behind to maintain the ship, and few of them had arms training, though some might be taken to help maintain the equipment. Regulations of 1859 suggested that the seamen be formed up into companies of 80 men under a lieutenant, two mates or midshipmen and three petty officers. Their boots were found to be unsuitable for long-distance marching and they borrowed others from the military. They wore canvas leggings, carried bandoliers and rolled their goods in blankets, which were not comfortable in warm weather. Casualties were relatively light, little more than might be caused by accident on board ship, but there was often a serious risk of disease.

## THE FLEETS

For the men of the lower deck, each of the main fleets was very different in character and offered a very different kind of experience. The Mediterranean Fleet was perhaps the most popular. The men lived in a benign climate and had a great variety of experience around the different ports and cultures. Action was rare, but in 1860 twenty-year-old Ordinary Seaman Edward Turner was one of the captain's boat crew of HMS *Argus*, when the rebel leader Garibaldi and his redshirts landed in Sicily to overthrow the corrupt Neapolitan regime and begin the unification of Italy. Though they were only supposed to support the British residents, feelings were running high in support of the rebels. When a Neapolitan frigate arrived, Turner helped row his captain out to it to negotiate, but on the way back, 'when we had only proceeded about a hundred yards away the ship fired a broadside of grape and canister, some of which nearly struck our boat. Our Captain jumped and shook his arm at the Neapolitan and said "Give-way boys". We were quickly aboard and everyone on board was on the alert wondering what our next move would be.' As Garibaldi's men landed, the British ships stayed close to the harbour of Marsala and prevented the Neapolitan warships from getting in close. They followed the rebel progress on the island and on the mainland, and Turner concluded, 'Although we took no part in the actual fighting in this campaign, there cannot be the question of a doubt but that the moral support we rendered by our presence at Garibaldi's landing at Marsala, and the presence of British warships at Palermo, and our ship's presence at Messina, Catania and Syracuse greatly encouraged the cause of the Garibaldians and equally weakened and depressed the cause of their enemies ...' In addition, some of the sailors deserted to join the Legion of British Volunteers.[53]

The Mediterranean Fleet was regarded as the most important one, with some of the most up-to-date ships. According to James Wood,

The Mediterranean was in 1886 as a naval station rapidly nearing the zenith of its glory. Here was to be found the very pick of the British Fleet, and the Grand Harbour, Malta, presented a scene of continual animation, for it was here that – except during the brief summer cruise – the fleet spent the greater part of its time.[54]

The Mediterranean Fleet was also the great centre for races between ships' boats, virtually the only sport the navy encouraged at this time.

One never-ending theme of discussion in ships of the Mediterranean Squadron was boat pulling. What horse-racing is to the ordinary civilian, boat pulling is to the Navy, only more so, for everyone can not only witness the races, but also take part in them ...

Nowhere in the Navy was boat-racing indulged in to the same extent as in the Mediterranean, and sometimes enthusiasm on a race rose to a pitch that no Derby could command.[55]

Signalman John Daggett enjoyed his rather innocent runs ashore from *Alexandria* in the Mediterranean in 1883–5. At Trieste the crew were very popular:

I took advantage of a fine day and went with a companion onshore, where we enjoyed ourselves very much. Hiring a horse and trap we sent into the country where we received numerous presents of fruit (so much so) that we came back with the appearance of marketmen. A number of women volunteered to give the clothes we had on a wash if we cared to have had it done, but seeing the way they washed it thought it advisable not to.

Malta was more used to the Royal Navy and had many entertainments specially tailored to its needs:

> Where too [sic] Jack; Silver Eagle; away sped the cab to another part of the island called Floriana and we set down at the desired point
>
> You ask what place it is, why a dancing saloon for Jacks who flock there in great numbers to have a spin round together to the strains of four or five fiddlers and the like number of guitars.
>
> Being tired of dancing we adjourned to the singing room, where we find Jack standing upon a raised platform, giving vent to his feelings in the Balaclava Charge, Death of Nelson, or some such like ditty.[56]

In the home ports, men attached to the depot ships came into three categories. There were permanent crew, such as police and instructors, who would stay there for some time. The great majority of men were young and simply wanted to get to sea, to do something useful and see the world. A few, perhaps ten per cent, were older men who had settled their families in the area and wanted to stay as long as possible, perhaps bribing the ship's police to allow them.

The Channel Squadron, the most active part of the big-ship navy at home, was a smaller force than the Mediterranean Fleet, unless it was mobilized for the annual manoeuvres with the use of coastguards and reserves. From the 1860s onwards it often undertook an annual cruise around the British Isles and northern European waters, visiting ports such as Liverpool, Scapa Flow and the Clyde. This would not have been possible in an earlier age, but now steamships and the electric telegraph allowed the quick recall of the fleet in case of a sudden emergency. The highlight of the first cruise was at Liverpool, where 40 shipowners each gave £10 towards entertainment for 800 sailors and 200 marines, and more than 57,000 people visited *Warrior* alone. John Grant, a petty officer in *Royal Oak* rose to address a company fuelled by Alsop's Pale Ale, and referred to the women's habit of wearing stays under their dresses.

> They say we live in iron age. No doubt of it; many of us present live in ironclad ships, but we are not the only ones, for I believe the fair sex can boast of that as well as us (roars of laughter) ... Now I hope for a little drop of the royal, not forgetting the stunsail booms, and we'll all drink success to every female in Liverpool (convulsive laughter), also to our worthy chairman and our kind entertainers. I know my fellow shipmates, both seamen and marines, will join me in returning their heartfelt thanks, and let us give three hearty cheers. 'The Lady Mayoress, and all the ladies of Liverpool.'[57]

One seamen was impressed on seeing a procession through the city. 'Blow me if I ever see'd such a sight as this. Just let them attack Liverpool and send for the Channel Fleet, that's all.' [58]

The cruises were quite popular with the sailors, though they sometimes became extremely bored during long receptions held by local authorities and preferred to spend time in the local pubs and music halls. In 1868 the fleet spent a few days in the Clyde; selected men were entertained, but their patience was tried:

> A dinner was given yesterday by the people of Greenock, to the men of the fleet, which went off capitally. The men (500) marched up, headed by our band, and were all seated by two o'clock, very comfortably. Then there was a delay, and till half past three they sat talking and listening to the band. No end of porter and beer and cigars were placed before every one, but though the dinner was a long time in coming no one touched either bottle or meat till a clergyman was called on to say grace, and they fell to with a good will.[59]

## LIFE ON BOARD

Thomas Holman's description of life on board a small ship in the tropics in the 1870s could easily have come from an earlier age. The men are roused at 4 a.m. by the boatswain's mates and go up to scrub the decks. 'Divisions' are held after breakfast, and the men and their kit are inspected by officers.

Plain sail is set, and lookouts are posted at the mastheads. An able seaman stands to windward of the steering wheel, with an ordinary seaman or boy to leeward for training. The men exercise with rifles and cutlasses, though a machine-gun has been added to the armoury. The carpenter and his crew are working away at repairs, and in the afternoon the men of the watch below are 'for the most part, making their clothes, or some fancy articles for wives, sweethearts, or mothers at home'. Holman is several hundred words into his description before he encounters 'the head of a leading stoker up for breath. You ask him if it is warm below. Through the grating you might see the stokers cleaning up the engines and boilers under the superintendence of the Engineer.' Later the captain deals with defaulters, sentencing them to cells or stoppage of leave instead of flogging, but the ship continues in time-honoured fashion.[60]

In contrast, the geography of the new battleships and cruisers was different from that of the old sailing ships, and inevitably that had an effect on shipboard life. They were subdivided by bulkheads, so lower-deck life became more fragmented. This was augmented by the increased number of specialists, and stokers and seamen were invariably kept apart for reasons of culture and cleanliness. Marines were already separated so that they might be used against the seamen in case of mutiny. So too were domestics and writers, to prevent them passing on gossip to the ship's company. The new signal ratings were kept apart for similar reasons. The seaman gradually lost his right to choose his companions in his mess. Much more space was taken up with engines, coal and turrets, so living space was often as restricted as ever. Compared with wooden ships, the new iron ones had both advantages and disadvantages as places to live. Iron and steel hulls were less likely to be infested with rats and cockroaches, but they were more subject to changes in temperature, so they became too hot in the tropics and too cold in the northern winter. Without adequate means of ventilation, they were often stuffy and suffered from condensation.

In early ironclads such as *Minotaur* and *Agincourt* of 1863–5 the men were able to move up from the orlop to the lower deck, about which they had mixed feelings:

the move up in iron vessels was an improvement from a sanitary point of view, as giving more light and air. But it was not popular with the men, who got all the air and light they had any use for in the fore and main top, and preferred that their messes should be what they called 'snug'. Moreover, mess tables slung between guns had to be cleared away not only at weekly General Quarters but also at battery divisional drills, which disturbed the watch below.[61]

Unlike gundecks, turrets were not suitable for living in except for short periods in action, though the casemates of some of the smaller guns could be used as messes. In the central-battery ship, the battery itself often divided the officers completely from the crew, as in *Monarch* of 1866, which had a main messdeck forward of the battery on the main deck and a smaller one for stokers below that. However, the men gained in that their mess spaces were not interrupted by guns. In *Bellerophon* of 1865 the guns were more concentrated – the battery was less than 100 feet long, leaving considerable space for the 600 men.[62] The crew of the ill-fated turret ironclad *Captain* lived in a poorly ventilated and lit space at waterline level, subdivided by numerous bulkheads, which did not prevent the ship sinking in 1870.[63] *Temeraire* of 1876 was much more comfortable: 'Forward of the battery and extending to the bows lay the fore mess-deck, where the majority of the ship's company were berthed. This was better than in the majority of vessels of the period both as to space, light and ventilation; and above all in head room.'[64]

## THE SEAMAN ASHORE

Sailors naturally made up a large proportion of the population of the dockyard towns, even though at any given time most of them were at sea or on foreign stations. The Census of 1861 recorded that there were nearly 6,000 sailors of the Royal Navy in the Plymouth district, more than two-thirds of them in the dockyard area of Devonport. Together they made up more than sixteen per cent of the male population, more than the army and Royal Marines put together, and nearly four times as many as the dockyard artificers. Most of them still lived in the ships and hulks, but a growing number rented small flats and houses ashore for their families, which might account for large pockets of relative poverty and overcrowding in Devonport, with more than ten people to a dwelling house in many parts.

'Why do women marry sailors?' asked Cicely McDonnell at the end of the century. Certainly Jack had his attractions, with 'a breezy freshness about him that is very captivating'. He also had guaranteed employment over a period of years with an employer that was not likely to go bankrupt, and a pension at the end of it. But any naval wife would have to put up with 'a simple, frugal, and somewhat lonely life'. Her husband was likely to be sent abroad on a three-year commission. While an army wife might be borne 'on the strength' so that she could live in married quarters and be shipped out to a foreign station with the troops, the navy had no married quarters, and it did nothing to support wives who might want to follow their husbands – even among officers' wives. Only a minority could afford the passage, and it was out of the question for the wives of ratings.

A sailor's wife may not live on board. She can only go as a visitor to her husband's ship, and this is one of the great differences between the services. The Navy is strong, but it has no 'strength'; the wives are practically ignored, though officially provided for by pension should their husbands die in active service ...[65]

Sailors' wives had a profound effect on the dockyard towns. Their husbands were poorly paid compared with the skilled civilians in the dockyards, so wives usually had to work to boost the family income. In Portsmouth the clothing trades were dominant. The navy itself created a certain amount of demand, wages were lower than in London, and plenty of naval wives were available. In 1847 it was stated that 'the female sex at Portsea and Landport are employed in the manufacture of shirts, stays and other necessary articles of outfit for sea. One house at present employs nearly 2000 hands.'[66]

Only a minority of lower-deck sailors were happily married, and most sought quick enjoyment as soon as they came ashore. In the early days at least, they enjoyed a scrap. One day around 1860 the young Henry Capper clung to his mother's skirts in terror as he watched a crowd of seamen, just paid off after a long foreign commission, were holding a posse of police at bay in the generally quiet street where we lived. The police had a very rough time, for, as well as being greatly outnumbered, and armed only with truncheons ... they were opposed to men of great agility and daring, provided too with ample ammunition from the stone heaps before them.

In 1864 he saw another ship's company just after it was paid off:

They engaged every available cab in the town and formed these up in procession on Common Hard. With each man was his 'long-haired chum' – generally a woman of the town. The cabs were decorated with flags and pennants, each box seat holding one or more men, a similar number being mounted on the roof. A few men were astride horses, and two of these to show their independence sat facing the tails of their beasts, which were towed in procession by lines to the horse or cab next ahead. The procession went, accompanied by the tooting of horns and the strains of chanties sung to fiddle accompaniments, to some of the villages surrounding Portsmouth, Fareham or Botley, where unreportable orgies took place.[67]

In Plymouth in 1871 there were 503 prostitutes registered under the Contagious Diseases Act, and there is no way of knowing how many were operating illicitly or on a casual basis. The Census of that year showed a few examples, for example Mary Beval and Emma Oliver of 78 Fore Street, Stonehouse, and Emma Davis, living with her one-year-old son at number 164.[68] Of course there is no reason to believe that all their clients were naval, by any means. The three towns of Plymouth, Devonport and Stonehouse had plenty of visiting merchant seamen, while there were many men in all walks of life who did not live up to the Victorian ideals of chastity, fidelity and family life. But naval seamen had plenty of money when their ship paid off, they had spent months or perhaps years away from feminine company, and they had little or no time for conventional wooing.

At Chatham there were 287 registered prostitutes in 1869. The most notorious areas were Red Cat Lane and Holborn Lane until these were built upon in the 1860s and '70s. This left The Brook, where in 1899,

'Courts and alleys are plentiful, and there are many back-to-back houses. There are 17 licensed houses in the area, and 13 registered lodging houses with accommodation for 461 people.'[69] As well as the aptly named Fullalove Alley, there was the King's Head, with 'a most remarkable history of sin known in most parts of Greater Britain!' It had only one entrance from The Brook, but nineteen doors on the ground floor opening into a dark back yard. 'There may also have been secret stairs leading from an upper room, the uses of which were revealed, as far as possible, only to the initiated! All so convenient to the lodger (?), and so perplexing to the police!'[70]

# 4
# STABILITY AND TECHNOLOGY
## 1875–1889

The battleship continued to evolve. The 'Admiral' class of the early 1880s used the barbette instead of the turret, which protected the magazines and the passages to them rather than the guns themselves. Armour plate and increased gun power raced for supremacy, and technological change created a great variety of ships, so it would have been impossible to form an effective line of battle during this period. The steam warship usually carried its guns on a single deck, so the old term of 'frigate' became redundant. It was replaced by the 'cruiser', a medium-sized, fast, long-range ship to patrol the trade routes, scout for the main fleet and control the empire. Armoured cruisers evolved with *Shannon* of 1875, and some of them were as large as battleships. Protected cruisers were built by the late 1880s, with limited armour and coal distributed so as to keep out enemy shot. Meanwhile another navy served in the rest of the world and especially among the British colonies. Sloops and gunboats were far more conservative in design, usually with wooden hulls, which could be repaired away from the facilities of a dockyard, and they combined sail and steam power because coal was scarce in the outposts of empire. These still deployed the traditional skills of the sailors and shipwrights, as well as the newer ones of engine room artificers, who might have to do repairs or make new parts on their own initiative.

## RECRUITING

The officers' dream of a navy composed of healthy and unsophisticated country lads was never to be realized. In 1880 it was accepted that 'with very few exceptions, the boys are recruited from the towns'. It was still hoped that 'the raw material for our navy would be much improved by a far larger admixture of country lads', but there was no easy way of getting them.[1]

In 1875 Sam Noble was a rare recruit from Dundee, taken on by a Royal Marine sergeant attached to HMS *Unicorn*, the Royal Naval Reserve drill ship:

> He then drew such a picture of the sea: how I should have nothing to do but sit and let the wind blow me along: live on plum-pudding and the roast beef of old England: lashings of grog and tobacco: seeing the world the while and meeting and chatting with princesses and all the beautiful ladies of other lands – ah! It was a gay life …![2]

Three years later James Wood was also recruited by a marine sergeant, in the Swan and Horseshoe pub in Westminster. 'He was a well set-up man with a black, neatly trimmed beard and piercing black eyes which seemed to fascinate the boys to whom he used to spin sea yarns in the little back room of the above-named pub.' He had 'cultivated the art of descriptive lying to an extent that would have put Baron Munchausen to shame'.[3]

A poster of 1883 for 'Stout, healthy boys' outlined what was wanted. Minimum height and chest measurements varied with age but the youngest, aged from 15 to 15½, needed to be 5 feet tall and 30 inches round the chest. The authorities worried that undersized young men might try to pass themselves off as younger than they were, and the navy would be stuck with 'stunted men instead of growing lads', so birth certificates were insisted upon.[4] Entrants would start on a pay of £9 2s 6d a year and have a minimum of £28 17s 11d as able seamen, with the possibility of eventually rising to £53 10s 7d as a chief petty officer, or even £164 as a warrant officer. Each boy would receive a gratuity to buy his clothing and bedding. He would be able to send money home to his parents. The navy now had no full-time recruiting organization of its own, but a boy could apply to one of the training ships at Devonport, Falmouth, Portsmouth, Portland, Sheerness or Queenstown, or to a coastguard ship, a Royal Naval Reserve drill ship or one of the Royal Marine recruiting stations in the major cities.[5]

The navy continued to seek new areas for recruitment, not always successfully. In 1883 Captain Kennedy of the Coastguard visited Orkney in

HMS *Lord Warden* but found that the past still lingered: 'absurd as it may seem, the terrors of the press gang are still remembered by the older inhabitants and related to the younger ones, so the arrival of HM ship, with the avowed intention of seeking recruits, was a signal for all likely youngsters to hide themselves, and to remain 'perdu' during the stay of the ship in the port.'[6]

Despite the setbacks, the navy's recruitment policy was a success, even if it was largely restricted to boys in the cities and the dockyard towns. In 1887 the First Lord of the Admiralty told the House of Commons,

> The Navy now seems to be a very popular service. A high standard and restrictions on the number of entries have been imposed to prevent an undue influx of boys, but the competition is, notwithstanding considerable. It is worthy of note that, simultaneously with the growing popularity of the Navy with parents as a career for their sons, there is a dread of dismissal from the Service which previously did not exist. Mutilations and misconduct not unfrequently [sic] in the past were deliberately adopted for the purpose of insuring dismissal, whereas the present tendency is in the opposite direction.[7]

## THE TRAINING SHIPS

By 1884, boys were trained in *Boscawen* at Portland, *Ganges* at Falmouth, and *Impregnable* and *Lion* at Devonport. All were old wooden ships mostly built in the early years of the century, which never put to sea any more. A boy who joined *Impregnable* in 1885 found that she was

> one of the old 'wooden walls'. She had three gun decks besides the upper deck with its raised poop and forecastle. She had five decks in all – upper, main, middle and lower and, above the holds the orlop deck where the bags, etc were stowed. There were three masts, that is, three lower masts with topmasts and topgallant masts above each; and, during the sail-drill season she had the sails, ropes and gear of a full-rigged ship.[8]

An inquiry of 1880 suggested that the boys were being given 'a superficial knowledge of many things without their being grounded in the more elementary parts of their work'. Instruction cards were issued for a new syllabus, though it was left to the discretion of instructors as to how they were used. They included salutes, standing rigging, boat pulling, bends and hitches, compass work, lead and log lines, sea terms and helm instruction. The inquiry resisted pressure from the gunnery branch to include training with heavy guns:

> The light gun drill, now taught, gives him a knowledge of the principles of pointing, sponging, loading, and the use of gun-tackles; and is very valuable in teaching precision and smartness in obeying words of command, besides furthering muscular development without overstraining. The boys, when older and stronger, are initiated into the use of the heavy guns on board the Gunnery ships.[9]

Each of the training ships had a brig attached to it, a small 500-ton sailing vessel with two masts. They were supposed to be ready for sea by 1 April each year. During the spring and autumn they would usually make short trips each day, but in the summer they might be away from base for up to two weeks at a time, generally anchoring overnight or in bad weather. The regulations showed some kind of consideration for the boys, most of whom had never been out of harbour before:

> Weighing [anchor] before breakfast is to be avoided as much as possible, as most of the boys are liable to sea sickness and cannot afterwards touch food; were the brigs to weigh three or four days successively before breakfast, utter prostration would ensue; whereas, if they weigh after breakfast, their being sea sick will be a matter of small import, inasmuch as their system will have been warmed and stimulated by the morning meal.[10]

To a boy from *Impregnable*:

> Life on board these toy ships, as they seem now, was a continuous round of practical seamanship. Speed – up to the limits of motion in young, healthy human limbs and muscles – was the great consideration. I refer, of course, to the speed at which we boys flew about the decks and swarmed aloft to lie out on the yards, loose, furl or reef the sails and so forth. 'Sharp's the word, quick's the motion', was the rule in those days. It worked well.[11]

James Wood was not alone in disliking his time in the brigs intensely. It was 'the most miserable six weeks of my life':

It was late autumn when I went, and the Channel winds already had a touch of approaching winter in them in which our scanty duck or serge suits, with just a flannel underneath, quite failed to rob of keenness. The comfort of boots was not allowed, the wearing of boots being strictly forbidden both day and night, while the good and ample meals of the training ship were replaced by hard ship's biscuit and salt meat on most days.[12]

But the boys invariably returned to the training ship with a swagger, having been to sea, unlike their juniors.

A boy helps a seaman with 'serving rope',
from Nares' *Seamanship*.

## THE STATUS OF THE PETTY OFFICERS

The transition from sail to steam was causing many difficulties in the selection of petty officers. Admiral Martin at Plymouth found that men were often rated up in small ships that were 'mere steamers' even if they had no real knowledge of seamanship. After that they might be transferred to depot or gunnery ships and then distributed throughout the fleet. For example, a quartermaster in a gunboat was able to steer a course under steam but might be useless as a helmsman under sail. One man in the gunboat *Flamer* advanced from ordinary seaman to quartermaster in eleven months and held on to that rating in his next ship but was soon found not to be a true seaman. Because of this, Captain Foley had found it necessary to change the ratings of some quartermasters drafted from *Cambridge* to *Defence*, with their consent. Martin commented, 'A system that admits of men obtaining first class petty officer ratings on board vessels in which seamanship is neither valued not tested, and in virtue of ratings so obtained passing to ships whose safety may often depend upon seamanship alone, seems full of mischief.'[13]

It was reported in 1889:

> In former days Seaman Petty Officers were perforce selected for their skill and experience as seamen, rather than for their trustworthiness and steadiness of conduct. This state of things no longer exists, and in our Petty Officers we now have a body of men trained entirely in the Service, who are in every way equal in character and conduct to the Ship's corporals, and their superiors in professional ability. Every extension of responsibility that has hitherto been imposed on the Petty Officers has been attended with the very best results …[14]

But not everyone agreed, and many thought they were too close to the junior ratings. The master-at-arms of *Iron Duke* reported, 'There is too much of the Bill, Dick, Tom and Harry business with them when they are on deck; there is too much familiarity between them.'[15]

The Admiralty was keen to increase the status of petty officers, and in June 1868 it issued a circular ordering that chief petty officers should mess separately from the rest of the ship's company, while petty officers first class should either join them or form a separate mess as was most convenient, with boys to attend as cooks of the mess. They were exempt from searches by the ship's police and were to fall in separately from the rest of the men – even their washing was to be hung on different lines in the rigging. Chief petty officers were separated yet further. They were allowed to wear gilt buttons instead of black on their cloth jackets and were to be automatically considered as special leave men.[16]

Despite their gains of 1868, the chiefs of HMS *Caledonia* approached their captain two years later with further requests. Despite their long experience, they were paid no more than the skilled but inexperienced artificers of the engineering branch, and their pension rights were no greater than those of a petty officer first class. They also wanted a new uniform with hat, shirt, jacket, waistcoat and cap instead of the seaman's frock and cap – 'it would be a boon, and enable them to frequent better class houses of entertainment from which they are now debarred, sailors not being admitted to them.' The captain was reluctant to back their requests, stating that the artificers had learned their trade by apprenticeship at their own expense, whereas the chiefs had been trained at cost to the crown. He also felt that some of the men holding the rating were 'certainly wanting in tone for the position', even though the orders of 1868 had allowed captains to disrate any man 'found incompetent to discharge his duties'. The Admiralty preferred to go in the opposite direction. The CPO's status was greatly increased in 1879 when he was allowed a jacket with collar and tie and a peaked cap to separate him from those below him and associate him more with the officers.

But not everyone agreed about the value of the chief petty officer. Admiral Martin did not think they were the equal of the sergeant major in the army, who was sometimes seen on troopships and was treated as 'an exceeding dignitary'. In the navy, much of the work of the sergeant major was done by the junior officers, who supervised the men at work and saw to 'the details which in the army devolve upon the non-commissioned officer'. Martin thought that the CPO did not improve discipline: 'Their casual interference with the 1st class petty officers, who really conduct the men of their watches, by night as well as by day, is often vexatious, and will never be necessary if the officers attend to their duties.' Moreover, the rating of chief petty officer was deterring suitable candidates from applying to become warrant officers.

## DISCIPLINE AND PUNISHMENT

The late 1870s and the 1880s showed a general decline in severe punishments, though the figures supporting this are never conclusive – they only record offences brought to trial, but some officers complained that they were deterred from using the full force of the law by Parliamentary pressure. On the other side, the lower deck often complained that the ship's police justified their status by prosecuting men for trivial offences. In any case, 237 seamen and marines were tried by court martial in 1878 and only 149 in 1887. Mutiny was almost extinct, but cases of striking a superior officer varied over the years, though generally fell during those years from 75 to 45, despite a larger navy. Cases of threatening language actually increased and disobedience was variable, peaking at 104 in 1883. But the great majority of disciplinary offences were dealt with by summary punishment. 50,400 petty officers and seamen were treated in this way in 1878 and only 42,285 in 1887, despite the fact that the number of seamen had risen from 41,556 to 44,895. In 1885 for the first time, there were fewer punishments than seamen in the fleet.[17]

## UNIFORM

The new naval uniform of 1857 took time to become popular, and one pamphleteer wrote:

> The opinion is strong in the service that the dress is ungainly in appearance. It is known to be uncomfortable to wear … What man possessing the faintest tinge of manly feeling would dare to walk through one of the public streets in any of our naval ports, having his wife or any respectable female in his company?[18]

This was published in 1877 and was perhaps a little out of date by then; in any case, the anonymous writer was clearly an embittered man. Joining as

A chief petty officer of around 1870.

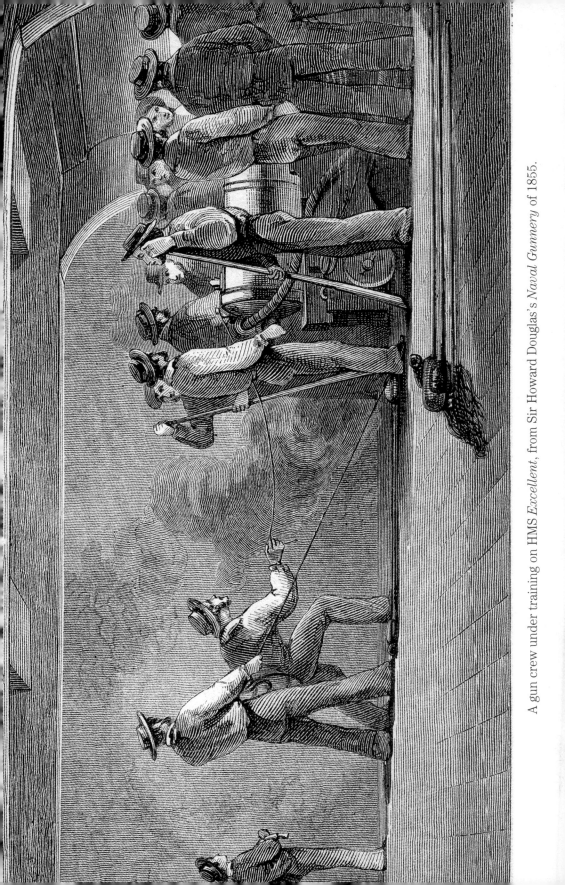

A gun crew under training on HMS *Excellent*, from Sir Howard Douglas's *Naval Gunnery* of 1855.

The first Victoria Cross ceremony in Hyde Park in June 1857, with several seamen in square-rig uniform in the presence of Queen Victoria. (National Maritime Museum Neg. No.58_1067)

The drill ship *Fame* in front of the Queen's House in Greenwich, now part of the National Maritime Museum. (National Maritime Museum A 1727)

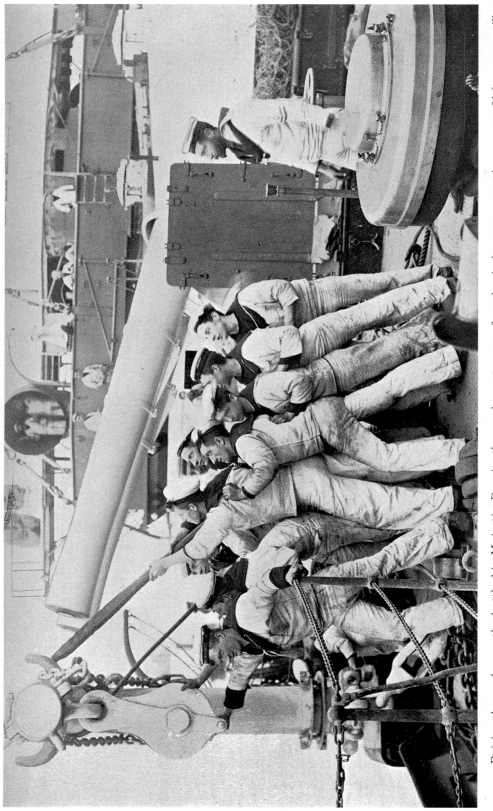

Raising the anchor on the battleship *Majestic*. Despite the much greater use of mechanical power, a certain amount of labour was still needed in such an operation. (*Navy and Army Illustrated*)

A naval brigade, formed from the crews of *Euryalus* and *Carysfoot*, repulsing an attack in Upper Egypt in 1884. (National Maritime Museum PU 9373)

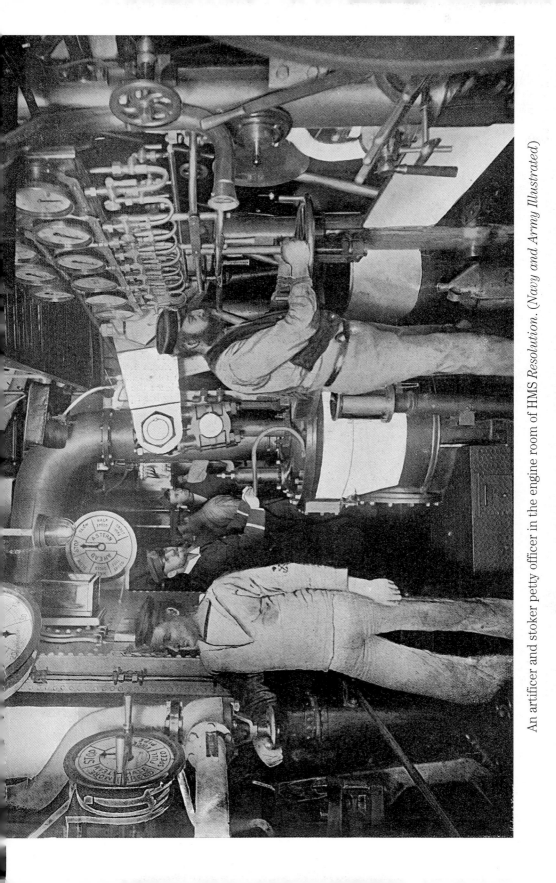

An artificer and stoker petty officer in the engine room of HMS *Resolution*. (*Navy and Army Illustrated*)

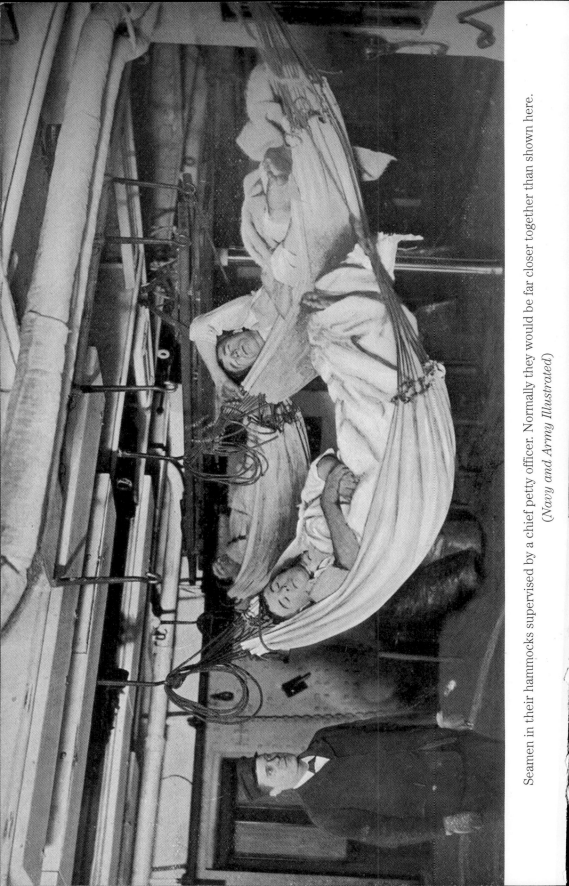

Seamen in their hammocks supervised by a chief petty officer. Normally they would be far closer together than shown here. (*Navy and Army Illustrated*)

a boy second class in 1872, Thomas Holman was only too glad to get into the uniform: 'I was installed on board one of Her Majesty's ships, and advertising it to the world by a suit of blue serge, which I fondly believed gave me all that look of picturesqueness that I had often admired in others similarly clothed.'[19]

It was not only in discipline that the seaman was treated as a child. Sailor suits were also worn by young boys, and in 1879 *Queen* magazine reported, 'Sailor suits are always popular … and ever since the Prince of Wales's two sons have adopted the naval uniform the preference has increased.' It was no less so in 1887, when *The Lady's World* commented, 'A boy before he rises to the dignity of trousers and jackets is never so happy as in a Middy's suit or a Jack Tar; and these suits are now selling in thousands.' Certainly the boys themselves preferred them to the 'Little Lord Fauntleroy' suit that parents might try to inflict on them.[20] But it also reinforced the image of the sailor as a childlike creature.

There is no doubt that the uniform became increasingly beloved by the public over the years, partly because the seaman himself modified it to make it more attractive. He found this easy to do, for several reasons. In the first place, the uniform was the sailor's personal property, paid for and maintained out of his earnings. This, he felt, gave him a moral right to modify it as he wanted. Secondly, every true seaman was adept with needle and thread, and if he was not he could easily find someone on board who was. Thirdly, ships were often a long way from established authority, and an over-strict officer would have to fight a lonely battle. Often the sailors were involved in shore expeditions, which demanded dress modifications; or they used eccentric dress for filthy tasks such as coaling. Fourthly, the printed uniform regulations were quite short and left much to the imagination – they were described in a single page of the *Navy List* up to the 1879 amendments. They occupied less than two pages after that, but the increase was mainly due to the number of uniforms now worn by the chief petty officer grades. True, there were sealed patterns, but these were lodged in the home ports and were not easily accessible to an inspecting officer. Finally, the modified seaman's uniform undoubtedly looked much smarter than what was issued by the purser and quickly became established as what a seaman ought to wear.

The seaman disliked the frock and the way it had to be tucked into his trousers. He hated the waistband that held the trousers up, for there were no braces or belt to support them in any other way. He liked his trousers wide, often twelve inches at the foot and the knee. He found it difficult to keep his collar clean and tended to attach it to a 'dickey' rather than the full checked shirt that regulations demanded, as this made it easier to wash. New regulations of 1879 went some way to meeting his desires. He was now allowed a 'jumper', which was to be worn outside the trousers and to extend two or three inches below the hip, with a pocket on the left breast.

The sennet hat caused many problems – it was very heavy, weighing eleven ounces, and was often as hard as wood. It was difficult to stow in a crowded ship, and the sailor often used it to hold such loose articles as soap, tobacco and towels. It was difficult to keep it clean, especially during coaling. The pattern varied, and those made in Malta were noticeably more round rather than oval in shape, causing the men to tilt them back to make them more comfortable – 'flat aback', as it was known to the seamen.[21] The seaman also had his cap, 'made round, of No 1 cloth, and partially stiffened across the crown, similar in shape to that worn by Officers, without the peak'. It was nine inches in diameter across the crown for men, eight inches for boys, and a white cover was issued for use in warm climates. It was quite soft round the rim in those days and more comfortable than the hat. According to regulations it was only for wear at night, and at sea when ordered.

The jumper was still intended mainly for working wear. The frock was worn for inspections and ceremonial, on leave and on Sundays. The blue jumper was used on working days aboard ship and at night, while the white duck suit was paradoxically worn during coaling and cleaning, and at times when 'better clothing would be spoiled.'

The most dramatic change in 1879 was the introduction of a long jacket for the chief petty officer, perhaps to allow him to keep up with his rivals in authority, the ship's police and the artificers. He had a white shirt with collar and tie, and four brass buttons down each side of his jacket, the upper ones being covered by the lapels. He continued to wear the laurel wreath, crown and anchor on his left sleeve, with a non-substantive badge on each lapel – those without gunnery or other qualifications wore a crown and anchor there.

## GUNNERY AND *EXCELLENT*

Ships' main guns continued to get bigger and more complex. Steam power was introduced to train turrets with *Monarch* of 1868, followed by hydraulic power in *Thunderer* of 1877, which was soon used for laying the gun as well as powering ammunition hoists to lift shells of up to 16.25-inch diameter and 1,800 pounds in weight from the magazines. It was suggested at the end of the 1880s, 'In ships carrying few and enormous guns, where firing is necessarily slow, and the throwing away of a shot disastrous, an able Captain of a turret is of incalculable value ...' He also had to take charge of a highly complex mechanism, rather than the muscle-powered contrivances of the past. However, there was no special course for his job, and he was usually selected from among the ship's gunnery instructors.[22]

This did not reduce the need for smaller guns in smaller ships throughout the empire and for defence of the bigger ones against torpedo attack. The rating of captain of gun was instituted for them in 1883, to be chosen from among the best shots with gunnery qualifications. He needed 'coolness, nerve, and quickness of eye, which some men have naturally, and others never can acquire'.[23] Technological change had altered the art of gunnery, from an athletic exercise to a skilled craft, and the navy expected a good deal of its gunnery ratings, as technicians, marksmen and disciplinarians. In 1879 some officers felt that the emphasis on good character was irrelevant: 'We see no reason why the present restriction of the Seaman Gunner class men of at least "good" character should continue; it is more than possible that a man bearing only a "fair" character might prove himself a skilled gunner.'[24]

To most seamen, selection for a gunnery school was an important stage in a naval career. Not everyone agreed with the basis on which it was done; to James Wood it was the naval Mecca to which every young sailorman turned his eye. To be a seaman gunner, and perhaps a torpedo-man, was to be one of the select, besides which, there was a growing inclination on the part of the Admiralty to have all petty officers selected from the gunnery ratings. On the other hand, to be a general service man was to be one of the mob, a kind of unskilled naval labourer.[25]

Some seamen possibly missed their best chance for a course because their ships were abroad at the age when it might have benefited them most. James Wood was selected in 1883 but missed the start of his course due to a misunderstanding about his leave, which set his career back.[26] When he finally joined his first course in *Excellent* in 1884, it was still largely based in the ship, though the course also used Whale Island in Portsmouth Harbour. Mostly an artificial creation from the spoil of the new docks, at that time it was 'simply a small mud bank infested by rabbits. The men of the *Excellent* had levelled off a part of it, which was used as a drill ground for field exercises and squad drill; there was also a house, built by the blue-jackets, in which lived the resident gunner …' When he returned some years later, it had been developed. Whale Island was just beginning to assume the proportions of a shore establishment; the first few blocks, of what is today [1908] a magnificent pile of buildings, had been erected, and men permanently established in them, though the bulk of the men and the principal officers still lived on board HMS *Excellent.*' Wood enjoyed the course, as did Thomas Holman:

> I class the twelve months I spent in the *Excellent* as among the happiest of my life; the days were only half long enough to squeeze all the good things into. True, we were at instructions all day long, but then it was being instructed among many young men of my own age and temperament that made it so delightful; always a keen competition among us to be first at drills and always a keen competition also as to who could play the biggest joke.[27]

The increasing use of the shore base at *Excellent*, and the need for sailors to be trained in land warfare, also led to an increasing emphasis on military drill at the gunnery schools.

HMS *Excellent* was training about a thousand men a year by 1889. It served as the depot ship for gunnery ratings in Portsmouth, as *Cambridge* did for Plymouth. This meant that the men who had not trained in gunnery were sent to the general depot ships, for example *Duke of Wellington* at Portsmouth. There were complaints that this creamed off some of the best men, as all seaman gunners had to be of good character and would lose the rating if they fell below certain standards. The general depot ships were thus filled with a high concentration of failures or rogues and had discipline problems.

But gunnery training was not always reflected in the fleet at sea, especially in the Mediterranean, where sail drill was still predominant. There were reports of ammunition being dumped overboard rather than used as set down for practice. James Wood noticed the poor standard of gunnery training, as at the annual prize firing, 'no-one took any notice of the fact that the target was in the same condition when we left off as when we started, though a certain amount of "hits" was always recorded'.[28]

## THE EFFECT OF THE TORPEDO

The self-propelled Whitehead torpedo was developed in 1868, largely by a British engineer working in Austria. It could be launched from a small, fast vessel and sink a large ship with a hit under the waterline, so it was an obvious threat to British naval supremacy. By 1871 Captain Hood of the Admiralty was suggesting separate torpedo instruction under the auspices of HMS *Excellent,* and by 1872 HMS *Vernon*, an old 90-gun ship, was serving as a tender to *Excellent* as a torpedo training establishment at Portsmouth. It became an independent command in 1876.

On the face of it, the torpedo and the gun were very different weapons. Powered by compressed air, the torpedo was a self-propelled one-shot weapon needing little in the way of fixed structure but requiring a good deal of maintenance. It raised the possibility of night attack by small craft, and the main way of detecting that was by searchlight. After trials in various ships, HMS *Alexandria* was the first to be completed with searchlights as standard in 1877, and three years later eighteen ships had two searchlights apiece, and four more had one each.[29] Ships were also fitted with electric lighting for domestic purposes, which greatly reduced the risk of fire, and the torpedoman began to take on responsibility for its maintenance. Compared with the gunner, he required less parade-ground discipline and a good deal of intellectual ability to understand the theory of electricity.

Despite this the Admiralty continued to believe that torpedo training was an adjunct to gunnery. In 1882 they decreed that 'all seaman gunners should, as far as possible, combine a knowledge of torpedo and gunnery and ... there should not be two classes of seamen gunners and torpedo men in the lower grades ... Every seaman gunner is to be a trained torpedo man, and ... those seamen gunners who fail to qualify as torpedo men are to cease to be seaman gunners.'[30] An extra course of 60 working days, or 12 weeks, was grafted on to the normal gunnery course – 6 days of lectures, 10 of practical work in the classroom, 26 working on boats, 16 on the Whitehead torpedo and 2 for the examination. Men who qualified with a 1st class mark in both gunnery and torpedo were to be given 6d pay per day. Those who gained a first in one or the other were to be known as seamen gunner torpedomen (SGT) second class, with 4d per day, and those who got seconds in both were seamen gunner torpedomen second class.[31] Above that was the rating of leading torpedoman (not necessarily a leading seaman) instituted in 1885 and selected from men who did well in the SGT course. After a further 60 days of training they were the true torpedo experts, and key men aboard their ships. It was initially planned to train 36 per year, but this was soon increased to 60. The gunnery badge now incorporated the torpedo crossed under the gun, or over the gun in the case of leading torpedo men and those who intended to specialise in that direction.

HMS *Defiance* was commissioned at Devonport in December 1885 to cope with the increased demand for such training, and meanwhile at Portsmouth another ship replaced the *Vernon* hulk, but took on her name. There were difficulties in finding enough instructors among the torpedo ratings. A hundred were needed, but only 64 were available in 1885, including 21 who qualified in the previous year. Ambitious men were reluctant to get so deep into a torpedo career, which at that time offered no route to warrant rank except by re-qualifying as a gunner, so the warrant rank of gunner (torpedo) was established. Torpedo artificers were recruited to do the more advanced work on torpedoes and electricity, mostly men retrained from engine room artificers and based in the dockyards in the first instance.[32]

In 1885 James Wood found that the course at *Vernon* was a complete change from that at *Excellent*. In those days, 'the torpedo may fairly be said to have been in its infancy; and our knowledge of electricity was not what it is today. But even then, the *Vernon* was little else than a series of lecture rooms, a studious atmosphere pervading the whole establishment.' In the theoretical part of the course, 'the men were taught the whole theory of electricity as then known, and the uses to which it could be put in war'. In the practical part, they learned about the use of mines, while '"Whitehead" covered the whole field of the uses of the automobile torpedo'. According to Wood, 'The work was engrossingly interesting, though all day long in an open boat in Fareham Creek laying and weighing mines was no sinecure.'[33]

In addition to torpedoes carried in larger ships small specialist torpedo boats were developed, often launching a single torpedo from a tube in the bows. John Daggett describes a ride in one off Malta in 1883:

> The boat is nothing but machinery, a small cabin for the officer and the same for the crew of five men, being the only places not taken up by it ...
>
> The crew are allowed a pair of heavy top coats and an oilskin (from the naval stores) for their protection from the inclemency of the weather, and I might add, I think they want it very badly ...
>
> If it is rough the boat is almost as much under the water as she is above, and it is only by holding firmly (if on the upper deck) that you keep yourself from being washed overboard altogether, but even if not you have the delirious sensation of feeling now and again that you were almost gone, which does not add to the comfort of those suffering from 'Nausea'.

He had a ducking 'in the shape of a great sea (which travelling at the rate we were) did not go under but over us. Another signalman with me lost his hat ...'[34]

## THE ENGINE ROOM

By the mid-1870s there was greatly increased demand for engineering staff at every level. The new 'mastless' battleships showed that steam could no longer be considered as an auxiliary in the battlefleet, if not in the farther reaches of the empire. The compound engine was far more fuel efficient that its simpler predecessor – *Inflexible* of 1881 needed 2.74 pounds of coal to generate one horsepower for an hour, while *Warrior* had needed 5 pounds. The triple-expansion engine was already common in merchant ships and was even more efficient. There was a great increase in auxiliary motors during the decade – *Devastation* of 1872 had 16; *Inflexible* of 1882 had 82. Ships relied on engineers, not just to provide the motive power but to operate steering gear, pumps, ammunition hoists, turrets and electrical generators.

It was necessary to raise the status of the engineer officer, by better training and by relieving him of manual duties. More engineers were also needed at a lower level. The triple-expansion engine was far more complex, boilers operated at much greater pressures and needed a good deal of attention, and the numerous auxiliary engines needed constant skilled maintenance. The engine room artificer was seen as the man to fill both these gaps, and greatly increased numbers were to be recruited. The battleship *Sultan* carried ten engineer officers and four ERAs, and it was planned that she should have six engineers and eight artificers in the future. A committee was set up in 1875, just as most of the 1868 recruits were beginning to think about their future, in or out of the navy, after ten years' service. They expressed a good deal of dissatisfaction and recommended increased pay and changes in conditions.

This was very obvious when the question of the ERA's uniform arose again in 1878, and it was ordered that they should wear the crown, anchor and laurel wreath of the CPO on their arms. However, they regarded this as a 'badge of servitude', and a group of them in HMS *Sultan* threatened to leave the service if forced to wear it. The Admiralty considered their comments to be improper in tone, inaccurate and a 'question of discipline' at first, but soon gave way. The ERA was to wear no badges on his jacket, while the chief ERA was to have three brass buttons on his cuff. These did not constitute a badge in themselves, so they were not objected to; indeed, they were already worn by certain warrant and commissioned officers in combination with gold stripes, so they might even be seen as raising the ERA's status. They were the origin of the device that came to denote all chief petty officers in later years.[35]

The navy hoped to have 835 engine room artificers in the wake of the 1875 report, and with improved conditions it does not seem to have had any difficulty in recruiting them. By 1889, after a further expansion of the fleet, there were 1,063 of them, far outnumbered by the 5,779 stokers.[36] The rise of the ERA meant that the status of the stoker tended to be lowered, and there is no sign that skilled men entered for the rating after 1868. However, the stoker did have a clear promotion path, which in many ways was superior to that of the seaman. He would normally enter as a stoker second class, unless he had previous experience, and he could expect promotion after a year. The stoker had good prospects of further promotion, and there was a high proportion of leading stokers. In 1866 the battleship *Bellerophon* had seven leading stokers in charge of 28 stokers, a proportion of 1 to 4; the 176 ordinary and able seaman and 20 leading seamen were headed by 27 petty officers and chiefs, a proportion of more than 1 in 7. The rating of chief stoker was reintroduced in 1885 as a supervisor of the stokers rather than as a highly skilled man. It was considered necessary to have a reliable man, either an artificer or a chief stoker, in charge of each boiler room on each watch. This created a considerable demand for chief stokers, as most battleships of the period had eight to twelve boilers.

## 'NON-COMBATANTS'

In 1887, Admiral Lord Charles Beresford complained about the number of 'non-combatant' ratings in the navy. He was perhaps being a little unfair, as everyone on board took an equal chance in the event of battle or shipwreck, but he was a very influential figure, and the Admiralty looked into it very seriously. It excluded stokers from the list of non-combatants, as they were now trained in weapons. It found that there were 2,490 artisans of various kinds, and 3,730 men still known by the old term of 'idler' (so called because they did not have to keep watch overnight), these including police, cooks, writers, sick-berth staff and ships' bands. A committee reported on ways of reducing these numbers to 1,505 artisans and idlers, but few of its recommendations were adopted, and the numbers were not greatly reduced.[37]

By the Regulations of 1862, a candidate for the rating of ship's steward, the paymaster's chief assistant, was to be examined by three paymasters in the presence of a captain, 'as to his ability to read, write and keep accounts'. He should have served at least two years as a steward's assistant, and if he passed he became the equivalent of a chief petty officer. His promotion path was from the third class to the second and then the first, in an increasingly larger ship. In addition to his wages he was paid a victualling stores allowance while on board a ship, because of his responsibility, and a committee of 1872 felt that this had not risen enough over the years – the steward was less well rewarded than a writer, but had more responsibility. There were 461 of them in the navy in 1888, and unlike other classes the Committee on Ratings did not recommend any reduction in numbers.[38]

Most writers started as boys, then were classed in three grades: third class, equivalent to an AB; second class, equal to a petty officer second class; and first class, equivalent to a chief. They were often kept on for very long service, particularly in static flagships in the home ports. Normally, like stewards, they were expected to change ship every three years, but a regulation of 1883 allowed posts of 'permanent character' to selected pensioners up to the age of 60. It would perhaps have been better to employ civil servants in such roles, except that the ships were afloat, if not actually at sea. By that time the navy employed 58 writers on foreign service, 19 in the reserve, 116 in the home ports and 8 boys.

The schoolmaster often shared a mess with the ship's steward and cook. At sea he had the duty of teaching the ship's boys, but this proved less than successful. Most boys were literate before entry and had received yet more education in the training ships. It was difficult for the boys at sea to find time for further instruction, and by 1887 there were only 18 schoolmasters in seagoing ships. It was decided to confine them to training ships, where 45 were in service. Any further education at sea would be conducted by volunteer ratings, with extra pay.[39]

The old style ship's cook, an aged petty officer serving out an 'honourable retirement' after losing a limb, survived until 1873, when a new system was introduced, with proper training on board *Duke of Wellington* in Portsmouth. The cook first class was the equivalent of a chief petty officer, and 'competent to cook for 300 men and upwards; and understand baking'. A cook second class was the equal of a petty officer first class and was in charge of the galley in a smaller ship. He was assisted by a cook's mate first class, roughly equivalent to an able seaman, or second class, equivalent to ordinary.[40] There were 58 ships' cooks first class in the navy in 1888, and 112 second class.

The sick berth attendant, the descendant of the old, untrained 'loblolly boy' of Nelson's time, was established on the recommendation of a committee chaired by Sir Anthony Hoskins in 1883. He wore the symbol of a red cross on a white background, twenty years after it had been recognized by international convention as denoting medical personnel. Originally the candidates were selected at the age of 17 from among the boys in the training ships, but these proved unsuitable and they were recruited from the shore among men between the ages of 21 and 25. The Sick Berth Attendant was trained in Haslar Hospital, near Portsmouth, and the length of his course was reduced from twelve months to six, then three.[41] He had prospects of promotion to sick berth steward, equivalent to petty officer, or to chief. There were 219 men in the branch in 1888.

The artisans were different from the artificers in that they pursued trades that had equivalents on shore. They tended to have less status, with the basic rating of petty officer rather than chief, and the ordinary seaman's uniform. The carpenter group included ten different ratings, such as the carpenter's mate (so called because he was an assistant to a warrant officer), caulker, shipwright and carpenter's crew. By 1888 it was recognized that these trades were in decline with the increasing use of steel ships, though there was still a certain amount of work in connection with ships' boats and fittings. The other artisans were the blacksmith, armourer, plumber, painter and cooper, with several levels of skill and appropriate mates and crew. It was recognized in 1888 that the metalworking trades were most important and that, 'the efficiency of blacksmiths is a matter of growing importance, while their present pay shows a marked inferiority to that of other Petty Officers of the Artisan Class, and there is no prospect of advancement during their service.'[42] Armourers were likewise restricted in their prospects until a new rate of chief armourer was introduced. In 1890 the navy advertised for men from the trades of 'White Smith, Blacksmith, Engine Smith, Shipsmith, General Smith, Carriage Smith, Gunsmith, Fitter, Turner (Metal) and Millwright', offering advancement to chief armourer and £91 5s per year.[43]

As to music, the practice of appointing boys as buglers proved unpopular. It meant that they were taken away from their seamanship training, which made it all the more difficult to qualify for AB when the time came, while the seamen regarded it as boy's work and were not interested in doing it. Some of the larger ships also employed a band, but these were not well regarded. According to the Committee on Ratings, 'It is very difficult to obtain men to fill the position of "Musician," and those who do so enter are, usually, of so inferior and objectionable a class, as to be entirely unfit to hold the rating of Petty Officer.' It was proposed to abolish all bands except on flagships and to train musicians within the navy; however, that was not approved by the authorities, and the problem continued until the Royal Marines took over naval band duties in 1903.[44]

There were other workers on board ship, such as barbers, shoemakers and tailors, whose ratings were allowed to die out in the late 1880s. Boatswain's mate John Buckley of *Agincourt* believed that barbers were unnecessary, as most sailors cut their own hair, and there was 'hardly any shaving going on' in the heavily bearded navy. As for the tailor, his shipmate Josephin Howard thought that he was unnecessary for the lower deck's needs: 'You will find that, as a rule, in the band there are men who can do all the tailoring that is required; and it is mostly for the officers; the blue-jacket mostly makes his own clothes.' Petty officers were more positive about the role of the shoemaker, though Howard believed that the sailors did not need him: 'When they come to England they get their shoes, and those last for some time; and when they wear out, they get new.' Shoemakers could always be found among the marines, so a seaman rating was unnecessary. The lithographer was even less useful – there were only four of them in the navy in 1888, all attached to flagships, and other methods of reproduction made them unnecessary.[45]

## LIFE ON BOARD

Signalman John Daggett is rather brief in his description of the accommodation in the last of the central battery ships, *Alexandra*, in 1883, but he cannot help convey the feeling of overcrowding: 'From here we enter the "mess deck" which is capable of receiving some seven or eight hundred men, some of whom must however sleep in the batteries. Leading from this deck are the torpedo shoots which when not in use are triced up overhead to allow some three or four messes to fill up the vacancy.' Below was 'the Stokers Flat, so called because the stokers live here, in the centre of which is an electric machine for working the electric lights on the upper deck'.[46] In fact, *Alexandra* was less comfortable than most ships. The deck was only about 40 feet wide forward of the battery, compared with 60 feet aft in the officers' quarters, and the stokers' mess below had no light except candles.[47] Cruisers were equally cramped. In *Terpsichore* of 1890 there was a small forecastle with room for a miniscule messdeck, but the rest of the crew lived below, just above the armoured deck, in three messes, which became increasingly narrow towards the sharp bows. The CPOs had a small cabin partitioned off for themselves. Much continued as before in the new metallic atmosphere, where the men continued to hang mess tables from the deckhead above, to sling hammocks at night and to stow them in the daytime. Meals were still prepared by the cook of the mess and taken to the galley for heating.

The Admiralty began to encourage the setting up of canteens on board ship where men could drink coffee as an alternative to alcohol. The men of HMS *Achilles* turned down the chance to have one, but most ships were in favour. The crew of *Lord Clyde* drank up to 200 pints of coffee per night. According to the captain of HMS *Revenge*,

It gives them, for less money, a superior quality of drink than they can get on shore (beer only is allowed) – a superior means of recreation, a clean, comfortable and healthy place to enjoy it in (tables and stools on the main deck) thus inducing many to remain on board who would otherwise go onshore and fritter away their money in semi-intoxication ... the social evil the bane of all sailors, and other temptations which they are exposed to without a warning voice or hand to help and keep them straight.[48]

Life on board could be violent, and a man might literally have to fight to establish his status among the crew. According to Sam Noble,

Sometimes an argument would crop up, bringing twenty or thirty into it all trumpeting their opinions at the same time. Talk about a shindy ... Sometimes a quarrel took place, and then you would hear a few pithy sentences, fairly well flavoured with salt, regarding one or other of the contestant's fathers or mothers or grandmothers ... Sometimes there was a real fight: a regular downright bout of fisticuffs. This was usually settled on the fo'c'sle, and the captain winked at it, believing that the men would be better friends when it was over.[49]

Noble also had to defend himself, as the only '*known* Scotchman' in the ship:

I wasn't long from school then, and being fairly well up in history, the things they said about Scotland put my back up ... So I needn't tell you that I had a fight nearly every day. First with Tom, then with Dick, then with Harry. But it was always me who figured in these fracas. Billy, the first lieutenant, used to give it to me hot for coming before him so often.[50]

### SEAMEN'S WELFARE AND AGGIE WESTON'S

Agnes Weston was born in 1840, the daughter of a wealthy barrister. She began her charity work by corresponding with soldiers, and then, though a series of chances, which she was happy to attribute to divine intervention, became the century's leading philanthropist for naval seamen. She went aboard many ships to spread the temperance message, with a certain amount of success. In 1874 she and her friend Sophia Wintz were approached by a group of ratings and asked to set up a temperance house, a 'public house without the drink', near the gates of Plymouth Dockyard. This proved a great success, and soon it was offering overnight accommodation on an informal basis. Miss Weston was expert at fundraising and claimed that nearly a million pounds had passed through her hands by 1909. She was able to open a large-scale Sailors' Rest at Portsmouth in 1881. She was sponsored by Queen Victoria herself, and one of the rooms in the Portsmouth Rest bore her royal plaque. She campaigned fiercely against public houses near the dockyards, especially the *French Maid* in Portsmouth.

> The 'Maid' was very dangerous to the susceptible sailors, and was well frequented. Many a fight took place outside in the street, and our building was more than once bespattered with blood and hair. Young seamen frequented it largely; men, according to the police reports, from eighteen to twenty-two years of age, the very lads that one wants to save, for their own sakes as for their mothers' sakes.

The pub's license was withdrawn, and she was able to buy the property and incorporate it as a block of the Rest, containing 200 cabins.[51]

Miss Weston knew that the seaman would not respond to a blatant attempt to impose religion or teetotalism on him, and so she kept these activities distinct from her pure welfare work. Alcohol was, of course, not allowed in the rests, but drunken seamen were not turned away, and even the geography of the buildings reflected the separate aims.

> The work, whether at Devonport or Portsmouth, consists of two departments, but both linked together. The Hall, with its evangelistic work, Bible-classes, gatherings for sailors' wives and children, temperance and other social meetings; and the Institute, with its refreshment bar, dormitories, baths, smoking, dining, reading rooms, billiard room, &c., the two departments to be kept distinct, and yet united; conveniently near, and yet not interfering with each other.[52]

In a philanthropic age, she was providing some of the services that perhaps the Admiralty might have taken responsibility for – family welfare, relief payments and so on. If naval barracks had been built earlier to replace the hulks, and made a little more comfortable, then 'Aggie Weston's' would have been less necessary. Nevertheless they became an institution, and the lady herself, despite her chaste, unmarried status or perhaps because of it, loved being called 'mother of the navy' by the host of seamen.

Miss Weston and Mrs Wintz set up homes briefly at Portland and Sheerness but decided that their effort should be concentrated on the two at Devonport and Portsmouth. Chatham had its own benefactors, and in 1900 Navy House was opened with 101 beds, to be followed by the Royal Sailors' Home near the Town Hall and the Welcome Soldiers and Sailors Home with 120 beds. Echoing Miss Weston's success at Portsmouth, the notorious *King's Head* was taken over to become the 'Victory Hotel and Temperance Café'.[53]

But still the seaman was not always placid when he was ashore. In Chatham in 1882, the gunboats *Constance* and *Linnet* were about to set off for the Far East when their crews came ashore one Sunday evening. Churchgoers were horrified when they formed up in fours led by their 'marshal', marching through the streets singing lewd songs as a parody of the Salvation Army. They stopped at many pubs and gathered a crowd of locals behind them. When the civilian police and a naval picket tried to stop them there was a pitched battle with fists and truncheons. It was serious enough to cause an enquiry by the Commander-in-Chief at the Nore, but by that time the ships had sailed, and it was implied that the police had over-reacted.[54]

In Plymouth the favourite destination for sailors with money was Union Street, originally built to link the three towns of Plymouth, Stonehouse and Devonport but now filled with pubs, theatres, dance-halls and brothels. A policeman who served around the year 1900 reminisced:

> Union Street was rough – afore they went on night duty they used to go in the George Tavern and have bread and cheese and two or three pints before they went on duty – they used to say that they were fit for anything after that.
>
> They were just keeping law and order. Usually it was around the pub's turning out time. Then it was always rough and almost always fighting

going on; there were so many pubs. The men would be egged on by the ladies of the town – they used to argue over the ladies and get jealous.[55]

In 1884 the Admiralty added two years to the standard ten-year period of enlistment, and this was reinforced by Act of Parliament[56] – the expression 'roll on my twelve' became common among discontented seamen. By 1889 the system of continuous service was so well established that it seemed completely permanent. Nearly two generations of sailors had passed through since it was first set up more than 35 years earlier, and even the most experienced men now in the service had been trained by continuous service men and had no memory of the previous age. The naval service was in its most stable period ever – but outside factors were soon to change that.

## 5

# THE AGE OF EXPANSION
# 1889–1904

### THE NEW NAVALISM

After being unfashionable in the middle of the century, imperialism had become more popular than ever by the late 1880s. The term 'jingoism', meaning extreme patriotism, arose during a crisis with Russia in 1877–8, with the music hall song,

> We don't want to fight, but by jingo if we do,
> We've got the ships, we've got the men, and we've got the money too!

All classes and many different political groups were united in favour of imperialism. Joseph Chamberlain, the radical mayor of Birmingham, transferred his allegiance to the Conservative Party in support of it. From the extreme left, H. M. Hyndman of the quasi-Marxist Social Democratic Federation believed in the future of the British Empire and the need for a strong navy. The role of the navy in national defence had never been questioned, and its work in creating and defending the Empire had almost equal public support by the end of the century. This helped recruiting as much as anything else, but it also meant that articulate young men who were not necessarily of a conservative disposition became naval ratings.

By the late 1880s the torpedo boat was perceived to be less of a threat than had been feared, and interest in the battleship began to revive. France was still the main rival. Her naval strength was not increasing, but a new group of slightly smaller naval powers was beginning to emerge, including Russia, Italy and Austria-Hungary – they would be followed by the newly-industrialized and unified United States and Germany. Parliament passed the Naval Defence Act in 1889 to sanction the building of 70 new warships.

This began 25 years of international rivalry, with increased naval budgets in almost every year. It was a time of great technological change, with the battleship concept being perfected in *Dreadnought* of 1906. At the same time, aircraft and submarines were being adopted for the fleet, new engines and gunnery systems were being developed, and wireless telegraphy presented the possibility of communication with ships beyond the horizon for the first time in history.

The total naval budget rose from £13 million in 1889 to more than £53 million in the 1914 estimates, but not much of that went on personnel. The two main parts of the estimates that directly affected seamen's conditions were Vote 1 on wages, and Vote 2 on victualling and clothing. In the 1888–9 estimates these totalled £4,069,100, or £74 per man; by 1914 that had risen to £12,789,662, or £87 per man, a rise of some 17 per cent. In the meantime, real wages in the rest of the country rose by 25 per cent between 1889 and 1914, and the cost of living by 10 per cent.[1]

The act of 1889 put forward the two-power standard – that the Royal Navy should be kept up to the strength of the next two greatest powers. It coincided with the building of seven battleships of the *Royal Sovereign* class, with higher freeboard and therefore more seaworthiness than their predecessors. They would set the pattern in battleship design for the next fifteen years. This led to the navy and the general public becoming obsessed with the number of ships, particularly battleships, compared with the other naval powers. The Navy League, formed in 1895, campaigned for greater public interest in the navy. It attempted to appeal to all classes, particularly the working classes, who were now beginning to turn towards socialist parties with pacifist leanings. It pointed out that command of the sea was as important as ever, since the country was now dependent on imports for most of its foodstuffs and raw materials. It was highly successful over the next twenty years, as when it organized demonstrations to demand more battleship building in 1909.

Amid all this, the lower deck of the navy received little public attention. The sailor was still seen as a heroic but rather naïve figure. In general the admirals were not interested in any reform of lower deck conditions, and few politicians made much impact on the arcane world of the Admiralty.

## NEW AREAS OF RECRUITMENT

In 1891, most of the seamen still came from traditional sources:

> The boys are mostly of the class of skilled mechanics, a large proportion being the sons of warrant officers, and petty officers who have been through the work and know what the service is like from experience. Sailoring runs in families, even more than soldiering; and in Portsmouth, Chatham and Devonport there are families who have sent five or six generations to the lower deck. The boys come from all parts of the Kingdom, the majority from the south coast.[2]

The new ships of the Naval Defence Act demanded larger crews and a great expansion of the navy, which put traditional recruitment methods under strain. In 1897 for example, the First Lord of the Admiralty, George Goschen, admitted to 'many sleepless hours' worrying over possible shortfalls in men, after he was shown a document showing 'deficiencies in a startling form all along the line' and containing 'no suggestion how to act in the face of such facts beyond the increase asked for which still leaves a large deficiency'. By late 1899 a shortfall of 6565 seamen and 4300 stokers was forecast for 1902.

One possible remedy was to revert to an old practice, by taking on merchant seamen directly into the navy. In 1894 it was decided to recruit 800 men from this source, but within a year the First Lord had to admit that it had not been successful, and very few men had joined in this way. It was therefore decided to recruit youths, slightly above the age for boy entrants, who were to be trained in the armoured cruiser *Northampton* of 1876, as she sailed around the coast, picking up more recruits on the way. This proved far more successful, and 670 boys were entered during 1895–6. In the fleet they became known as '*Northampton* riggers.' The First Sea Lord told Parliament:

> Reports have been received from the captains of H.M. ships of the Mediterranean Fleet, to which boys passed out from the *Northampton* have been drafted. These reports are exceedingly satisfactory, and state that, on the whole, the boys compare well with those trained in the other

training ships. There has been some difficulty about their learning to swim, but steps are being taken to mitigate this as far as possible.[3]

As a result the old corvette *Calliope* was used to supplement *Northampton*. Charles Cutler describes his training in 1902:

> Aboard the ship we were taught to run the rigging, compass and helm, how to steer a ship, etc., how to take sounding with the hand lead and boat pulling. These were the main seamanship things we learnt there, breaking us in gradually. We did three months of that and we were then sent to sea for three months in a sailing ship, the Calliope ... when we learnt seamanship proper – that is setting sail.[4]

Another policy was to expand the geographical area of recruiting. It had long been recognized that very few men and boys were recruited in Scotland, though the maritime commerce of that country was flourishing as never before. In 1892 the First Lord told Parliament:

> The increase in the number of boys in training will require an additional training ship. At present all the ships engaged in this work are located in the south of England. A training ship is a recruiting attraction, and the districts in which they are placed consequently contribute more than other parts of the country to the manning of the fleet. A large proportion of the hereditary seafaring class is now to be found in the northern districts of the country, and with a view of obtaining recruits from this natural source of supply, the new training ship will be placed in the Firth of Forth at Queensferry.[5]

This was HMS *Caledonia*, the old 98-gun ship *Impregnable*, which had been the training ship at Plymouth before being towed north and renamed. The policy was reasonably successful, and after recruiting cruises round Ireland it was decided to set up another training ship at Queenstown near Cork. *Black Prince* of 1861, sister to the famous *Warrior,* was adapted to accommodate 450 boys. In the same year, the length of the course for boys was reduced from twenty to sixteen months, partly to reduce pressure on accommodation, partly to accelerate the supply to the fleet.

Another tactic was to improve the image of the naval recruiting office, which had moved on very little since the days of the rendezvous and the press gang. By 1897 there was a policy of making them look more like government offices, 'usually a separate office with room or rooms in a business neighbourhood, where a respectable recruit can enter into his contract without the former bad adjuncts'.[6] Recruiting staff officers were appointed from among retired officers to supervise the nine recruiting districts, while petty officer recruiters were taken on to supplement the work of the Royal Marines, who tended to put a favourable gloss on their own corps at the expense of the navy as a whole – some went even further, and in 1889 P. Howick found he had joined the marines instead of the navy by mistake.[7]

Recruitment was aided by the fact that life was often very insecure for the unskilled working class and for the children of large families, so the prospect of permanent employment seemed very attractive. One man joined the navy because 'there were tons of people out of work' in his home town of Bishop's Stortford. Stanley Munday's father was a skilled carpenter, but, 'He had too many kids and he couldn't keep them all.' James Austin's father was far less skilled, as a bricklayer's labourer, and like most building-trade employees in those days 'he was out of work a lot'. William Prayle was brought up in the workhouse after his father deserted the family and joined as a stoker because he was hungry. 'I thought, "See the world in comfort"; a bit of a rise, eleven and something a week.'[8]

## TIDYING UP THE RATES

By the last years of the nineteenth century there was a general urge for tidiness, which was reflected in naval administration. In May 1889 many of the old rating titles, such as chief captain of the forecastle, captain's coxswain and captain of the hold were abolished, and all seaman petty officers were known as chief petty officers and petty officers first and second class. Older titles such as gunner's mate and quartermaster were still used, but the posts were allocated to individuals on board ship.

By this time there were 26 different non-substantive badges, which were awarded for specialized skills (as distinct from substantive badges, which denoted a man's rate as leading seaman, petty officer, etc.) in use, not counting those awarded for rifle-shooting ability. Basic badges consisted of the gun crossed over a torpedo for seaman gunner torpedomen and gunnery instructors, with the reverse, the torpedo over the gun, for leading torpedomen and torpedo instructors. The basic seaman gunners wore a

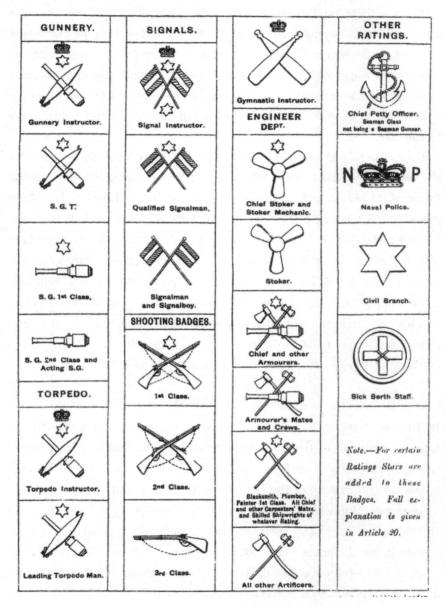

Ratings' badges, from a report of 1901.

single gun, while signalmen had crossed flags. Stars and crowns were used to indicate higher proficiency within the non-substantive rate, with a crown over a star for the highest in each group, and a star for the next rate. The newly established gymnastic instructor had crossed Indian clubs and a star. The stoker was given the three-bladed propeller, but the stars were used differently, partly to indicate substantive rate – a chief stoker had one, and so did a stoker mechanic. A seaman chief petty officer who did not have any non-substantive rate wore an anchor on each lapel. Other artificers and artisans had badges based on a crossed axe and hammer, with a torpedo superimposed for torpedo artificers and a gun for armourers, while plumbers, painters, blacksmiths and so on wore the basic badge. The naval police had a crown with the letters 'NP', while the men of the civil branches adopted a six-pointed star – gold for schoolmasters, stewards and writers, silver for cooks. Sick-berth staff continued to wear the red cross on a white background.[9] The question of a badge for ERAs was raised, but Captain Bedford remembered previous troubles and commented, 'The Engine Room Artificers, the most numerous and influential body of Chief Petty Officers, would resent the addition of badges to their uniform. It was

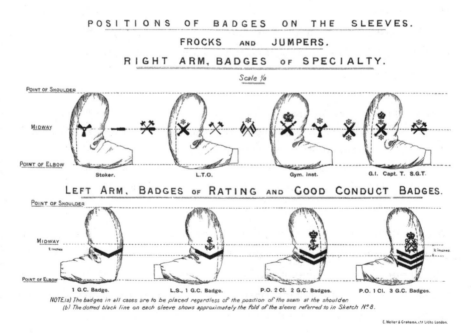

The correct way to wear badges in 1901.

tried once and had to be given up.' Instead, their status was indicated subtly by putting a purple background to their cap badge, the same colour as worn by engineer officers between their sleeve rings.

## THE ROLE OF THE GUNLAYER

Ship's guns were now increasingly large, with long barrels and high-explosive, which made longer ranges possible. In 1892, Professors Barr and Stroud of Glasgow University invented a new kind of rangefinder using mirrors, and ratings of the gunnery branch were trained to use it. Nevertheless, ships' guns were were nowhere near their full potential for long-distance firing. The Mediterranean Fleet was still the natural home of the 'spit and polish' navy until close to the end of the nineteenth century, when Captain Percy Scott of HMS *Scylla* showed what could be done with good aiming of the ship's guns and careful training of their crews. This was the beginning of a new gunnery revolution. Scott's ideas spread through the navy, and good gunnery rather than cleanliness became the means of measuring a ship's efficiency. As one seaman of the time put it, 'The Gunlayer was the man in those days, before director shooting came out. The Gunlayer had to make all his own corrections to hit the target.'[10] He might become a hero, like Petty Officer Walter Grounds of HMS *Terrible*, trained personally by Scott in the first years of the new century.

> His shipmates had nothing but praise for his generosity, his steadiness, his intense devotion to the science of shooting. 'Give him a box of 1-inch cannon tube' (ammunition for a small bore barrel, placed inside the gun for practice shooting) 'and he was happy', they said. He would work away at it, marking the result of each shot and trying various ideas he had.'[11]

In 1903 such skill was recognized by the First Lord of the Admiralty in his annual statement on the Navy Estimates. He acknowledged 'the overwhelming importance of proficiency in gunnery' and agreed that 'the whole of the Navy are striving, both officers and men, to reach the highest standard'. He announced the institution of a medal to be worn for a year by the most successful gun captain in each ship.[12] In 1905, Admiral Sir

Charles Beresford wrote of a potential battle that seemed almost Nelsonic in its tactics:

> The result of an action (after the Admiral in Command of a Fleet has placed that fleet in a position of advantage) will depend on the Captains of Guns of a Fleet; on their accuracy of eye, readiness of resource, and strict discipline the fate of the Empire will depend, should the British Navy ever be engaged in warlike operations.[13]

This placed new emphasis on gunnery training, and on the role of the schools at *Excellent* and *Cambridge*, and the new one near Sheerness.

The gunnery instructor was an important figure in the schools and also on board ship:

> To become a Gunnery Instructor a man must go through a long and varied course, comprising some theory as well as practice. He must be absolutely at home in every detail ... so he is able to take a class in any subject ... From being constantly accustomed to drilling bodies of men, he is a good and trustworthy man to send in charge of others on detached duties.[14]

Two practice gun turrets were set up at *Excellent* in 1906, and numerous simulators were devised by Scott for the training of the men. With the 'dotter', for example, a board was placed in front of a gun and moved up and down to simulate the rolling of the ship. The 'deflection teacher' taught the layer to aim off to allow for the target's movements.[15]

In 1901 it was finally decided to separate gunnery ratings from torpedomen. The basic seaman gunner wore a single gun without any addition. Gunlayers wore crossed guns, with stars and crowns according to their class, while at the top of the tree the gunner's mate and gunlayer first class wore a crown and star above and two stars below. Men could also be rated as gun captains and second captains, and as sightsetters. In 1907, however, it was noted,

> in visiting the various gun positions in a battleship that, whereas in one case the Gunlayer is the Senior man, in the next the Trainer or Sightsetter may occupy that position. Who under these conditions ... is to be the

person responsible for order, discipline, and the accurate working of the casemate?[16]

## UNIFORM

Naval uniform was another matter that had developed by accretion over the years, and had to be regulated. An official committee on uniforms reported in 1890. It started by looking at the sealed patterns for clothing and comparing them with what was actually worn by the men. It found that the square-cut bottom of the seaman's frock was difficult to tuck into the trousers, and the men were resistant to doing this. Most of them shortened it and made it tighter, a pattern that was adopted by the committee. The men rarely made the front of the frock double as was required, but put in a false seam, and this too was adopted. The trousers were supposed to be ten inches at the foot and nine inches at the knee, but most seamen made them twelve inches at both foot and knee. The committee compromised with ten inches at the knee and eleven inches at the foot. The general effect was to make the dress tighter above the waist and looser below. The lower deck had largely had its way, not for the first or last time.

Plenty of other problems were identified. Gold badges were often made of inferior material, which turned black in service. There was much discussion on the shape of boots, which were found to be 'quite unsuited to the shape of the seaman's foot' and were difficult to stow on board, so a new pattern was recommended. The sennet hat remained an object of dislike.

The committee of 1890 was obviously well-intentioned in giving the ratings almost all they wanted, but unfortunately the effect was to make the rules far more detailed: the Regulations, which had previously taken up two pages of the *Navy List*, now occupied more than eight pages. Moreover, it gave increased opportunity for martinet officers and corrupt policemen:

> the new regulations fell on deaf ears, commanding officers, with few exceptions, were much too busy with paint and bright work to interest themselves in tailoring affairs; it was left till the end of a commission, when

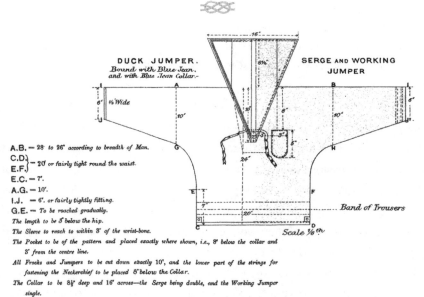

DUCK JUMPER.
*Bound with Blue Jean.
and with Blue Jean Collar.-*

SERGE AND WORKING
JUMPER

A.B. — 28" to 26" according to breadth of Man.
C.D.
E.F. } — 20" or fairly tight round the waist.
E.C. — 7".
A.G. — 10".
I.J. — 6". or fairly tightly fitting.
G.E. — To be roached gradually.
The length to be 5" below the hip.
The Sleeve to reach to within 3" of the wrist-bone.
The Pocket to be of the pattern and placed exactly where shown, i.e., 8" below the collar and 3" from the centre line.
All Frocks and Jumpers to be cut down exactly 10", and the lower part of the strings for fastening the Neckerchief to be placed 8" below the Collar.
The Collar to be 8½" deep and 16" across—the Serge being double, and the Working Jumper single.
The Working Jumper to be of exactly the same size and pattern as the Serge, but the edges are to be plainly hemmed.
*NOTE.*—The dotted lines represent stitching. No fancy stitching or embroidery allowed.

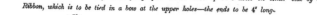

All Trousers to be made with a Waist Band 2" deep the lower seam of band to be just above the hip.
The Flap to be 5" deep. —— All Trousers to be from 9" to 10" across at the Knee and 10" to 11" at the Foot, but the Measurement across at the Knee is to be always one inch less than at the Foot.
The Gusset at back to be 2" at top when fully open—to be laced up in 3 holes on either side by a Ribbon, which is to be tied in a bow at the upper holes—the ends to be 4" long.

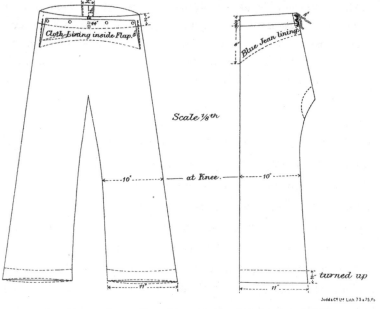

The correct patterns for ratings' jumper and trousers, 1890.

men returned to their home depots for the regulations to have full effect, they found themselves thrown on the tender mercies of a ship's corporal who had powers to mutilate each offending article unless he was paid to stay his hand.

Soon this spread among some of the officers. 'Quite likely some of the younger officers saw in a strict attention to the uniform of the men of their division a road to promotion, others probably took it up as a new fad owing to a lack of professional subjects to occupy them ... There might be several other lieutenants in the same ship who, taking no interest in the uniform regulations, would ignore them altogether; a state of affairs which ... would mean that the majority of men were contented; a small minority cursing the navy and all connected with it.'[17]

The naval salute was changed in 1890. In 1864, boys were told: 'The purely naval salute is taking the hat or cap off, or touching the hat or cap. By touching the hat or cap is meant holding the edge with the forefinger and thumb, as if about to take it off.'[18] This was changed after Queen Victoria saw something of German drill practices, and a much more formal salute was instituted:

> The naval salute is made by bringing up the right hand to the cap or hat, naturally and smartly, but not hurriedly, with the thumb and fingers straight and close together, elbow in line with the shoulder, hand and forearm in line, the thumb being in line with the outer edge of the right elbow, with the palm of the hand turned to the left, the opposite being the case when using the left hand.[19]

## THE NEED FOR STOKERS

The new triple-expansion engine of the 1880s was far more economical of fuel than its predecessors, so sails were not needed as a back up. Many of the older battleships and cruisers had their masts removed or reduced in the 1890s, and no more sailing ships were built. The gunboats were withdrawn from Empire from 1905 onwards, and another survival of sail ended, at almost the same time as the sail training brigs were abolished. Stoking was no longer a part-time activity, for the engines were in constant use while the ship was at sea.

There was some concern in 1889, when Stoker Charles Colwell of HMS *Alacrity* died during full-power trials in the Far East, and six more stokers were seized with cramp. It was suggested that the deaths were 'due to the cold air from the fans playing upon the bodies of men perspiring freely at the time, men who from debility or exhaustion possessed but little power of nervous shock'. Enquiries showed that nearly all ships operated the stokers in three watches, unlike the seaman, who were usually in two. This was only possible at full power if extra men were added to the complement. Even so, the work was gruelling, with temperatures of up to 120 degrees Fahrenheit (49 Celsius) being recorded. With the assistance of a trimmer working in the bunker and keeping the stoker supplied with coal, each man was assumed to be capable of shifting up to 2.4 tons of coal during a four-hour watch.[20] Early in 1891 the Admiralty issued an order that stokers were always to be worked in three watches, except in cases of 'real emergency', in which case they were not to be in two watches for more than 24 hours. Seamen could be sent down from the deck 'when coal is unavoidably in the less accessible parts of the bunkers and high powers are required ...' However this was regarded as exceptional, and in general the engineer officer was to make sure that 'sufficient coal is brought near the stokeholes from the more remote parts of the bunkers so that trimming difficulties should not immediately arise if the vessel is required to proceed at or near full speed.'[21]

It became increasingly difficult to build up a reserve of stokers from the merchant marine. A large proportion of it operated through the Suez Canal, and shipping companies found that lascars from India and 'seedies' from Africa could stand the heat of the stokehold much better. But the culture and technique of stokers, even British ones, were very different from those required by the Royal Navy. As the shipowner Lord Brassey observed,

In the Royal Service it is possible to raise a superior class for stokehold duties. Entered at an early age, systematically trained, accustomed to the strict discipline of a ship of war, worked only at intervals at full pressure in the stokehold, inspired by the prestige of the Royal Service, and encouraged by the prospects of promotion and a pension, a stoker, as we find him in the Navy, is a man of a different stamp from the stoker of the Mercantile Marine, who shares none of his advantages.[22]

This was largely confirmed by an officer who had to deal with the stokers of the liner *Teutonic* in 1916: 'They are without exception the lowest scale of humanity found in Great Britain. They have been accustomed ... to be treated ... as animals necessary to the steaming of an Atlantic liner. They have no patriotic, social or moral conceptions ...'[23]

Up to 1891 it was not unknown for stokers to be recruited from 'reformatory' ships for wayward boys, though seamen were never taken on from such sources. Some officers defended this practice, as boys could be sent to such ships by local authorities for fairly trivial offences, or simply because they were homeless. One officer even considered them 'a far superior class of man than those generally received from the recruiting officer'. But a survey showed that out of eighteen received from *Cornwall* during 1888–90, six had deserted, one had been invalided and another sentenced to 90 days' imprisonment for theft and was dismissed the service as 'objectionable'. The practice was stopped.[24]

Stokers had a reasonably good disciplinary record on board in the 1890s – Fisher claimed it was because they were too tired to do anything else. They tended to desert at a higher rate than seamen: 9.66 per cent ran before completing their first engagement by 1891, compared with 6.33 per cent of seamen. They were subject to injury, and nearly 15 per cent did not complete the engagement for that reason, compared with 9 per cent of seamen. However, they apparently liked the pay and conditions, for 72 per cent of them signed on again in 1894, compared with 67 per cent of seamen.[25]

## THE CIVIL BRANCHES

Domestics were non-continuous-service men, which allowed officers to take trusted servants from one ship to another. They were conscious of their own status and carefully graded, and no less than 26 different ratings could be identified in 1888. At their head was the general mess steward, a kind of naval butler. He was included in the first class domestics, including admirals' and captains' stewards and general messmen, who were rated as chief petty officers, and others who were equivalent to petty officers, 'as regards traveling by Rail or Steamer, share of Prize Money and Privileges as to Smoking and other Accommodation on board ship'. Domestics second class were grouped with ABs, or leading seamen after three years service. These were captains', commanders', secretaries' and engineers' servants. Below them were the assistant cooks, the wardroom and gunroom servants. Domestics third class were equivalent to ordinary seamen and boys. Many were warrant officers' servants, working for a class of men who were not used to dealing with domestics and who could not afford to pay substantial tips as other officers did.[26]

The navy was experiencing its own 'servant problem', reflecting the situation in upper- and middle-class society as a whole. It could not use women, who made up 95 per cent of 'indoor' servants and 95 per cent in 1871 – the navy had little use for male 'outdoor' servants such as grooms, coachmen, gardeners and chauffeurs.

The navy got its domestics from several different sources. Some were recruited on foreign stations – the Chinese and Goans were considered very satisfactory, the Maltese were popular, though less clean and more inclined to move from ship to ship, and the Royal Marines were often used, and not just for their own officers. In 1905 it was complained, 'It is said that good marine servants are becoming scarce. The men are no longer of the same class as formerly, from the fact that old soldiers will not now volunteer, largely because they are forced to parade &c.' Seaman boys lacked proper training for the job and were likely to move on before they became proficient. This left the men who had been recruited to the navy specifically as domestic servants. They were one of the last groups to be kept on non-continuous service because that allowed greater flexibility for an officer to keep his servant on as he moved from ship to ship without going through the drafting system. Often the servants were paid privately by their officers in addition to their naval wages. In 1905 a captain's steward or a wardroom steward might make up to £48 per annum in this way. At the other end of the scale, warrant officers' servants made between £3 and £12.

The domestics third class were the biggest problem in 1905. They were often recruited with very little training and discharged when found to be unsuitable. They usually served in the warrant officers' messes, but many of them were 'nothing but dirty scallywags' who could not even keep themselves clean. They suffered from lack of proper living space, as did many domestics of other classes. Most of them ate, washed and dressed in the pantry and slung their hammocks as close to it as possible. It was recommended that they have an enclosed mess room on the lines of a 'servants' hall' in a country house.

By 1905 the domestics were beginning to demand better conditions. They held a meeting in Portsmouth in February asking for better training, a more suitable uniform and an increase in wages to reduce the dependence on private payments, which did not count towards a pension. They also disliked the title of 'domestic' and suggested its replacement with 'steward', 'cook', etc.[27]

In contrast with the domestic, the sick berth attendant was well trained within the navy. A committee of 1899 recommended that the training period be restored to six months and physical standards and pay greatly improved. The probationer sick berth attendant went to one of the naval hospitals at the home ports for a course of lectures, which included anatomy, wounds and fractures, fits of insensibility including alcoholism, the carrying of wounded and infectious diseases. He was trained in invalid cookery, including beef tea, fried fish and rice water. He spent each morning under the nursing sister in a ward, rising at 6 a.m. to make the beds and then carrying out various duties until late in the morning, when he would leave for instruction, squad drill, physical training or to write up his journal. He was given ten practical demonstrations and twenty lectures in the dispensary, including the Latin and English names of various medicines, their doses and uses, and the antidotes to poisons.[28]

## THE PORT DIVISIONS

All the great naval bases – Chatham/Sheerness, Portsmouth and Plymouth – had been in existence for more than two centuries, and a great deal of naval and social culture had built up around them. Sailors and dockyard workers made their homes there, pubs, dance halls, theatres and brothels opened to cater for the nautical market, and each town looked to the navy as its main economic activity. Each area was a large command headed by an admiral, and in the 1888 Naval Estimates the Admiralty planned to use that as the basis for mobilization in the event of war. Each port was to have a specific number of reserve ships allocated to it, and the country was divided into three districts. In the event of mobilization or war, all the reserves from that district would be sent to a specific port.

In 1893 the Admiralty began to extend this system to the regular ratings (though not to the officers):

During the year preparations have been made for definitely appropriating petty officers and men of all ratings to the three home ports, in order that each port may be self-supporting and capable of manning and providing for the care and maintenance of all ships attached to it. A complete establishment for each port has been drawn up, and the numbers voted have been divided between them in proportion to their requirements. New entries from the shore, and boys on completion of their training, will be appropriated to a port, according to the numbers required to complete the respective port establishment. It is hoped that the establishment of these port divisions will eventually provide for the actual needs of each port, facilitate mobilisation, and enable recruiting to be placed on a continuous and satisfactory system.[29]

Each of the ports was to become a self-contained naval base, with a yard, a large harbour to lay up ships, accommodation for men awaiting allocation, marine barracks, armament and victualling depots, and training schools for every type of rating. Most of these facilities were already present, though the Chatham command had no gunnery school, and one had to be set up at Sheerness, where it was given the rather inappropriate name of HMS *Wildfire*. All this was modelled on the regimental system of the army, though on a very different scale.

In May 1893 the seamen were told that they would have to be attached to one of these divisions. In the past they had been allowed to choose which depot they wanted to be attached to each time their ship paid off. Now they were to be told clearly that 'their election is final and they will only be subsequently allowed to be transferred to another Port on giving sufficient reason for it, or by exchange'. Boys on completing their course in the training ships were to be allocated to a port division, mainly according to the area in which they had been recruited. The London recruiting area included all the counties around the city, including Kent and Oxford. Half its recruits were to be sent to Portsmouth, a third to Chatham-Sheerness, and a sixth to Devonport. Otherwise, the Portsmouth men would come from Wiltshire, Dorset and Hampshire. Chatham would take the whole of Scotland and the North of England as well as East Anglia and north Wales, while Devonport would have the West Country, Ireland, the English Midlands and South Wales.[30]

The Portsmouth Division was planned to be the largest, with 10,066 seaman and 4,408 stokers, with other grades in proportion. Devonport was next with 8,465 seaman and 3,359 stokers, while Chatham had 6,619 seamen and 3,328 stokers. It was necessary to transfer large numbers of gunnery and torpedo men to Chatham to achieve these figures, and training schools had to be set up. The system was regarded as complete by the time of the Naval Estimates in March 1895. Each of the port divisions would take on its own identity over the years, particularly Devonport, which was much more rural in its recruitment than the others and whose ships tended to be dominated by men with West Country accents:

> It is common knowledge though difficult to convey to anyone who has not had personal experience of it, how different are the characteristics of a ship manned by a 'West Country' Crew and one manned by a Chatham crew, principally recruited from London or Liverpool and district, Portsmouth crews holding a place midway between these 2 extremes ...
>
> The somewhat stolid discipline of the home loving and cautious West Country men finds an admirable counterpoise in the vivid intelligence of the east Country crews with their superior education and acute qualities that may be so readily guided into good or bad channels.[31]

Portsmouth was known as 'Pompey' for reasons that have always been the subject of debate. Devonport was 'Guzz' for equally obscure reasons, and Chatham was less imaginatively known as 'Chats'.

## THE NAVY COMES ASHORE

It was only in the 1890s that the navy truly 'came ashore', with the building of training schools and barracks to replace the old hulks. There were plenty of buildings in the Royal dockyards and armament depots, but these were civilian-manned workshops and storehouses – the only dwelling houses were for yard officials and port admirals. Traditionally the navy had favoured accommodation afloat, as it was cheaper, it made it more difficult to desert, men were away from the power of the civil courts, and it gave the men some feel for shipboard life. But these reasons tended to decline as the nineteenth century progressed. Desertion and civil lawsuits were far less likely with the end of impressment, and the old 'wooden walls' were very different from the steel steamships in which the men would do their active service. The wooden ships could not be kept afloat for ever, and there were doubts about whether the first generation of ironclads, with so much space taken up by engines and with considerable subdivision, were suitable for the role of training ships. The ships took up valuable space in the wet docks of the yards, and were unsanitary by modern standards. Shore barracks would be good for discipline and would allow more options for training. But, as with many things, the navy's coming ashore began almost by accident.

Whale Island in Portsmouth Harbour was tiny until it was expanded using the spoil from the dockyard extension of the 1860s. It was then used by the men of HMS *Excellent* for rifle training and target practice, and its first building – 'The House that Jack built' – was erected in 1864 to the designs of Chief Petty Officer William Tribe to provide meals and storage. Captain Percy Scott had the land levelled, and gun batteries were erected for training. Barracks had followed by 1880, and eventually the island had a wardroom, drill shed, summer and winter parade grounds and was connected to the mainland by a bridge. The ship *Excellent*, now an old gunboat formerly called *Handy*, remained in commission, and the men based on Whale Island continued to wear 'HMS *Excellent*' on their cap tallies, a practice that would be followed by all shore bases in the Royal Navy.[32]

It was only natural that shore barracks should follow for men between commissions, especially after 1891 when gunners and torpedomen awaiting draft were allocated to the depot ships rather than continuing in the gunnery schools. There already was a small barracks at Sheerness and one at Keyham for the Plymouth men, opened in 1889 after many delays caused, it was suggested, by the old-fashioned officers' belief that sailors would soon lose their skills if they spent any length of time ashore. It was somewhat out of the way, but a 'dockyard train' could take men to their duties. It had eight barrack rooms, each with space for 125 men, who lived as if they were still on board, with mess tables and hammocks. It also had recreation facilities, such as an American-style bowling alley and even a billiard room – the officers' reluctance to let ratings play what was then an upper-class game was countered by the need to keep them out of the seedy clubs of Plymouth. The barracks became more important in 1891 when it became the home for the men of the steam reserve and the depot ship *Indus* was no longer needed.[33]

Barracks at Portsmouth had been suggested as early as 1862, and a site was selected with room for 4,000 men, but as always the navy found it difficult to raise money for bricks and mortar. Another plan was prepared in 1879, but a site large enough could not be found. Nine more sites were considered, including one on the peninsula of Tipnor, but the medical officers disapproved because of its proximity to a chemical works. There were plans to acquire the Anglesea Barracks from the army, but these fell through.[34] Finally in the Naval Estimates of 1891, the First Lord announced:

> The naval gunnery establishment and barracks at Whale Island, Portsmouth, will be completed by the end of the current year. It is proposed to commence the construction of new Naval Barracks at Portsmouth to accommodate 50 officers and 1,000 men. The favourable results anticipated from the substitution of commodious buildings on shore for the old hulks in which the seamen were previously accommodated have been fully realised in the case of Whale Island and Keyham Barracks, and the extension of the system of naval barracks is recognised as a matter of urgent necessity.[35]

Portsmouth Barracks opened with some style in September 1903, though they were still not complete:

> The hulks were vacated with no ceremony or regret as they were unpleasant and miserable quarters ... After dinner the men mustered in four companies – Chief Petty Officers, Seamen, Stokers and Marines. There were four bands present from the Naval Barracks, H.M.S. *Excellent*, H.M.S. *St. Vincent* and the Marines. At half past two the bugle sounded to go and the men marched off. There were immense crowds of spectators and difficulty was experienced by the Mounted Borough Police in keeping the road clear. Once inside, the gates were shut and the crowd besieged the railings to see what was to follow. The men were formed in a huge hollow square. Commander Stileman gave a few orders and closed with an intimation that there would be general leave that evening, an announcement which called forth a cheer. Then, to some lively tunes, the men marched off to their quarters.[36]

At Chatham, an old convict barracks was to be taken over from the Home Office, but that plan had fallen through by 1894, when plans for a new building for 3,500 men were announced. Still there were delays, and it was not until April 1903 that the Chatham Barracks were occupied. They were not popular with seamen and stokers, except those who found themselves a 'cushy billet.' Harry Hemmingway recalls, 'I didn't like it in barracks. We used to call it the Stone Frigate and I got out of there as quick as I could. There were too many crushers and they seemed to pick on the stokers.'[37]

## PHYSICAL TRAINING

The new sail-less fleet needed to find a new way of giving its men exercise in the confines of a ship at sea. In 1889 the Admiralty issued a circular on a new system of 'Physical training or Swedish gymnastics'. Instructors 'of good physique' under the age of 25 were to be chosen at the gunnery schools and go through a special course. They were issued with a manual of instructions.

> Every exercise comprised in the present handbook has been selected for its value in one of two aspects; the first, or elementary aspect being the

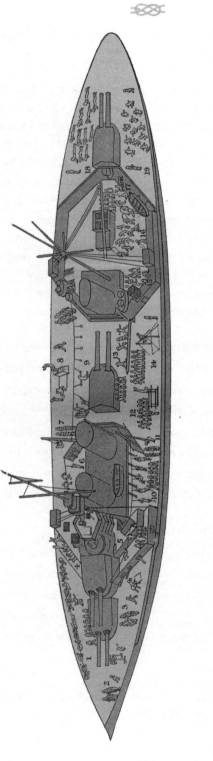

1. Tug of War.
2. Jump.
3. Buck.
4. Wall Bars.
5. Horizontal Climbing Rope.

6. Vertical Climbing Rope.
7. Trapeze (Coaling Derrick).
8. Horse.
9. Travelling Rings (Awning Jackstay).
10. Vertical Climbing Rope.

11. Rings (Coaling Derrick).
12. Parallel Bars.
13. Balancing (Coaling Derrick).
14. Horizontal Bar.
15. Shelf Drill.

16. Skipping.
17. Shelf Drill.
18. Swedish Drill.
19. Swedish Drill.

William James had some imaginative ideas for exercises and games on board a dreadnought battleship.

manner and degree in which it tends to cultivate the physical resources of
the body; while the second, or practical aspect, is the manner and degree
in which its practice may be brought to aid directly in the professional
duties of the seaman.

Instructors were to form their men in squads of ten to fifteen and were
urged to be reasonably tactful:

> The instructor will repress all laughing at the mishaps or unsuccessful
> efforts of beginners calculated to discourage or annoy or distract attention;
> and will strictly forbid the slightest attempt to baulk, hinder or otherwise
> interfere with anyone during the performance of an exercise; but this need
> not be allowed to mar the full enjoyment and free expression of interest felt
> in witnessing each other's performance, successful or unsuccessful.[38]

Fourteen years later, Admiral Fisher was equally keen on physical training
now that the fleet was completely sail-less. His unmistakeable style forces
its way through what should have been a staid official report:

> We are 'Babes in the Wood' compared with foreign countries in the matter
> of gymnastic exercises – so important for health and physical development.
> Observe our slouching boys and pot-bellied Petty Officers ... Much is hoped
> from the improvements proposed to be effected in physical training on the
> return of the Superintendent of Gymnasia from Sweden, where he will
> obtain full details of all requirements.[39]

There were several hundred petty officers first class holding physical
training ratings in 1908, and it was complained that, 'Gymnastics has been
rewarded by far greater substantive advancement than the other Branches,
though its importance as a factor of fighting efficiency is less.'[40]

Exercise on board ship always called for a little ingenuity, but
Commander William James produced a diagram of a battleship (see facing
page) showing no less than nineteen different activities in place in different
parts of the ship – tug-of-war on the forecastle, climbing ropes alongside
the funnels, a vaulting horse amidships, a rather terrifying demonstration
of balancing on a coaling derrick, Swedish drill on the quarterdeck and

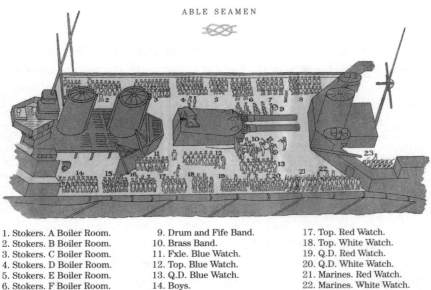

| 1. Stokers. A Boiler Room. | 9. Drum and Fife Band. | 17. Top. Red Watch. |
| 2. Stokers. B Boiler Room. | 10. Brass Band. | 18. Top. White Watch. |
| 3. Stokers. C Boiler Room. | 11. Fxle. Blue Watch. | 19. Q.D. Red Watch. |
| 4. Stokers. D Boiler Room. | 12. Top. Blue Watch. | 20. Q.D. White Watch. |
| 5. Stokers. E Boiler Room. | 13. Q.D. Blue Watch. | 21. Marines. Red Watch. |
| 6. Stokers. F Boiler Room. | 14. Boys. | 22. Marines. White Watch. |
| 7. Stokers. G Boiler Room. | 15. Fxle. Red Watch. | 23. Marines. Blue Watch. |
| 8. Stokers. Engine Rooms. | 16. Fxle. White Watch. | |

The ship's company at divisions, according to James.

many others. As if that were not enough, he also included a drawing of various recreational activities including a swimming pool on the forecastle improvised from a canvas awning, cricket amidships and officers' quoits on the after platform.[41]

## LIFE IN DESTROYERS

By the early 1890s the navy was thinking of ways to counter the menace of torpedo boats, particularly those of the French, who were developing faster and more seaworthy boats, and the Royal Navy evolved the torpedo boat destroyer or TBD. It was larger than the torpedo boat and could operate for a few days away from its bases, perhaps raiding across the English Channel, but it had a very narrow hull and minimal accommodation. Destroyers, as they became known, got larger and faster over the years, though a theoretical speed of 30 knots, for example, was not always achieved in real conditions at sea.

Destroyers were always uncomfortable even by naval standards. At one stage it was planned to have some of the men sleep in the engine room, but that was abandoned. Instead, the crew lived in a mess in the bows, as described for the 27-knot class of 1893–4: 'The mess fittings consist of a cupboard and plate rack for each seamen [sic] and a bread tray for every two men. Lockers of special pattern are fitted so as to be readily removed, one for each man. No provision is made for ditty boxes or bags. Hammocks are stowed overhead on the hammock beams.'[42] Things became distinctly hazardous when at high speed: 'Against a heavy sea a TBD steaming at 17 or 15 kts would tear all her packing out, sweep everything off the upper deck, carry away the platform and bridge rails, and probably sweep someone off the bridge. She would race, jump, kick, labour, eventually lose her steam, and after a short time be a mass of defects.'[43] Another officer remarked, 'The behaviour of the ship and the accommodation is such that no cne gets undisturbed rest at sea even in fine weather and in bad weather of course there would be very little rest for any one so that I should (except in very exceptional circumstances) recommend a limit of five nights at sea ...'[44]

Ships got larger, and the River class of 1902 was fitted with a high forecastle, which made seakeeping much better. But now their main job was to escort the battlefleet, so they were expected to do more, to stay at sea longer and in worse weather, and there was no less hardship for the crew. Nevertheless, many seamen preferred service in destroyers, where discipline was less rigid and ratings were allowed more responsibility. Larger numbers of destroyers were ordered, and more than two million pounds was spent on them in 1913–14, compared with less than half a million in 1905–6.[45]

The torpedo boat created the new category of torpedo coxswain, the senior rating on board, to be selected from among leading torpedomen at *Vernon* and *Defiance*. He developed into an important figure on board as torpedo craft got bigger and bigger, and his role was extended to the new destroyers. He was trained intensively in the Torpedo School at *Vernon* and afloat in Portsmouth Harbour, but the Ratings Committee of 1905 pointed out that he had very little to do with torpedoes as such, and each vessel already had torpedomen to deal with technical questions. His main job in action was to steer the ship, and at other times he had to act as 'ship's steward, master-at-arms, sick-bayman, etc.'. According to the captain of the destroyer depot ship *Sapphire II* at Devonport, 'What is required is a good steady petty officer of a certain age, who will not lose his head in an emergency and who has a good command of men.' He was to be 'useful to the Commanding Officer of a torpedo craft', rather than 'a man stuffed full of special torpedo knowledge'. Despite protests from the torpedo branch, his training was transferred to the destroyer flotillas, and the rating was opened up to seamen gunners as well as torpedomen. They were to be experienced men, recommended by the captains of sea-going ships and 'steady and reliable Petty Officers, good disciplinarians, and possessed of a sufficiently good education to keep the Destroyer accounts, and have shown ability in handling steam boats'. They were given 80 days of training, including the management of torpedo boats and destroyers, and accounting and the internal economy of ships.[46]

## SPECIAL SERVICE AND THE RESERVES

The Royal Fleet Reserve was founded in March 1901 as a means of allowing pensioners and other time-expired men to continue with some form of naval training. Pensioners were liable to recall up to the age of 50 and were automatically put in Class A, where they would be given some rather desultory training in a local RNR drill ship. They, and men who had not served long enough to earn a pension, were eligible to join Class B, which involved a strict medical examination and a week's far more thorough training at a naval depot, in return for payment. The Admiralty considered the terms to be very advantageous, but in 1904 it was surprised that less than a thousand pensioners had transferred to Class B, and nearly 2,500 had not.[47]

In the meantime a Committee on Naval Reserves headed by Sir Edward Grey was not yet ready to deliver its report, but the Admiralty asked it for some views in advance, so that it could plan the active service numbers for 1903–4. The committee suggested a move away from the principle of long service, which was almost sacred to the navy by that time. It was proposed that 1,500 men be taken on for five years, to be followed by seven years in the Royal Fleet Reserve so that they would not be lost to the navy. As well as helping solve the immediate recruiting problems, it would help to increase the numbers available in wartime. It was to start on a small scale, with 375 seamen and 625 stokers in the following year, and the relevant legislation was passed through Parliament. By the beginning of 1904, 261 seamen and 328 stokers had already been found, and the Admiralty was confident of getting the full number.[48] The title of 'special service' was chosen instead of 'short service' as it seemed more positive and reflected the long-term role with the reserves. They began to rely more on this method in years to come, though the twelve-year engagement was still expected to provide the core of the navy and the great majority of petty officers.

By the early 1900s the navy was trying to reduce its expenses, but at the same time it needed stokers rather than seamen, so the latter were positively encouraged to give up their permanent engagements to transfer to the RFR. Men with eight years' service were allowed to transfer without payment; those with shorter service had reduced fees. Initially this had a limited uptake in Portsmouth and Plymouth but was popular in Chatham. However, over the years the strength was built up, and by the end of 1912 the Royal Fleet Reserve had 7,500 men in Class A and 16,000 in Class B, with a new intermediate class of 2,000 men who did up to 28 days' training per year and were liable to recall in an emergency that did not justify calling out the full reserve.[49]

## THE NAVY IN AN IMPERIAL AGE

The Mediterranean remained the grandest naval station during the 1890s. It was here that Petty Officer Thomas Lyne was a witness to the greatest naval tragedy of the age. He was on board the battleship *Victoria* when she accidentally rammed and sank HMS *Camperdown* off the coast of Lebanon in 1893:

> Vast quantities of spars, wreckage, etc., shot up to the surface, wounding many who were fortunate to get away from the ship, and were now struggling in the great upheaval of water. Then, and not until then, we in the boats were ordered to proceed to the succour of Officers and men in the water. Then there was a further upheaval, which appeared to be the boilers exploding, causing a swell of water, carrying with it spars and other forms of wreckage and making the efforts of rescue by boats most difficult.

Many poor fellows, evidently seriously injured, were seen to drown within a few yards of my boat, which was unable to reach them through the wreckage.[50]

The navy ended the century with two notable operations on shore. In 1897 a naval brigade from nine ships captured Benin in Nigeria after the army failed to mobilize a force in time. Thousands of half-starved slaves were liberated, and the British Empire seemed at its best.

The South African War with the Boer republics of Transvaal and the Orange Free State began very badly as the irregular but skilled and effective Boer armies advanced against the ill-prepared British. To the west and south they besieged the towns of Mafeking and Kimberley and threatened to advance into Cape Colony. In the east, the cruiser *Powerful*, on the way home from China, landed a naval brigade with four 12-pounders and two 4.7-inch guns to go inland by rail to help defend the town of Ladysmith. They were just in time as the Boer siege began, and the 4.7s, named 'Lady Anne' and 'Princess Victoria', were the only weapons big enough to counter the Boers' German 'Long Toms'. At Wagon Hill on 4 January 1900, Gunner Sims rallied the thirteen men under his command with the cry of 'Naval Brigade! Extend in skirmishing order to the right and left – forward!' and repelled a Boer attack, which was already running out of steam.[51] In the meantime the cruiser *Terrible* had arrived at Durban and landed men and guns to form the main defence of the port against Boer attack.

The navy was responsible for organising the sea transport services that brought a greatly increased number of troops into the region. The war was unpopular in Europe, but there was no real prospect of a major power intervening in favour of the Boers, so it was possible to form more naval brigades. A party set out from Cape Town in October:

> All hands on board manned and cheered ship, and a hearty reply was given from every boat as it pulled ashore laden with its khaki-clad bluejackets, stokers and marines ... There were many dismal faces among those left behind, nothing but cheerful smiles on the faces of those chosen as they formed 'fours' and wheeled through the dockyard gates on their way to the station.[52]

This proved a false start, but the men from *Doris, Powerful* and *Monarch* landed with an initial complement of 400 men and four 12-pounder guns. The sailors were dressed in khaki issued from the army stores, while those who could not find clothes to fit had to dye their white uniforms with coffee. They took the train north to help in the relief of Kimberley and took part in several battles. Two 4.7s, 'Little Bobs' and 'Sloper', were sent to join them. As they moved overland the sailors learned how to control teams of oxen:

> They learnt to drive as well as the natives, learnt the names of the individual oxen belonging to their especial wagon or gun team, could crack a whip with the best, and were almost able to pick out any particular ox with the lash without touching any other. They copied the unearthly noises with which the Kaffirs stopped and restarted them, and not only that but they took great pains to teach these natives the most fearful and effective oaths they knew.[53]

The sailors foraged for geese and sheep to improve their diet, and stokers seemed to be best at this. They hauled guns up hills, as their ancestors had done. They dug out gun emplacements and ribbed the Royal Engineers with cries of 'How about the blooming sappers now?' They adopted pets, such as a dog which was fitted with a cap ribbon from *Doris*. There was no end to their resourcefulness, for as a naval surgeon commented,

> our men seemed to adapt themselves more readily to varying circumstances, to forage more for themselves, and to be better able to cook what they received than could the soldiers.
>
> Every man in the navy has, of necessity, to be a sufficiently good cook, whilst the soldier does not have the same opportunity to learn, and therefore to gain experience in making a little go a long way.[54]

During nine months ashore, these brigades travelled nearly 800 miles besides their rail travel and used their guns on 25 separate occasions, including at the Battle of Paardeberg, in which more than 500 rounds were fired over eight days.[55]

Meanwhile in the east, a relief column for Ladysmith was being organized, with the naval element comprising 39 officers and 403 men from the crews of *Forte*, *Terrible*, *Tartar* and *Philomel*. *Terrible's* contingent had a 6-inch gun manned by 3 petty officers, 19 seamen and 29 stokers; two 4.7s each commanded by a chief petty officer with 2 petty officers and round 20 seamen; and a dozen 12-pounders, each commanded by a petty officer or leading seamen with about 10 seamen. In addition there were two ambulance parties, each with a sick-berth attendant and about seven stokers, and two miscellaneous groups of blacksmiths, armourers, carpenters and signallers. During the hard-fought battles on the approach to Ladysmith, Petty Officers Veness and Taylor, each in charge of a 12-pounder, challenged one another to knock out a Boer gun. Taylor, a noted marksman, was the winner, and the soldiers cheered as his target toppled over.[56] At the end of February 1900 the troops and sailors entered Ladysmith to finish a siege of 112 days. Naval involvement in the war would soon come to an end as army reinforcements arrived and it entered a new guerrilla phase in which heavy guns were less useful. The last naval detachments were withdrawn in October 1900, so the navy had no direct involvement in the policy of 'concentration camps' which sullied Britain's reputation in Europe.

*Terrible* completed her voyage to China, where she was in time to take part in the multinational expedition to Beijing to relieve foreigners besieged there during the Boxer Rebellion. Captain Scott recommended landing four of his 12-pounders, but his admiral, Sir James Bruce, only took one, which was later regretted.[57] It proved to be 'a most effective weapon' with a crew 'from South African experience, thoroughly acquainted with its capabilities'.[58] Naval brigades, including nearly a thousand British sailors and marines, formed a large part of the forces landed in China in the early stages. A German officer was impressed when sailors from HMS *Endymion* drove off a Chinese attack with bayonets. At the siege of Tientsin, a customs launch manned by a naval coxswain, an able seaman, an ERA and some stokers, a French engineer, an American interpreter and an incompetent pilot managed to get letters out of the city, though the sailors had to undertake the last part of the journey on foot. Inside the city, naval

144

engineers and stokers worked to repair the boilers and engines that kept the water works and gasworks running. The bluejackets got on well with their colleagues from other nations, particularly the Germans.[59]

## RECALLED FROM EMPIRE

These were the last of the navy's foreign adventures for now, as attention was focused nearer home. In 1903, Prince Louis of Battenberg pointed out that the principles of foreign service were at least 50 years old, and the traditional three-year commission was obsolete. 'When ships were first commissioned for continuous service in peace the process of enlisting the crew and fitting out the ship was in itself a long one. The passage to distant stations took many months, and it was long before the ship was thoroughly efficient.' But now everything was changed:

> Most of the causes enumerated above, which necessitate a long commission, have now practically disappeared. Ships are commissioned for foreign service from the 'A' Division of the Fleet Reserve in so complete a state of readiness to proceed that a week is generally sufficient between the hoisting of the pennant and the ship leaving England. On the other hand the crew which is drafted on board consists for the most part of highly trained men, already familiar with the internal arrangements which in our days differ very slightly in the various classes of ships. Again, the time taken to reach the distant station only takes days, where it formerly took weeks.[60]

Many officers agreed that a ship's company would become bored and stale by the third year of a commission. Battenberg's proposals for two years were largely adopted, but were soon overtaken by events.

Initially it was not just the fear of Germany that caused concentration nearer to home waters – that threat was only one of several that might develop in years to come. The First Lord told Parliament in 1905 that the United States was 'forming a navy the power and size of which will be limited only by the amount of money which the American people choose to spend on it'. The Russian Navy had been 'greatly increased', while the new German Navy was 'of the most efficient type and is so fortunately circumstanced that it is able to concentrate almost the whole of its fleet at its home ports'.

The Royal Navy, on the other hand, was still dispersed. 'The principles, on which the present peace disposition of His Majesty's ships and the arrangement of their stations are based, date from a period when the electric telegraph did not exist and when wind was the motive power.' Numerous colonial gunboats were to be scrapped, and a new disposition of battleships was proposed. The Home Fleet was to be renamed the Channel Fleet and have a strength of twelve battleships plus cruisers. The Channel Fleet of eight battleships was renamed the Atlantic Fleet and would be based permanently at Gibraltar. The Mediterranean Fleet of eight battleships would remain at Malta.[61] In 1909 the Channel Fleet was increased to sixteen battleships, and it was closely associated with the six of the Atlantic Fleet. By early 1913 the concentration had gone much further. The *Entente Cordiale* with France meant that it was no longer necessary to guard the Mediterranean so strongly, and the fleet was reduced to four battlecruisers and supporting ships. The main force at home, now renamed the Home Fleet, was to be increased to 33 battleships including all the new dreadnoughts, a battlecruiser squadron, three armoured cruiser squadrons and eventually five flotillas of destroyers with around twenty ships each. [62]

Combined with this was the nucleus crew system, by which second-line ships were to be kept ready for war. Under the old system, 'such ships as were not fully manned were entirely without officers or crew, and left laid up in the dockyards, which they never left until their turn came for full commission.' In the new system, as described by the First Lord in the 1905 Estimates,

> They will each have a captain, second-in-command, and a proportion of the other officers, including engineer, gunnery, navigating and torpedo officers. They will have a nucleus crew two-fifths of their war complement, but in that two-fifths will be included all the more expert ratings, especially the torpedo ratings and the principal gun numbers, and each ship will periodically proceed to sea for the purpose of gunnery practice and testing her machinery. They will be grouped homogeneously at the three Home ports according as their destination may be determined for reinforcement in time of war.[63]

Prepared in this way, it was hoped that the ships could be fully manned from the naval barracks and training schools and be ready to put to sea in a few hours.

For the lower deck all this meant less foreign service, which was attractive to family men; but sailors tended to live far more cheaply in the Empire and this had an effect on their purses. The changes brought a good deal of prosperity to the home ports. They also meant, according to some officers, that they were less focused on the job. It was claimed that Admiral Sir Charles Beresford, Fisher's greatest rival, had started the problem when commanding the fleet at Portland. Courting popularity, he allowed extensive weekend leave to let married men visit their families in Portsmouth, 'by which the ships at Portland were rendered absolutely inefficient for war from Friday to Tuesday and efficient only on Wednesday and Thursday each week'. As this spread, 'in the Home Ports it is quite impossible to keep all hands up to the mark.'

> Every officer and man and most of the Captains have one eye on the shore permanently. The liberty men come off at times varying with the weather for 8 to 10 am only to return at four to the shore having spent the previous hour thinking about it ... Demands for ordinary leave, special leave out of turn, and for varying periods urged with every excuse reason and ingenuity can suggest are absolutely endless ...[64]

A few years later William James, from his experience as commander of *Queen Mary* at this time, longed for 'a return to the days when a man's ship was his home and not a place of business to be left at every opportunity'.[65]

# 6

# THE ROAD TO WAR
# 1904–1914

### THE FISHER REFORMS AND THE NEW SEAMAN

Admiral Sir John Fisher served at the Admiralty as Second Naval Lord, in charge of personnel, in 1902–3 and took over as the professional head of the navy in 1904, as possibly the most dynamic First Sea Lord of all time. He remains a controversial figure because, rather like Margaret Thatcher eighty years or so later, he made many enemies and carried out his reforms with no little disruption, dividing the navy in the process. He built radically new ships, reorganized the system of officer training, abolished sail training and recalled much of the navy from the Empire. His biographers tend to make light of the lower deck aspects of his reforms, though they continually quote his dictum, 'The scheme, the whole scheme and nothing but the scheme!'

One of the tasks he set himself was to get rid of obsolete practices. In 1904 the First Lord told Parliament,

> The boys in the training ships will no longer receive any instruction which is solely applicable to the management of sailing ships, and in place of the training they have hitherto received on masts and yards there has been substituted a more extensive training in gunnery and an elementary training in mechanical and stokehold work.[1]

The training brigs were abolished, and the final demise of naval sail led to an identity crisis among the traditional seamen. As the First Lord of the Admiralty quoted to the House of Commons in 1903,

> Everything in the modern Fleet is done by machinery, be it steam, hydraulic, compressed air, electricity, to which will probably be added in the

near future, explosive oil and liquid air. Not only are the ships propelled solely by machinery, but they are steered by machinery. Their principal arms – gun and torpedo – are worked by machinery. They are lit by machinery, the water used by those on board for drinking, cooking, and washing is produced by machinery; messages which were formerly transmitted by voice-pipe, now go by telephone. The orders which the Admiral wishes to give to the Fleet could formerly only be made by flags in the day and lamps at night; they are now made by electricity, that is by wireless telegraphy and electric flashing signal lamps. Orders which were formerly written out by hand are now produced by typewriter or by the printing machine. Formerly the Admiral visited another ship in his pulling barge; now he goes in a steam-boat. The anchor, formerly hove up by hand, is now worked by an engine. The live bullocks which were formerly taken to sea are now replaced by frozen carcasses maintained in that condition by machinery. If a fire breaks out in the ship the steam pumps drown it. If the ship springs a leak, steam pumps keep down the water. The very air that those on board between decks breathe is provided by a fan driven by machinery.[2]

There was still plenty for a seaman to do, but it did not provide the constant readiness that had been needed in handling and trimming sails. Men were needed as lookouts and helmsmen, but that only took up a small number of men during each watch. Most of them were needed when the ship raised anchor, but that only took a short time and did not affect what happened when at sea. In harbour they manned the numerous boats, but at sea they only had to provide a crew for a single one on each side, to be used if a man fell overboard. The seaman was no longer the man who made the ship go, and unless he found a subsidiary job as a gunner or torpedoman he was likely to be left behind for promotion. One captain went as far as to say that 'the ideal "Man of war's man" should be a "stoker gunner"'.

## THE LIFE OF A STOKER

By the 1900s the navy's greatest need was for extra stokers rather than seamen, and they could be recruited from a wider age group and a slightly lower standard. As a result, there were occasional gluts of seamen boys. In 1905 seamen were invited to transfer to the stoker class. Two years later, in the only years in which the numerical strength of the fleet was reduced, the entry of boys decreased to 1,500 per year but the intake of stokers was kept up. By 1910–11 the expansion had resumed, and the navy entered 11,770 ratings in addition to 1,092 marines – the largest entry for many years. Two years later it had risen to 15,844 ratings and 2,124 marines as the world accelerated towards the Great War. By these methods, the navy was able to keep up a continuous increase in numbers over 25 years, and overall it increased from 64,405 men in 1889 to 151,000 in 1914.

But standards began to decline as demand increased. Entering in 1904, George Wells noted that, 'The big four-funnel ships were coming in then and they wanted Stokers at any price.'[3] In 1913 the commodore of the Portsmouth Barracks complained,

> There are 7000 men here, one way and another. About 6000 are short service 2nd Class Stokers, five year engagement. Their only qualification is strength and ability to shove coal into the ship's furnaces … The recruiting Officers don't ask too many questions as to their past. They're a tough lot, and discipline has to be strict accordingly.[4]

'Clinker Knocker' trained as a stoker in 1910. He did two weeks of drill and indoctrination in the Portsmouth Naval Barracks and was sent to the old battleship *Renown* to learn the job:

> We are taken into the boiler-rooms and taught how to fire boilers. The boilers are not in use, and we shovel stones instead of coal into the furnaces by numbers. At the command ONE! the shovel is thrust forward and filled with stones. TWO! the shovel is brought backward. THREE! the stones are hurled into the furnaces; and FOUR! brings us back to the READY! Position again. Some of our number are a long time before they can hit the open furnace, and we look along the handle of the shovel in the throwing of the stones, as if we were firing a rifle. The naval method of firing boilers is: LIGHT, EASY and BRIGHT, therefore, getting every ounce of energy from the fuel.[5]

Sidney Knock describes the work in the stokehold before the First World War:

The men look magnificent; their figures, through the gloom pierced by the light of the fires, show up grotesque, weird; their features wear a tense, drawn expression. Through an open furnace door, one is dextrously shovelling coal into the voracious mouth. The movements of his supple, sinuous body are distinctly alluring. At each movement, in methodical time, the shovel rebounds upon the dead-plate. We are told that this movement is necessary. It is a mystery of the craft.

At the next boiler a stoker, armed with a poker, or 'slice,' some nine feet in length, and thick in proportion, thrusts and lunges it into the fire, shaking and breaking a mass of clinker, while another stands by holding a shovel in front of the furnace door to protect the other's face from the terrific heat … A foul oath escapes from his clenched lips as he prises at the resisting clinker. It comes free. The slice, now red hot, is withdrawn and flung smartly into a rack above his head. … The hot ashes are drawn, damped down, and flung into the rear, skid upon skid of coal emptied in place. Other fires need attention; the skids of coal skim across the chequered plates. So the feverish activity continues.[6]

The stoker's work was far more intense than the seaman's, and he was doing heavy and constant manual labour throughout his watch. Engineer Rear Admiral Davis testified in 1905, 'In these days there are no "idle" times below deck like those possible on deck. When the ship is at sea the engine-room staff is fully employed pushing the ship through the water and on arrival in harbour it is busy making good defects.'[7]

Admiral Fisher remarked, 'The seaman complement is assessed on the requirements of "action" only, the stoker complement is assessed on peace requirements only.'[8] Stokers were paid more than seamen, a minimum of 1/8$d$ per day compared with 1/3$d$. It was necessary to attract a suitable class of men, though standards were not the same as for seamen. The stoker had the advantage of better medium-term promotion prospects. For promotion to first class, he would have to be efficient as a fireman when the boiler was working at full power, able to lubricate a bearing, to know the names of all the tools in the engine room and to use the more common ones, to plait gasket for packing and to have 'a fair knowledge' of the 124 pages of the *Stoker's Manual*.[9]

At this stage a man might well qualify for stoker mechanic, roughly equivalent to a seaman's non-substantive rating in gunnery. To earn it he had to acquire some skill in the use of tools, and he would be employed as an assistant to an ERA on repair work, or working with the auxiliary machinery, which needed a good deal of attention. When the rating was established in 1871, it was estimated that 300 would be needed. There was no formal training scheme, and they were examined on board by the captain and the engineer officer, with no restriction on numbers. By the early years of the twentieth century there were more than 23,000 of them.[10]

The system of substantive stoker ratings changed in 1908 to bring it into line with the seaman class. The old leading stoker first class became known as stoker petty officer, while the new leading stoker was equivalent to leading seaman. Further promotion was usually in the hands of the man's officers on board ship:

> as soon as possible in a ship's commission the Engineer Officer selects the most promising of the stokers 1st Class and puts them through a special course of instruction in auxiliary machinery. Men so trained who give good promise of the qualities necessary in a Petty Officer are rated Acting Leading Stoker by the captain of the Ship on completing two years' service as Stoker 1st Class ...

After that the leading stoker went to the Mechanical Training Establishment at Chatham or Devonport, where he might be selected for the rank of mechanician. If not, he was confirmed in the leading stoker rate and advanced to petty officer in due course. The number of petty officers was no higher than in the seaman branch – precisely 20.3 per cent in 1903–4. However, far more chief stokers were needed because there had to be a chief or an ERA in charge of each boiler space to take on the vital and responsible job of monitoring the water level – a typical battleship of the period had eighteen boilers. As a result, the stoker branch had 6.2 per cent of chiefs, compared with 1.8 in the seaman branch.[11] But promotion stopped there. The only path to warrant or commissioned rank was to train as a mechanician after the leading stoker course, so the branch had many chiefs with no hope at all of promotion.

The introduction of the turbine engine with *Dreadnought* of 1906 did nothing to relieve the pressure on the stoker. There was a steady increase in fuel efficiency and *Dreadnought* herself needed only 1.52 pounds of coal to maintain one unit of horsepower for an hour, whereas *Royal Sovereign* of 1892 had needed 2 pounds. But this was swallowed up in the far greater horsepower needed. *Royal Sovereign* had 9660 horsepower and would need 19,320 pounds of coal to maintain full speed for an hour. *Dreadnought* had 27,720 horsepower and would need 37,544 pounds, all of which had to be shifted by the stokers. It was calculated that the whole fleet had 2,687,000 horsepower in 1905, rising to 5,665,000 by 1913, and it was projected to reach 8,328,000 by the following year.[12] The *King Edward* class, one of the last groups of predreadnought battleships, needed 273 able and ordinary seamen compared with 120 stokers. In the battlecruisers of the *Invincible* class of 1907 the proportions were reversed – 163 seamen and 244 stokers.[13]

One possible solution was to bring the seaman and the stoker closer together. Fisher wanted to go so far as to merge the two classes, as he was trying to do with officers, so that up to able rate the seaman and the stoker would be interchangeable.[14] This would have undermined the recruitment system, for boys could not be used efficiently as stokers until they were fully grown. Stokers were already given a certain amount of weapons training, and in action only two thirds of them would be needed in the engine room: the others would be available for damage control or to assist on the guns. In return, seamen could be sent below to the stokehold when high speed was needed, though Rear Admiral Davis was sceptical about their value. 'Owing to inexperience and lack of special knowledge the seamen cause some hindrance as well as help.' He estimated they were only worth about a quarter of their numbers compared with trained stokers. This was to be remedied in the new scheme of training started in 1904 by which every boy seaman was to learn how to work in the bunkers and stokehold and use simple tools.

But the expansion of the stoker branch continued. By about 1910 they outnumbered the seaman in the navy as a whole. This rapid expansion led to a certain lowering of standards and problems of discipline. It is not surprising that stokers under training were responsible for the most publicised outbreak of unrest in the period, the 'on the knee' incident in the naval barracks at Portsmouth in 1906 (see page 182). By 1913 it was necessary to reduce the physical standards, but nevertheless it was reported, 'Recruiting for Stokers shows a steady falling off of late, and considerably increased entries of that rating will be needed to make up for the lean periods through [which] we are now passing.' One answer was a coloured poster designed by George Falkner & Sons of Manchester, who were already producing picture postcards of naval scenes. It had nine vignettes including a dreadnought battleship, foreign travel in the Mediterranean and China, men playing football, the possibilities of promotion, sailor at 'make and mend clothes' and stokers in surprisingly white uniforms striking dramatic poses in the boiler room. The poster was 'superior to anything which has been used by the Navy before', but such recruiting was soon to be overtaken by world events.[15]

## Boy Artificers and Mechanicians

Fisher was constantly concerned about the ERAs and how much they were influenced by their trade unions ashore. In 1903 he found part of the answer – to recruit boys and train them for the role. They were to be selected at the age of fourteen to sixteen by examination conducted by the Civil Service Commission, in the same way as dockyard apprentices, and preference was to be given to boys from Greenwich Hospital School. If successful, they would be signed on for twelve years from the age of eighteen and would begin training in the Royal Dockyard at Chatham, where they would live on board a hulk. They would spend the first two years learning a trade in the workshops – mostly as fitters, with a smaller number of boilermakers, coppersmiths and engine-smiths. Much supervision was needed 'or habitual laziness will result'. After the first two years, they would go out among the ships in the reserve and under repair to learn their trades on the engines. After a total of four years, each successful boy artificer would be promoted to the equivalent rating of petty officer second class and sent to sea for a year's practical training. After that, or at the age of 21, he would sit a stiff examination and become a fully fledged artificer.

This was not an instant solution. Obviously it would take at least five years for the first of the artificers to take up their role, and their numbers were quite small to start with. A hundred and twenty artificers were needed per year to cover normal wastage, and half of these would come from the boys trained within the navy. Ninety boys were to start each year to allow for failures.[16]

Fisher also proposed to tackle the issue from another direction, by training up selected men from within the stoker class. He did not give them the title of engine room artificer but revived the ancient term of mechanician, meaning a mechanic or artisan. They were to be selected from men doing the leading stoker's course. They would work for two years in the dockyards and reserve fleet learning a trade then be promoted to mechanician, equivalent to a chief petty officer and ranking just under an ERA. They would be eligible for promotion to warrant rank, unlike their former colleagues of the stoker class.

As with most of Fisher's schemes, this was met with a good deal of opposition. The chief stokers had already passed the point for selection for mechanician and saw this as 'the downfall of their hopes of attaining warrant rank, which they have been counting upon'.[17] There was a deeply ingrained belief that a skilled trade could only be learned by starting at the age of around fifteen, and this was reflected in the views of Engineer Rear Admiral Davis: 'As the mechanician cannot – except in special cases which do not affect the question – have more than a smattering of trades, he cannot be considered a substitute for an E.R.A., but solely as a supplementary rating.'[18] Naturally the ERAs themselves were not any keener on the proposal, and they regarded the mechanician as an intruder to their craft. But in practice they proved quite successful. They were already trained in naval discipline and were carefully selected at leading stoker level, 'thus minimising the risk of uselessly training an inexperienced man'.[19] They were less skilled with tools than the ERAs but equally competent at engine operation.

## LEADING SEAMEN AND PETTY OFFICERS

Officers continued to worry about the role of the petty officer. When they worked with the army or the marines, they were constantly impressed about how much more control the NCOs had over the men, while the petty officers mingled too closely, or relied too much on the ship's police. In 1890 the Commander-in-Chief of the Atlantic Fleet thought that the position was getting better:

> Undoubtedly in the days of masts and sails, the younger seamen looked up to, and trusted, the Petty Officers more than they do now; this was of course natural, as their lives often depended on the knowledge and ability of the petty officers; nowadays, the men do not feel that they have to depend on them in the same way, except on the rare occasions of boats being under sail. In the engine room it is different, and there, in my opinion, the petty officers have better command. The sudden and large increase in the service also tended to lower discipline, as men without much experience, often rather young, had to be rated Petty Officers, and to deal with very young and raw ships companies. The struggle to maintain discipline was very marked, and I consider that matters are now improving.[20]

But the general opinion was less optimistic, and Admiral Fisher complained,

> Petty officers are required primarily to command those junior to them; therefore the chief attribute of a petty officer should be 'power to command'. It is not unfair to say that in a large number of our present petty officers this attribute is conspicuous by its absence ... One never hears in the army a non-commissioned officer addressed as 'Ere, Shorty', or ''Ullo Ginger' (to quote the most mild of unparliamentary modes of address on the lower deck.[21]

A committee of 1908 addressed the problem in some detail. It noted that the petty officers second class usually messed with the men, while those of the first class were kept separate. Artificers were no help in enforcing discipline, despite their high rating – 'their ignorance of the customs of the

Service and their disinclination to assume responsibility for discipline tend to lower the prestige which should attach to the Petty Officer's position.' The pay rise on promotion to petty officer was quite small. In the British service it was 37 per cent between AB and petty officer, though that was often overborne by non-substantive pay, which might be lost on promotion. It was pointed out that the difference was 125 per cent in the German navy and 150 in the Austrian; though in reply it was noted that these were largely conscript services, in which the petty officers were regulars.

The committee began to focus on the petty officer second class and his relationship with the leading seaman, who had taken on a new role since being established in 1853 as a superior class of skilled man:

> In the process of time the Leading Seaman has come to be regarded as a sort of inferior Petty Officer of slightly lower grade than Petty Officer 2nd Class, and he performs practically the same duties. Unlike Lance Corporals of Marines, however, he has never been regarded as a 'superior officer' within the meaning of the Articles of War.

One answer would have been to abolish the leading seaman, or at least make it clear that he was a skilled man rather than a junior petty officer. The committee considered this, but chose another route, the abolition of the petty officer second class. This would save some money as the leading seaman was paid less, though the committee did not state that as one of its reasons. The lack of legal authority vested in the leading seaman was paradoxically considered an attraction. Offences of striking petty officers were prevalent, and each case demanded a court martial for striking a superior officer, with all the bother that entailed. If the junior petty officer was replaced by the leading seaman, cases could be tried summarily under the authority of the captain.[22] This was agreed, and the rating of petty officer second class was allowed to die out. Future petty officers, all wearing the crossed anchors and placed in a single class, were also to have an educational test, which was quite stiff for men of moderate education. Once promoted, his status was to be increased. For example, petty officers and men were not to be in the same class in schools such as HMS

*Excellent.* 'When a dull P.O. is classed up with intelligent A.B.s, and in the course of drill is frequently corrected, and set right, his position as a P.O. is weakened.'

It was also agreed that petty officers should be called by their titles. The committee did not address the problem that five syllables did not trip so easily off the tongue as, for example, 'sergeant' in the army or marines. The ratings committee of 1888 had suggested the antiquated and respectable title of 'yeoman' instead of 'petty officer', but this found no favour at the top. Instead, 'Ships and establishments were informed, and the strict formality of the sister service was introduced. It was made known that a false step in this direction would be treated as a serious offence.' This was not popular on the lower deck, and Stoker Sidney Knock complained, 'Now here was a fine state of affairs! Leading Seaman Knight must no longer be addressed as 'Bogy', Petty Officer Miller was no longer known as 'Dusty Miller''[23]

By 1910 there were doubts about the wisdom of relying too much on the leading seaman. Rear Admiral Lowry of HMS *Shannon* was 'impressed by the large number of Able Seaman wearing two or more good conduct badges who are in all respects recommended for advancement by their Captains, and yet who decline to present themselves for examination for Leading Seaman'. He attributed this to several factors: the pay increase was small in comparison with non-substantive pay available; and, on the other hand, the increase in responsibility might be considerable.

> Owing to the small number of Petty Officers (Seaman Class) borne, nearly all the Coxswains of Cutters, Pinnaces, etc., are Leading Seamen, and they also frequently have charge of a part of [the] ship. As leading hands of messes they have to spend a considerable time over the canteen accounts. Consequently they have to do much of the work previously done by Petty Officers 2nd Class (old system) but they have neither the position nor the pay to support them.

Thirdly, a leading seaman would probably have to wait some years for promotion to petty officer, now that the intermediate grade had been abolished. According to Admiral Lowry, 'There was a well nigh universal wish among the men to see the 2nd Class Petty Officer rate introduced again ...'[24]

Able seamen were eligible for the examination for leading rate after two years man's service including one year afloat. To qualify for petty officer, a man had to spend at least a year as a leading seaman, have good character ratings from his captain and have at least an acting seaman gunner's or torpedoman's rating. He also had to pass the educational test, which involved writing a passage from dictation and passing 'a simple paper on the first four rules of Arithmetic (simple and compound) with vulgar and decimal fractions ... calculating the average points obtained at practices, making out mess bills, etc'. The first tests were held at the home ports in December 1907, with more ad hoc arrangements at Portland. Approximately 700 out of 900 men passed, which was regarded as 'a very satisfactory result on the whole'. Eleven men obtained full marks in all subjects, and it was noted that nine of these came from the signals branch, already known as 'the brains of the navy'.[25]

But it was difficult for some, and Leading Seaman Albert Hemmingway needed special tuition:

I know nothing about education – sums and figures – but I was all right on the professional side – compass and degrees. We had to be passed by the Padre of the parent ship. He gave us twelve sums and I remember sitting on my ditty box doing these sums and all the old able seamen know that I was a dunce – all trying to advise me what to do ... I remember the First Lieutenant asking me if I had done my sums, and he said, 'Yes, very good, I'll give you twelve more tonight!'[26]

Eventually he passed by these means.

Finally, the potential petty officer had to be recommended by the captain of a seagoing ship, and all naval officers were convinced that this was the best way of assessing a man's real character, as distinct from his book learning. The captain also had the power to promote a qualified man to fill a vacancy in the complement, but in 1911 it was found that men nearing the end of their careers were usually drafted to harbour ships, so such vacancies rarely occurred at sea. New orders banned that practice, to open

The Royal Sailor's Rest at Portsmouth, from Agnes Weston's *My Life among the Bluejackets*, 1909.

Boys on board HMS *St Vincent* training in furling sail with a very small and low yardarm. (*Navy and Army Illustrated*)

Above: The naval recruiting office just outside Portsmouth Dockyard. From John Blake, *How Sailors Fight*, 1901.

Below: The hulk *Defiance*, used as a torpedo training ship at Devonport in 1898, with *Perseus* astern of her. (National Maritime Museum NO4687)

Sailors in Spartan condition in a mess room of HMS *Excellent*, Whale Island, Portsmouth. (CPL)

Life could be uncomfortable and hazardous in a torpedo boat at speed, as off-watch sailors try to get some rest and shelter.

From Fred T. Jane, *The Torpedo in Peace and War*, 1898.

**Left:** A sailor and his family near the end of the nineteenth century. (CPL)

**Below:** The hulk *Tenedos* at Chatham around 1903, with some of the first artificer apprentices and their instructors.

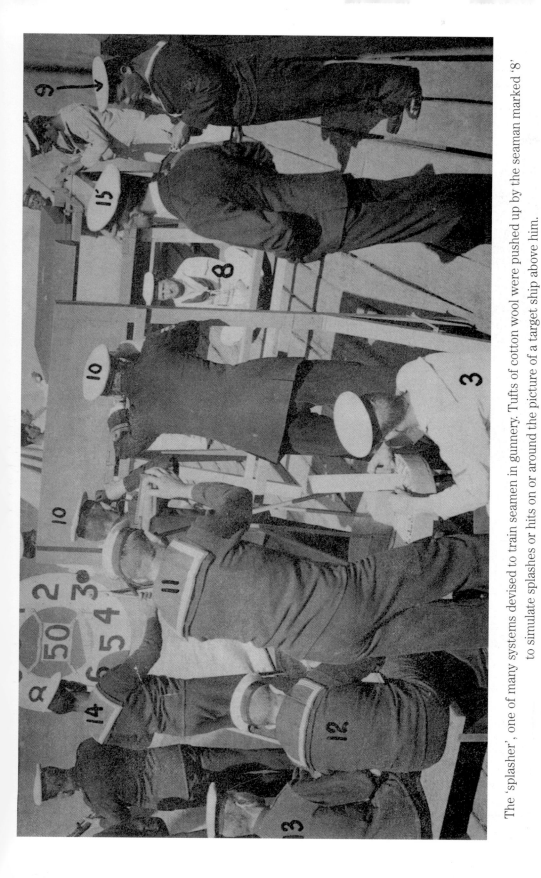

The 'splasher', one of many systems devised to train seamen in gunnery. Tufts of cotton wool were pushed up by the seaman marked '8' to simulate splashes or hits on or around the picture of a target ship above him.

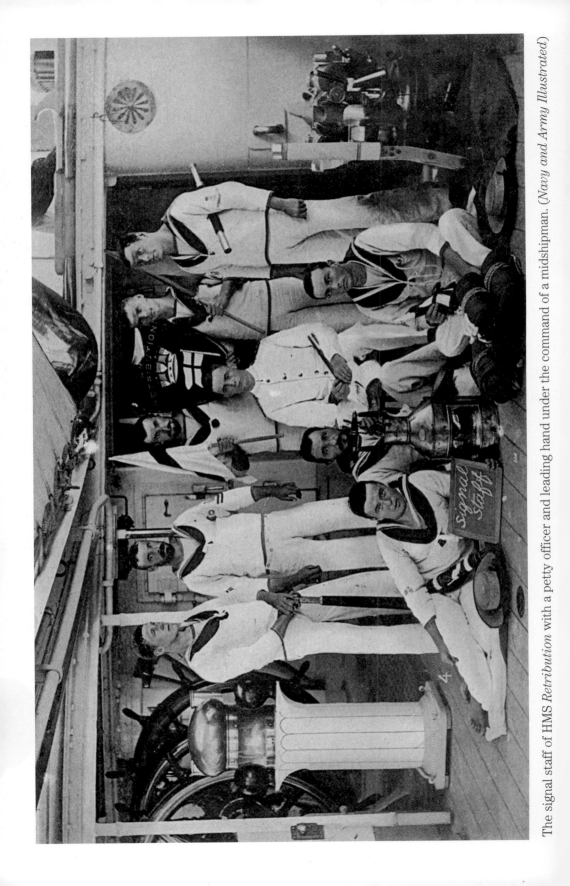

The signal staff of HMS *Retribution* with a petty officer and leading hand under the command of a midshipman. (*Navy and Army Illustrated*)

up possibilities for promotion at sea. Meanwhile the men in the depots and barracks were promoted when they reached the head of a roster, based on the date on which they had last been promoted, rather than on when they had qualified for advancement. It was unpopular with the seamen: 'there is a certain amount of suspicion of advancements made from the Port Rosters. The dislike of the Roster system on the lower deck is in our opinion chiefly due to the existing differences of method in the administration of the system at each port, to ignorance among the men of the conditions under which their advancement is regulated, and to the fact that a man is never sure of his position on the roster. As he is nearing the top of it, senior men who have passed later may be placed above him.'

Chief petty officers were mostly promoted by the roster system. By the time he was eligible, a man had probably served about eleven years as a petty officer; he was 'well advanced in years and in service', and he had given up any chance of promotion to warrant officer.

Though the committee of 1908 was mostly concerned with the seaman, its report had effects on other branches. In particular, the leading seaman was given an equivalent in other areas, for example leading cook, sick berth attendant and writer. The term of petty officer was also applied to other branches, so that there were stoker petty officers, petty officer cooks and so on.

## DREADNOUGHT AND THE NEW GUNNERY

The next stage in the gunnery revolution began with the building of HMS *Dreadnought* in 1905–6, with a main armament of ten 12-inch guns. It was intended that they would be fired in large salvoes in order to ensure hitting the target at long range, but for the moment aiming was still in the hands of the gunlayers in each turret. A typical turret had two 12-inch guns and was commanded by an officer and two midshipmen. Its crew comprised a turret gunlayer, two turret sightsetters, 40 seaman gunners and 24 other ratings. Practice with these guns could be a terrifying experience for a new member of the crew:

I was one of the loading numbers in this twin turret and I didn't really appreciate what it was because I had never seen a big gun. We had drilled

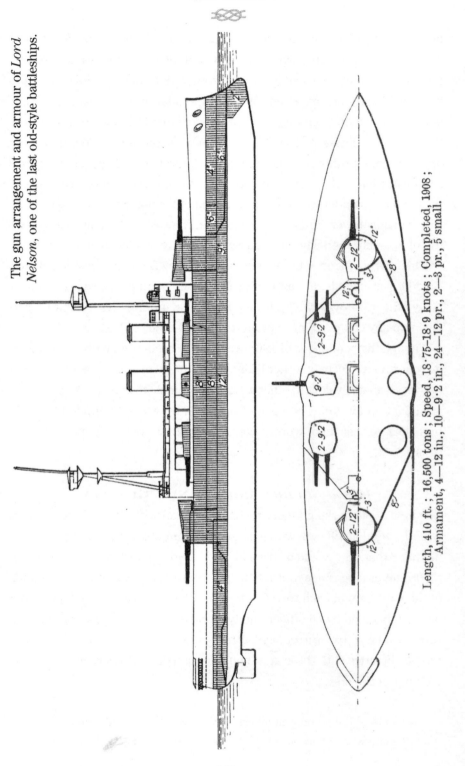

The gun arrangement and armour of *Lord Nelson*, one of the last old-style battleships.

Length, 410 ft. ; 16,500 tons ; Speed, 18·75–18·9 knots ; Completed, 1908 ; Armament, 4—12 in., 10—9·2 in., 24—12 pr., 2–3 pr., 5 small.

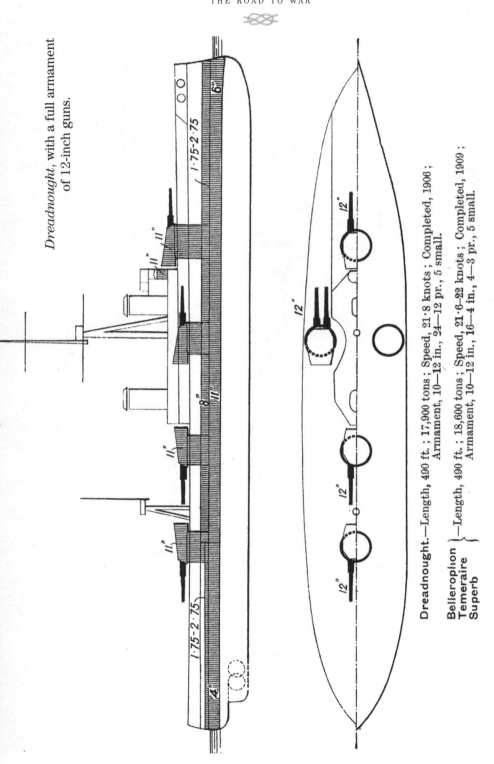

*Dreadnought*, with a full armament of 12-inch guns.

**Dreadnought.**—Length, 490 ft. ; 17,900 tons ; Speed, 21·8 knots ; Completed, 1906 ;
Armament, 10—12 in., 24—12 pr., 5 small.

**Bellerophon**
**Temeraire** }—Length, 490 ft. ; 18,600 tons ; Speed, 21·6-22 knots ; Completed, 1909 ;
**Superb** Armament, 10—12 in., 16—4 in., 4—3 pr., 5 small.

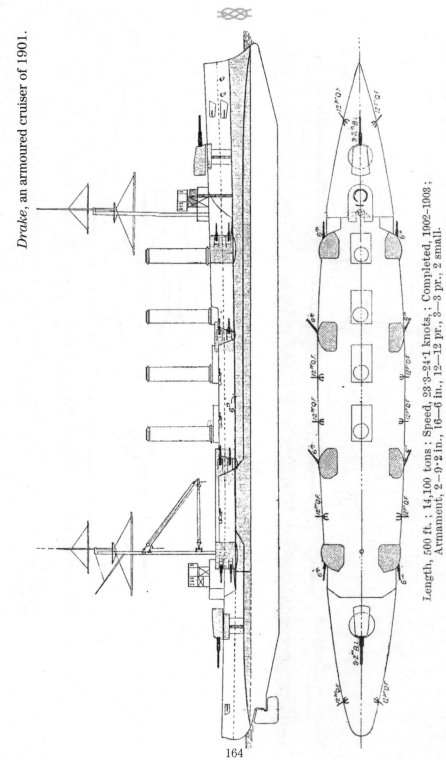

*Drake*, an armoured cruiser of 1901.

Length, 500 ft. ; 14,100 tons ; Speed, 23·3–24·1 knots, ; Completed, 1902–1903 ;
Armament, 2—9·2 in., 16—6 in., 12—12 pr., 3—3 pr., 2 small.

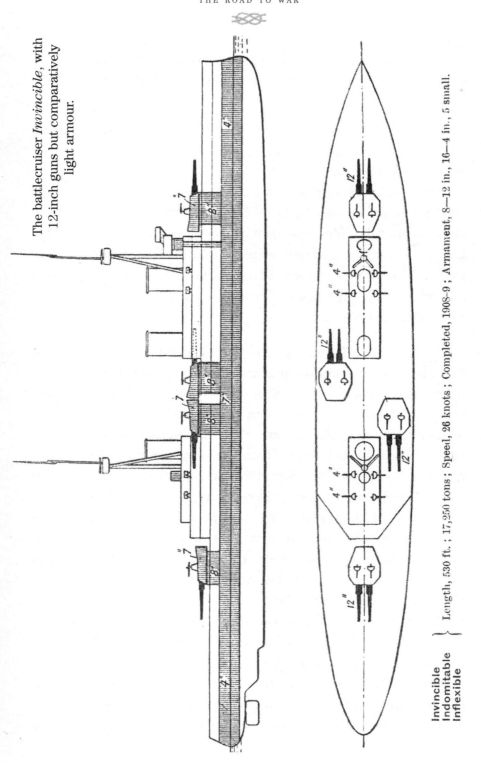

The battlecruiser *Invincible*, with 12-inch guns but comparatively light armour.

Invincible
Indomitable
Inflexible

Length, 530 ft. ; 17,250 tons ; Speed, 26 knots ; Completed, 1908–9 ; Armament, 8—12 in., 16—4 in., 5 small.

with 6" but not with 12" and we hadn't been in the Mars long when we went out for firing practice. And the first time that thing went off and the whole world recoiled about four feet I thought the world had come to an end.[27]

Each ship also had a secondary armament of lighter guns to defend against torpedo attack, such as a 4-inch gun, which was manned by a gunlayer, a sightsetter and seaman gunner.[28]

There was a great increase in the size of guns over the next few years: the 12-inch was replaced by the 13.5-inch and then the 15-inch as new dreadnought battleships were built at great speed in an arms race with Germany. British propaganda emphasized the rapid improvement in gunnery, and a *Punch* cartoon of 1906 showed the German Kaiser being astonished by the latest figures – an improvement from 42 per cent to 71 per cent hits in two years.

## SIGNALS AND TELEGRAPHY

The invention of wireless telegraphy was closely linked to the Royal Navy. In the 1890s, Captain Jackson of the torpedo school at Portsmouth conducted experiments with waves, his main aim at the time being to distinguish friend and foe in battle. Guglielmo Marconi moved to Britain largely because he could see the greatest use for wireless with the British merchant marine and Royal Navy. His most important single contribution was to demonstrate that low-frequency waves could be sent well beyond the horizon, which opened up vast new possibilities for naval use. The Royal Navy used Marconi sets in its 1899 manoeuvres and set up shore stations to communicate with ships. The value of having wireless sets and trained operators on board ship was becoming increasingly obvious. However, the system had its limitations. Morse code transmissions were used, since voice transmission was still unreliable over any distance. And only a limited number of frequencies were available, as any transmission tended to block out other signals over a wide band.

Obviously the Morse code skills of the signalmen were useful in operating the new wirelesses, and for a few years it was the custom to deploy the senior signal ratings, usually yeomen of signals or leading signalmen to this role. In 1906 it was agreed that the operators were to be trained as a separate branch. Signalmen usually worked under the eyes of the officers and tended to earn promotion by 'a display of their activity on the bridge'; wireless operators would be in a sealed room away from the noise. The operation of sets was to be a separate task from maintenance, which was to be done by established groups such as armourers, electricians and ERAs. The wireless telegraphist, however, needed some knowledge of electricity. The possibility of recruiting from the Post Office was considered, but trained telegraphists were well paid and it was not possible for the navy to match that. The Post Office also employed large numbers of telegraph messengers, who had no guarantee of employment beyond the age of sixteen, when they would be ripe for naval recruitment. However, their job was to deliver telegrams on foot or by bicycle, and they knew little of the techniques of an operator. The majority of naval telegraphists would be recruited as boys in the normal way.

The new branch was formally set up by an Admiralty circular of August 1907. It was to be 'exclusively for wireless duties' and 'quite distinct' from the signal branch. Its men would work under the supervision of the torpedo officer, and with the electrical party when not needed in the wireless room. In the long term it would be recruited from boys selected after three months in the training establishments, but for the moment about a hundred ratings from other branches, not necessarily signalmen, would be allowed to transfer to make up a core of petty officers and experienced men and set the branch on a 'proper footing'. A flagship would have four operators; a battleship would have three, comprising one petty officer telegraphist and two telegraphists; a destroyer would have a single petty officer telegraphist.[29] In July 1908, after some experience, it was decided that WT operators had to work in four watches of two men each, with no more than two hours on the set at a time in order to avoid loss of concentration. Since there were not enough trained WT operators to do this, signalmen were to be drafted in as needed to assist.[30]

But soon the 'quite distinct' status of the telegraphist branch came under question, for there was confusion when signals could be treated through two different routes. In 1910 it was decreed that all the signal ratings should be under the same officer, and the telegraphists should fall in with the signalmen for divisions. The dilution of the telegraphist branch continued when it was ordered that,

> Commanding officers are also to take steps to secure, if possible, further interchange of duties between the Wireless and Signals Staffs, by employing wireless ratings off watch for two or three hours a day on the bridge. It is considered that the ordinary day's work of wireless ratings need not necessarily be limited to a maximum of six hours in the wireless room, and that a turn of employment on deck would be of advantage.[31]

## POLICE AND PUNISHMENT

Rates of crime and punishment in the navy remained very high, despite the careful selection procedures for entry. As Lionel Yexley pointed out, the seaman was quite carefully chosen, and habitual criminals or weak characters were not likely to find themselves in the navy. Moreover, the crime rate, in the conventional civilian sense, was quite low – 219 men were found guilty by court martial during 1908, out of 112,751 men in the navy. But the picture for summary punishments was very different – every year from 1903–8 there was slightly more than one punishment for every sailor or marine afloat. The problem was highlighted by the statistics for the marines. When ashore, 1,706 men were punished out of 7,275 in 1908, or 23 per cent; when afloat, this rose to 13,057 for 10,726 men or 121 per cent. As Yexley wrote, 'It is not possible to believe that this force, as soon as it steps afloat, commences to misbehave itself, and as soon as it steps on shore loses its bad ways. The real difference lies in the different ideas of discipline that animate the naval and military mind.' Punishment fell especially heavily on the seaman class, who were working constantly on deck under the eyes of the officers and were subjected to far more rigid dress regulations than the others. It could go to extremes in an unhappy ship. Yexley cited a cruiser in which there were no less than 337 punishments during three months of 1909 – some were committed with a view to getting out of the ship, for 'prison life was preferable'.[32]

Punishment took many forms, including restriction of leave, loss of good conduct badges and extra duty. One of the most hated was known as '10A', in which a man was ordered to stand facing the paintwork for two hours every evening, after doing extra duty. To Yexley it simply confirmed that the official view was that the seaman was a child 'the punishment of our nursery days, when very naughty children were stood in a corner'.[33] Lieutenant Bevan of the Signal School at Portsmouth had 'much correspondence' about 10A. In his view it was 'most distasteful and therefore probably excellent if properly carried out'. But this seldom happened in his experience. 'The practice of allowing men who ought to be facing the paintwork to do odd jobs is very bad, I think as they can loaf or slip away unless carefully superintended.'[34]

To some, including Bevan, the police were part of the problem rather than the solution:

by their position in the ship they take the responsibility for the control of the discipline and conduct of the lower deck away from the C.P.O.s and P.O.s who ought to be the men to maintain it. That therefore the C.P.O.s and P.O.s do not usually attempt to check (in silent hours more especially) what they know to be against the regulations, eg,
Men going on deck improperly dressed
Men spitting on the deck
Men smoking after 'out pipes'
I think any experience of defaulters will at once remind one that P.O.s never do report that nature of offence, altho' they must have many chances (confining themselves to reports of men turning up slack in parts of the ship or actually disobeying them) ...[35]

To Yexley the problem was more complex and sometimes originated with the officers. True, the police were used mainly for 'espionage on the ship's company', but he also cited the example of a captain who was obsessed with polishing:

and always wanted a body of black-list men for burnishing stanchions, etc. These not being forthcoming he sent for the master-at-arms ... and complained that more men were not reported. Later he had all the ship's police and petty officers on the quarter-deck, and told them they were not doing their duty because 'there isn't a half-dozen damned black-list men in the ship'; so to save their own positions these people, of whom I was one, had to manufacture offences and soon there was a plenitude of men doing 10(a) punishment.[36]

When he commissioned the new battlecruiser *Queen Mary* in 1913, Captain 'Blinker' Hall carried out the bold experiment of doing without the ship's police. Initially his commander, William James, was surprised at this, and even Yexley's newspaper *The Fleet* was critical. But Hall benefited from what he saw was an improvement in the standard of petty officers:

> The gunnery renaissance had produced splendid opportunities for Seamen Petty Officers; there were many well-paid new ratings; the Warrant Officer branch was being rapidly expanded and so candidates for the Police branch were neither so numerous nor of such good quality as formerly. Furthermore, the Petty Officers, now better educated, could undertake clerical work hitherto a responsibility for the Police.[37]

The experiment worked, partly because of the captain's willingness to back up his petty officers:

> Hall had no patience with men who refused to obey their Petty Officers' orders or who in any way questioned a Petty Officer's authority and he invariably gave the maximum punishment permitted by the regulations. Before a week had passed everybody knew where they were, the Petty Officers knew their officers would support them through thick and thin, and we were on the high road to becoming a thoroughly happy ship.[38]

Of course punishments were not equally distributed. Some men never suffered, others were habitual troublemakers. Despite the careful selection procedures, there were always plenty of seamen who were prepared to test the system to the limit. 'Clinker Knocker' was one:

> I affected an air of bravado which was entirely foreign to my nature. To be noticed and respected by my shipmates I felt I must do something out of the ordinary, and the only way was to 'kick over the traces'. There is a certain glamour in rebelling against the rigid discipline of battleship

routine, and the *St. Vincent* had more than her share of 'hard cases', or 'birds' as these reckless individuals are called. Many were just habitual leave-breakers. Others carried their delinquencies to extremes, to answer 'defaulters', crimed for insubordination refusing duty and mutinous conduct. They kept the half-dozen cells always tenanted.[39]

The system of imprisonment was reformed in 1911. Only Bodmin was retained as a naval prison, but detention quarters were built in the three home ports. It was made clear that this was a different kind of punishment, that detention did not carry the same kind of stigma as imprisonment, and that the emphasis was on training. 'Clinker Knocker' endured three weeks of this at Portsmouth in 1916. He was drilled by a 'powerfully-built, bull-necked' marine sergeant who was 'a picture of brutality':

I've read out the rules, and now listen! This is not a prison! You are not criminals! What you are here for doesn't interest us! We neither know nor Care! This is a detention quarters, and you men are sent here to be corrected of your faults.

'Knocker' was soon counting the hours until his release:

The food was good and wholesome, and the training was absolutely the finest in the world. As a gun's crew on the six-inch loader we were the smartest in the universe ... Physical exercises were more like high-speed acrobatics, and we could get over the eight-foot wall like a race-horse taking a fence.

Sergeant Brimstone was not half a brutal as he professed to be. In fact we got to like him.

Nevertheless,

I was determined to make those three weeks a closed book in my life, and forget all about them. Neither have I ever had the inclination to serve another sentence for background to write about. Twenty-one days was more than sufficient in a short span of three score years and ten, and twenty-one days seemed a lifetime to me.'[40]

## MESSDECK LIFE IN A BATTLESHIP

As First Lord of the Admiralty from 1911, Winston Churchill visited many ships and kept in touch with lower deck opinion. He was well aware of the growing problems:

> The sailor's life is one of exceptional hardship. Service in a ship of war is not only strenuous but more uncomfortable than twelve or fourteen years ago. Instead of seeing something of the world, the young sailor knows nothing but the North Sea and a few war anchorages round the coast. The construction of the modern warship renders it extremely uncomfortable and even unhealthy as a living place. Nothing is possible in the nature of a recreation room on board, nor are there facilities for any kind of rest, privacy or amusement. A man has only the mess deck to go to, where he is herded with several hundred others in messes of about sixteen. If he wants to read and write in quiet there is no place for him. Now that armour has been carried to the upper deck, he has to subsist on artificial light and ventilation. If he wants to smoke or see the daylight he has to go on deck, where there is scarcely any shelter. When the majority of ships were abroad in good climates this would not have mattered so much; but the life of the bluejacket and stoker in our finest ships of war around the British coasts and in the North Sea is one of pitiable discomfort, which cannot, while the present competition in armaments continues and the present types of warship construction prevail, be effectively alleviated.[41]

At the beginning of the twentieth century the navy still used the antiquated messing system, which had almost merged with the canteen system. A mess consisted of 12 to 25 men, usually of one type – seamen, stokers, signalmen, stewards, and so on. It was quite possible for a mess to live on standard rations of meat, vegetables, bread, chocolate, tea, coffee, milk, sugar, ham and corned beef. This would produce a typical day's diet beginning with a basin of hot cocoa on turning out; coffee and bread for breakfast; rum, meat, vegetables, mustard, pepper and salt for midday dinner; tea, bread and jam for tea and corned beef and bread for supper. This was an adequate diet, but monotonous, so most messes drew only part of the ration and used the money to buy other goods from the canteen. Each would appoint a caterer to keep its accounts – sometimes for a month at a time, but more often a man who had some aptitude for 'housekeeping' would be given the job for the whole commission. It involved a good deal of clerical work, and caterers rarely knew whether they were in debt to the purser or not.

The use of canteens expanded greatly over the years. By 1907 the authorities were concerned about this. The canteen system was largely under the control of the men themselves with the cooperation of Maltese contractors, and the officers suspected corruption. Moreover, it would be necessary to stop the system in wartime, or at least curtail it, and for planning purposes the Admiralty had little idea of what was really needed to supply each ship. A new system was adopted, with increased supply of most articles, while the canteens were regulated more closely, with standard Admiralty contracts and a committee of officers and men appointed by the captain in each ship.[42]

Preparing the food was still in the hands of the mess itself. Each would provide two cooks of the day, who were free from other duties but would prepare meals and take them to the galley to be cooked. These men knew nothing about cookery except what they had picked up casually, and there were several complaints as to their incapacity. A new man had to learn how to prepare a meal: 'you had to start another apprenticeship under the tutorship of one, who through the course of years had become somewhat efficient at being able to prepare a 'straight bake' and make a duff, two primary items on the dinner menu.'[43]

A Committee on Naval Cookery reported in 1905, and it was recognized that 'Until recent years no attempt had ever been made to provide a sufficient number of Cooks in H.M. Ships to undertake the preparation of the men's meals. The Staff was only sufficient to look after the fires and keep the Galley clean.' It was agreed to train a greater number of cook ratings who would actually prepare the food, but in the meantime the old system was only replaced gradually. In any case, it was necessary to appease the sailor's traditional conservatism, and the fear that his food was being taken out of his control. By 1907 the system of 'general messing' had been set up in many of the training bases, and in the battleship *Dreadnought* and cruiser *Hampshire* at the request of the ships' companies.[44] Soon it would spread throughout the big-ship navy, but not to the destroyers.

## THE SUBMARINE SERVICE

The Royal Navy's submarine service was founded in 1901 with the purchase of *Holland No. 1* from its American inventor. Originally they were intended mainly for harbour defence, but rapid progress was made over the next decade, and seagoing and ocean boats were planned. The eight-man crew of the *Holland* had already doubled by the C class of 1906, and reached 25 for the D class, which followed. Initially submarines operated from Portsmouth, where Fort Blockhouse was taken over as headquarters. The first idea was that each would have a double crew, as life on board was considered so exhausting; eventually it was agreed to have one spare crew for every three boats.

All submarine crews were volunteers, often attracted by the extra money. This was at first intended as 'Hard-lying' money on a temporary basis, but it soon became clear that many skilled men would leave the service if it was withdrawn. It would almost double the income of a chief petty officer from 2/8 per day to 5/2; of an ERA from 5/6 to 8 shillings; and an able seaman from 1/7 to 3/7. In every case this was far more than a man could get in destroyers. Other incentives were the informality of the submarine service, where relations between officers and men were casual to a degree that would never be tolerated in a battleship. The boats made short voyages and they were usually home in Portsmouth by 4 o'clock each afternoon, so it was a suitable position for married men. But life on board an early boat was hard, as Captain Hall recognized in 1910:

> Clothes cannot be dried, fires are not permissible, in cold weather it is difficult to keep reasonably warm, the amount of fresh water precludes any attempt at personal cleanliness and the roar of the Engines is all over the boat and though the Officers and men are normally in watch and watch there is no certainty in the watch off. To many the smell inside a submarine after she has been a short time at sea, which is absolutely peculiar to itself, is most revolting, All food tastes of it, clothes reek of it, it is quite impossible to wear any clothes again after they have been used in it.[45]

Conditions began to improve as boats got larger, but, as with destroyers, they were then expected to go on much longer voyages.

The submarine service needed a high proportion of skilled ratings. Besides two officers, a boat of the C class needed a chief or petty officer first class as coxswain, plus two leading and five able seamen. At least two of these should be torpedomen, mostly to maintain the electrical power, but in practice nearly all the ratings drafted were from the torpedo branch. There were two ERAs or mechanicians in charge of the diesel engines, plus a stoker petty officer and three stokers.[46]

Conditions were primitive in early boats, with no toilet facilities at all, according to Telegraphist Halter:

> In *C18* and *D4*, we had no heads. Our Captain used to say 'everybody below', and they'd carry it out on the bridge, then come down, dive to twenty feet, wash it away, and then come up again. But the conning towers were hollow, only casings. You could go down there in a bucket, and empty it through the holes in the side ... Down below doing extended diving, you used a bucket quarter full of diesel oil. It wasn't offensive at all then.[47]

## THE GROWTH OF THE LOWER DECK MOVEMENT

In retrospect, the Edwardian age provides an image of peace and stability compared with the devastating war that was to follow, but it did not seem so at the time. The suffragettes demanded votes for women and turned to increasingly illegal means to draw attention to their case. The Catholics of southern Ireland were in revolt against British rule, but any attempt to placate them tended to lead to opposition from the wealthier minority in the north of the island, supported by many army officers. And, most important for the navy, the working class movement was increasingly strong and was beginning to flex its muscles through strikes.

The navy was not entirely separated from the trade union movement at the beginning of the century. Nearly all the lower deck came from working class backgrounds, and many of them, especially stokers, had been union members before joining, or their fathers and brothers were. The need for reform was at least as obvious in the navy as anywhere in industry, and the privileges of officers were greater than those of private employers. The navy was far more powerful than any other employer, with its men on board ship for most of the time and subject to strict discipline. The issue of a naval trade union was not taken seriously at this moment, but the lower deck wanted a way for its views to be represented on such relatively uncontroversial matters as the design of badges as well as on pay and working and living conditions.

The informal leader of the lower deck movement was James Wood, who had joined the Navy in 1878 at the age of fifteen and trained in *Impregnable*. He served off Zanzibar, with the Mediterranean Fleet and trained as a gunner and a torpedoman at Portsmouth. He loved the navy but hated much of the way it was run – the arrogance of many of the officers, the low pay, which had not been increased since 1853, inadequate food, the corruption of the police and the way in which sailors had to pay for their own uniforms. He transferred to the Coastguard in 1884, which gave him more freedom of expression to write articles on lower-deck conditions. Then in 1897 he resigned to take up full-time journalism. He adopted the pen name of Lionel Yexley and changed it legally to fight an election in 1918. He edited a newspaper called *The Bluejacket* and founded another called *The Fleet*. It was, by his description, 'a literary bridge to span the gulf that discipline fixes between the ward-room and the mess-deck.'[48] That rather understates the campaigning role of the newspaper, which attained a circulation of around 20,000 and a much greater readership than that. Notwithstanding the paper's careful policy of avoiding becoming 'anti-officer', there were many officers who saw it as a rabble-rousing rag and had greatly exaggerated ideas of both its influence and its radicalism. Despite this, by 1912 Yexley was in contact with both 'Jacky' Fisher and Winston Churchill, who was then First Lord of the Admiralty.

Churchill was as dynamic as political head of the navy as Fisher had been a few years earlier as its professional head. Among many concerns about the preparations for a coming great war, he was aware of the lower deck's problems, much to his credit, though this is barely mentioned by most of his biographers. He campaigned for better pay and conditions for the men, who had not had a substantive pay rise since 1853:

Meanwhile, outside the naval service everything has advanced, and the relative position of the bluejacket compared to the soldier, the policeman, the postman, the fireman, the railway man, the dockyard labourer – in fact, with everyone with whom he comes in contact at the great ports, has markedly declined. This comparison would prove more invidious if extended to skilled artisans, such as those engaged in the shipbuilding industry, or in dangerous trades like coal-mining. The concentration of the Fleet in Home Waters has diminished the sailor's opportunities of saving money, and led him into constant expenditure. It has induced a greater proportion of marriages. The serious rise in prices of the last twelve years, amounting to 15 per cent, has increased the stringency of life in the dockyard towns. Owing to the movements of the Fleet, a large amount of railway travelling is necessary for the men to get to their families, and this alone is a new and heavy drain upon their resources. On the other hand, the service becomes more strenuous every year; the number of practices and exercises of all kinds continually increases, and the standards are raised.[49]

Another element in the equation was the lower deck societies. Any attempt to form a trade union would be a serious breach of discipline, but these groups started mainly as friendly societies intended to support members in cases of illness or hardship. Warrant officers had been organized in this way since 1792, and the artificers followed in 1872. From the 1880s, societies were set up for various petty officers and the more educated part of the lower deck, the writers. There were 124 different societies by 1910, and they played some part in producing an annual petition to the Admiralty asking for better conditions. In 1912 the movement spread to seamen and stokers. The benefit societies only represented about ten per cent of the lower deck at most, but in the atmosphere of the time they contributed to a feeling that naval discipline, like order in society in general, was about to break down. Very few sailors had the vote because they were not ashore long enough to qualify as householders, but nevertheless J. Jenkins, the Labour Member of Parliament for Chatham, had much support from the lower deck and could raise issues in Parliament. It was reported in the *Daily Chronicle* that 'numbers of men, disappointed by all parties alike, have jumped from old-time naval conservatism to political views in advance of radicalism'. And in 1912 a lower-deck correspondent in the *Portsmouth*

*Evening News* claimed that, 'There is only one thing for the bluejackets to do, they must combine themselves with the trade union movement.'[50]

Churchill had a certain amount of success in reforming lower deck conditions in 1912–13, and Yexley was jubilant, but he had not succeeded on the biggest ones – on marriage allowance, on uniform or on pay. He did manage a rise of 3*d* per day for an able seaman after six years, but that was recognized as a compromise and not adequate to meet the rising cost of living or the increased awareness of it among men on ships serving at home.

## COMMISSIONS FROM THE LOWER DECK

The gap between officers and men had greatly widened during the long years of peace, and for most of the nineteenth century it was virtually impossible for a member of the lower deck to rise to commissioned rank. It was commonly believed that the last was John Kingcombe in 1818, but in fact he had entered in 1808 as a first class volunteer, which suggests that he was always regarded as a candidate for a commission.[51] In any case, there were no more for the rest of the century. Of course, only a minority of lower deck seamen would ever seek commissions, but the lack of any promotion prospect beyond warrant officer in a more democratic age was becoming increasingly anomalous. It also tended to widen the huge gap between the rating and the officer. James Cox transferred into the navy from the merchant service training ship *Warspite* and found that the role of the officer was very different:

> The officers in Warspite were fathers to you. You could always go and talk to them. Of course you always gave them respect, they always insisted on that. But in the Navy, the officers were entirely apart. You very seldom addressed an officer unless he addressed you. All your contact with officers in the training ship was through petty officers. All the petty officers were severe. It's a kind of upstairs, downstairs. The cook doesn't go straight to the missus; she goes to the butler first. It was the same then in the Navy.[52]

The gulf between officers and men meant that there was no large middle-class element in the peacetime navy:

At one end of service-life we have the officer recruited from that comparatively small class that is wealthy enough to spend £700 on a boy; at the other end we have the men recruited from the poorer artisan and labouring class. In between lies the pick of the nation. It will not send its sons on to the lower-deck because of the great limitation in the facilities for advancing; it cannot send its sons in as officers through lack of money.[53]

It was the naval officers themselves (and their families) who were strongest in their opposition to lower deck promotion. They had invested a good deal of money and effort in getting their sons through an expensive training at Dartmouth and were not going to have that devalued by opening up the officer ranks to outsiders. They did not have a trade union like the engine room artificers but were equally determined to protect their privileges; they also had much more powerful connections in state and society. They did not want to mix socially with men of lower origin, and this was shown by the example of Henry Capper, who joined as a rating from a middle-class family and had cousins who were naval officers. When he found himself on watch with one of them he tried to strike up a conversation and was rebuffed harshly – 'If you ever have the presumption to address me except on duty I'll have you caned.'[54]

The families, as much as the officers themselves, were determined to protect their position. Capper campaigned to open up commissioned rank, and the mother of a sub-lieutenant said to him, 'I have the greatest sympathy with you personally in your desire to rise, but you have chosen the wrong service. The Navy belongs to us, and if you were to win the commissions you ask for it would be at the expense of our sons and nephews whose birthright it is.'[55]

When it found itself short of officers, the navy did not turn to the lower deck. In the 1890s it offered regular commissions to RNR officers from the merchant marine, the 'hungry hundred', followed by the 'famished fifty'. In 1913 it began much shorter courses to 'special entry' cadets who were recruited directly from the public schools. There were other incidents that annoyed the lower deck. In the famous Archer-Shee case, which was settled in 1911, the family of a wrongfully dismissed naval cadet sued the Admiralty successfully. There was no prospect of a lower-deck rating doing anything similar, and indeed Yexley was himself sued by Captain Kemp of the battleship *London* in 1914 and lost the case, despite several ratings from the ship giving evidence in his favour.

One officer claimed in 1913 that 'the general wish of the lower deck is to be officered by gentlemen of the upper and middle classes. Not that they wish to close the door to the "ranker"; but they prefer that, other things being equal, their officers should be men trained in the traditions of the "gentry".'[56] This might sound highly patronizing, but it is borne out by 'Clinker Knocker', a natural rebel if there ever was one. He served under a string of conventional upper-class officers who were often amazingly tolerant of his escapades. The only martinet he encountered was an ex-ERA who was 'abhorred by the whole engine room department ... We were fortunate to have real gentlemen by birth and breeding in higher positions than the senior [engineer], or it would have been harder for us.'[57]

Of course the rank of warrant officer was always open to the lower deck, but that was still declining in importance. In the days of iron and steel, the carpenter was no longer the man who kept the ship afloat, and his successor, the warrant shipwright, was far more dependent on dockyard facilities. The boatswain had less to do in the new sail-less ships, while his disciplinary function was largely taken over by the ship's police. The gunner was sandwiched between the gunnery lieutenant, who had taken an advanced course at HMS *Excellent,* and the chief gunner's mate, who was closer to the lower deck. He could, however, find a very worthwhile role as skipper of a small torpedo boat, as Thomas Lyne did. For specialists there were new warrant ranks like artificer engineer and signal boatswain, but even then the warrant officer's life was often a lonely one, and his position between the lower deck and the quarterdeck was awkward:

In a small ship the one Warrant Officer lived in a cabin placed forward on the men's mess deck, generally some seven feet by six feet in size, the floor space seven feet by two and a half feet: this was dormitory, dining-room, bathroom, and office combined. In many ships he was entirely isolated from the remainder of the Officers, not even being included in the common smoking circle on the upper deck; and his position made it imperative that he should not associate familiarly with the senior Petty Officers who lived outside his cabin door.[58]

Nevertheless, it was warrant rank that provided the first opportunity for lower deck commissions, albeit at a very late stage in a man's career when was too old to ever get beyond lieutenant. From 1903, a few selected chief warrant officers were commissioned as lieutenants.

Again it was Churchill who began a serious reform by introducing the 'mates' scheme in 1912. This would enable,

> warrant officers, petty officers and seamen to reach the rank of commissioned officer at an early age. The candidates selected undergo courses of instruction at Portsmouth, and on passing are given the rank of Acting Mate. They then proceed to the Royal Naval College at Greenwich for four months' instruction in navigation, followed by two months' instruction in pilotage at the Navigation School at Portsmouth. On passing the examination at the termination of this course, they are confirmed as Mates and are embarked in sea-going ships for two years, at the end of which time they will be eligible for promotion to the rank of lieutenant. Their duties as lieutenants will be the same as those of other lieutenants, and they will be considered for promotion to commander with other lieutenants on their merits.[59]

By the spring of 1914, 44 men had been commissioned as mates or acting mates. It was a small beginning, but an important one.

## MUTINY

Discontent, and the lack of the means to express it legally, led naturally to a revival of mutiny – there were 24 recorded incidents between 1900 and 1914. All of them were local and concerned with affairs in an individual ship, fleet or base, but they had many features in common. Often gun sights were thrown overboard, since it was no longer possible to roll shot about the deck as had been done in Nelson's day and in the Crimean War; occasionally a boat was cut from its falls. There were three main causes of mutiny – lack of leave, excessive work (especially cleaning) and excessive punishment. In all, 75 men were tried by court martial; a few were acquitted; most received terms of imprisonment of up to two years' hard labour.[60]

The most publicised incident, and the only one to take place in a shore base rather than on a ship, was at Portsmouth Naval Barracks in 1906. It was a wet Sunday afternoon in November when the seamen and stokers paraded for evening quarters, and many of the young trainee stokers, not yet familiar with naval discipline, were murmuring questions about why the parade was not held in the nearby gymnasium; these got louder when the parade dragged on longer than usual. When they were struck by a sudden squall, some of the stokers broke ranks and dashed for shelter. Lieutenant Collard, in charge of the parade, dismissed the seamen but kept the stokers to give them a lecture on discipline. He gave the order 'On the knee!', which was often used to let the men of the rear rank see better, but Collard had an unfortunate manner, which would dog him throughout his career – the stokers interpreted it as an attempt to humiliate them. That view was later supported by the Admiralty. The stokers called out 'No!' but Collard persisted until all but two of the men had obeyed.

In the mess that night the seamen treated it as a joke, and someone called out 'On your knees!' to the stokers' tables. This infuriated them even more, and two dozen of them tried to get out through the gate with the object, apparently, of crossing the road to the officers' mess to demand an apology. They were prevented by the guards, and eventually the commodore restored peace. There was an incident involving a warrant officer and a small group of men in the canteen late in the following evening, and the men were turned out on parade. The commander, realising a mistake had been made, dispersed them, but they began to create disorder on the parade ground. Meanwhile men returning from leave found themselves locked out, and they joined with civilians to create a further disturbance outside the gates. Marines had to be called from the barracks to quell it.[61] The affair was widely reported in the press, as far afield as New York. There was a series of courts martial in which Stoker First Class Edwin Moody was sentenced to five years in prison (later reduced to three) and ten others to shorter periods. Collard was tried for conduct prejudicial to good order and naval discipline in that he used 'a drill order for other than drill purposes' and was reprimanded. Privately the Admiralty was prepared to admit that he had been guilty of 'want of judgement'. Three of his superiors were removed from their posts for failure in the performance of their duties.[62]

The most serious incident was in the battleship *Zealandia* early in 1914. Large numbers of stokers refused to obey an order in protest at the harsh discipline of Captain Walter Cowan. A dozen men were apparently chosen at random, and eight of them were sentenced to two years' imprisonment, the sentences subsequently being annulled on a technicality. In the middle of the year the *Morning Post* was of the opinion that 'in the test of war the discipline might conceivably fail. In the opinion of not a few naval officers it would fail.'[63] And the test was not to be long away.

# 7

# STALEMATE AT SEA
# 1914–1916

⚓

## THE OUTBREAK OF WAR

At 9.36 on the morning of Monday 13 July 1914, the Commander-in-Chief at the Nore received the signal 'Prepare to test', and a carefully laid plan went into action. As the signal implied, it was a test mobilization of the reserve fleets, planned some time in advance and not directly related to the ominous events in Europe – for Archduke Franz Ferdinand of Austria had been shot at Sarajevo in Serbia just two weeks earlier, and in the Balkans a crisis was brewing that would soon draw in all the major European powers.

Regular seamen (known as active service ratings) already in the barracks at Chatham and Sheerness went off to man minelayers and the port defence flotilla. At 11.56 the following day the signal 'Test' was received, and the plan sprang fully into action. Pensioners and men of the Royal Fleet Reserve were called out by telegram and newspaper advertisement. William Jenkins left his wife and family in Swansea after 'twelve months of bliss' since his discharge. He took the train to Portsmouth, where he encountered card sharps and his old friend Josh, with whom he spent a pleasant evening. He entered the Royal Naval Barracks again on the 14th, to be 'pushed around the barracks getting kit, hammock, etc. In the afternoon got rushed around the parade ground'. At 5.30 he was one of a party sent into the dockyard to commission HMS *Leviathan*, but the ship had suffered engine trouble on the way round from Chatham, so the men went back to the barracks, where the authorities closed the wet canteen, 'doubtless thinking all the Levi's belonged to Miss Weston's Temperance Society'. *Leviathan* finally arrived and was commissioned the next day.[1]

The remaining regulars in the barracks were sent out to complete the complements of the reserve ships of the Second Fleet, which were held in readiness. These included five predreadnought battleships and four cruisers at Chatham and Sheerness alone. *Lord Nelson* at Sheerness, for example, needed 155 ratings and 21 marines to complete her complement. Meanwhile 3,700 men of the Royal Fleet Reserve arrived on the 15th to man the older ships of the Third Fleet, which were only partly stored – the crews had to get them fully coaled, though the work of getting the fuel on board was done by civilian contractors, and the sailors only had to 'trim' it into its proper bunkers. Dozens of destroyers and torpedo boats were got ready, and their crews were put into trains to take them as far afield as Dundee, the Tyne, Portland and Devonport. That day five battleships sailed from Sheerness, along with three minelayers. Seven cruisers would sail the next day, and the last ship, the Scout cruiser *Pathfinder*, left port on the 17th after a week of intense administration and preparation. It was considered a great success for the Fisher reforms: 'Owing to [the] great advance which has been made in recent years in the general state of preparedness of ships not in full commission, the operation of Mobilisation of such ships has considerably diminished in magnitude'.[2]

The ships were headed for Portsmouth, where they would combine with more from there and the other dockyards, making a total force that included 59 battleships. Anchored in up to five rows in the Solent, they filled the seven-mile space between Portsmouth Harbour and Southampton Water. They were to be reviewed by the King and would incidentally provide a demonstration of the readiness and strength of British sea power as the crisis in Europe developed. There was also a display of the brand-new Royal Naval Air Service, which brought Farman and Short biplanes down to Calshot Castle from bases on the Isle of Grain, Dundee and Yarmouth. His Majesty arrived on Saturday the 18th and spent two days cruising around the ships in the Royal Yacht *Victoria and Albert*. 'Clinker Knocker', in the destroyer *Hind*, was impressed, even though his crew had to interrupt a football tournament at Harwich to get there:

A glorious July evening in 1914. The sun shines brilliantly from a sky of cloudless blue, reflected in the sparkling splendour on the bright metal work of the ships of the mightiest armada the world has ever seen, lying in the anchorage between the Isle of Wight and the mainland. Line upon line of battleships, cruisers, destroyers, torpedo-boats, submarines, depot ships, and auxiliaries, each class in perfect formation ready for His Majesty King George V to inspect. Practically every ship stationed in home waters in the great assembly.[3]

Arrangements were made for the crews of the Portsmouth Division to have leave on shore, but in view of the short time they were away from port and the large numbers of reserves on board, those of the Third Fleet were not allowed to go. Meanwhile a team of petty officers had toured Portsmouth looking at private houses, temperance hotels and lodging houses where men could find accommodation for a shilling a night, 'a separate bed being provided for each man'.

On Monday 20th the fleet began to get ready to put to sea, led at first by 5 royal yachts, 5 battlecruisers, 29 battleships in two columns, 16 cruisers and 57 destroyers of the First Fleet, followed by even more of the Second and Third Fleets. After that the ships returned to their home ports. *Hind* went back into Portsmouth, where some of her crew were given leave.

On the 29th Petty Officer E. F. Locke of the battleship *Vanguard* was called up at 5 a.m. at Portland:

I had been disturbed several times during the night by people moving about and talking near my hammock and soon found out the cause – a signal had come from the flag-ship 'Iron Duke' during the night ordering all ships to discharge supernumeraries to their respective barracks, and all men on the sick list who were likely to remain so, to the hospital.

The postman was ready to land to send and bring off the last mail before we sailed, and all were bundled over the gangway into the picket boat alongside, which soon after shoved off and made for the shore, going to Weymouth Pier.

At 5.15 we unmoored ship and waited for the signal to weigh anchor, which came about 6.45 am. By 7.00 am we were ready to proceed, and the fleet passed through the breakwater and shaped course westerly; but after getting out of sight of land we altered course to the east ...[4]

'Clinker Knocker' came ashore at Portsmouth late in the month and found the town strangely quiet. He saw a headline proclaiming 'GRAVE WAR NEWS', and ran into a tearful sailor who was due to be discharged the next day and knew it would be postponed. Characteristically, Knocker took his time to get back to his ship, despite orders from a naval patrol. A few days later he was at sea in the destroyer *Hind*, steaming out of Harwich when the crew heard cheering from the boys of *Ganges*. '"Come on deck, fellers!" yelled a voice down the hatch, "we'll be meeting the German Fleet any time now, the bloody war's been declared."'[5] But nothing happened.

> That first trip to sea on the outbreak of war was a great disappointment, and we lost all respect for the German Navy. For years we had been led to believe that our former friends were eager for 'DER TAG,' which their officers drank to, and freely boasted about. But after keeping us on tenterhooks for the past few years, they refused to meet us in battle. All that took place was the sinking of the Königin Luise, and a submarine was rammed and sunk by the light cruiser Birmingham.[6]

William Lovell was one of those called to action:

> We knew things were brewing up over this Sarajevo business though we never thought it would come to what it did come to. I was down doing middle watch in the stokehold, hulking coal out of the bunker for someone else to sling into the furnace, and we were just on domestic supply to keep the dynamos going, when in came the Chief Stoker, 'Light up all round. We're on the move!' Instead of coming off watch at four I was on till about seven, by which time we were at sea, and we go to that delectable resort, Scapa Flow, where there was a great big Collier waiting – two thousand tons.[7]

Some of the crews were very mixed. In the old cruiser *Crescent*, Midshipman Alexander Scrimgeour complained, 'We have an extraordinary mixed assortment of men – C.G.s., R.N.R., R.N.V.R., R.F.R. men and boys under training, with a smattering of active service ratings. Not much of a crew, I am afraid, but we will get them into shape.'[8]

## THE FIRST BATTLES

H. A. Hill soon got tired of being briefed by the officers during the first weeks of war. 'Sound off "Clear Lower Deck" ... If there was anything important the Commander would say, "The Commodore will be up and speak to you in a few minutes" ... This happened scores of times. "Tell me the old, old story".' But finally there was real action.

Eight o'clock, 'Clear Lower Deck!' and [Commodore Sir William] Goodenough told us that he had heard the Germans were out having a go at Roger Keyes's Flotillas. Between half past nine and ten we went to General Quarters again. My Action Station was up in the fifth funnel – a platform behind the after funnel – and I operated the Dumeriques [Dumeresque] from there. Below in the well we had two 6" guns manned by Marines, the sergeant Major being one of the Gun-layers ... Then we saw smoke on the horizon and about a quarter of an hour later you could see a ship, a Cruiser. Goodenough made a signal to the Cattle Bruisers (the Battle Cruisers) and we eased up to let the Battle Cruisers come up. In about half an hour we saw them – *Lion, Princess Royal, New Zealand* – weren't they coming it! ... the *Lion* got nearly opposite to us and we altered in towards her, when all of a sudden she opened fire, with her foremost guns. We looked towards where this was going and there was the [battlecruiser] *Derfflinger*. She opened fire on us and projies started falling on our starboard side, so Bill [Commodore Goodenough] altered course and got out of it ... we watched the *Lion*. When those projies hit, they hit first just abaft the after guns. There was a flash, incandescent it was, and when we looked there weren't any guns. When they did that, there were some stokers down below me, and they threw their caps in the air – we were doing about fifteen knots – so they came down miles astern! ... This went on for some time, but the *Derfflinger* got away and left us with the [cruisers] *Köln*, *Mainz* and *Ariadne*. Then you heard the dialogue down below from the Marines. Language! – you never heard anything like it. They were calling out for more ammunition ... and as fast as the Sergeant Major could fire his gun they were shovelling it in. We watched some of our projies go aboard the *Mainz*. They were armour piercing stuff but they exploded on impact. They hit and got just inside and then exploded. We were firing amidships and the first thing that went down was her second funnel. When that happened there was a cheer from all the guns that couldn't do anything.[9]

This was the battle of Heligoland Bight, in which three German light cruisers were sunk, but the main fleets were never engaged.

On 22 September, seven weeks after war was declared, the Germans had their revenge. Three old cruisers *Aboukir*, *Cressy* and *Hogue*, built at the turn of the century, were patrolling off the Dutch coast in an operation that was even more old-fashioned than the ships themselves – in the age of the submarine, mine and torpedo they were attempting a close blockade of the enemy as the navy had done in Nelson's day. The German submarine *U-9* sank them one by one, as the captains, with old-fashioned courtesy, came in to rescue the crews of ships already hit. As a result 62 officers and 1,397 men were lost, and the navy had a salutary lesson about the power of the submarine. The cruisers were old, but as Admiral Beatty commented, the men could 'ill be spared' in the crisis. According to Midshipman Hereward Hook of *Hogue*,

> The ship's company was made up almost entirely of Royal Fleet Reservists, and two or three badge Active service men, real seamen every one of them, practically the pick of the Navy, and I would never have believed it possible that there could be so little panic or excitement amongst them. I do not think I saw a single man running on the upper deck.[10]

It was even worse because, by coincidence, all three ships were from the Chatham Division, so that losses fell very heavily on that area. The losses highlighted one of the faults of the home port system; within a few months it would be overtaken by far worse losses to the army on the Western Front.

### LIFE IN THE GRAND FLEET

The great mass of the Royal Navy's sailors were concentrated in the Grand Fleet, as the Home Fleet was now known, which planned to use Scapa Flow as its base. But this had no anti-submarine defences, and the loss of the three cruisers in September 1914 raised concerns about its safety, so the fleet was evacuated to Loch Na Keal, on the Isle of Mull, and Lough Swilly in Ireland. Admiral Beatty described the position to Churchill:

we have no place to lay our heads. We are at Loch na Keal, Isle of Mull. My picket boats are at the entrance, the nets are run out, and the men are at the guns waiting for coal which has run low, but ready to move at a moment's notice. Other squadrons are in the same plight. We have been running now hard since the 28th July; small defects are creeping up which we haven't time to take in hand. 48 hours is our spell in harbour with steam ready to move at 4 hours notice, coaling on an average 1400 tons a time, night defence stations. The men can stand it, but the machines can't, and we must have a place where we can stop for four or five days now and then to give the engineers a chance. Such a place does not exist, so the question arises, how long can we go on, for I fear very much not for long, as the need for small repairs is becoming insistent.[11]

The defences of Scapa were eventually ready, and life in the Grand Fleet settled into a routine. After nearly two years training in *Impregnable* at Plymouth, one ordinary seaman was pleased to arrive at Scapa to join the cruiser *Liverpool*: 'it was a great spectacle to see the mighty fleet which were there when our ship arrived which formed only a portion of our mighty navy.' He was soon disillusioned when his ship put to sea in bad weather. 'The whole crew turned out, for almost three days and nights sleep was impossible for anyone the ship tossing about more like a cork on the water than anything I myself have experienced.' [12]

But life at Scapa soon became intensely boring. According to A. W. Ford, 'we had no world outside the ship.' Some settled down to that, like John Beardsley:

The routine aboard H.M.S. *Hercules* was interesting enough and in spite of a thousand hands on board the space provided for each fighting unit did not under the circumstances seem inadequate. All of us were well fed, with plenty of fresh veg., butter, meat, and our own bakery, distilled water, a good comfortable hammock, complete with warm blankets; in fact we were really comfortable whilst lying at the Flow. However we were subject to what was known as *eighteen at one* – in other words we had to be able to raise steam for 18 knots at one hour's notice.[13]

Trips ashore were rare and hardly worth the bother:

Apart from the fact that it meant a long trip in a drifter, as the one boat called at a number of ships on her way, there was only the one canteen (where one guzzled a large amount of beer, usually roaring out ribald songs that one couldn't sing anywhere else) but the place closed at 8.30 P.M. (invariably ending with a fight or two), and then there was the job of picking out your own drifter from the many at the pier, the long trip back to the ship, and having to pass the Officer of the Watch before you got back 'home' to your mess.[14]

Leave was even rarer and was according to the needs of the ship rather than the men. If it started from Scapa it involved a rough ferry ride across the Pentland Firth, then a journey in a closed train, the 'Jellicoe', named after the commander-in-chief of the fleet. It might take up to two days to reach the naval bases on the south coast:

In the afternoon and more particularly at night, the whole train was strewn with 'bodies' trying to sleep. The air was dense with smoke and smelt more like a ship's bilges than a train; but the thought of having a window open, even if one could get to it, was out of the question and asking for trouble. Little or no heat was provided by the train and it was a case of putting up with any discomfort to keep warm.[15]

The Battlecruiser Fleet under Beatty was based in the Forth, where there were slightly better facilities, though the ships had to be kept at constant readiness. Ratings were allowed only an hour or two ashore, often confined to the limits of Lord Elgin's park. At one stage his lordship found a seaman in a compromising situation with one of his housemaids and remonstrated with him – 'The naval Don Juan in reply to his protests told him to go to hell and get a girl for himself.'[16]

Ships normally coaled up as soon as they came back from an operation, when the men were already tired. It was a filthy, laborious business:

The ship had barely dropped anchor when the collier *Mercedes* came alongside and was made fast. Again the bosun's pipe – 'Hands to supper and clean into coaling rig. Coal ship in half an hour's time.' Away we hurried to eat and change into that most hateful rig.

The bugler sounded 'The General Assembly, at the double' ... As soon as the watches were reported present the Commander gave his orders. 'The country is now at war. We have to take in 2,500 tons of coal at utmost speed. The squadron gets under weigh at dawn. Hands coal ship! Carry on.'

Away we doubled to the sound of 'The Charge' on the bugle. The competitive spirit to try and get the first hoist inboard made us work like slaves. Each hoist consisted of ten bags, each containing two hundredweight. The hold gangs began shovelling furiously to get the bags filled. Soon the winches began to work and up went the first hoist ... Throughout the night the shovels were working and the winches rattling away, whilst the inboard gangs were clearing the dumps at the double to have the coal tipped into the bunkers. Those poor devils in the bowels of the ship were trimming the bunkers as the coal shot into them. The stokers were enshrouded with an indescribable cloud of dust, which got right into the lungs, and they had only a Davy safety lamp to guide them...

At length the 'Cease Fire' sounded on the bugle and a tired and dusty ship's company downed tools and had a breather. Not for long, however. Soon came the pipe 'Clear Collier', followed by 'Stand by to cast off collier'. Shovels and coal bags were hoisted across, the collier's holds covered and a tired crew climbed inboard.[17]

J. J. Eames did not enjoy his time at Scapa and wrote as he came back from leave, 'Return, it's a sad, sad world after 12 days at home, I wish I could sign on for two pensions, I don't think.' Life in Jellicoe's flagship brought no joy, as W. C. Hales recorded:

I didn't like the *Iron Duke* very much. She was the Fleet Flagship and you had more crew, more Officers, because of the Admiral's staff and three Admirals. We carried out our ship's routine as though it were peacetime. All the other ships made some concessions – make and mends when you were in harbour – but all we got was one on a Saturday and if something cropped up on a Saturday or we were at sea, you lost that and they never made it up to you. And it was a strict routine.[18]

In the same ship, AB Arthur Sawyer found that the admiral was 'a very nice gentleman', though he was only seen occasionally, exercising on the upper deck. Sawyer tried to make the best of the situation on board.

> In our world between decks we got to know each other. We were together for so long and we were very young. We never seemed to see the sun – it was so bleak up in the Orkneys, barren and bleak – just bloody heather everywhere and cold grey seas. You never saw a girl. You had to make your own enjoyment. The officers had their deck hockey and we used to run around the upper deck and do exercises. Then in the evening we'd play cards and housey-housey (bingo). And we had concert parties.[19]

Trystan Edwards describes the atmosphere on the messdecks:

> The most obvious characteristic of the broadside mess is that its inhabitants have no privacy. It is a noisy place, in which a large family of men partake of the fullness of social communion. There is no mumbling nor talking in undertones here. While Able-Seaman Smith and Able-Seaman Brown sitting next to each other may be indulging in a 'naval argument', a form of converse which has rather unjustly been described as 'vehement assertion followed by flat contradiction and personal abuse', Leading Seaman Robinson may be exchanging witticisms over three had [?] of his mess-mates, with Leading Seaman Baker three tables away. Stoker Woods passing down the gangway flings a jibe at his friend Able-Seaman Miller, which leads to roars of laughter. This evokes a reply, swiftly conceived yet apposite, and Stoker Woods disappearing round the corner, at this distance being obliged to raise his voice to shout out a Parthian shot.[20]

## THE FALKLANDS

The start of the war was just as dramatic in ships on foreign stations, such as the cruiser *Glasgow* off South America, as Leading Seaman W. T. C. Hawkes recorded:

> Sunday August 2nd. Received the orders to prepared [sic] for war. Telegram arrived at 3 o'clock this morning, the hands turned out at 4 o'clock and started work. One watch coaled ship, about 250 tons, the other watch dismantle ship, all wood-work and everything out of the captain and

officers cabins and all moveable articles was pass[ed] into lighters. Other hands employed in snaking down the rigging and stays and securing everything aloft. Carpenter unshipping all wooden decks. After tea hands rigged splinter nets all over the guns and cleared away all article below the water line.[21]

*Glasgow* was soon in action, when she and the cruisers *Good Hope* and *Monmouth* met the larger German ships *Scharnhorst* and *Gneisenau* off the Chilean port of Coronel. As a gunlayer, Hawkes had a good view as the action developed:

> In the first ten minutes the *Good Hope* and *Monmouth* were on fire. The *Monmouth* had her fore turret blown over the side. After a while there was a terrible explosion and we saw the whole of the midships part of the *Good Hope* blow up, the fire must have spread to her magazine. It was a shocking sight. After that her 9.2 fired about twice, and that was the last I saw of her. *Monmouth* was in flames, and she pulled out of the line. We carried on firing for about ten minutes.

Hawkes was distressed as the *Glasgow* made her retreat:

> It was a miserable night all round after we got away rushing at 24 knots against a head sea and leaking badly and shipping big seas. All we could do was think about our Comrades we had left behind at the bottom of the sea and thank God he had brought us out of it.[22]

Heavy British ships, including the battlecruisers *Invincible* and *Inflexible*, were sent to deal with the German squadron. First Writer Henry Welch was in the cruiser *Kent* as the squadron under Vice Admiral Sir Doveton Sturdee sailed out to meet the German cruisers off the Falkland Islands in December. As captain's clerk, he stayed on the bridge to take notes and had a good view of the action. There was a timeless mixture of fear and elation as battle became imminent:

> Things were now getting exciting, and I think the men were jolly delighted with the chance of a scrap. The thoughts came crowding in – home, wife,

child and all that a man has dear to him. The possibilities of the day occurred to me, but there was no time to think of the danger. All that seemed to trouble me was that the other ships in harbour were so long getting under way. The business in hand gave one little time for thoughts. I had to write all that was taking place. I fear that my hand was a trifle unsteady with the excitement, but I got plenty of detail down.[23]

Soon the *Kent* was in the thick of the action:

Now we were at it in deadly earnest. The crash and din was simply terrific – our first broadside going off and shaking our bodies to pieces, deafening, choking, and nearly blinding us; then the shells from the enemy hitting us and bursting, throwing death-dealing pieces of shell and splinters of steel in all directions and nearly poisoning us with the fumes. Shells were screeching all round us, and as they whizzed by the bridge and the deck I could feel the rush of air. Some were going through the funnels. One hit the corner of the fore turret casing, glanced off and tore through the deck into the sickbay, crumpling and tearing steel plating as though it was paper. One went through the chart house just over my head. Another burst just outside the conning tower and sent a perfect hail of pieces in round us.[24]

But the British force had overwhelming strength and was soon victorious. Welch's feelings were timeless again as he helped rescue men from the defeated ships:

After dark the captain dismissed me, as there was nothing else to record, so I went down to the aft deck where the German survivors were being restored to vitality. I worked hard on one of them for more than an hour and a quarter with Dr Schäfer's method [of artificial respiration], but could get no life into him. Only seven of the ten could we bring to after much hard work and hot stimulants.[25]

Even amongst this comradeship of the sea, there was the characteristic hatred of the Germans as he thought about the previous action at Cornel, in which the British had been outnumbered:

So, truly, we have avenged the *Monmouth*. I really believe it was in the *Nürnberg's* power to have saved many of the *Monmouth's* crew. Instead she simply shelled her until the last part was visible above water. Noble work of which the German nation should feel proud. Thank God I am British.[26]

## IMPROVEMENTS IN CONDITIONS

To aid recruiting in competition with the army, as soon as the war started, the Admiralty began to offer a series of concessions to seamen, potential seaman and those returning to the fold. Men who had been out of the service for less than a year were given their full non-substantive ratings if they returned. Deserters were offered an amnesty if they turned themselves in to one of the home ports by 4 September; they would be issued with a free kit and their debts to the crown would be remitted. Promotion was made much easier in several different branches, largely because there were no opportunities for the usual training and examination. For example, 'Ordinary Seamen recommended for advancement may for the time being be advanced to the rating of Able Seamen without further qualification than a recommendation for such advancement.' 'In order to afford the Royal Navy every facility in the present crisis ...' duty free cigarettes were to be made available on board ship, Woodbines were sold at 1½d for ten, Players at 2¼d. Canteens no longer had to be sealed up in harbour, and the men were allowed their duty-free goods as if at sea. The rules on leave were relaxed:

> During the present hostilities, whenever a ship returns to her Home Dockyard to refit or dock, the whole of the work in connection with docking is to be undertaken by the yard, in order to allow the Officers and men to have an opportunity of taking as much rest and leave as possible.[27]

The railway companies offered cheap fares, on the basis of a return for the same price as a single fare, and at Christmas the men were offered free travel. Most important of all, the men were now paid separation allowance, which for practically the first time recognised their married status. Able and leading seamen had 6*s* extra a week for a wife, rising to 8*s* for a chief petty officer. Two shillings were paid for the first and second child, and a shilling for every other one.

The naval detention quarters were closed, though that was not entirely philanthropic, as 'the desirability of not losing the services of men who may commit offences during the present war' was recognized, and other punishments were to be used instead. But Bodmin prison was soon filled with naval men, and in October the DQs were re-opened.[28] The effect of using recovered deserters was not always good, as they tended to be sent to whatever ships were fitting out at the time. One victim of this was the battlecruiser *Tiger*, completed in October and hurriedly fitted out and manned. Admiral Beatty later complained that she had 73 recovered deserters out of a crew of 1,121, plus 10 more who had been sent to prison already. She also had 46 Short Service seamen who had joined just before the war, 50 RNR stokers, 65 boys and 50 newly joined marines, making for a very weak ship's company of whom at least a quarter were untrained. He told the Second Sea Lord, 'it was an uphill task for the captain to pull them together in war time, and the same efficiency could not be expected from the *Tiger* as from the other ships.'[29]

## BOYS

By the end of 1914 the navy needed 8,000 men for new ships already ordered in peacetime and coming off the stocks. Four new battleships of the *Iron Duke* class were completed that year, along with the battlecruiser *Tiger*. Two large ships building for Turkey were taken over, and the great battleships of the *Queen Elizabeth* class would begin to enter service in 1915. In the meantime, the light cruisers of the *Birmingham*, *Arethusa* and *Caroline* classes were almost ready, along with dozens of destroyers. There was no question of manning them by taking older ships out of service, as might be done in peacetime.

One solution was to draft in training-ship boys who had not completed their courses, but in the Grand Fleet Jellicoe found this was not an adequate answer. As he wrote in April 1915,

> In regard to the drafts now being sent to the fleet to replace the young able seamen sent to gunnery and torpedo schools, the large majority consists of

very young boys – sixteen is probably the average age – who have little strength or stamina, nor can they be expected to develop much for a year or so. A great many ships have already received large drafts of these boys, and it will not be possible to continue much longer exchanging them for men without loss of efficiency.[30]

Meanwhile recruitment of boys continued at slightly more than the usual peacetime rate. One great advantage was that they could be promised action at an early age, which was very popular during the first months of war, when young men feared it would all be over before they had a chance to prove themselves. As Stan Smith found in Norwich,

The whole population seemed to be caught up in war fever. All the young men were rushing to join the Forces for everybody said the war would only last six months at most, and it seemed like a good thing to be part of it.

Swept along on this tide of feeling were two 15 year old youths filled with a determination to help the war effort in whatever way they could ...

We did our best to join the Army, but were 15 and enthusiasm wasn't enough. In fact, we got the distinct impression that they weren't that hard up for recruits! ... We fished around for information and found out that we could join the Royal Navy at 15 years and three months.

He and his friend got round the problem of parental consent by the time-honoured tactic of forgery. They were signed on and ordered to report to the recruiting office next day with only the clothes they stood up in. Shipped to Shotley, they came under Petty Officer Slyfield, 'a sailor of the old school, a tough old salt who believed that sailors were not born but hewn out by the vigorous application of discipline':

Once we were at drill he exhibited an ability to swear which, in my experience, has never been equalled; a command of language which was, in itself, a part of my education which left a lasting impression.

But it was his job to make sailors of us, and quickly, for there was a war on. And, for our part, we got on with the job. We learned gunnery, signalling, wireless and many other mysteries of the sea.[31]

## RESERVISTS

Just before the war, Jellicoe had written as Second Sea Lord, 'Great Britain has 36,636 Reservists who have served a term in the Navy, with an addition of 16,667 RNR men; a total of 53,303. The RNR men cannot be said to be comparable in efficiency to the remainder, and only a small proportion of them are available on mobilization.'[32] This was typical of the Admiralty view – that the Royal Fleet Reserve was far superior to the merchant seamen of the RNR, and the amateurs of the RNVR did not count at all.

Officers seemed quite satisfied with the RFR and RNR ratings called out at the beginning of the war. Admiral Sir Rosslyn Wemyss wrote of his flagship *Euryalus*, 'Nice officers and a fine ship's company. The reserve men throughout seem a splendid lot of men and far beyond anything I expected. Their average age of course is a good deal higher than the regulars, but what they lack in activity they make up for in solidity.'[33]

Building a reserve of wireless telegraphists posed some difficulties for the navy. It was a very new art, so there had not been time to build up adequate numbers through the Royal Fleet Reserve. Whereas the regular navy trained the brightest boys in the training ships for the role and gave them few privileges beyond those of the seaman, the merchant marine tended to treat them as officers. A special section of the RNR was formed for them by royal proclamation in February 1914, and they were to be given the uniform of chief petty officers.[34] Their actual status was unclear, and it was not fully resolved by an Admiralty Order of October:

> It is to be clearly understood that this high rating is given to these men in order that they may be entitled to messing conditions and general accommodation more in keeping with those to which they have been accustomed in civil life.
>
> The Admiralty fully appreciate the patriotic spirit that has brought so many men forward in answer to the request for volunteer operators, and are confident that such men will be the first to recognise that they cannot be as capable of conducting Wireless Telegraph signalling in a large Fleet as the Naval Service operator who has had years of experience and training in that difficult situation.
>
> In all cases, therefore, when the complement of a man-of-war includes both Active Service Telegraphist ratings and W/T Operators, R.N.R., the

senior Active Service rating is to be in charge under the Signal Officer, of all matters relating to the Wireless Telegraphy signalling and maintenance of instruments.[35]

The Trawler Reserve, founded in 1911, became increasingly important, as such boats were found very useful for minesweeping and anti-submarine work – more than a thousand were in service by the end of 1915. The Admiralty was reluctant to draft ratings into this reserve from general service, as trawlers posed special problems of seasickness and rough accommodation to those who were not used to them. When a man was transferred from a yacht to a trawler, 'it takes him a further four or five weeks to get over the seasickness and discomfort produced in small vessels of this type'. A 'special section' of the reserve was set up in April 1915 to take in men who would not normally qualify. There were 200 ratings of the Newfoundland RNR, noted for their hardiness at sea, as well as Shetland RNR men who were equally well regarded. Volunteers from the RNVR depot at Crystal Palace were also to be accepted, and any fishermen between the ages of 18 and 55 who could be persuaded to join. Normal fitness rules were waived: 'Candidates who are reasonably fit are to be accepted without any regard to the standard physical requirements laid down in the existing instructions.' Even Sea Scouts were to be taken on as signal boys, and boys from the industrial schools, normally turned down as being too close to the criminal classes, might be taken on as deck or cook boys, though not signal boys.

A number of very large yachts were taken over in 1914, as owners such as the Dukes of Leeds and Sutherland, Lord Howard de Walden, Lord Iveagh and Sir William Beardmore, as well as companies such as Camper & Nicholson and Cole & Baker offered them free of charge for three months. Some of the owners were commissioned in the RNVR, while their crews often remained on board as RNVR ratings. There were 85 of them in service by the end of 1915.

The Motor Boat Reserve was founded just after the start of the war, when various boat-owners offered the services of their craft. It had two officer ranks, lieutenant and sub-lieutenant, and two ratings, chief motor boatman and motor boatman.[36] In 1915, 550 motor boats were ordered from the Elco company in New York, and manning them posed something of a problem. Deckhands could be found by returning the miscellaneous collection of motor boats to their owners, and many fishing drifters were paid off at the same time – 'Their slow speed and high maintenance costs do not, in many cases, justify their continuance in service.' Engineers were a different problem, for the new boats had 'high-powered twin-screw engines and auxiliary starting and lighting plant', which were far more sophisticated than most of the older craft. The smaller boats needed a crew of nine, including two officers and five deckhands. Each engine room was to be manned by a chief motor mechanic with at least 'five years practical experience in work shops and a high knowledge of internal combustion engines and their repair', and two motor mechanics with two years' experience. They were recruited from other sections of the navy, and in New Zealand and Canada. Those eligible for promotion to chief, after at least four months' service and the recommendation of a commanding officer, were to be brought forward. Base staffs were to be reduced, and it was to be remembered that the chiefs could do a good deal of their own maintenance, while officers were warned: 'Motor Launch complements should not be transferred to, or used in, yachts, drifters or any other vessel but their own Motor Launches, for which work they have been specially trained.'

The yacht, motor boat and trawler reserves were mostly employed together, along with parts of the RNVR, in the Auxiliary Patrol Service around the British coast. The standard unit in October 1914 was expected to be one yacht, four trawlers and four motor boats, though that could vary greatly. The Patrol Service's function was 'to examine the coast, harbours, and inlets in waters where their sea-going capacity enables them to work, with a view to preventing their use by hostile craft'. Senior officers were warned, 'It is not intended that they should be used for the service of ships and harbour establishments.' Soon their aims were extended to include minesweeping, anti-submarine patrol and eventually convoy escort.

The provision of signalmen was a problem for the patrol service generally. It was planned to have a wireless telegraphy operator in each yacht, and in one trawler in six. Men were trained with two months in

*Impregnable* and one in *Vernon,* but they often found the conditions in trawlers intolerable. For visual signals, boys were recruited from the merchant navy training ships such as *Mercury* in the Hamble River, *Warspite* in the Thames and *Arethusa* at Greenhithe, but regulations demanded that they should only be posted to vessels with a commissioned officer on board 'to supervise their morals'. This meant that the majority of trawlers were without any full-time signaller, though pensioned yeomen of signals were employed to train selected seamen, who would be paid 2*d* per day extra if successful.[37]

## THE ROYAL NAVAL DIVISION

As the battle developed in Belgium during the second week of the war, Churchill began to advocate a strong force of sailors to fight on shore, 'in order to make the best possible use of surplus naval reservists'. He planned for two brigades consisting of 3,000 amateur seamen of the RNVR, 2,500 recalled naval men of the RFR and 1,500 merchant seamen of the RNR. It might be seen as part of Churchill's ambition to lead a great land battle in person, one which never really left him. He set up a camp near Deal in Kent, where the forces assembled, and told them of his plans. The RNVR men, who had joined the force because of their enthusiasm for the sea, were not pleased and sent a deputation to their leader, the Marquis of Graham:

> They said they had been cheated and made the only 'conscripts' in all the British Forces. They demanded to be sent to sea at once, or sent home with authority to join up with their home regiments and friends. They went so far as to threaten downing arms on parade, or making a wholesale desertion if their wishes were not met in a sympathetic way.[38]

The issue of the Royal Naval Division did at least crystallize thinking in the Admiralty on the role of reservists and the need to maintain and expand fleet strength. By September it was becoming clear that the war would not be settled suddenly by a quick battle by land or by sea. In the Grand Fleet, Jellicoe was finding it difficult to cope with a large influx of boys, and in April 1915 he wrote, 'If available for the fleet, it is thought that men recruited for the Royal Naval Division would do very well; they have been initiated to naval discipline and given some training, and probably many would volunteer for service afloat.' [39] The last phrase was something of an understatement. But it was not to happen, for the Western Front was always hungry for men. And as the submarine war developed, the RNVR men would have been even more suitable for the small craft that were fitted out round the coasts; but 21,000 of them were still serving in France in 1917.

## THE HOSTILITIES ONLY MAN

At the start of the war, amidst a great flood of patriotism that led to huge queues of men outside army recruiting offices, former naval seamen who were no longer on the reserve lists began to offer themselves at their home ports. It was quickly agreed to take them on 'for hostilities only', and soon the phrase came to take on much greater significance. It was also suggested that 'men with very exceptional qualifications who have never served may be entered under the same conditions from the shore'. They would fill in the same form as continuous service men, but the question on length of engagement should be answered as 'for the period of hostilities only'.[40]

From the Grand Fleet in April 1915, Jellicoe soon came to demand ordinary seamen 'of better physique and improved development' compared with the boys he had been sent so far. He suggested, 'Special efforts should be made to recruit Ord. Seamen for the period of hostilities age 19 to 30, with a minimum height of 5'4", chest 35". These Ord. Seamen to be offered similar inducements as regards advancement to A.B. as now offered to those entering the R. N. Division, viz:– advancement to A.B. after 3 months service, if satisfactory, and recommended.' This was already beginning to happen. Since January, 574 men between the ages of 18 and 25 had been recruited for special service, and 65, aged 18 to 38, 'for period of hostilities'.[41] In the end, more than 74,000 men were entered for hostilities only, many of them with little or no experience.[42] One of them was F. W. Turpin:

It was on the morning of January 10th 1917 that I entered the gates of the Royal Naval Barracks at Chatham and was enrolled as an ordinary seaman in the Royal Navy. It was with trepidation that I passed through as I knew that I was leaving all my little home comforts and liberty behind me. Well for about two months I was drilled and instructed in the elementary part of seamanship and then I was drafted to Rosyth ...[43]

Another was W. Wise, who left Rochdale with his brother early in September 1916, having volunteered as an alternative to being conscripted into the army. He stayed in the 'Aggie's' at Devonport – 'a sort of temperance institute or hostel where sailors on shore leave may find cheap means of refreshment recreation etc and even a nice little bed in a cubicle for fourpence the night', though he was still in his civilian clothes and felt conspicuous there. Next day he reported to the naval barracks, too late for a bath and fumigation but in time to have a medical. Dinner was on board the old gunboat *Eclipse* – 'I think it was unfit for pigs so they gave it to us ... we scarcely touched it but bought cake at a fabulous price from the canteen.' He paraded in the barracks, then back to *Eclipse* for tea, which was at least better than the dinner. Then, 'At the pipe "Stand by hammocks" the whole mob of us dash below and after about one hour of pushing and fighting in a dirty dingy flat and signing our names we manage to secure a prize viz a bundle of dirty rag and string which when untied and straightened up turns out to be or once was a hammock'. The brothers used their clothing and boots as pillows so they would not be stolen.

They were woken at 5 a.m. with the traditional cry of 'Heavo, heavo, lash up and stow hammocks'. They went to the New Entry Office, where they sat around and wrote letters until called, then went back to the barracks for a literacy test and to be entered formally into the service. In the afternoon particulars were taken down for making up kit and identity discs. Crafty as always, Wise dodged fire practice and potato peeling by going out to the jetty for his first wash since joining. He spent a leisurely evening with his brother, and they mystified some Cardiff men with a card trick and got some rope to make quoits. Next day he made out the form to allot his wages to his family and signed the pledge against alcohol with 'one of Aggy's disciples', but it did not last long. The day after he felt very unwell. He was detailed to scrub out a marine sergeant's cabin, and was given a tot of rum, which he justified on medicinal grounds. He spent a whole day in barracks and finally volunteered for cook of the mess, 'not having cheek enough to dodge it any longer." He was one of 230 men vaccinated and had a sore arm for weeks afterwards, which he did not hesitate to use to get out of unpleasant duties.

After a week the men were drafted into the barracks and issued with their kit. Wise had a rather undemanding life by his account, with frequent visits to Aggie's, the YMCA and Goodbody's Cafe. They did 'physical jerks' one day, paraded on an old cruiser to learn anchor work on another, and did knot-tying and compass work, then learned dhobying, or clothes washing, though Wise was often excused duty – when the class went for boat pulling, he stayed behind to sew buttons on his pants. After a month the class moved into C Block and was dispersed. Wise was paid his first 2 shillings since joining, learned more seamanship, rifle drill and laying out kit for inspection. Somehow he wore out his boots and had them repaired by the shoemaker. He continued to dodge duty when he could, but at the end of October he was detailed as messenger to the petty officer in charge of new entries and killed a rat in his cabin. On 13 November he passed the doctor as suitable for drafting and was issued with his winter clothing – sea boots, stockings and socks, gloves, muffler and helmet. All leave was stopped, and the men left the barracks on the 14th for the day-long journey to Invergordon, where they were split up between various ships. He was one of a dozen men sent to the battleship *Ajax*, where, 'we are kept busy till late at night passing the doctor, having our gear fumigated and victualled up. We are then placed under the care of a regular sea-dog, Leading Seaman Stevens, who puts me in charge of the mess account.' He was allocated his action station in the after 4-inch magazine, followed by seamanship instruction by 'Stevo'. On 22 November he sailed for the first time, but found the rolling motion of the ship 'a bit trying'.[44]

On board ship the HO men were known as 'Cuthberts' and tended to be seated at the opposite end of a mess table from the regulars. Trystram Edwards entered as one despite his public school background and was soon absorbed into naval culture:

While in the Army, civilians who volunteered to become 'cannon-fodder' take precedence in popular imagination over the much smaller number or professional fighters, in the Navy it was otherwise. Granted that towards the end of the war a large proportion of the ships' companies in Dreadnoughts, cruisers and even destroyers consisted of ratings who had signed on "for hostilities only," these latter did not establish for themselves a prestige separate from that of the professional Navy. On the contrary, they were completely absorbed by the latter and cleaved to its traditions.[45]

## THE STOKERS

Early in 1915 it was easier to recruit stokers than seamen because of their higher wages.[46] This did not meet naval needs – more oil-fired ships, such as the new *Queen Elizabeth* class battleships, were being built and older ones were being converted to oil. 'Clinker Knocker' did not like his first experience of an oil-fired destroyer: 'I could not get used to the burning of oil-fuel. The fumes made my head ache, and I longed to get back to coal-burning ships.' But during the war he came to appreciate the advantages:'the poor fellows "carrying on" under war conditions in a coal-fired craft must have gone through hell.'[47] For many the change from coal to oil was the most important reform in naval conditions. As a result the number of stokers was now declining. In March 1914 there were 38,500 continuous service seaman ratings and just 500 more stokers. By March 1917 the number of stokers had declined slightly to 36,400, while seamen had increased to 46,000.[48]

Hostilities only stokers (known as firemen in the merchant service) were not always well adapted to naval conditions:

One of the coal-trimmers [who got the coal out of the bunkers for the stokers] was a merchant-ship fireman, and he had no use for the naval method of firing boilers. Darky Bagshaw liked to cram the furnaces with coal. The light, easy and bright method he could not get used to, so he trimmed coal for others.[49]

'Clinker Knocker' describes his companions in the stokehold of a destroyer, a mixture of regulars and HO men and all proud of their toughness:

Our section of boilers was cut off, and we settled down to an easy four hours of attending banked fires. The six of us who operated the boilers were chatting with the two coal-trimmers near one of the bunker doors. Jim Bottomley, the petty officer in charge of the watch, was pacing the boiler-room plates, carrying a wheel spanner. By his attitude, his mind was far away in Wakefield, Yorkshire, with his wife and children. Although a first-class petty officer, he was also a hard case, as befitted the petty officer of the 'cranky blue watch' ... Daisy Dormer, the leading stoker, sat on an upturned coal-skid, gazing vacantly at the gauge glasses on the boilers. He was also a diamond in the rough, and only his prowess in the boxing ring was the cause of his still being able to sport the anchor on his left arm ...

Shelley stood alone. He feared nothing! Some men thought him mad. Then there was Birdie Harris, cockney, born within the sound of Bow bells, and proud of it. He had eleven years of service to his credit, but had never yet been granted his first good conduct badge ... Bill Chaney comes next on the list, and his troubles came from the periodical raids which the ship's police staged on many ships. Bill had his stock-in-trade confiscated, and languished in a cell for a few days for operating a 'Crown and Anchor' board.

George Gadsby was a rough, uncouth coal miner from Northumberland, and had enrolled for the duration of the war. He had not served in the *Achilles* long before he was 'crimed' for refusing duty, and his excuse was that he joined the navy to fight, not to be roasted alive ... Now he was recognised as the best fireman in the ship ... Chuck Beasley ... was formerly a regular in the army ... wounded at Loos, and on his discharge from hospital he had somehow managed to join the navy instead of going to France again. He complained that another Jutland did not materialise, and he wished he had stayed in the army.[50]

## THE DARDANELLES

By the end of 1914 there was stalemate on the Western Front in France and Belgium. Inspired by Winston Churchill, it was decided to send the fleet into the Black Sea, hoping to force Turkey out of the war and open up a passage to the ally Russia. The first plan, executed on 18 March 1915, was to send a fleet of British and French capital ships, mostly predreadnoughts, through the Dardanelles despite Turkish forts and mines. Petty Officer George Morgan watched from *Ocean*, one of the reserve ships. At first his comrades were contemptuous of Turkish gunnery – 'Why my sister could shoot better than that!' They were exultant as the British

ships opened fire. 'Salvo after salvo made us dance with delight. "Oh! look
at that beauty," and "lovely" and all sorts of similar remarks. We were like
youngsters on Guy Fawkes days.' *Ocean*'s turn to move up arrived, and
Morgan was in the magazine. '"What the Dickens was that?" said one to me
as a monster shell must have struck the armour plating. "Oh! someone's
false teeth must have fallen in the shell room."' But the French *Bouvet*
blew up, and the British battleship *Irresistible* hit a mine. *Ocean* was
ordered to take her in tow, but she too hit a mine. 'I was about to hand out
a charge for the loading tray, when bang!! The force of the blow lifted me
off the floor with the charge in my arms. We didn't need to ask what it
was.' Morgan managed to escape and was rescued by a destroyer.[51]

Lieutenant-Commander Kitson of *Swiftsure* worked hard to keep his
gun crews in their stations:

> My station was not a good one for seeing everything that was going on
> outside the ship & what I did see was by looking out of the gun embrasures
> or by going on the upper deck – which I did from time to time to see that
> men were not straying away from their stations … Curiosity is it seems the
> strongest of impulses and it is almost impossible to prevent both officers
> and men from coming up to 'have a look' no matter what the penalty or
> how dangerous.

But some of the gun crews were more relaxed:

> Men at their guns on the disengaged side frequently dropped off to sleep,
> others sat down and read books or chatted just as one had been
> accustomed to see them do at target practice or other peace manoeuvres.
>     Others such as gun layers or sight setters took advantage of their
> telescopes to see all there was through their gun ports and frequently
> would make facetious remarks on what they observed outside.[52]

The attempt to force the Dardanelles failed, and the campaign entered a
new phase. Troops, largely Australians and New Zealanders, were to be
landed on the beaches of the Gallipoli peninsula. There were no specialized
landing craft. The nearest thing was the converted collier *River Clyde*,
with ports cut in her side to let men out. A bridge would be formed to the

land, either by the hopper *Argyle* or by a series of unpowered lighters. But *River Clyde* grounded too far out and came under fire. Able Seaman William Williams of the RFR went out with his captain to help tie the lighters together but was killed. Able Seaman George Samson spent the day on the lighters, exposed to enemy rifle fire:

> Samson was most prominent through 25–26 April. He effected many daring rescues of the wounded, stowed them carefully away in the hopper, and treated them himself until medical assistance was forthcoming. In the intervals he devoted his time to attending to snipers and was prominent in the close fighting on 'V' beach on the night of 25 April. He was eventually shot by a Maxim machine-gun and wounded in nineteen places.[53]

Both he and Williams were awarded the Victoria Cross.

The rest of the troops were landed by conventional ship's boat. Petty Officer William Main was coxswain of the cruiser *Bacchante*'s picket boat and had a good relationship with the midshipman in charge. To guide the inexperienced youngster, he tapped his bare foot to signal when it was time to pass orders to the engine room, from where Stoker Petty Officer 'Bogey' Knight looked out occasionally to ask what was going on. Australian troops were embarked in the picket boat, which also towed a launch loaded with troops, one of twelve leading the attack on 'Z' Beach, later known as Anzac in honour of the troops who landed there. Leading Seaman Worsley and Able Seaman Rice kept a good look out through the darkness from the bows and were ready to sound the depth using the boat hook as they came in close, while the launch was rowed in with muffled oars.

> A bugle call from the shore gives the alarm. We've been seen! 'Very' lights are set off and a star shell, too. The enemy opens fire and down comes a rain of bullets. It is just dark enough to see the flashes of the rifles and machine-guns and light enough to recognise the Turks moving about on shore. ...
>
> There is no cover for our soldiers, and several are wounded before the shore is reached. I see some of them fall back into the crowded boats as they stand up to jump out. Thank goodness there are only a few more yards to go.

The moment their boat grounds, they leap out. In some cases further out than they imagine, and they have to wade ashore up to their waists in water. A few unlucky ones are completely out of their depth, and their heavy equipment is carrying them under. But the majority are reaching the shore in safety, and I have a glimpse of them lying flat on the sand behind their packs and firing, then rising with a cheer and charging up the beach.[54]

George Burtoft, a gunlayer in the predreadnought battleship *Queen*, watched in horror as the troops landed:

About three o'clock they were all lined up. We were afraid of the moon but it cleared all right. Not one soldier knew what he was going to meet when he got on shore. He didn't know the terrain. We had our telescopes. I could pick out all the ravines but that was all one could see at the front. When they got on top they hadn't a clue. Not a clue! It was chaos. But the Turks never fired. With the gun-sight telescope you could see everything. It was awe-inspiring. I've never had the feeling. But when the light came, it was just slaughter. There were not many of the Anzacs who would go home and tell about it.[55]

Boy Telegraphist Blamey was in *Lord Nelson* helping with the latest techniques:

We had aeroplanes and seaplanes up all day giving us directions by wireless where to fire. As yesterday we packed up at 9 pm, but remained where we were all night just off V Beach. Every now and then Asiatic Bill [one of the Turkish guns] would send a huge shell whistling in our direction, and more often than not it fell on the beach among stores, provisions and the Red Cross place.

It was hard and uncomfortable work for the boys:

Aeroplanes are up spotting again today & here on Lord Nelson these spotting signals from the aeroplanes are received by Dyer and myself, two boy tells [telegraphists], and we are down below near the fore 12-inch magazine, with all the watertight doors closed on us, so if the ship went down we may as well say our prayers. The office is only about 4 feet 6 inches by 3 feet 6 inches, so with all the doors closed on us and with hot water pipes running all over the office and below it the heat can well be imagined. We have to keep our flannel, jersey, shirt, cap, boots & socks all off & then we sweat as if we were in a furnace … Our watch was only an hour, it was impossible to stay on longer, & so we worked an hour and hour about. We only man it during the day, as we do no firing by night for fear of hitting our own troops.[56]

Petty Officer George Morgan was sunk again in *Triumph* and was sent to help with beach parties, where he worried about the small stature of many of the British troops compared with the gigantic Australians and New Zealanders. On 13 August he was attempting to salvage a boat when a shell burst near him and he was riddled with shrapnel:

I passed out for a minute or so, and on coming round found myself in a sitting position about to fall overboard. I had been struck in the right arm by one bullet. Another had passed through my right breast and lodged just under the left shoulder. A third had struck me below the right shoulder blade and had come out through my left breast. A fourth struck me lower down on the back coming out of the abdomen above the left hip; and a fifth had caught me in the small of the back paralysing the use of my legs. I was in a tidy mess.[57]

Again the operation had failed. The troops were finally withdrawn early in 1916.

## GUNNERY

Until well into the war, the Admiralty continued to publish the names of those ratings and marines who had been awarded medals for good shooting on a wide variety of guns. But in fact the day of the independent gunlayer, a naval hero since the days of the Armada, was about to come to an end, for the big guns at least. The change in the layer's role was implicit to a certain extent in the design of a dreadnought, for it was expected that all of the 12-inch guns that could be brought to bear would be fired in a single broadside. If each was independently aimed, it would be more difficult to assess how accurate the individual shooting was. Moreover, the view of the gunlayer was often obscured by battle smoke and was likely to be limited at increasingly long ranges. The answer, as devised by Percy Scott and tested late in 1913, was to control the guns from a director mounted high in the ship, on the tripod mast. The director trainer, usually a warrant officer, would keep it trained on the target while an experienced gunlayer turned the assembly on which they sat to point at the enemy. The other ratings in the director were the sight setter, who adjusted them for deflection and other factors, and a phone man to convey messages. The whole system was under the control of the gunnery officer in the spotting top above, assisted by the spotting officer, who reported where the shot were falling, and the rate officer, who reported on changes in the target's speed and direction.

Ranges of up to 12,000 yards were already expected when the war started, and would get much longer in practice – a shell might be up to a minute in the air before it hit or missed the target. Clearly the assessment of range was very important. The British rangefinder had two mirrors some feet apart, which split the target in the horizontal plane. When the two halves were lined up, the range was read off on a dial. The trade of rangetaker, a new rating in the gunnery branch, was only recognized in November 1914. There was no time for theoretical training: men who were already doing the job were to be appointed at the rate of up to nine per battleship, until the gunnery schools were ready for them. The British rangefinder was found to be inferior to the German in practice, but that was not the fault of the operators – the British rangefinders had too short a base, mostly nine feet or less.

All this information, on the range, direction, speed and course of the target and many other factors, was fed down to the bowels of the ship, where the marine bandsmen fed them into a mechanical 'computer'. The final results were fed to the layer and trainer in each turret, who only had to follow a needle on a dial to aim the gun, unless the director system was put out of order and the guns had to be laid and trained independently again. Only eight battleships were fitted with directors when the war started; all but two of those in the Grand Fleet had them by the middle of 1916.

There was still plenty of hard work to be done in the turrets and magazines. Every man was concerned with the detail of his own action station, where he might someday fight and die, like F. W. Turpin in *Agamemnon*:

> My station in battle is down in the bowels of the ship in the shell room of our after 12″ guns. There it is my duty to help load up high projectiles weighing nearly 1000 lbs each. Picture us loading up to feed the gun up above. We are hideously attired in masks and with goggles, respirators and anti-gas apparatus resemble demons from the nether world. Gloves protect our hands from the flashes, there is an awful din, the crashing of iron doors and clanging of machinery punctuated by the deafening roar of the guns. You feel the deck reel under your feet from the terrific effect of a broadside and you realise to the full that war is a monstrous thing. I am fairly safe in my shellroom from direct fire but if anything should cause the ship to sink fairly quickly this diary would remain unfinished.[58]

Exercises were common, and J. E. Attrill describes a typical day in 1917:

> At 9 am our division proceeded outside in the Pentland Firth. At 10.28 the first pair, *Emperor of India* and *Benbow* opened fire and finished at 10.34 firing 40 rounds of 13.5. At 10.35 us and the *Iron Duke* opened fire, range about 18,000 yards. At 10.49 we had to cease fire on account of the target being obscured through smoke.[59]

# 8

# JUTLAND AND AFTER

## JUTLAND

On the morning of 30 May 1916, the Grand Fleet began to leave Scapa Flow, planning to link up with other ships from Invergordon and with Beatty's Battlecruiser Fleet from the Forth. They were following up an intelligence report that the Germans were coming out. As the battlecruiser *Queen Mary* left the Forth, the crew were sceptical about the possibilities of action, according to Petty Officer Francis: 'Of course the usual 'buzzes were started, but I now know that no one had any idea we were on a big errand.' When the gunnery officers briefed the turret captains they 'made a joke about "old guns" trying to make us think "they" were really out.'

It was the battlecruisers that came across the enemy first, in the afternoon of the 31st off the coast of Denmark. For Jeames in *New Zealand*, the action began at half past three when the cruiser *Galatea* signalled that two enemy light cruisers were in sight. The fleet altered course in their direction and increased speed to twenty knots. Twenty minutes later they were called to action stations: 'everything ready for action, will we win? Will we come through allright? What's going to happen? These are a few things we are thinking of.' At 4.25 they loaded the guns and stood by, and fifteen minutes later they altered course to begin the action. 'Order comes port 110 enemy battle cruisers, stand by – The Huns fire, we fire. What a noise. The Huns have got us, shells are firing all around us, can anyone live through it?'

Beatty's battlecruisers, heading south, were now in action with their German counterparts, though neither side knew that the other was backed up by its main fleet. Beatty's ships were slow to get the range, while the powerful ships of the Fifth Battle Squadron were heading off in the wrong direction due to a signalling error. Worse, the lack of armour and faulty safety procedures in the battlecruisers began to have an effect as *Indefatigable* blew up. The High Seas Fleet appeared over the horizon at quarter to five, and Beatty had to withdraw north to bring the Germans on to the guns of the main force of the Grand Fleet. But his troubles were just beginning:

> 531, HMS *Queen Mary* blows up. What a sight, what was once the best firing ship is now in pieces, her after deck is floating by, two men are crawling along on their hands and knees. Paper is flying about. Her after deck turns over and explodes. Every soul on board must be blown to pieces. It's hardly creditable ...

In fact Petty Officer Francis was one of 'quite a crowd' who clung to the starboard rail as the ship began to capsize. He took to the water and was about fifty yards away when there was a 'big smash' and a series of shattering explosions. He was sucked under by a huge wave but managed to struggle up. He clung to a hammock and then a wooden target until rescued by the destroyer *Petard*. One of eight survivors, his eyesight was permanently damaged by oil fuel.[1]

Alexander Grant, gunner of Beatty's flagship, *Lion*, observed that,

> for men in big ships a sea engagement is a particularly trying experience. There they are cramped and confined down below in so many small compartments, with no certain knowledge of events. If they have work to occupy their minds they are fortunate, but in such a well organised community many have not so much to do during the actual battle. They listen to the thud of one enemy shell and the explosion of another. This unavoidable lack of occupation, together with the rumours that get about (and they certainly do get about) to the effect that some ship has been blown to pieces, is more than enough to arouse uneasiness in their minds. It is the bounden duty of all those in authority to dispel these rumours, even if they know them to be true, and so keep up the men's spirits to the job in hand, the annihilation of the enemy.[2]

Petty Officer Dan Sheppard was high up in the director of the same ship, but his view through his gunlayer's telescope was restricted, and visibility was often poor so he had very little idea what was going on as one enemy ship after another came into his sights:

> Next trained to Green 90. From there trained left onto a battlecruiser, left hand ship, which looked like the *Moltke*, I forget how many gun flashes she showed, lost the target and found it again at Green 110 or thereabouts. We lost this target and was ordered to another bearing. I could barely see the object and reported – there was a considerable smoke about and also mist, so we had a lull, trained fore and aft and had a check on director readings. All found correct. About 6.30 p.m. Stand by again Green bearing. Could not do much, fired a couple of salvoes, lost the target in the mist, enemy in sight again further aft – this was also stopped by mist. There appeared a lull in the enemy's fire; he burst out again in 2 gun salvoes, we were ordered to take the rear ship. Here I fancy we picked up a battleship as target, she had 5 turrets. Next we got a shift to battle-cruiser. Here I lose myself, I do not know what training we were on. It was battle-cruisers, but the conditions were about as bad as one could imagine. We were ordered to train on a light cruiser, but she was very hard to see, and appeared to be someone else's target – this would be somewhere about 9 o'clock.[3]

In fact he had had a confused view of the climax of the action. The British battlefleet had entered the action around 6.10, coming to the rescue of the beleaguered battlecruisers and getting into a perfect position to 'cross the T' of the enemy and inflict maximum damage. The cruiser *Chester* was caught in an exposed position and battered by five of the enemy. Her engine room was largely undamaged, but as Leading Stoker Bert Stevens came on deck he found a scene of carnage, for the gun crews had suffered heavily: 'when I came up from down below, the sight I saw I'd never like to see again. It was a terrible sight because they had smashed us up. They'd slaughtered us – the upper deck people.'[4] Among the casualties was Boy First Class Jack Cornwell, who had stood by his post on an exposed gun despite the death of all around him and his own wounds – he died later but was awarded a posthumous VC, becoming perhaps the most famous lower-deck character of the war.

At this point the battlecruiser *Invincible* was the third to explode and was split in two. As they passed her bow and stern sections sticking out of the water, the crew of *Hercules* assumed she was German and cheered, until the captain called from the bridge, 'Stop that cheering – that's one of our ships!'[5] But the Germans turned away on seeing the main force of the British fleet ahead of them. Cut off from their bases, the Germans retired to the east, hoping to find a way through the British line, but again, just before 7 o'clock, they found the whole of the Grand Fleet ranged in perfect order in front of them. They turned away again, and this time the Admiral ordered a daring attack by his torpedo boats. This caused the ever-cautious Jellicoe to turn away himself, an action that was probably correct but was subsequently widely criticized. Darkness was coming down, and there ensued the night action that Sheppard witnessed. The situation was very confusing for ERA Legatt in *Galatea*:

> It was a weird and wonderful business. You only saw the square mile you were in, but I have never seen anything so quick as the way a Destroyer would appear, fire a torpedo and go up in a sheet of flame and there'd be no Destroyer. Everything was at super speed; they would be overcome by enemy fire and where you looked there was a patch of troubled water but no Destroyer and that was a couple of hundred men.[6]

Charles Gifford, a signalman in the light cruiser *Castor*, was a lookout and had a better view. At about 10.30,

> I spotted the mast of a ship coming towards me. I shouted the alarm. I told the Commodore where it was, but none of them could see it, they had not been trained for night spotting like I had. But the Commodore took no chances and ordered his gunnery officer to train the guns on the bearing I had given. Then I saw two more cruisers following up behind. To me they seemed less than half a mile away and they were definitely German cruisers that had crossed the line ahead of us and were steaming home as fast as they could.
>
> Our guns fired their first salvo into the German control tower and bridge which flashed up like an explosion, then the second and third ship started to fire on us.

*Castor* suffered much damage from the four ships of the Second Scouting Group, and they escaped into the night.

Boy First Class Stan Smith was a sight-setter on one of the 4-inch guns of the destroyer *Spitfire* when she launched a torpedo attack:

Up to that point we had not been spotted but the act of firing pinpointed us for the Germans ... We were spotted on the turn, and before our smokescreen could cover us, all hell broke loose.

We were hit several times. I was on the after gun, which was on a 'bandstand' raised some three feet from the deck ... The shell that did the damage to us on the gun hit the searchlight tower just 'forrard' of the bandstand and when it exploded it threw the whole gun completely on its side; shield, mounting, the lot.

I was slung over with it and it was quite some time before I managed to get clear. When I eventually got out I found that all the rest of the gun's crew had been killed; some blown almost to pieces.

It was then that I felt conscious of a pain in my leg. Taking my shoe off, I found it was full of blood – and I fainted.[7]

By 3.25 next morning men were wondering if battle would be resumed. 'Thinking of meeting the Huns again, shall we?' wrote Jeames. But during the night the High Seas Fleet passed astern of the British and made its way back to its bases. As the sun rose the sight was not pleasant:

During the day we passed through hundreds, aye thousands of dead, friend and foe alike, some clinging together, others in small boats, could anyone live in such a fight? ... We have come safely through the biggest naval action ever known. Thank God

As the fleet arrived back at Scapa, most of the men were still in the dark about the result:

We on the lower deck had no means of telling the outcome of the Jutland battle, and we were quite confident that the German Fleet had been sent to the bottom ... But now, back at Scapa, amidst the bustle of re-fuelling, reports were fluttering through that the honours were with the Germans, and that we had suffered a moral defeat. It was beyond belief, and we concluded that the news was German-inspired; but it did have a somewhat chilling effect on our self-confidence.[8]

In fact the British, despite their superior numbers, had lost three battlecruisers against one German battlecruiser and one predreadnought battleship; eleven other ships against nine, and 6,090 men against 2,550. But the Germans had fled from the scene, and their plan to trap an isolated squadron of the British fleet had failed miserably. Arguments about who really won at Jutland, and whose fault it was that the British had not been more triumphant, would split the navy for the next twenty years.

## THE SUBMARINE WAR

The Germans experimented with 'unrestricted' submarine warfare (attacks on merchant ships without warning) in 1915. One early reaction was to use Q-ships, disguised warships that would only reveal their true nature after a U-boat surfaced to attack them by gunfire. Stan Smith was posted to one at Hartlepool, and he and his fellow crew members found themselves in frequent conflict with the locals because they were obviously of military age but not wearing uniform. The ship itself was not comfortable:

> The unwieldy old vessel would plough up and down the length of England in the trade routes. Her screw and rudder were only one third in the water, and, although she had ballast, she would spin and yaw all over the place in a strong wind and a decent sea.
>
> Food was not good, either. We only carried fresh provisions for five days and after that we would be on corned beef and biscuits ...
>
> The routine had us doing about ten to twelve days at sea at a stretch before going in to coal and water. Coaling was quite easy because we would go under the chute.

There were many ingenious devices to fool the enemy. One of the crew was dressed as a woman and had to hang washing on the forecastle line. Containers of explosives were arranged around the ship to be ignited while under attack and thus give the impression of hits when under shellfire.[9]

Able Seaman Hempenstall was drafted to *Baralong*:

> We had two 12-pdr guns on each quarter, and later a stern chaser ... We had name boards with various names painted on them, and national flags,

Greek, Spanish, etc. to suit the name of the ship we were operating. If we had the name board Ulysses S Grant up we would fly the American flag. Sometimes we would repaint the funnel at night with different shipping line colours.

*Baralong* was involved in a very controversial incident in August 1915, as the steamer *Nicosian*, carrying a load of mules, was sinking ahead of her:

> The alarm bell sounded, and we closed up to the guns, lying on deck out of sight ... The order to clear away the guns was given the US flag came down, the name boards were dropped, and the White ensign was hoisted. As we cleared the Nicosia, the submarine came in view. He fired a shot across our bow to stop us, and that was the last round he fired.
>
> Our first 12-pdr Lyddite shell hit his conning tower, exploding. The Marines positioned round the ship where they could get the best shots opened fire with their rifles scattering the submarine's crew, who dived over the side. We fired until there was nothing to fire at. It didn't last long, the nose-fused Lyddite soon put a stop to that.

The marines then shot most of the survivors from *U-24*, perhaps believing they were armed and incensed by reports of German atrocities including the sinking of the liner *Lusitania*, and apparently encouraged by their officers. Hempenstall did not take part, but was not unhappy about it: 'The RN ratings supported them, and would have done the same if given the opportunity. We didn't think killing U-boat crews a big issue, it was perfectly reasonable.'[10] No one was punished for the incident. It was used by German propaganda, and made U-boat captains far more wary – they now tended to sink on sight by torpedo rather than surfacing to use gunfire.

The Germans gave up unrestricted warfare under pressure from neutrals and especially the United States, but after their lack of success at Jutland it was revived. With a far greater number of U-boats available, it would cause the biggest threat of the war to the British. To counter it, many different types of vessel were used in patrols and as convoy escorts, including trawlers, motor launches and destroyers. One specially built type was the P-boat, a kind of utility destroyer with a very low freeboard, a tight turning circle and a resemblance to a submarine in silhouette. 'Clinker Knocker' joined *P 47* in 1917:

> Everything pertaining to the engines was of Lilliputian proportions; even us who had served in destroyers were amazed by the toy-like smallness of everything in both engine-rooms. The ship in appearance looked like a submarine, and at sea nothing more than a conning tower-like superstructure would be visible from a distance. The funnel was built into the superstructure, from which the stern tapered away like the tail of a fish. The bridge, with its short stumpy mast, constituted the fore part of the superstructure, and on a small platform in front of the bridge was a business-like four-inch gun. The bows were equipped with a deadly-looking ram, and it would be bad for any U-boat to make the acquaintance of it.[11]

Petty Officer E. F. Locke found his name on the notice board in Chatham Barracks and was sent to join *P 29* at Hartlepool. He expected something new but was disappointed to find her armed only with an old 4-inch gun and two equally old fixed torpedo tubes. Escorting a small convoy off Start Point on the south coast of England in August 1917, he felt helpless when a ship was lost:

> I heard dull report to starboard, and thought it was distant gun-fire, the look-out man (Rowden AB) at once reported ship torpedoed on starboard bow.
>     I went up to him, and borrowed his glasses and picked out the ship struck about 1½ miles away. We turned towards her at full speed, but had not gone far when it became clear that she was sinking rapidly, her forecastle already being awash; a minute later and her stern rose to a nearly vertical position, and without any hesitation she dived beneath the surface, an explosion occurring, probably her boilers bursting; as she disappeared two dark objects probably boats with the crew in them were seen to leave the ship and get clear, and must have been picked up by the P-boat nearest to them, by now it was quite dark. The submarine had done its work at the best time for them, between the lights and had probably gone to the bottom till the morning.[12]

One ship of the convoy turned and made for land without orders and had to be pulled up. Two more had lost contact, so only one ship was escorted into Plymouth that night.

From 1915 the Admiralty began to concentrate on the hydrophone, a passive listening device, as a means of detecting a submarine underwater. It was hampered by the fact that a submarine's electric motor made very little noise, that there were strong currents and tides making their own noise in most parts of the United Kingdom, and that any submarine noise would be blotted out by other ship noises, including the one in which it was mounted. For that reason most of the early hydrophones were shore based, in crucial areas such as the Firth of Forth and Harwich, though 25 stations had been set up round the coast and in Italy and Malta by the end of the war. The scope of the instrument was increased in the second half of 1917 when the fish hydrophone was introduced. It could be operated from a ship that was was barely making steerage way, with equipment rigged out on a spar just ahead of the bow.

Hydrophone listeners were selected from among RNVR recruits in the depot at Crystal Palace but, in the early days, after the better-established gunnery, signalling and wireless branches had taken their pick. They obviously needed good hearing, but also the ability to assess the direction from which the sound was coming, to pick out one sound against a mass of noise and to detect the difference in sound intensity. Out of 6,200 men initially selected, only 570 eventually passed all the tests. Several training stations were set up, including Hawkcraig on the Firth of Forth, Granton across the estuary and HMS *Sarepta* at Portland on the south coast. Training was carried out in four stages. Lectures were given in the theory of sound, then the trainees listened to gramophone records of underwater noises, and for the third stage they listened at a shore station. After that they went to sea in a motor launch to be tested practically. Altogether 2,731 ratings were trained in the Forth or by travelling parties in addition to 590 trained at Portland.

By the middle of 1918 it was planned to fit hydrophones to 'all sorts and sizes of ships, including capital ships, armed liners and merchant ships, a much wider field than now obtains'. At this point the Admiralty became worried that virtually all hydrophone listeners were RNVR or HO men and that there would not even be the nucleus of a branch once the war was over. Furthermore, there were very few leading seamen and petty officers with the necessary skills. A total of 42 continuous service ratings were to be selected for training, though it was recognized that it might be unfair to pick out boys and youths when there was no actual branch to put them in. The training was incomplete when the war was finished. In any case, the art of submarine detection was in its adolescence, and a new instrument, the echo-sounding asdic, was already on the way. The setting up of a proper anti-submarine branch had to wait for some years yet.

From 1916 the depth-charge was established as the main means of destroying a submerged U-boat. Great faith was placed in its large explosive power, even though methods of aiming it were still primitive. Leading Seaman John McConnel of the trawler *Whitefriars* describes the dropping of some, in the path of a submarine that was already believed to be damaged:

> As we got closer I took particular notice of the oil that was rising and as we got right over the place I could smell it very strongly. The Lieut. then order[ed] the 'A' type depth charge to be dropped. We steamed around until we came over the spot again. This time there were large quantities of oil rising to the surface and numerous large bubbles. The 'Cambria' spoke to us telling us that he had struck something which grated right along his port side. Lieut Irvine then said he would drop the second charge as it was a new type of charge. I went off to see if it was properly set to xx feet depth. It exploded about 13 second[s] after it was dropped and I noticed and called the guns crew to observe that there was a very large mass of thick oil which almost resembled the bilge oil of a steamboat.[13]

## DESTROYERS

Many sailors still preferred destroyers, which were now larger and able to undertake long voyages, even if they were badly affected by rough weather. According to an aged chief petty officer reminiscing from the time of the next war, it was

> a pretty rough life. I've 'ad good times in destroyers, even in the last war. On quiet days you sit up on your gun and watch or read or smoke in the sun. But you don't get many quiet days. Either the sea's so rough you can't stand, or you're out on some job or other and have to keep your eyes skinned. No, you'll find it hard all right.[14]

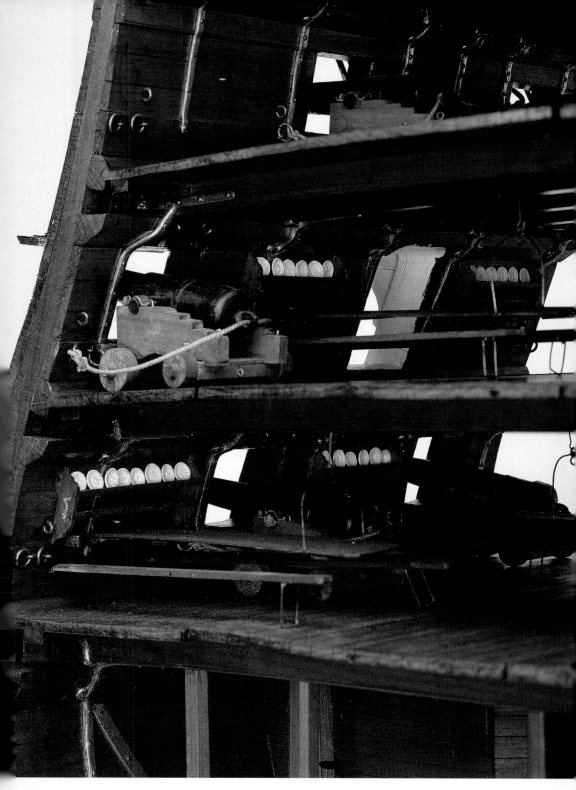

A sectional model of the ship of the line *Queen* of 1839, showing the crew's mess tables and plates between the guns. She was converted to a screw ship in 1859. (National Maritime Museum D7870)

Queen Victoria visits the fleet in 1853 on board the paddle yacht *Victoria and Albert*, with the new screw battleship *Duke of Wellington* to the left. (National Maritime Museum PAF 6120)

An old 74-gun ship, *Gloucester*, serving as a receiving ship at Chatham *c*.1880. (National Maritime Museum PW 2025)

Sailors manning guns on shore at the bombardment of Sebastopol in 1854. (National Maritime Museum PW 4906)

HMS *Edinburgh*, a turret ship of 1882, has torpedo nets out in an exercise against torpedo boats in 1887. The boats have the spar torpedo, which exploded on contact with the ship under attack. (National Maritime Museum BHC 1674)

Sailors are roused ungraciously from the hammocks during an night alarm exercise. (National Maritime Museum PW 3742)

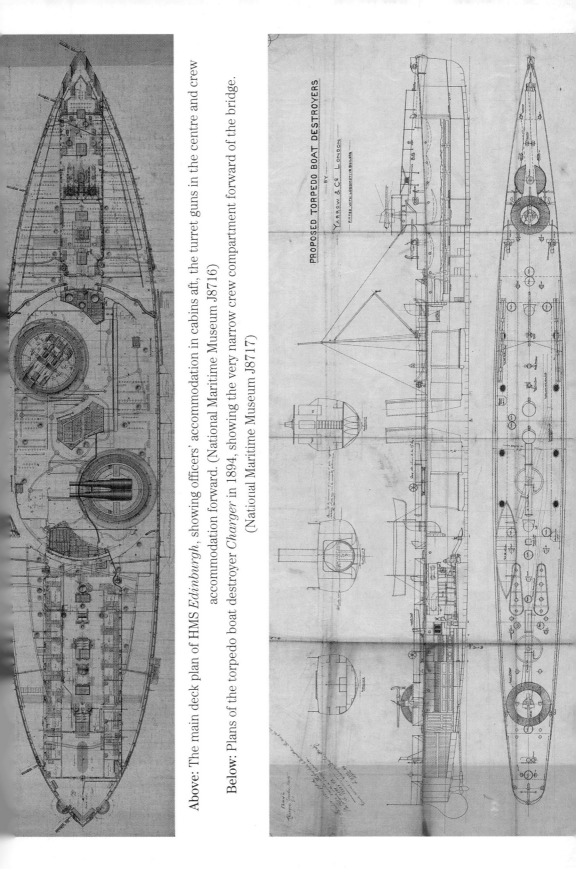

Above: The main deck plan of HMS *Edinburgh*, showing officers' accommodation in cabins aft, the turret guns in the centre and crew accommodation forward. (National Maritime Museum J8716)

Below: Plans of the torpedo boat destroyer *Charger* in 1894, showing the very narrow crew compartment forward of the bridge. (National Maritime Museum J8717)

PROPOSED TORPEDO BOAT DESTROYERS

BY

YARROW & C.º LONDON

FITTED WITH LOCOMOTIVE BOILERS

Battleships and cruisers engage the Turkish forts in the Dardanelles in 1915. (National Maritime Museum PW 0900)

Much depended on the character of the coxswain:

Men of my type who could stick the sea always volunteered for destroyers. I never liked big ship life. There was more discipline in a big ship. In a destroyer you got no Naval Police, the only man aboard to discipline you is the coxswain. He's a busy man, he's a seaman, he's the purser, he takes the ship in and out of harbour, and looks after the charts. Everybody had his job to do. If he didn't do it, no one else did. We'd come in from the sea, and the captain would say, 'You can't go ashore for the weekend until the ship's cleaned up'. The ship would be spick and span before you left it. As soon as you'd done your job you were free to go.[15]

According to another seaman,

When you went to a small ship, like the *Thisbe* destroyer, with only seventy-eight people on board, you lived a different life, you counted for more as a person, than you did in a big ship, and the rules and regulations were not so strict. The man who's most responsible on a destroyer is the coxswain. He can make or mar the happiness of a ship. On the *Thisbe*, I went on after the *Lord Nelson*, we had a very fine coxswain.[16]

## SUBMARINES

British submarines were never likely to be as significant a strategic weapon as U-boats, because the Germans were far less dependent on the sea. Nevertheless, 74 were in service at the beginning of the war, 147 more were commissioned during it, and 54 were lost. The E-class, introduced in 1912, was a great improvement on earlier boats because they were expected to operate for much longer periods. As Telegraphist Halter noted, 'In *E17* we did have a heads right aft. One of the exhaust pipes ran through it and you got boiled if you went in there. But because we'd got so little food and drink you could go.'[17]

Despite the free and easy lifestyle, there was less role for the lower deck hero, for in battle only the captain could see what was going on.

When a submarine is submerged, her captain alone is able to see what is taking place; the success of the enterprise and the safety of the vessel depend on his skill and nerve and the prompt, precise execution of his orders by the officers and men under his command.[18]

It could quickly turn into a scene of horror if the submarine was sunk by enemy action or accident, and only a few lived to tell the tale. When the large steam submarine *K-13* sank in trials in the Gareloch in 1917, Professor Hillhouse of Glasgow University was on board and calculated exactly how long the oxygen would last before everyone died.

> As the air in our submerged prison became more impregnated with carbonic acid, so did our breathing become more and more difficult, and we had to inhale and exhale with painful rapidity. For some the process was only carried out under great pain and difficulty. Many found standing the easiest posture, while our good pilot, Captain Duncan, during almost the whole course of our imprisonment, walked to and fro in the control room as though still in command on the bridge of a surface craft. The great majority, however, were rendered more or less inert and apathetic, and lay down anywhere and everywhere, half asleep, half awake, and breathing stertorously. There were a few berths, and each of these usually had two or three occupants ...[19]

Petty Officer Moth commented more tersely, 'What a bloody rotten way to die.'[20] But the boat was salvaged, and most of the crew were saved.

Petty Officer William Brown was a survivor when *E-41* sank after a collision. 'He was by himself, in almost complete darkness, with the gradually rising water, receiving electric shocks and, towards the end, suffering from the effects of chlorine gas and a badly crushed hand ...' At last on his seventh attempt at escape,

> I now considered it impossible to attempt to blow myself out by means of internal pressure. Therefore I knocked the dogs off the deadlight and allowed the Boat to flood as quickly as possible, with the idea of flooding the Engine Room completely and then raising [the] hatch and escaping ... I allowed the Engine Room to flood till the water was up to the covering of

the hatch. I then raised the hatch and escaped, rising to the surface and being picked up by HMS *Firedrake*.[21]

## THE AIR SERVICE

Aviation had made great strides since the Wright brothers first flew in 1903, though it was almost untested in war, or indeed for any practical purpose. Just before the start of the war the Admiralty issued orders for the manning of the Royal Naval Air Service, which would soon sever its links with the army's Royal Flying Corps. As well as taking on officers as pilots, it soon began to recruit men for the new rating of air mechanic. Men already in the navy were invited to volunteer, but only youngsters with a certain amount of experience and no non-substantive rates. Petty officers would be drafted in, but only until the air service was mature enough to produce its own. The terms were not particularly attractive: men would be returned to general service after four years and would not be eligible for petty officer rates before that. And the Admiralty clearly had no faith in the lower deck to produce the kind of men they wanted, for it anticipated large numbers of failures: 'This will not necessarily imply that any blame is attributable to the man. The special nature of the duties peculiar to the Air Service renders essential a very high standard of mental and physical fitness, which individuals may not be capable of maintaining, although there may be no fault found with their character and zeal.'

The Admiralty placed more hopes on recruits 'from the shore'. They advertised for men with previous experience of aircraft, though these were few at the time. For the wooden and fabric-covered biplanes of the age, it could also use carpenters, cabinet makers, boat builders and fabric workers. For engine work it was prepared to train fitters, motor mechanics, coppersmiths, electricians, cycle mechanics and motor drivers. Those with high trade qualifications might be entered at the CPO rate, as with engine room artificers. Others would start as air mechanics first, second and third class, equivalent to leading, able and ordinary seamen. There were prospects of promotion to petty officer and chief petty officer air mechanic. As a result the service had 708 ratings at the beginning of the war, rising to 41,597 by November 1917. Less than a thousand of these were from the pre-war reserve, the vast majority of the rest having been recruited from the shore.[22] Henry Allingham had initially promised his mother that, as an only son, he would not get involved in the war. She died of cancer, and in 1915 he was inspired to join the RNAS after seeing an aircraft circling an aerodrome near Chingford in Essex.[23]

According to the orders of 1914, a new entrant would go to the naval depot at Sheerness for 'instruction in naval discipline and customs', for it was felt that their early instruction should be 'freed from the distraction of the sight and sound of aircraft making flights'. During six weeks there they would be selected for work on aircraft, seaplanes, airships or kite balloons, and then most would be sent to nearby Eastchurch, at that time the centre of naval aviation, for practical instruction. They would learn about the internal combustion engine and the theory of flight and do practical work on the care and maintenance of engines, on adjustments and repairs to aircraft, aircraft handling and the use of tools, as well as naval subjects such as signalling and boat work.[24] Air riggers were responsible for the 'truing' of the fuselage of their aircraft, for adjusting the numerous wires that braced the wings together so that they were set at the correct angle of incidence. They adjusted the controls and fitted propellers. They were told that 'the pilot's life, the speed and climb of the aeroplane, its control and general efficiency in flight, and its duration as a useful machine all depends upon the rigger. Consider that while the engine may fail the pilot may still glide safely to earth *but* if the aeroplane fails, then all is lost.' When the engine was started, one air mechanic was stationed on each wingtip with a good grasp of the outer strut, while at least two more sat on the tail. Another mechanic came forward to start the engine with 'one good downward swing of the propeller blade', after which he had to stand clear. The pilot checked that everything was all right with his fitter and rigger, then the senior mechanic checked that everything was clear, with no other aircraft taking off, and the flight could begin.[25]

Henry Allingham was sent to Sheerness for assessment in August 1915:

I was joined there by 14 other hopefuls, including two Americans, two Australians and two new Zealanders. That first night we were each given two blankets and told to sleep on the floor of a hut ... But the next morning we were allocated beds. And, although the first week was boring, the remaining three weeks at the camp were a real challenge. We did written and practical tests. I felt that in some areas of maintenance, the RNAS was not as advanced as its engineering equivalents in civvy street.[26]

Apart from their early training in 'naval discipline and customs', the air mechanics did not necessarily have much contact with the traditional lower deck. They wore the 'fore and aft' rig uniform of the domestic, medical and administrative branches, with a special cap badge. They were issued with breeches and puttees like soldiers, for they did not always serve at sea. They were not subject to the same snobbery and excessive discipline as the regular navy – Allingham was amused when his commanding officer at Great Yarmouth, 'Snakey' Oliver, ordered young officers into the water to help recover an aircraft. When some Australian ratings failed to salute an officer they went unpunished: 'if Snakey had got to hear of the exchange, I doubt they would have got into trouble. In that way the men of the RNAS were a new breed.'[27]

The orders of 1914 stated that 'the selection of a man for service in the Naval Wing does not necessarily imply that the man will be trained as a pilot', though up to 2s a day extra was allowed for men who qualified. In fact, very few ratings would do so, for nearly all pilots were officers, mostly recruited directly from civil life. So too were most observers, for the navy preferred the 'back-seater' to take responsibility for sighting and deciding when to attack. This did not stop ratings getting into the air, especially in multi-seat aircraft – bombers, flying boats and airships – which were used in large numbers by the RNAS. Henry Allingham describes the experience:

If it was available, you'd smear Vaseline on your face to protect it from the cold weather. If that wasn't available, then it was whale oil or engine grease because you were flying in an open cockpit with only a small windshield for protection. You wore gloves to protect you from frostbite. It was so noisy. I do remember the deafening throb and the chap on the ground shouting, 'Chocks away!' Then we were up, the freezing wind gushing past my face as we climbed steeply, my heart in my stomach as we banked. It was a great adventure for a bloke like me.[28]

One officer commented:

> I think a word ought to be said for the observer ratings who accompanied
> us on patrols. They were of all ages – from Chief Petty Officer Heywood,
> who was a naval rating of many years service ... down to the youngest
> apprentice signaller who came to us out of the training schools. It was their
> duty to accompany as passenger any pilot on patrol; which, in view of the
> very mixed batch of pilots we had, was a serious undertaking indeed.
> Nearly all of them got 'ditched' at one time or another. It must be
> remembered that the passenger had no control over the machine if the
> pilot failed, and ... there were some of the younger ones whom it could
> have been no pleasure to accompany.[29]

But even an expert pilot could get into trouble, as Allingham found:

> Everything looked all right as we were coming down but as we touched
> the ground the nose dipped. We lost half our undercarriage and the plane
> ended up half buried in the ground. Major Cadbury and I scrambled out
> quickly. I heard a torrent of expletives from the major that included words
> I've never heard before or since. Parachutes had been invented but they
> were never issued to crews in the RNAS.[30]

The rating of aerial gunlayer was formally established by the end of 1916,
though in practice ratings had operated as machine-gunners in aircraft since
the beginning of the war.[31] W. Jones shot down six enemy aircraft in this
role.[32] Wireless operators were also needed in the air, and the training of the
first twenty warrant officers and ratings began on board HMS *Campania*
early in 1916. Though only fifteen of them were successful, they formed the
nucleus of the Grand Fleet's 'W/T/Operator Observers'.[33] By 1918 it was
becoming increasingly difficult to find enough officer observers, and it was
proposed to train more ratings, but at the same time the intake of aerial
gunlayers was declining. 'A large number are perfectly useless and in many
cases do not want to go in the air again after their first flight. The material
for this important work is slowly getting worse and I have already pointed out
that unless steps are taken to get young, healthy and active ratings from the
Navy or some other source the situation will become serious.'[34]

The RNAS operated airships in patrols in the North Sea and other areas, though Britain was a long way behind Germany in the development of the rigid airship, and nearly all the ones operated by Britain were non-rigid and therefore small and slow. The Sea Scout or SS, the original 'blimp', was improvised at the beginning of the war and employed an officer as pilot, and usually another officer as observer. The Sea Scout Zero of 1917 used an officer pilot and rating wireless operator and engineer. The Coastal class was larger, with officer pilot and co-pilot and rating coxswain, wireless operator and engineer. The division of labour was generally that the pilot controlled height (a complex matter involving the trim of the gas as well as use of the elevators) and the coxswain steered. Up to this point all the crew were in open cockpits, usually in adapted aircraft fuselages. The North Sea class of 1918 had some enclosed accommodation and a double crew. It could operate for up to 24 hours, and a watch system was adopted, rather like on a ship. The standard crew was a pilot, co-pilot, two coxswains, two wireless operators, two engineers and two gunners.[35] Crews of Coastal and North Sea airships had the chance to log up some very long tallies of flying hours. When *C9* landed at Mullion airship station in Cornwall in 45-knot winds after a 10½ hour flight, her coxswain, Petty Officer Charles Regan, had already flown 840 hours in the craft. Petty Officer G. N. Mills had logged 900 hours as wireless operator.[36]

Landing an airship involved most of the ground crew and could be quite a dangerous operation in itself, according to Air Mechanic Bert Adams:

When it was about 500 feet above us, the airship's crew threw out a landing line. We caught hold of it and started to pull it down. The rope had wooden toggles so that you could get both hands on it and pull. There would be perhaps fifty men on the starboard side and fifty on port all pulling down. Well, sometimes the wind would catch the airship and if the pulling was not greater than the lift, then you'd find yourself hanging on going up and up. People would panic and drop off. But of course the more who dropped off the higher it would go, with others hanging on for dear life. In one case one of our men held on too long, drifted off and was killed when he could hang on no longer.[37]

Seaplanes, both floatplanes and flying boats, were operated from shore stations. Chief Petty Officer Frederick Tadman was the engineer of a Curtiss H-12 Large America flying boat in June 1917, along with two officer pilots and a rating wireless operator. A submarine was sighted off the Scilly Isles and attacked. It retaliated by firing three bursts at the aircraft with its machine-gun, but the pilot was satisfied as it sank by the bows. Then he saw CPO Tadman signalling frantically and pointing to the starboard engine. Its radiator was leaking fast and the engine would soon overheat. Tadman climbed out on to the wing between the spars and bracing wires, and held a cloth over the leak so that the aircraft did not have to land in the rough seas and made it back to base. He was awarded the Conspicuous Gallantry Medal.[38]

The main job of the patrols was to spot submarines and either sink them or force them to 'keep their heads down'. This required a good lookout by all the crew, and a captain was enjoined to 'keep his crew interested in the work, and to pay the greatest respect to what they sight and report, not to discourage them by hasty denunciation, as crews have often been treated for pointing out as a submarine a trawler or a whale'.[39] It was very rare to spot the periscope of a submerged submarine, but for some reason seagulls seemed to be attracted to them in the Atlantic, but not in the North Sea. A submarine might well be sighted underwater in the clear waters of the Mediterranean and even in the Western Approaches to the English Channel, but it was highly unlikely in the far muddier waters of the North Sea. The best hope was to spot one on the surface and attack before it had time to dive. Leading Air Mechanic T. W. Thirwell was the first to spot a conning tower on patrol off Cornwall in *C22* in February 1917, about a mile away in poor visibility. He watched as the first bomb was dropped on it, but it did not explode. His was attention was diverted by a leak in the petrol tank, but he was able to see the second bomb dropped where the submarine had been seen. The bomb exploded a little way under the water, sending up bubbles of oil along with water, and it was believed that a submarine had been damaged if not sunk.[40] But often the main effect on the submarine was to the morale of the crew. Leading Mechanic Bill Argent was in a flying boat that spotted a U-boat on the surface in June 1917: 'The captain obviously panicked because he gave the order to "down hatch" and abandoned some of the crew on the deck.'[41]

Back at the base, it was hard and dangerous work getting a seaplane back on to a ramp:

> The waders, clad especially for the occasion, pushed the trolley further down the slipway into the sea. The tide frequently caught it and carried it to the side. The work was hard for them – almost armpit deep in the water – and if the trolley went over the edge of the slipway it had to be retrieved before another start could be made. The waders had one of the worst jobs at a seaplane station, and they were very 'stout fellows', for imagine this job, at night, in winter, in a four-foot sea (no uncommon thing at Yarmouth) and a cross-wind, both of which rocked the boat in all directions.[42]

A seaplane also needed a great deal of help:

> The petrol party arrive. There are 300 gallons to be sieved through chamois leather into her empty tanks, for the petrol is poured through the leather to prevent any water from getting into the petrol tanks, because failure of the petrol system in rough weather might easily result in the total loss of the boat at sea.
>
> A party of engineers look to cleaning the petrol and oil filters – the magnetos and valve springs are overhauled. Aircraft riggers run over the controls, examine the wires, the fabric, the fittings. Armourers look to the guns, clean them, and replenish the ammunition trays. The working party wipe down the hull and clean the inside of the boat.
>
> One or two hours later the shed doors clang. The Duty Petty Officer reports to the Duty Officer – 'Everything all correct, Sir.' 'Thank you, is everything ready for the dawn patrol?' 'Yes, Sir.'[43]

The RNAS was merged into the new Royal Air Force on 1 April 1918, but it took a year longer to absorb the airship service. Despite this, Henry Allingham still considered himself 'a Royal Navy man'.[44] A huge amount of aerial experience was lost to the navy, but a certain amount of naval tradition was absorbed by the RAF – for example, a flight sergeant was commonly known as 'chiefy', after his equivalent in the RNAS, the CPO.

## THE GROWTH OF THE NAVY

By October 1917 there were more than 420,000 men serving in the navy and marines, but nearly a third of them were in various branches that had little connection with the lower deck as it was usually understood. There were 3,000 coastguard plus 17,000 marines afloat and an equal number ashore. The air service took up a total of 46,000. There were a similar number in the Trawler Service, who certainly had their share of sea time but who had never been regular Royal Navy sailors and knew little of naval discipline. And there were still nearly 21,000 officers and men in the Royal Naval Division, most of who would have welcomed sea service but were unlikely to see it. More than a third of the men in the navy were not really part of it in the usual sense.[45]

The seamen were restored as the largest branch of the 'real' navy. With 111,692 men estimated for 1918, they had overtaken the stokers, who numbered only 68,977 as a result of the increased use of oil fuel. Nearly three-quarters of the seamen were 'active service' regulars, recalled pensioners or Royal Fleet Reserve men who had already served time in the navy. Of the rest, there were more than 10,000 RNR and 18,000 RNVR who had avoided the Western Front to find a place at sea, or at least close to it. Even more of the stokers, 78 per cent, were regulars or ex-regulars. Seven thousand of them were RNR; very few were RNVR. For the future, there were 3,853 seamen boys under training on 1 October 1917, not very different from the peacetime figure. The lower deck, despite three years of war, was still largely composed of regular seamen.

## THE WRNS

In 1914 the energy that had gone into the suffragette movement was largely diverted towards the war effort, and women found new roles in factories as well as augmenting older ones in offices, schools and kitchens. It was the army that first put them into military uniform with the Women's Auxiliary Army Corps, to free soldiers from domestic and office work. At first, the Admiralty asked to use the services of some of them but got tired of waiting for the War Office to reply and formed the Women's Royal Naval Service – a fortunate choice of title which soon led to the acronym 'Wren'.

It began its formal existence early in 1918, but already it was planning to lose some of its members to the new Royal Air Force. Originally women were to be 'immobile', living at home and not liable to transfer to a different base, but soon 'mobile' members were recruited to live in hostels, barracks and converted hotels and schools. As well as officers (who wore light blue stripes instead of gold) they were supervised by section leaders, chief section leaders and superintending section leaders, the equivalent of petty officers. The ratings' uniform consisted of a rather loose dress with a seaman's collar and a hat that was said to be based on a yachting cap. Some complained that the more formal officers' uniform was more attractive, though it was dominated by a very wide-brimmed hat.

There was no question of women working afloat on a regular basis, and indeed they were proud of their enigmatic motto, 'never at sea'. Instead they trained as clerks, typists, telephonists, cooks, waitresses, sailmakers and drivers. They also cleaned boilers in some naval bases, acted as porters and repaired mine nets or gas masks. Scandals over immorality in the WAAC tended to reflect on the WRNS, but it tried hard to establish a separate identity. The authorities tended to be compassionate with women who got pregnant or contracted VD. The slogan 'free a man for the fleet' was popular in the country but not necessarily with the men concerned, who were often 'barrack stanchions' at the naval bases who had spent the last few years contriving ways out of active service. One WRNS driver, let loose on a Bedford ambulance found that 'every job taken over by a Wren meant that a man was released for sea service – and by 1918 few men had any stomach for further fighting. So we were discouraged; this took such forms as disconnected terminals, air let out of tyres, water in the petrol tanks, and so on.' But often the men were won over eventually. 'In spite of some prejudice against women taking the place of Service men, everyone in that office, and in fact the whole ship's company, was most respectful, kind and helpful.'[46]

At its peak the WRNS had a strength of 438 officers and 5,054 ratings, and had built up a remarkable esprit de corps. It was disbanded with the end of the war, but its members often kept in touch and would be ready to form the core of a new service two decades later.

## DISCONTENT AND MUTINY

The early wartime wave of patriotism was gradually overtaken as the men had to cope with more pressing realities. It did not take long for William Jenkins and his fellow reservists on board the cruiser *Leviathan* to become unhappy after their recall was extended indefinitely due to the war. As they hoisted some bullocks on board on 21 August 1914, he noted that they 'had the appearance of being tired of life, a natural existing state aboard here, all hands living on bread and "suck"'. He had already become disgruntled with Captain Hill ('Marcus' to the crew behind his back), who had almost burst into tears when announcing that war was likely. He made things worse early in 1915 when he made a speech complaining that the crew's letters home, as opened by the censor, were far too gloomy. Later he 'had the audacity to order men to pull their trousers up to see if they had any socks on ... treating us more like training ship boys than married men with families'.

A new commander had taken over in November and was instantly known as 'Bully Pierson' – in December at Cromarty he had the men taking their sea-boots off while washing the deck in freezing temperatures to avoid 'disturbing the admiral in his beauty sleep'. But the new first lieutenant, 'Odd Trick' or 'The Human Hairpin', was even worse. He supervised work on the foredeck, though he 'knew as much about anchors and cables as an elephant does about deer stalking'. He disappeared in rough weather, and it was alleged that he was seasick. In port he searched the corners of the messdecks with his electric torch and proclaimed, 'he would give us no rest until our kettles shone ...' Jenkins complained: 'Verily our prayers not answered, viz, that we should be reading a burial service at sea, with the 'Odd Trick' sewn up in the hammock.' [47]

At the end of 1914, Ordinary Seaman P. Rook of the battleship *Canopus* off the coast of Brazil was already disgruntled and wrote:

Christmas Day (at Sea). Signal from Admiral wishing us a very happy Christmas, which proved a very miserable one. Our officers had a very good one, best of food, drinking and singing all day, while the men were on corned beef and hard biscuits and manning the guns all night. Personally I felt very sad that day, as I recalled the happy one I had on the previous Christmas ...

27th (Sunday) ... Took 1,100 tons from coal from collier (Indian transport), finished at 11 pm. This has been our hardest coaling as we were working in the sun and the temperature was 90 degrees in the shade; quite a lot of men collapsed during the day, and our captain expressed his gratitude by telling us that the coal must damn well come in faster, if not he would walk round himself and we would know what that meant – yes, we all knew what it meant, he would get his suit dirty, and could not drink so much whisky.

4th. ... Whisky boat hove in sight, our officer went on board. She proved to be a mail boat from Montevideo to England; loaded our cutter with bacon, turkey, butter, cigarettes and whisky; all got on board and carefully watched to see that it all went aft to the officers – nothing for the boys.[48]

Sailors always grumble, but soon it began to grow into something more. Jenkins's comrades in *Leviathan* contented themselves with occasional cat-calls and hooting, for which selected men were savagely punished. But by 1916 there were at least three known mutinies, in *Psyche* when the stokers refused duty, in the auxiliary ship *Teutonic* when eight men were court martialled after discontent over pay, and in the cruiser *Dartmouth* for refusal to carry out a punishment. There were yet more mutinies in 1917 – a relatively mild one in the battleship *Resolution* in the Grand Fleet, when two men lost good conduct medals and badges for supporting an anonymous petition, collective disobedience in the sloop *Fantome*, for which seven men were given detention, and non-violent mutiny in the same ship, for which a dozen stokers were given twelve months' hard labour. More serious was the affair in the minelayer *Amphitrite*, when 62 men refused duty in protest against excessive punishments, and eight of them were sentenced to between eighteen months and two years' hard labour.[49] Since wartime censorship prevented the publishing of details of any that did not come to court martial, it is quite likely that there were many more.

By this time it was much more than a question of failure of leadership by individual officers. Early in the war, patriotism had papered over many of the cracks in society, but some were beginning to show again. Suffragettes had diverted their energies into war work and improved the position of women that way, but the Irish issue was revived with the Easter Rising of 1916, during which the patrol boat *Helga* shelled the rebels.

Trade union leaders were co-opted into the war effort, but this led to a gap that was exploited by shop stewards' movements in cities like Glasgow and Sheffield. Prices and rents rose rapidly in wartime, and government pay was inflexible – many sailors' and soldiers' families were living in near-poverty as munitions workers next door made huge wages from overtime. The Russian Revolution of 1917 found an echo in Britain, and leaders like John Maclean in Glasgow had to be imprisoned to reduce the threat. The sailors were not totally insulated from society at large, and this discontent was reflected in the navy, to add to the sailors' own grievances.

One problem was that there were many different types of ratings on different engagements and plenty of scope for jealousy. The writers were perhaps the best-educated men on the lower deck, but promotion was very slow. Around 1,200 men were brought in as accountant officers 'from the shore' or from shipping companies, whereas experienced writers had no prospect of a commission. The Admiralty responded by offering commissions to one or two a year, until a total of ten was reached. The continuous service men complained that promotion to petty officer was often offered disproportionately to RNR and RNVR men. The Admiralty replied reasonably that it could not afford to promote too many CS men or it would be left with a surplus after the war. Lionel Yexley agreed with this: 'If you were to fill all these positions with active service ratings look at the fearful stagnation in lower deck promotion that would follow the war.'[50] Several issues were raised by James Hogge in Parliament in April 1917, and by October the Admiralty had offered a number of concessions. Pay would no longer be stopped when a man was in hospital for a long period; men who qualified for pensions during the war would now be paid them in addition to their wages; and substantive pay was increased by between $2d$ and $5d$ a day – but this was much less than the 50 per cent rise that lower deck petitions had demanded.

Perhaps the most important long-standing issue was that of payment for kit. Sailors were now issued with kit free on entry but had to pay for replacements. The obvious answer was to issue and replace uniform free, as was done in practically every other armed service in the world, and it was agreed at the Admiralty: 'Such a system would have the advantages of ensuring equality of treatment for all classes and avoiding any contentious questions as to the sufficiency of an allowance.' However, it might prove more expensive, and experience with the marines suggested that a man would have 'no inducement to take care of his clothing'. Furthermore, it would cut across naval tradition and might be resented by the lower deck. Chief petty officers, wearing class I uniform (collar and tie, with brass buttons), and writers, stewards and so on in class III (black buttons) nearly always bought them ashore in any case. Seamen and stokers in class II uniform often tailored their own clothes or had them made up by their messmates. It was decided to pay a kit allowance of £5 10s per annum for class II men and £7 for chiefs. Lionel Yexley agreed that it was 'admirable in every way', except that the payment was quarterly rather than annual, for payments tended to be seasonal.

> The man who has to pay out say £1 in one quarter and pockets 10/– on each of the other quarters will be dissatisfied because of what he has 'paid out'. The same man who has not had to 'pay out' at all during the year and only pockets say 1/– at the end of year will be satisfied because he will reckon he is in pocket.
>
> That is lower deck philosophy and lower deck psychology. You see if it does not work out at that.[51]

The Admiralty made sure that the ratings knew about all these concessions by having posters printed and hung up in every messdeck and depot. Perhaps it worked, for there were no major mutinies during 1918.

## THE ARMISTICE

The end of the war came suddenly with the German request for an armistice and was just as memorable as the beginning. 11 November began with normal routine for F. W. Turpin in the predreadnought battleship *Agamemnon* in the Mediterranean, until the news arrived. He wrote that, 'the greatest event of many centuries has occurred. An armistice with Germany our greatest enemy has been signed ...'[52] There was just as much excitement in the Grand Fleet that day: '8 pm. We learn that an armistice has been signed by Germany. All the foghorns of the fleet are blowing –

what a noise – search lights are burning, rockets, dancing, singing (and drinking?).'

*New Zealand* and other ships put to sea ten days later to meet the German High Seas Fleet, a large part of which had to surrender under the terms of the armistice:

21 Nov 1918

3 am, To sea, everything ready for action if they give any trouble we're ready

9 am We (Grand Fleet) met the Huns – no panic. 5 battle-cruisers, 9 battle-ships, 7 light cruisers and 49 destroyers have surrendered to us, it is a sight, they are made to steam in between our two lines of ships. We bring them to the Firth of Forth and anchor off Leith ...

22nd

Search parties sent aboard each Hun ship (ours being SMS *Derfflinger*) Crews very friendly, a lot of them have spent many years in America, some in England, before the war and can speak English, said they were glad it was all over, and if they knew it was coming to this, they would have done it two years ago ...

24th

Battle cruisers leave Largo Bay, Leith for Scapa, 1st BS as escort. I wonder what they'll think of that beautiful place, it's just the place for them.

Yeoman of Signals J. E. Attrill took part in the inspection of the battleships *Kaiser* and *König* on 9 December. He found that the fire-control instruments had been removed, and the turret machinery was nearly all electric. The ships were 'filthy smelling and hot and generally very unhealthy', but he excused that on the grounds that German sailors rarely had to live on board for long. He was disturbed by the attitudes he found on board. 'Some of the crew seem to be quite prepared to start building another navy with the object of BEATING us in the future.???? Some of them expressed the opinion that the German army had fought the whole nation and not been beaten.'[53]

# 9

# THE AFTERMATH OF WAR
# 1919–1925

## DEMOBILISATION

The first task after the Armistice was to reduce the navy to a peacetime level. In November 1918, 379,000 men were serving, excluding the Royal Naval Division. Of these, 235,000 were reservists, Hostilities Only or time-expired men whose engagement automatically ended with the war, and practically all of them were entitled to be discharged. It was not possible to release them instantly, and Admiral Beatty outlined the policy for the first batch of men to be released in January 1919. General demobilization had not yet been ordered, but 'demobilizers', whose assistance as civilians was required in the actual demobilisation process, and 'pivotal men', who were urgently needed in industry, would have early release whether a relief was available or not. Most ships were to be reduced in turn to three-fifths of their wartime complement, so eligible men could be released as soon as that happened. 'Contract letter men', those who had been promised employment with the employer they were serving with at the start of the war, would also be given priority. So too would those operating one-man businesses, provided their wives filled in the appropriate forms.

In the meantime the Admiralty had prepared a booklet 'to acquaint men about to be demobilised with the principles adopted for demobilisation of men of the Naval Service'. Seamen were cautioned that some of them would have to be kept on for clearing the seas of mines, and that would cause trouble later. The captain of each ship would choose the men according to certain principles:

After the 'Demobilisers' and 'pivotal men' have gone home he will make up his draft from men for whom he has received release slips, i.e. men for

241

whom definite jobs are known to be waiting. If he had thirty 'slip' men left in his ships those thirty men would go. If, however, he had say, forty, he would give preference to men whose Industrial Groups stood highest in the list of priority and to married men. In the same way, if he had only twenty 'slip' men he would make up the other ten from 'non-slip' men according to the priority of their Industrial Groups. In both cases he would include a proportion of men who are pensioners or time-expired pre-war active service ratings, whether they have jobs waiting for them cr not, or whether they belong to priority groups or not.

The last sentence was rather unclear, and the scheme as a whole might be criticized for giving too much priority to the needs of the navy and the country, as distinct from the men themselves. Moreover, it was largely a matter of chance whether one happened to be in a ship with a large or small proportion of men due for demobilization, or on foreign service, or retained for minesweeping duty.

By March 1920, only 700 reservists, HOs and time-expired men were still in service, mostly with the trawler reserve. Even that was not enough to get the navy down to a peacetime scale, and in November 1919 the Admiralty allowed free discharge to any ratings over eighteen years of age, except in certain technical and administrative branches.[1] The navy had had fewer demobilization problems than the army, where there were several mutinies over the issue, for the navy had a much higher proportion of regulars and no real conscripts. The main trouble came from a group of men in the Grand Fleet minesweepers, who refused to put to sea until they were paid a £2 per week bonus. But there was also a certain amount of disgruntlement among men who were kept on for other reasons. After a mutiny in HMS *Vindictive* in the Baltic, Captain Edgar Grace complained that the original order on discharges 'raised the hopes, and unsettled the work, of ratings of all descriptions by the rash offer of free discharge to all and sundry, made apparently in total disregard of the inevitable result'.[2]

## THE INTERVENTION IN RUSSIA

The biggest source of disaffection in the navy came from a rather different cause. It was Winston Churchill, now Secretary of State for War and Air, who urged intervention against the new Bolshevik regime in Russia, which he regarded as 'plague-bearing'. Naval forces were engaged in the north at Murmansk and Archangel, and in the Black Sea. They found themselves in a very complex situation in the Baltic, with Latvia, Lithuania, Estonia and Finland all trying to establish their independence against Russians and Germans. But there was no formal declaration of war, as the cabinet was not united behind Churchill, and the naval forces were left in a very ambiguous position. Moreover, the servicemen were looking forward to demobilization and had no wish to get involved in yet another conflict.

This led to a series of mutinies. The first one, at the end of 1918, was by Royal Marines, who were supposed to be a barrier against mutiny. The Sixth Battalion, at Murmansk, refused duty, and men were savagely punished by court martial. The crew of the gunboat *Cicala* refused to sail up the River Dvina, and Admiral Cowan had to threaten to fire on them. The men of the cruiser *Vindictive* demonstrated on the quarterdeck in Copenhagen after being refused leave, and two stokers tried to sabotage the engine room fans to prevent the ship sailing. And the crew of the flagship *Delhi* protested against poor food and locked themselves in the recreation area, as described by one of the officers:

Up the gangway tripped the trim little figure of Walter Cowan ... As he came over the side he barked out in his little nasal voice, 'Prepare for sea at once, please, Captain Mackworth; we are returning to Biorko.' Even the most loyal among the ship's company felt this was 'a bit 'ard.' No Christmas shopping, no run ashore, nothing but an immediate return to bloody Biorko. So when the Commander ordered, 'Both watches prepare ship for sea', the response was very poor; only about 25% of the ship's company obeyed the bugle.[3]

Among the men affected by mutiny was Herbert Greatwood, who had already had a hard war in destroyers and risen to leading seaman before he was sent to the Baltic:

After a while we came back and tied up at Queensferry and there was a long pier there and all the destroyers were there. The war was over. We'd just come back from Russia. All of a sudden we had an order 'Proceed with full dispatch to Russia.' 'We're not going back to Russia, the war has finished' they were saying. So I proceeded, and all the boys there, over the side. The Coppers tried to stop us. And the Coppers ran. So we got down to Edinburgh. We forged a pass and we come down to Euston and we were finally arrested by all the Y Division of the London Police. They were saying: 'Don't cause no trouble, Jack! Don't cause no trouble!'[4]

He was one of 44 men who made the journey out of about 90 who left the ships. They were mostly long-service regulars, partly because Greatwood 'had told the youngsters to go back'. A petition had been drawn up by Leading Seaman Henry Baker:

> After due consideration we have decided to come straight to Whitehall to have our grievances investigated and settled. It must be clearly understood that we have not in any way refused to work or cause unnecessary disturbance, but we have taken the only possible course open to us under such short notice to have our grievances settled.[5]

But the men gave in to the police (actually at King's Cross rather than Euston), were formed up in fours and sent to the detention quarters at Chatham Barracks. Greatwood was bitter about his treatment:

> I was court-martialled and got six months ... They sent me to Perth jail. I done six months and came out and had a terrible nervous breakdown. I couldn't sleep; I couldn't do nothing. They discharged me with neurasthenia and I got £1 15s a week; that was fifty per cent pension.[6]

There is no evidence that many of the British sailors were positive supporters of Bolshevism, but they were weary of war and could not understand what they were supposed to do, when even the instructions to admirals were unclear about whether they were to engage in hostilities or not. In the Black Sea a Soviet propaganda leaflet was dropped by aeroplane on the destroyer *Tobago*:

> English sailors, you are the working people. All of you have neither castles nor factories. We have no enmity with you – just the opposite. We look on

you as brothers. Then why do you fire on us? Your capitalists are afraid of us. Also the feeling of oligarchy forces them to help Russian capitalists and sanctianamus who pray for help. This is why your Government keeps you in the Black Sea, far from your homes and families.

Despite the incomprehensible wording in places, it struck a chord with the seaman when the first lieutenant rashly pinned a leaflet to the ship's notice board. '... the sailors all read it and the mumble went around, "Why are we here?" And they mutinied, in a kind of way.' The men refused to turn out on Christmas Eve, and the first lieutenant had to intervene, according to Leading Seaman H. A. Hill:

> Old Gossage came along with his revolver, so I reported to him as I wasn't going to be in this. He shook each hammock and told the hand to turn out – of course he knew everybody's name – and he turned out and nothing was done except the Captain cleared lower deck and said, 'I fear there was a bit of trouble this morning. I don't know why it was, but you'll carry on the same (this was Christmas 1919) as if nothing had happened, but I'm afraid you'll only get very pusser's leave. You'll have to be off at four o'clock at night and there won't be leave like I've been giving you.'[7]

Able Seaman Stan Smith had far more reason to hate the Bolsheviks after he was captured in a working party in Baku. He was forced to witness brutal executions and imprisoned in appalling conditions:

> At the beginning we had to work. We were lined up outside our cell and chained together like a lot of convicts on a chain-gang. We were marched through jeering crowds to the railway station where we had to unload sacks of millet from the trucks and carry them to the waiting carts. Some men became so weak, they would collapse under the weight of the sacks. Too feeble to work we were of little use to our captors, so back in the unrelieved misery of our cells we went on reduced rations.

They were released after more than a year, but only 12 men out of 29 survived.[8] By that time the intervention had ended, partly because of protests from the services.

245

## SOCIAL UNREST

The months after the Armistice were a time of extraordinary social unrest. The working class movement was more powerful and better organized than ever before, and power lay not with the essentially conservative craft unions but with the mighty industrial unions, especially the 'triple alliance' of transport workers, railwaymen and miners. There had been a Communist revolution in Russia, which many of the working class admired before it turned into a new tyranny; there was near revolution in Germany and in other parts of Europe. In January 1919, when the striking workers of Glasgow raised the red flag in the city centre, it looked as if a British revolution was not far away, until it was put down by police baton charges, military force and the imprisonment of ringleaders.

Ominously for the authorities, the revolutionaries called on the soldiers and sailors for support – it was naval mutiny that had opened the first cracks and brought down the regimes in Russia and Germany. The Soldiers, Sailors and Airmen's Union seemed to be at the heart of the trouble in Britain, and its title had echoes of the soldiers' councils that had been active in Russia and Germany, though in fact it was mostly made up of men who had already left the service. The lower deck was better organized than ever before and was clear in its demands, expressed in an 'Appeal of the Petty Officers and Men of the Royal Navy' produced in December 1918. At the head of the list was a demand for an increase in pay, 1s.6d across the board so that it would help the lower rates more. It was also asked that pensions for the wounded and for widows should be allowed in the same manner as for officers. In a clause that would strike a chord with the lower deck in the next war, it was asked, 'That the promotion of Active Service Ratings be accelerated in lieu of the present system of entering inexperienced civilians as Commissioned Officers to fill positions for which there is an abundance of fully qualified Petty Officers and men on the Lower Deck.' The men appointed had 'almost invariably to depend upon the Petty Officers for instruction in the duties they are called upon to perform', and it was a 'remarkably poignant injustice'. In a similar spirit of egalitarianism, scholarships were to be provided for sons of lower deck men to train as officers.

It was the seventh clause that caused the most difficulty at the Admiralty – 'That the lower deck associations be recognised by the Admiralty as a means of direct communication with the organised and loyal thought on the Lower Deck.' The petitioners claimed that the associations were 'bodies of loyal and devoted workers, whose sole aim is to leave the Lower Deck a better and happier place for their influence ...'

## THE JERRAM COMMITTEE

Meanwhile the government needed the navy's support as possible strike breakers and was aware that its wages and conditions had not kept up with the rest of society. Just before the Armistice, the Admiralty had set up the Naval Personnel Committee, under Admiral Sir Martyn Jerram, initially to deal with relatively minor matters such as the discrepancies between different branches. At the end of the year its remit was extended to inquire into the general question of lower deck pay. It was composed of naval officers and did not include a more neutral statesman as some would have liked, but it had twelve ratings from different branches attached to it, who would listen to all the evidence and advise on the final recommendations. Only two of them, a leading seamen and a petty officer telegraphist, wore the square rig uniform; the marines were represented by a sergeant major; but there were no stokers, whose interests could hardly be said to be identical to those of the engine room artificers. A chief petty officer was the second representative of the seaman branch (besides the leading seaman already mentioned), but the group was heavily weighted in favour of the smaller branches such as artisans and writers, perhaps because of its origins in sorting out the anomalies. Nevertheless, the Committee was as close to democracy as the Admiralty had ever gone.[9] Moreover it was to listen to witnesses at the three home ports, elected by the lower deck. In January a hundred delegates from the various lower deck societies got together illegally in London to discuss the nature of the evidence. It was decided to ask for a rise of four shillings per day.

The committee met against a background of industrial unrest and threats of revolt during January, though the prospect of revolution faded after the defeat of the Glasgow strike at the end of the month. At almost the same time the committee announced an interim rise of 1s 6d per day. Apart from that, it boiled the men's demands down to 60 basic points. Eight of these were turned down flat, some were modified or were outside the Committee's remit, such as the request that writers should start with leading rate. Some were extremely trivial – it was agreed that rating interpreters should be paid the allowance given to officers and that men who played the harmonium during services should be paid whether there was a chaplain on board or not. On the most thorny questions, the men mostly had their way. Good-conduct pay was to be increased from 1d to 3d per day, selected non-substantive rates were to be increased to 1s per day, and the kit upkeep allowance was to be retained. The separation allowance was to remain in force for the time being until a final decision was taken. An able seaman without dependents would now get 4 shillings per day exclusive of good conduct and non-substantive pay. The average man could thus expect £2 4s 11½d, more than double his pre-war rate of 19s 3d. A married man with two children would get £3 11s 5½d, more than triple the rate. The Committee prided itself on simplifying the naval pay structure, but the report contained seven pages of detailed tables showing the pay rates of men in 24 different groups, not including the Royal Marines. The total cost of the package was nearly three million pounds, and at government level there was great debate about whether a country already heavily in debt after the war could afford it. The award was granted at the end of April, though only backdated to February, so that the men who had already left the service would not benefit from it. The men's representatives discussed the offer at another meeting in London, and were less than delighted with it. But soon the 1919 rates would become the benchmark for naval pay.

## Direct Representation

In 1919, under severe pressure from the near-revolutionary atmosphere in Britain and Europe, the Admiralty conceded the lower deck's right to be represented in decisions about its conditions of service. A total of 54 ratings, one elected from each branch of the service and each home port, would meet annually at one of the home ports. They could discuss matters of payment, living conditions, welfare and so on, but were banned from any mention of discipline or individual complaints. The lower deck benefit societies were seen by their members as a basis for this, so that the representatives could be chosen with some knowledge of what they stood for, but the Admiralty took a very different view:

> Any relaxation of the regulations will be but the thin end of the wedge which will split the discipline of the Navy. From an organisation for representing the aspirations of the Lower Deck it would be but a short step to one very much akin to the equivalent of the 'Soldiers and Workmen's Committee'.[10]

The first conference was held at Portsmouth later in the year with 307 points to consider, some trivial and some important. The Admiralty was slow to reply to the conference's requests, and the men began to mistrust the system. Meanwhile the lower deck societies were growing in strength: it was estimated that 42 per cent of ratings were members in September 1920, including 37 per cent of seamen and 33 per cent of stokers, while the ERAs had 100 per cent membership, and the chief petty officers had 77 per cent. The next welfare committee met at Devonport with the replies to the previous year's suggestions still not available – and when they arrived only about  a quarter of the requests had been agreed to. The welfare system collapsed amid great dissatisfaction from the ratings. There was a serious danger that they would link up with the left-wing movement ashore. The former suffragette Sylvia Pankhurst published an article on 'Discontent of the Lower Deck' in her paper *Workers Dreadnought*, as a result of which she and several others were arrested. The lower deck leaders took fright.

At the end of 1920 the Admiralty issued an order that grudgingly recognized the lower deck societies, which now had 'the full support and approval of the Admiralty so long as they confine themselves to their original and legitimate objects'. The last phrase was the important one, for the order went on to describe the limits within which they should work. They claimed to have 'documentary evidence showing that outside influences which are hostile to the discipline and good order of the service have fixed upon these Societies as a possible channel through which to work'; so far they had had 'no success whatsoever', but everyone involved should keep their guard up. In the meantime the Admiralty was setting up 'an efficient machinery to enable them to be informed fully as to the aspirations, grievances and disabilities of the Lower Deck', and the societies, it was made clear, were to confine themselves to their legitimate functions, 'promoting thrift by securing to their members, in return for regular contributions, specified benefits for themselves or their representatives in the event of disablement or death'.[11] The order removed any hope that the Admiralty would recognize any kind of trade unionism in the navy. The order was grudgingly accepted. The influence and membership of the benefit societies declined rapidly. A new and weaker system of welfare conferences was set up in 1922, but the strength had gone out of the lower deck movement. Len Wincott was elected to a committee but was soon disillusioned as it became bogged down in trivia.

> Now I knew why the sailors scoffed. Here was a serious body like the Admiralty spending its time discussing, and what's more refusing, simply asinine requests – such as permission for men to have cuffs on their number two suits as well as on their number one suits; or to wear sewn-round caps, because the sewn-round cap looks smarter than the non-sewn-round cap.[12]

### DISCHARGE BY PURCHASE

After the initial rush to demobilize, the Admiralty found that it was going too fast, and by the end of 1919 there was a shortage of seamen. The cost of discharge by purchase was raised to more than double pre-war figures, and it was only allowed in exceptional cases. The Admiralty warned that discharge 'cannot be claimed as a right, and may be granted or withheld in accordance not only with the merits of the case, but with the requirements of the service at the time'.[13] Discharge by purchase remained far harder to get for the rest of the period.

In 1923–4 only 192 men, or 0.237 per cent of the fleet, were discharged by purchase, compared with around 600 a year before the war, or more than 0.5 per cent. Of course, these statistics do not make clear how much of this was caused by the men's satisfaction with the service, or the inhospitable climate outside, or by Admiralty policy. By the mid-1920s the

Admiralty's attitude to discharge by purchase had very much hardened, and in 1927 officers were informed that, 'the grant of discharge must depend on the requirements of the service ...' and that 'no guarantee can be given that the Admiralty will be able to approve the request...' This led to pathetic cases such as Mrs. Williams of Bristol, who had lost her husband and a son in the war. Her son Harry was serving in HMS *Hood*, and she wanted him out 'to help me support my home and the younger ones which he cannot do if he remains in the Navy'. She cashed in her life insurance policies and sold furniture to raise the sum of £48 that the Admiralty demanded, but still the Admiralty refused. 'This news of disappointment drove the boy nearly mad and me too causing me to go to the doctor who told me that it was nothing but this case which was worrying me to death, but the Captain blames the boy.'[14] Incidents like this tended to make men feel they were trapped in the navy, with no option but to see out their term, while the sudden swings in policy reduced confidence in the system.

## THE NAVY AND STRIKES

The immediate post-war activities of the navy were often politically controversial, including intervention in national strikes, such as the railway strike that began suddenly on 26 September 1919 and threatened to bring the country to a standstill. All weekend leave was cancelled as soon as the strike began, and parties were sent to various ports, which were often owned by the railway companies. At Barrow-in-Furness the crews of submarines fitting out assisted in operating the dock. At Immingham they worked the power station; at Liverpool they took charge of the Mersey Tunnel. Often the seamen worked with great enthusiasm in a new field, for example at Methil in the Firth of Forth:

> It is interesting to note that when the men working the hydraulic and electrical plant struck they were complacently certain that the machinery could not be worked for about five days owing to its 'intricacies'. However, within two hours of the arrival of naval ratings they had the plant in working order, and a satisfactory rate of coaling has been maintained.

251

At Eastleigh, near Southampton, three hundred men operated the railways as goods porters, engine drivers and guards. They were mostly accommodated in the RAF station there, and 'allowed to work as Railwaymen i.e. as long as they turned to at the proper time, they were perfectly free to go where they pleased in their "off" time'. Petty Officers Wright and Sutton organized football matches with the strikers in anticipation of a famous game between strikers and police seven years later, while the seamen were invited to local dances. A year after forming the spearhead of the Grand Fleet in the North Sea, the First Battle Squadron arrived at Southend and landed men. It was planned to train 161 volunteer engine room artificers, mechanicians and stoker petty officers as engine drivers and 280 stokers as firemen, but this proved impracticable; however, many of the men already claimed experience of engine driving and needed no further training. Crews were assembled, and old destroyers took them to Tilbury, where they manned two ferry boats to disembark troops arriving back from overseas. They brought their hammocks with them and lived on board. When the crew's quarters were flooded, the officers moved into a hotel and the crew went into the comparatively luxurious, but now overcrowded, accommodation in the ship's saloon.

One of the greatest concerns was for the supply of yeast. It was essential in the making of bread, a staple food that was usually fresh-baked locally in those days and could not be stored for long, refrigeration being rare. Yeast itself would only last for a week after it was made, so the position could become critical during a long rail strike. The navy took on responsibility for this, as destroyers, minesweepers and trawlers carried hampers of yeast from ports such as Methil, the Clyde and Aberdeen to the major centres of population.[15]

If the regular navy did not openly revolt against strike duty, things were different with recalled men of the Royal Fleet Reserve. The men had their civilian work interrupted, might suffer financially and were taken away from their families. Moreover, they often had strong trade union links in their regular jobs. 'Clinker Knocker' was recalled from the reserves in 1921 and sent to Manchester with a group, still unclear about their role:

Whilst we were enjoying our mid-day meal, the captain of the battalion made a speech informing us that our duties were to guard property against sabotage. We were not going to fight our fellow workmen as many believed. It was very nice to know this, because about seventy-five per cent of the battalion were coal miners.[16]

Conditions for the seamen were not luxurious:

Life in the White City was a near approach to active service, with the exception of fighting. We marched out in the mornings to guard the railways, and at night returned to the ruins. Rations were very scarce, and the keeping of our bodies clean was an utter impossibility. Soon we became verminous, and many men went to hospital ... In spite of all these hardships, which seemed incredible in the midst of civilisation, and in post-war England, we were a happy body of men.[17]

A battalion of reservists was mustered at Portsmouth and sent to Newport, in Wales, in 1921 during a miners' strike. After two weeks living in makeshift billets in a school in the town, they had already been contacted by local strikers. There was considerable disgruntlement by 29 April, when the group was moved to a box factory two miles outside the town, ringed with barbed wire, which made the men feel as if they were being sent there as a punishment. After a very unpalatable lunch, the majority of the men refused to assemble for orders. According to Captain Edward Kennedy, in charge of the party, 'The grievances were, in the main, confined to victualling, leave, sanitary arrangements, and sleeping accommodation.' Food was a particular problem for men who had grown used to home cooking: 'The fare is always the same, i.e. stewed meat and seldom a second vegetable. There is not enough roast meat, the potatoes are black, and the bacon is bad. The breakfast ration is always the same.' But politics were not absent, and when Kennedy addressed them one man shouted out that 90% of the men were trade unionists and would lay down their arms if called to use them against their fellow workers. This got a 'murmur of assent' from the rest. Kennedy felt he had to negotiate with the men, and was eventually court martialled and reprimanded for it.[18]

The greatest confrontation between capital and labour was the General Strike of May 1926. The navy's role was peripheral compared with that of the army. It did its well-established duty of conveying yeast and using submarine crews to provide power in key areas, but apart from that its main role was to protect docks and harbour installations. There was little hostility from the general population in the pro-naval city of Liverpool, where 'no disparaging remarks about the Navy and its presence in the Mersey have been heard'. But the Newcastle area included many coal mines and was more militant. *The Flying Scotsman* was derailed there one night, while Captain Tapprell Dorling was horrified to see a tableau in a demonstration that contained

> two men dressed as labourers wearing placards 'We Are British workers. We demand bread and the right to live'. At the other end, facing them, were two men in blue-jacket's uniform – proper uniforms, one with an S.G.'s badge – and three men in khaki all pointing wooden rifles at the two workers … On either side the cart bore large placards 'Soldiers and Sailors, do not shoot your working comrades' or words to that effect. It was more ludicrous than effective; but it was tantamount to telling soldiers and seamen not to obey orders.

Relations with the strikers were mostly cordial and low key, though in Glasgow a naval guard disturbed a group of men attempting arson near Prince's Dock. In general, captains had nothing but praise for the lower deck. The conduct of submarine crews in London was 'entirely satisfactory'; and the captain of HMS *Westminster* reported, 'The behaviour of the ship's company throughout was excellent.' In Liverpool, 'The behaviour of men on shore was very satisfactory,' though in Glasgow there was a small amount of leave breaking and drunkenness, 'due to the foolish persistence in following the local habit of drinking neat bad whisky and washing it down with beer'.[19] The strike ended after ten days when the Trades Union Congress took fright and gave in, but the miners continued their own strike for many months, leaving a long-standing legacy of bitterness.

All that tended to make the navy as an institution less universally popular than before the war and to undermine the aim of the Navy League to win working-class support for it.

On 'Red Clydeside', the Recruiting Staff Officer for the area, Commander H. T. Strawbridge, found he had great difficulties:

> The political views and activities of the 'masses' in the Glasgow district is firmly believed to be the principal deterrent to Naval Recruiting in general. The great majority from whom recruits of all branches are taken are rabidly anti-service, so much so, that there have been cases where applicants have stated they dare not mention the fact that they were joining the navy to anyone in their neighborhood for fear of being 'roughed'.

He was heard politely by a meeting of the Amalgamated Society of Engineers, but he was informed 'how much the Services were hated and everything connected with them ...' Even managers of labour exchanges had 'Socialistic views' and did not encourage men to join the services, while local politicians were 'rapidly undermining the patriotic spirit which is so essential to the youth of the Nation, if suitable and voluntary recruits are to be obtained in the future'.[20]

## RECRUITMENT

The navy claimed that its recruits came from many different groups in society. 'The boys that enter are of many types and kinds; they vary from sons of farmers, hotel proprietors, commercial travelers, small shopkeepers, retired Warrant Officers, and chief and Petty Officers, to sons of fishermen, mechanics, miners, cotton operatives, lower naval ratings and labourers.' Five per cent came from Greenwich Hospital School, and more than 16 per cent from other training ships. Exactly 14 per cent came from secondary and grammar schools, but the great majority, more than 64 per cent, had only an elementary school education.

Demobilization after the war was soon found to be proceeding too fast, and the navy began to take on new recruits and recall older men. RFR men who wanted to complete time for a pension were allowed to re-enter, while the recruiting of boys was stepped up and the entry of youths was revived.

In the year up to March 1921, the number of boys under training doubled from 1,733 to 3,500. The ships of the fleet had some difficulty in accommodating them for the second part of their training, partly because of a new regulation that they were not to be employed on ships in the East Indies, which would have taken them too far from home. The new battlecruiser *Hood* was to take a total of 65 boys, light cruisers were to take 10 each, and the old battleships *Colossus* and *Collingwood* were used as additional training ships at Portland, under the command of the notorious Captain Collard of the 'on the knee' incident (see page 182).[21] Recruiting was closed for a time in 1922 and re-opened in April 1923. With full employment, it was difficult to raise enough seamen boys, so height and chest measurements were each reduced by one inch. Stokers were even more difficult to find. Depots were 'authorised to accept men slightly below the educational standard if they appeared sufficiently intelligent for their duties and were otherwise desirable', but that was still not enough, and they were allowed to accept men an inch below the height standard, which brought in just enough to cover wastage.[22] A new syllabus was drawn up to get them though the ordinary seaman grade to able seaman as quickly as possible, and a wartime destroyer base at Port Edgar in the Forth was used for boys' advanced training, so that they could go for short trips in destroyers based there. To ensure the flow of trainees it was necessary to utilize the ships of the Mediterranean Fleet to the full – 310 boys were transferred without warning from the Atlantic Fleet when the two fleets met at Gibraltar in February 1925. This was a brutal procedure, as the Commander-in-Chief of the Atlantic Fleet pointed out. It resulted in

> a large number of young ratings being drafted to foreign service for the first time without an opportunity of saying good-bye to their families and, in some cases, of settling their private affairs. This, I consider, may be thought a source of hardship by the ratings themselves and by their parents and give rise to a feeling of discontent at the commencement of their service.[23]

By 1925 the Admiralty was satisfied with its recruiting, though only nineteen per cent of the applicants were accepted, and the rest were mainly turned down for medical reasons. It was also considering reviving the policy of short service – seven years in the fleet and five in the reserve – as part of a campaign to reduce pay levels. Unemployment rose again and was never less than ten per cent between 1923 and 1940, so re-engagement rates were now 'extraordinarily high', with 64 per cent of seamen, 72 per cent of stokers and 98 per cent of ERAs signing on for an extra term. This compared very favourably with 1912–13, when around 50 per cent of seamen and stokers signed on again.[24]

There was another turn in the Admiralty's roller-coaster recruitment policy in 1926 when it was found necessary to recruit extra boys for the huge new battleships *Rodney* and *Nelson* and some cruisers that were about to be launched. Short service recruitment was re-opened with reluctance, and older ships had reduced crews. Harold Ackland was one of those who joined around that time:

I was working for a chap called Giddings, who lived on Chepstow Road, and I was going to be an apprentice. In the General strike the apprentices couldn't go on strike, so I was painting railings on Chepstow Road and a couple of chaps came along and they threatened, more or less, to fill me in if I didn't pack up. So I went back to Giddings and I told him, and I immediately went over to Corporation Road and joined the Royal Navy.

He soon found that medical standards were high:

There were so many trying to get in, and they was so particular, that if you had a tooth missing or a toe overlapping they would send you away. But these preliminaries in Corporation Road was nothing compared to the examination they had in Bristol.[25]

Later in the decade, unemployment boosted recruitment yet more. Hugh Morris joined from a declining middle-class family:

When I joined up I met people who had the option of staying in places like Jarrow, where there was appalling poverty, or joining the Navy. They had been brought up in really grim conditions, and seen their parents out of work. They had a different kind of poverty from us – I had mental richness, they didn't.[26]

On the whole the officers were satisfied with the quality and motivation of the boys of this period:

> The Boys of course vary and while many very likely are attracted by its being a safe job, there is no doubt that most of them come into the Navy definitely because they want to, and not because it is just something to do; they are keen and anxious to get on and in many cases are healthily ambitious. There are very few cases of serious offences while they are under training, the majority being offences against Regulations and the trouble that boys who come under discipline and control for the first time, would be expected to get into.[27]

## THE SPECIAL SERVICE SQUADRON

In November 1923 the Special Service Squadron left Plymouth on a tour of the British Empire, carrying their Royal Highnesses the Prince of Wales and the Duke of York. J. F. Clark was an Able Seaman in *Hood* and relished much (but not all) of the voyage. When addressed by the captain he concluded that, 'I think he will be all right to work for', but he had his moments of disillusionment. In Sierra Leone he was no more racist than one would expect from a sailor of the period: 'Very nice place as regards people ... blacks of all kinds resident there.' He watched the 'Seedy boys' diving for money alongside the ship and was amazed that they had got hold of songs like 'We have no bananas' so quickly. On 25 December in Cape Town he complained, 'Xmas day, ordinary routine, rotten Xmas', and things were no better on Boxing Day: 'Ordinary routine. Had visitors on board. Fed up. Got paid fortnight's money.' He soon cheered up by the 28th when a children's party on board was an 'enormous success'. By the end of the year he had helped at another children's party with 1,400 children in two sittings; he had received a card and a parcel from his wife and had gone 'surf bathing'; it was 'the last day of 1923 but the best'. He enjoyed the water, and in Fremantle, Australia, he was taken by a visitor to 'what he said was the biggest closed in swimming bath in the world. Water chutes, high diving boards etc. In my glory here with this fellow.' He enjoyed the visits laid on by the local Europeans in Kuala Lumpur – 'the finest time of my life. Visiting rubber plantations, tin mines, bathing, shooting galleries, sightseeing, dancing, singing, eating, drinking, in fact a grand time.' The trip had its share of tragedy, as when a stoker petty officer was killed in a charabanc accident in Ceylon, and the local people and ship's company contributed £273 for his widow. On duty guiding crowds around the ship he found a 'rotten job, very embarrassing'. It was estimated that 29,000 people visited the ship one day, but lack of crowd control led to the greatest tragedy of all – a mother was knocked over by the crush of people in the galley and her baby girl was scalded to death in a tub of boiling water. *Hood* sent fourteen men ashore to the funeral.[28] The ships crossed the Pacific, visited San Francisco and Vancouver, and returned through the Panama Canal.

## The Status of the Petty Officer

Officers continued to be unhappy about the role of the petty officer. After the mutiny in *Delhi* in 1919, Admiral Cowan complained,

> It is a fact that in almost all these outbreaks ... an unmistakable feature has been the inclination of the petty officers to disown all knowledge and responsibility, and to withdraw and keep out of trouble and avoid being involved, rather than to range themselves on the side of their officers and assist them to enforce the discipline and identify ringleaders.
>
> The fault lies largely with the officers for not, through the daily life of the service, correcting and instructing the rank and file through the petty officers. The almost invariable tendency is for the officer to check or correct the man himself rather than to do it through the petty officer, or to admonish the petty officer for not becoming aware of the man's fault ... [29]

Officers were taught naval history in those days and had rosy views about the old-style petty officer in the days of sail. In the old days there was 'the Captain of the Main Top in the days of masts and yards selected for his prowess aloft and retaining his position by proving daily before all hands his power of command and superior knowledge'.

> In the present year of Grace it is often difficult to find out exactly why a particular man became a Petty Officer: it is true that he has passed examinations in seamanship and school but there are a hundred and one

reasons for promotion; he may be a good gun-layer, he may be an efficient member of the electric light party or he may be the only leading seaman with 'passed for P.O.' on his certificates and 'nothing against him' and the roster at the barracks and the pressure from the Drafting Offices also play a large and not entirely satisfactory part in this matter.

One vital factor in the prestige of an army sergeant was that he lived apart from the men under him. The sergeant's mess was an important institution, usually in a separate building in the barracks and with facilities that almost matched those of the officers – sometimes exceeding them in practice, as dilettante officers in some regiments spent little time in their own mess. None of this was practicable aboard ship. Petty officers and even chiefs would continue to live in hammocks rather than bunks and there was no question of giving them individual cabins like officers. Petty officers in the navy were far more divided than army sergeants. There were separate messes for chiefs, for artificers and artisans, for stoker and seamen petty officers and often those of other branches, though this had to be modified in smaller ships. 'In many cases several categories of C.P.O.s and P.O.s must mess in a single enclosed space due to considerations of space, light, etc. As instances, Artisans P.O.s may have a mess in the same enclosed space as other P.O.s, and E.A.s, O.A.s and Shipwrights in the same enclosed space as other C.P.O.s'. Even in the biggest ships there was no space to put any distance between the petty officers' messes and those of the junior ratings, and even on the same messdeck it was not practicable to seal them off by barriers. In fact Admiralty policy was moving the other way. In 1923 it was noticed that 'in certain of H.M. Ships where various categories of C.P.O.s and P.O.s have been allotted a separate mess, the enclosing bulkheads have been carried right up to the beam, having the effect of depriving the mess decks of natural light and ventilation.' In future they were to be fitted with a 'dwarf bulkhead halfway up to the beam, supplemented by curtains where necessary'.[30]

Another problem rose from the officers themselves, and their inability to delegate:

The change from sail to steam witnessed the gradual process of centralisation until a state of affairs was arrived at in which ever the officer of the watch – probably a Lieutenant of three or four years seniority – could not call away the skiff without referring to the Commander and the pipe 'Clear up the upper deck' was the signal for the arrival of as many overseers as workers – a not uncommon sight was five or six men under a Leading Seaman and a Petty Officer sweeping up the deck being overlooked by a Warrant Officer, an Officer as Mate of the Upper Deck, the Officer of the Watch, and lastly the Commander.'

This kind of 'intensive overseeing' had tended to disappear during the war, as officers had far too many other things to do, but it was reappearing in peacetime. [31]

One possible solution was to give the petty officers some kind of training for the role. In 1920 the first experimental courses were held with the twin approaches of instilling the men with a 'pride in their profession' and teaching them to give orders – though they were not to be taught leadership as such: that concept was alien to the thought of the times. Half of the course of 8 weeks, 44 working days and 198 hours, was to consist of drill, taking charge and exercising command', though it is not clear how all the members were to learn this at once. The other half of the course consisted of lectures, which fell into two main categories. Some were subjects of practical use, such as the King's Regulations, the internal economy of ships, health and hygiene, and ship construction, as described by a member of the Royal Corps of Naval Constructors. The others used history to instil 'pride in their profession' among the petty officers. They had eight hours on the history of the seaman and two on the story of the uniform, with ten more on general naval history. Ten hours were devoted to 'Discipline and morale, the reason and value of; important part taken of Petty Officers in their maintenance, and the necessity for their understanding their status and responsibility in the efficiency of a ship.' Twenty more hours were devoted to:

Geography – British Empire – British trade – part played by the Navy in protection of Trade and shewing the Flag. Procedure of Government – the Naval Estimates – elementary finances of the Country – and how the Navy is paid for. Foreign Navies.

Some of the participants were delighted just to be taken into the official confidence in this way and to be told about subjects that were normally regarded as the preserve of officers. For one stoker petty officer from HMS *Tiger*, 'His pleasure in knowing something of Naval History etc was almost pathetic.' Some officers suggested lectures on Communism, 'in order to supply them with good arguments to rebut any Bolshevistic statements made on the lower deck'. Notes were prepared for a question-and-answer session on 'A brief Sketch of Bolshevism and its Results'.

Promotion was often quite fast just after the war as older men retired. In 1921–2 the average leading seaman was promoted after just over five years as an AB, at the age of 24–25. The average petty officer had been promoted after less than three-and-a-half years as leading seaman, and chiefs after six years and eight months. Promotion soon began to slow down. For most of the 1920s men were advanced to leading seamen after around six years, but for candidates for petty officers the situation gradually got worse. It took an average of more than six years by the end of the decade, and the typical man was 29 or 30 years old before he made the grade.[32]

## PETTY OFFICERS' UNIFORM

One of the suggestions put before the Jerram Committee in 1919 was that the petty officers' uniform should be upgraded to the fore-and-aft one of the chiefs. The petty officers of Devonport pointed out that there was 'insufficient distinction' between them and junior ratings: 'We contend that a distinction in dress would render our duties easier, as our prestige with Junior Ratings would be increased; thus reducing the occasions on which we require to call on Superior authority to enforce our own authority ...' It was agreed that, 'A conspicuous difference in dress would give them more authority over their men and prevent the latter being able to say "I did not know he was a Petty Officer".' Moreover, the ratings of the administrative, domestic and medical branches already wore an inferior version of the fore-and-aft uniform, and to outsiders they seemed to be senior to the petty officers of the seaman and stoker branches – 'if dressed as seamen they are denied entry to places of entertainment, etc., which is freely given to men such as Officer's Stewards, 3rd Class, Victualling Assistants and others of the relative rating of Able Seaman, who are not dressed in Blue Jacket's Rig.' This tendency was even more marked in India and the colonies. The C-in-C at the Nore was sceptical and wanted to make sure that 'whatever alterations are made in the uniform of Chief Petty Officers and Petty Officers the clearest distinction may be maintained between that of Officers and ratings'. Admiral Oliver, in command of the Home Fleet, went further: 'If they [the petty officers] are put into a dress similar to that of the chief petty officers, the latter will soon wish to be dressed as warrant officers, and the warrant officers as commissioned officers until, finally, everybody will be as gorgeously dressed as Australian and New Zealand port officials and pilots who carry as much gold lace as post captains.' The commodore on board HMS *Castor* did not concede the point about civilians mistaking the value of a particular uniform: 'it is not confined to Petty Officers. What Naval Officer has not been mistaken for a Railway Official? Recently I was, whilst dressed as a Post Captain, presented with a shilling when coming out of a London theatre, as an inducement to procure a taxi-cab.' But other officers did not agree that the distinction between petty officer and chief was the most important: 'the main change in a man's status from one who obeys to one who commands, is made when he becomes a Petty Officer, and it is at that stage that the uniform should be altered.'

There were others questions. Fore-and-aft rig uniform could not be folded away and put in a kitbag in the same way as square rig, so large numbers of lockers might be needed for the petty officers' messes. The petty officers naturally wanted the 'Class I' uniform worn by the chiefs, but many of the officers were only prepared to grant the inferior version known as 'Class III'. Then, what badges would the petty officer wear to distinguish him from the chiefs? One suggestion was that he should wear no substantive badges as such, like the chief, but the latter should be elevated by wearing the three brass buttons worn by chief artificers. Another was that the petty officers should continue to wear the crossed anchors, but with no good conduct stripes. As the captain of HMS *Excellent* pointed out, 'good conduct badges are often mistaken for rank such as Corporal etc, a young Petty Officer with one or two G.C. badges is often termed 'Youngster', and considered insufficiently experienced to have the necessary authority, sometimes placing the Petty Officer concerned in an awkward position.'

The Admiralty was moving towards a compromise by giving the petty officers the Class III uniform but made more distinctive by brass buttons instead of black. This ran into another problem, the rivalry between different branches, for the Admiralty was always anxious to placate the artisans such as plumbers and blacksmiths, who were recruited as adults and wore the Class III rig with black buttons. If the seamen and stokers were to be given Class III with brass buttons, would that not upset the artisans? To avoid this the Fourth Sea Lord claimed that, 'The only alternative that I can therefore suggest, to the refusal of the Petty Officers' request, is to grant the proposed Admiralty Pattern Fore and Aft Rig to Petty Officers after reaching a certain seniority as Petty Officer.' This is a little obscure: it is not clear why the artisans could not be given brass buttons as well to bring them into line, but the obvious saving in expense was attractive to a cash-strapped Admiralty. Three years seniority as petty officer was considered as the time to change over the uniform, but it was pointed out that many petty officers would be within a short time of the end of their first period of twelve years, so the money spent on the uniform would be wasted. The Admiralty therefore went for four years, but it undermined the point by ruling that men should not take up the new uniform if they were within a year of discharge in any case.

Eventually it was decided that petty officers of more than four years' seniority should wear Class III uniform, a disappointment to the men concerned on both counts. They would, however, be allowed gilt buttons to distinguish them from the lower rates in Class III, who had black buttons. They would adopt the badge, of an anchor within a circle surmounted by a crown, at present worn by the chiefs, who would get a new badge with the anchor surrounded by a wreath, which was much narrower than that worn by the officers to maintain the distinctions of rank. Petty officers would continue to wear their good conduct and rating badges in their new dress, which some of them considered would be 'too gaudy, and make them appear ridiculous'.

By the end of the year it was clear that the scheme was not working, however, and the Admiralty wanted to extend fore-and-aft to all petty officers:

> The number of Petty Officers in any individual ship who are in the one dress or the other depends on the chances of drafting; also that the feeling among the Petty Officers themselves is strongly adverse to the present distinction of dress within the rating, which is regarded as diminishing the authority of the Petty Officers during their earlier period of service as such when they need all the support that can be given them.

But this soon ran into opposition from the Treasury, who pointed out that it was not possible 'in the present financial stringency', for it would cost £100,000 to re-equip all the petty officers, plus recurring expenses of £10,000 per year. It was suggested that money could be saved by keeping men in square rig for the first year's petty officer, and treating that as a period of probation in acting rank – though the King's Regulations said nothing about acting status. There was some objection that a young petty officer needed all the status he could get in his first year, but after much hesitation it was agreed and enforced by an Admiralty Fleet Order of July 1923, so an estimated 4,400 seamen and 3,100 stoker petty officers changed into new uniforms.[33]

In 1920 the wearing of three brass buttons on the lower sleeve, previously confined to chief artificers, was extended to masters-at-arms. In 1925 it was ordered for all chief petty officers.

## THE NAVY IN SOCIETY

Despite a good deal of patriotic bluster, the war had done the image of the navy no good. The vastly expensive fleet of dreadnoughts had not deterred war. It had failed to bring the enemy to a decisive action, as the navy had allowed the public and press to expect. It began to emerge that the navy had only begun to tackle the submarine effectively after pressure from outside. It now had to live in an atmosphere of disillusionment in which war was regarded as futile and catastrophic, and in which money was scarce due to near-bankruptcy and the fear of depression.

In 1922 the navy reluctantly accepted the Washington Treaty on arms limitation. Abandoning the two-power standard, it now accepted parity with the United States in the number of battleships, with smaller rations for France, Italy and Japan. The British reaction to this was to build ships right up to the limits allowed by the treaties, so yet again the tonnage of battleships and cruisers became an obsession with the navy. Money for improvements in social conditions was as hard to come by as ever. The United States Navy transformed its personnel policies during this period, while the Royal Navy moved very slowly and suffered traumas as a result.

The British Empire had expanded to an even greater extent as a result of the war, largely by way of League of Nations' mandates to govern the former territories of Germany and the Turkish Empire, but some of these soon proved extremely difficult to control, especially Palestine and Iraq. The public as a whole had no great enthusiasm for empire, while the older 'white' dominions such as Australia and Canada became ever more independent, and Mahatma Gandhi's campaign in India was the first stirring of a movement that would ultimately end British rule in the subcontinent. The navy was only marginally involved in these events, but its old role as protector of the Empire was no longer fashionable as it had been in late Victorian times.

The old upper classes, who had traditionally sent their younger sons to become naval officers, were now financially stretched due to death duties during the war, and had lost a disproportionate number of sons. The working classes who had traditionally provided ratings were often disaffected. The rise of the middle classes continued as fast as ever during the 1920s and '30s. The financial and insurance sectors continued to grow even when the rest of the economy was depressed. In those days before computers, they employed large numbers, especially in London where they bought houses in the new suburbs. The numbers of men employed in commercial, insurance and finance business rose from 1,180,000 to 1,621,000 during the years from 1921 to 1931 alone – such people were not likely to want their sons to become naval ratings, while they were not usually rich or well-connected enough to start them on the road to becoming officers.

The navy had no more of a 'middle class' than in the past. Promotion from the lower deck to commissioned officer status had not got much easier. In 1920 a scheme was announced for young men to be selected at the age of 20 for training as mate so that they would reach the rank of lieutenant at around 23, at the same time as Dartmouth cadets, instead of at 28 or 29 as with the old system, but the numbers involved were never large. In the meantime, the first officers appointed in this way were reaching the time when they were eligible for promotion to commander; 32 of them were about to enter this zone in 1926. But, as the *Naval Warrant Officers' Journal* complained,

> the budding mate or accelerated promotion candidate is handicapped by having more years on his shoulders than his contemporary advancing through another channel. By the time he arrives at the promotion zone, age has robbed him, not of zeal, but of opportunity ... although it is possible to reach the highest rank, it is highly improbable.[34]

Only a hundred mates were allowed on the establishment, so they were not likely to dominate the officer corps. A committee looked at the matter in 1930. In order to extend the range of candidates it considered raising the upper age limit of 25, but instead it proposed to start from the opposite end, to seek out suitable boys at an early age in the training schools. The title of 'mate' was quite well liked by the officers themselves, as it had a good deal of history, but on promotion they were ever known as 'ex-mates' and the committee suggested changing it to 'sub-lieutenant'. However, they were aware that, 'in all probability some other name will be coined for colloquial use in the service itself.' They recommended that newly promoted officers should start off in the gunroom among the midshipmen and sub-lieutenants, to 'minimise the first bewildering effect of shyness and diffidence which is now felt on entering the wardroom'. They also maintained the rule that only unmarried men could apply. Early marriage, it was claimed,

> almost invariably prevents the young officer from giving his best endeavours to the service, but that if he is made to wait till much later in

his career when he has had the social opportunities which his officer's position will have given him he is likely to marry someone who will help him in his social life, and he will for ever bless those who deterred him from an improvident marriage.[35]

To the lower deck, the authorities appeared to put every possible obstacle in the way of candidates for officer rank, and when finally promoted such officers were in an unhappy position. They were often lonely in the wardroom, unable to afford the drinks bought by their colleagues, and socially awkward. Very few boys joined the lower deck with the expectation of becoming officers, and if they did they were soon disillusioned. Despite the more egalitarian climate in society as a whole, the navy did very little to close the gap between officers and ratings.

The status of the warrant officer continued to decline – he was usually too old for the mate scheme, while the ancient rank of boatswain was dying out. The writer branch, the nearest naval equivalent to the middle-class banking and insurance clerks ashore, was rather low in status – the Jerram Committee turned down a request that they should all start at leading hand status, and there was no path to commissioned rank for a writer.

# CRISIS AND REVIVAL
## 1925–1939

### 1925 PAY

The 1919 pay rates had been set in 'quite abnormal circumstances' of almost revolutionary disruption combined with high wages and cost of living during the short post-war boom. The cost-of-living index fell from 154.4 in 1920 to 100 in 1925. Meanwhile government spending cuts became ever more urgent, for deficit budgeting was not accepted in those days. Despite all this, the pay rates survived the 'Geddes Axe' of 1922, in which many naval officers were made redundant, and the Anderson Committee of 1923, which found that ratings' pay was too high.

Another committee was set up in 1925 to consider pay across the three services but soon found there were 'innumerable difficulties' in comparing one rank or rating with another, as the Admiralty and Air Ministry claimed 'at great length' that there were 'special features attached to sailors and airmen' as compared with soldiers. What the navy feared most was that one of the other services would attract its recruits by higher wages on entry. As Rear Admiral Kelly told the committee, 'The Admiralty believe they can get the recruits they want on the scale of remuneration that is offered, provided the other services do not offer greater inducements.' The committee decided that the best policy would be to coordinate the entry rates for each, which meant that the army rate should be cut by 10%, the RAF by 20% and the navy by 15%.

But it would be very difficult to apply any cuts to existing personnel. According to the Admiralty,

The men enter for a succession of contracts binding them to serve for a definite period of years. They are not allowed to leave the Service during these contract periods, except by special permission, and probably on payment. It is generally accepted in consequence of this that a man's pay cannot be altered to his detriment during the contract period on which he is serving.

It was also very difficult to discharge men against their will:

> It is certain that a large proportion of Naval ratings would never have entered the Service at all if it had not been a recognised thing that a man is allowed to serve on for pension if his ability and conduct are satisfactory. Whatever the strict law of the matter, it has been a bargain between the man and the State and if the State goes back on that bargain, shore labour, from which the Admiralty obtains its recruits, will have lost all confidence in the good faith of the Admiralty ...[1]

It was agreed that new entrants from 1925 onwards would be at a reduced rate of pay, with able seamen on three instead of four shillings per day, and higher ranks in proportion. But the pay of men who had entered before that was protected, avoiding a breach of faith and the threat of mass disobedience but creating a divisive two-tier system within the navy.

## NAVY DAYS

One answer to the navy's declining prestige was to publicize its role. The RAF was already highly successful with its annual air displays at Hendon, to the north of London, while the army had the Aldershot Tattoo. The first Navy Day was held at Portsmouth in 1928 during the late August Bank Holiday, when the Atlantic Fleet had its summer leave. It had the intention of 'bringing the Navy into close touch with the people who live in the inland manufacturing centres, so many of whom visit Southsea during the summer holidays'. It involved a special opening of the dockyard museum in Portsmouth and HMS *Victory*, with visits to modern warships conducted by naval and Marine guides. It was a great success, and the idea was extended to Plymouth and Chatham in subsequent years, though the latter suffered because of lack of facilities for the biggest battleships. But class divisions within the navy did not disappear, and there was controversy about how much of the proceeds from these events should be allocated to charities that were exclusively for officers.[2]

Navy Days certainly worked for Bob Tilburn: 'I was born in Leeds and when I was ten we went on holiday to Portsmouth to visit relations. It was Navy week and we went round all the ships. From then onwards, it was my one ambition to join the Royal Navy.'[3]

For many the greatest naval event of the 1920s was the placing of Nelson's old flagship, HMS *Victory*, in dry dock at Portsmouth in 1922 and her opening to the public in 1928. This attracted huge attention and confirmed the status of the navy at the heart of the nation; however, this was looking back on past glories and contrasted with the RAF''s custom of showing off its latest technology.

## LIFE IN THE TRAINING BASES

As recruitment began to revive, plans were also made to take over an old Royal Marine barracks at Forton, on the Gosport side of Portsmouth Harbour, and convert it to a boys' training establishment. It took some time to convert an old building, but in June 1927 it was commissioned as HMS *St Vincent*, taking the name of the training ship that had lain in Portsmouth Harbour until 1906. With *Ganges* now a shore base at Shotley, *Impregnable* at Plymouth was now the only one of the old hulks still used for naval training, but that was soon under question. By 1928 all the bases were half empty and *Powerful*, the old 1895 cruiser that formed the core of the base, was nearing the end of her life. It was hoped that £90,000 could be saved, plus £60,000 scrap value for the *Powerful* and other hulks. The last boys entered early in 1929, bringing an end to boy training in the West Country for the moment. By 1931, as the cuts began to bite even deeper, it was suggested that the recently converted *St Vincent* might be closed too and all training concentrated at *Ganges*. Against this it was argued that it would be dangerous to rely too much on a single base: for example, an epidemic, such as the catarrh that struck *St Vincent* shortly afterwards, could halt all boy training for a time. It was also argued that Hampshire was a vital centre for naval recruiting, and it would be damaged by the closure. *St Vincent* narrowly survived.[4]

271

Many recruits knew nothing of the sea before arriving at a training base. Approaching Harwich, one boy is said to have exclaimed, 'Whet a strong smell of salt', to which a companion replied 'What do you expect? That is the sea, you know.'[5] And despite his start in a training ship for orphans, Fred Copeman had no idea that HMS *Ganges* was a shore base:

> Crossing the harbour we became more aware of the outstanding points of the *Ganges*, a cluster of low buildings on a rather flat and treeless countryside with a tall mast of a ship, which looked as if it was growing out of the buildings themselves. I began to wonder how the ship got there, and thought maybe there was another inlet running in behind the buildings ...[6]

Though smoking was positively encouraged among adult ratings with the sale of cheap cigarettes, the authorities at the training ships tried obsessively to prevent it. John Whelan's first contact was with a petty officer in the Regulating Office at *St Vincent*:

> 'Got any fags, boys?'
> Eager to please, eight trembling hands proffered packets. The Regulating Petty Officer took them all. 'Any matches?'
> With less enthusiasm eight boxes were produced. They shared the same fate. 'Smoking's not allowed,' explained the R.P.O laconically. 'Now I'll take all your money except a shilling.'[7]

Later Whelan came under suspicion when he was found in the same room as a boy who was smoking, and his career suffered its first setback.

It is possible that the young men of the 1920s and '30s were a little more sensitive and less used to hardship than their predecessors. The first night in a training base was only the beginning of a hard experience:

> Curled under rough blankets in a strange, hard bed in a strange, harder world, my thoughts turned, inevitably perhaps, to my home. One cannot abandon the patterns, influences and familiarities of sixteen years in as many hours, and the dormitory, with its ice-blue nightlight, held the strange unreality of a bad dream ... My thoughts were disturbed by the sound of

sobbing from the next bed, and in the other boy's weakness I found strength. 'Cheer up, chum,' I whispered, and fell asleep.[8]

Such scenes could soften the hardest heart. 'Some lads who had come straight from home and were alone found it hard not to cry. When this happened you saw an immediate change in the men who previously had been rather harsh. A sailor has a big heart.'[9] As a Greenwich boy, Leonard Charles Williams was more used to naval ways:

> Altogether, they were exciting days. We slowly divorced ourselves from civilian life and learned to work together and to share our lives and experiences. We even began to speak a different language. One spiced and laced with nautical expressions foreign to the ordinary man in the street. We were sailors in the making and we were very proud of that.[10]

The syllabus was divided into four parts. Seamanship included knots and splices, the use of the compass and boat 'pulling' or rowing. At *Ganges*, 'All the boys had to climb the mast at least once a week and this became quite an ordeal for me. I never got the knack of running up the rigging at speed.'[11] Gunnery naturally included drill at the weapons, but also, under the influence of HMS *Excellent,* a large amount of parade-ground drill, especially in the beginning:

> It was a month of marching and counter-marching, of saluting to the left and saluting to the right, of moving at the double and moving at the slow march, of marking time and turning about, until Ginger remarked to the P.O. that he thought he'd joined the Navy and not the blasted Army, and was rewarded with a slap across the backside from the petty officer's stonickey: a twelve-inch length of rope with a large manrope knot at the end.[12]

Physical training had its terrors for some, especially those who could not swim. The rest of the time was taken up with school work. After the first few months, the boys were rated first class and wore the stiff cap rather than a soft one. Then they would be sent to sea, where they were segregated from adult ratings until the age of eighteen.

## THE ADVANCED CLASS

In the 1920s there was a new service, the Royal Air Force, competing with the navy for a certain kind of recruit. The army had its own target youth, somewhere between 'the scum of the earth, enlisted for drink' of Wellington's day, and the boy who was brought up with intense loyalty to his city or county regiment in which generations of his family had served. In addition, the army was much less technological (except in a few areas), and it could rely much more on short service. The RAF, on the other hand, was at the vanguard of technology, and in contrast to the traditional practices of the navy it gave off an air of modernity. The distinction between air and ground crews was less than it would become later, and most non-commissioned personnel could look forward to some flying time, either as air gunners or as sergeant-pilots. The apprentice system, a personal favourite of Lord Trenchard, the 'Father of the RAF', was aimed at boys from lower-middle-class or upper-working-class background, with a certain amount of education beyond elementary school. At entrance level, the RAF scheme was comparable to the navy's artificer apprentice system, but it was far more extensive – up to 1,200 boys a year were taken on by the RAF – the navy took about a tenth of that number in normal years. Artificers had a 'fast track' to the rating of chief petty officer, while RAF apprentices did well to pass out as leading aircraftmen, roughly equivalent to the old idea of a leading seaman but with no authority to give orders. The artificers were a small elite, but the RAF ex-apprentices were intended to be the core of the non-flying part of their service. The RAF was evidently poaching on traditional naval territory in its recruiting. Favourable terms were offered, not only to the small number of sons of RAF warrant officers and NCOs but also to the sons of army and naval families. There were eight centres for the examination, including the naval heartlands of Chatham, Portsmouth and Plymouth.

In competition with this, the navy offered direct entry to advanced class in the training ships. The Admiralty wanted 'increased recruitment from the central school type of boy, or even the secondary school type' in contrast to the elementary school boys who made up the bulk of new entrants. The scheme was also intended to attract boys from inland towns outside the traditional recruiting grounds. A booklet called *The Royal Navy as a Career* waxed lyrical about sea life: 'The call of the sea is a very mysterious thing. It is like red hair or a taste for boiled peas. You have either got it or you haven't.' The navy had a tradition of silence – 'the chief drawback of this silence lay in the fact that a lot of boys whom Naval life would have suited to a T, and with whom the navy could have done, grew up and passed into other trades and professions without knowing anything about the possibilities of the Navy ... To ensure that the Navy shall in future obtain a percentage of recruit rather above the average in education ... the Admiralty have instituted an examination for direct entry in the Advanced Class (at the Naval Training Establishments where all recruits spend their first year).' Either daringly or naïvely, boys were offered the chance to 'lead a vigorous, manly life in the company of your own sex'. The pamphlet outlined four possible careers under the scheme. An 'unsuccessful man' might not get beyond able seaman, and perhaps leave after twelve years. A 'successful man' might reach chief petty officer by the age of 35 and retire at 40 with a pension of £87 a year. A 'very successful man' would retire as a warrant officer, while an 'altogether exceptional man' might be commissioned as a mate at the age of 23 and retire at 50 as a commander.

In practice the advantages offered were not enough to attract large numbers. Headmasters of the schools approached soon spotted that speed of promotion was not commensurate with the qualifications needed, and they wanted a statement of numbers expected to become mates, chief petty officers and so on. The scheme failed to attract many recruits, and in August 1929 the Admiralty decided to discontinue it.[13] In any case, the value of the advanced class was questionable because it did not necessarily accelerate a boy's career. As AB Len Wincott put it, 'It is legitimate to wonder what the Advanced Class was for.'[14]

## THE BIG-SHIP NAVY

There were many who believed that the battleship was obsolete in the face of the aircraft and the submarine, but the navy remained faithful to it. There had been a tendency for capital ships to get larger ever since

*Dreadnought* was launched in 1906; the post-war navy was strapped for cash and could afford to maintain fewer than before, while the Washington Treaty of 1922 demanded wholesale scrapping in any case. There were 45 dreadnought battleships and battlecruisers in the navy at the end of the war: after two disarmament treaties, only 13 were left by 1930. As a result, the prestige of the navy depended increasingly on a small number of very large ships. *Hood,* the last of the battlecruisers, was launched in 1920 and became the pride of the navy. The battleships *Rodney* and *Nelson*, completed in 1927, were the heaviest gunned ships the Royal Navy ever had, the only ones with 16-inch gun batteries.

A young sailor had a thrilling experience when he joined a big ship for the first time:

> Coming aboard *Nelson* was like climbing the side of a mountain. After the relatively small *Centaur*, *Nelson* was a veritable colossus. She towered above the South Railway Jetty like a giant, and looking up at her vast bulk, I felt very small indeed!
>
> Arriving on deck, I looked towards her bows and wondered where they were going to terminate. In fact it would not have surprised me to see a bus drive from around her huge gun turrets. She gave one the impression of being in a big city, so great were her areas and spaces.[15]

It was not just her royal connections with the Special Service Squadron that made *Hood* the favourite ship of the navy and the public. According to D. A. Rayner she was 'the most beautiful steamship that man ever devised'.[16] When the Coombes brothers were drafted to her in 1935, 'we were thrilled when we heard that, with 6 others, we had been chosen to join the mighty "Hood", thinking it an honour when most of our class had been sent to the much smaller cruisers …' On arrival at Portsmouth, they recalled 'struggling up the long steep gangway with, first, our bags and after scathing remarks about our slackness, a run back down to fetch our Hammocks, we felt like flies on top of a dung heap'. And when they sailed out of the harbor, 'The pride we took in our first appearance as part of the crew of the "Mighty Hood" as she slid quietly and was quite close to the fortifications guarding the entrance to Portsmouth Harbour, with cheering crowds waving their farewells, was soon put into a matter of fact, with the remark that some of the crowd were glad to see us go and the order to clean ship on leaving land.'[17]

Very different were *Rodney* and *Nelson*. They were much shorter than originally intended because of the limitations imposed by the disarmament treaty and to the historically-minded they were 'the cherry trees' – cut down by Washington. Their lack of fore-and-aft symmetry and their angular shape caused the lower deck to adopt more basic nicknames – the 'ugly sisters' and 'the pair of boots'. One officer in *Rodney* had to agree that they were not beautiful: 'In these two ships there is not the faintest suggestion of the low pyramidical profile and jutting armament that gives so truculent an air to previous design. Instead, they suggest an L on its back, with a short tail ...'[18]

Not everyone liked big ships:

Big ships are lonely places. There is no camaraderie, no sense of intimacy. Knowing hundreds of people, you don't really know anyone. The upper deck of *Malaya* during the dog watches was as desolate and miserable as a wet night in Piccadilly Circus to the visiting provincial. Faces come and go, and even after eighteen months aboard her, there were still people I had never seen. On a big ship the fo'c'sle messes are as remote from the stokers' as if separated by hundreds of miles of ocean; quarterdeckmen and maintopmen are barely homogeneous. Everything is too big, too impersonal, too lonely.[19]

On the other hand, the traditional naval song, which occurred in many varieties, favoured big ships over destroyers:

Roll on the *Rodney*, *Repulse* or *Renown*
This two funnelled bastard is getting me down.

## Life in the Fleet

Statistics showed a much more law-abiding navy than before the war. In 1923–4 there was a desertion rate of less than half of one per cent per annum compared with 1.26% in 1912–13. Only 61 ratings were sentenced to imprisonment in the latter year, a fifth of the figure before the war, and

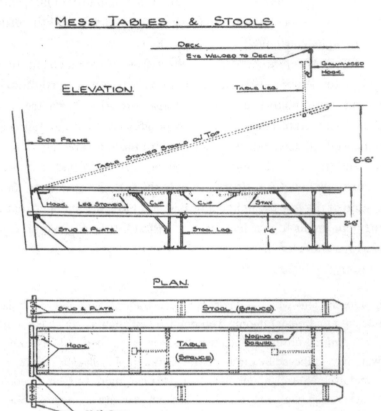

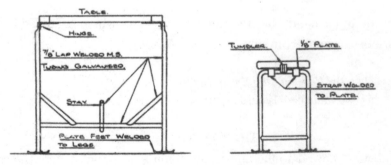

Standard designs for mess tables and stools, from *Practical Construction of Warships*, by R. N. Newton.

501 to detention, compared with 2,313 – overall a fall from 2.06 to 0.73% of the fleet. A reduction in crime by two-thirds is impressive by any standards.

But conditions on board ship were not necessarily any more comfortable. Ashore and in barracks, an allowance of 600 cubic feet per person was considered barely adequate – 300 cubic feet was allowed in 'common lodging houses' that were only occupied at night, and 400 in those that were occupied both day and night. In modern battleships, cruisers and destroyers the design provided for '200 cubic feet per man for all purposes, which would admit of an interval of 20 inches between hammock and hammock, but in the course of completing and equipping ships this allowance is unavoidable encroached upon, and the actual space available in completed ships is approximately only 150 cubic feet per man'. It would be impossible to increase this 'without unduly increasing the size of ships of given fighting power, and a very limited allowance of sleeping and working space is one of the necessities of naval life'.[20]

The messdeck was at the centre of life as always:

I was victualler in a mess, the members of which were mainly Irish or West Countrymen, since *Queen Elizabeth* was a Devonport manned ship. We were a happy-go-lucky lot and many were the times we had a mess sing-song, with a couple of our Irish members playing piano accordians [sic]. The Cornish and Devon types possessed a soft and pleasant accent which fascinated me, and one or two of them wore a single gold ring in one ear in the manner of gypsies. Some wore magnificent black beards, black and smartly trimmed. As the only Portsmouth rating in the mess, I took a lot of ribbing from them, but I was glad to be one of their number.[21]

Sport was a priority in the peacetime fleet, and Fred Copeman excelled at it:

Wrestling and boxing were favourites. Hockey was played with a piece of wood as the chucker – (a bucket of chuckers were always available as so many were lost over the side). And of course there was a tug-of war and 'Tombola', the only game of chance, other than betting on regatta days, permitted in the Fleet.[22]

Football was played incessantly in bases such as Invergordon, but for many the highlight was the inter-ship regattas:

> We were handicapped by carrying the heaviest cox'n in the fleet; a chief petty officer who weighed seventeen stones if he weighed an ounce. Yet, although we cursed as we laboured over our oars, we loved him dearly, and would have rowed him up the Styx had he asked us. He, in turn, was responsible for many minor miracles; we were excused scrubbing decks, had cocoa in our hammocks while the rest of the world worked, were provided with small boys to carry our oars to the boat, and were plied with gargantuan quantities of food.[23]

Ashore and between ships, a seaman had a certain amount of freedom:

> Liberty, as the right to go on shore is termed in the navy, was exceptionally generous at Devonport, in that we could spend all our free time on shore. All activities, study and working parties were ended at 4 pm, and anybody not on watch aboard was entitled to go on shore till seven the next morning. Such freedom I have never met in any armed force in the world. As a result many married men, returning from a foreign commission to be accommodated in the barracks, closed up their houses in their home towns, hired rooms near the barracks and lived with their wives the whole time they were at Devonport.[24]

As a result some of the older men tried to become 'barrack stanchions', with more or less permanent jobs in the home ports.

## THE BRANCHES

This was a rather static period for naval technology, with no radically new weapons or engines. There was no overall reform of the branch structure of the navy but some new developments on a small scale. The structure of the gunnery branch had become more complex than ever by the end of the war. As well as the basic seaman gunners, it had gunlayers and range takers, both of whom needed excellent vision, light director layers, each of whom was 'of higher standard intelligence' and 'capable of care and maintenance and operating a delicate and mechanical instrument', and sight setters. At the top of the tree was the gunnery instructor:

> A very highly trained Petty Officer or Leading Seaman. Trained to instruct, organise and take charge of large parties of men. Has a thorough knowledge of all types of drill used by the Navy. Has experience of using and good general knowledge of hydraulic machinery. Has an elementary knowledge of the principles of electricity. Has had more advanced educational and mathematical training than the average Petty Officer. Knowledge of keeping accounts and taking charge of stores.[25]

There was some attempt at simplification after the war, but the path to promotion remained quite complex. By 1932 a man became a seaman gunner (trained man), then had a choice of training on board ship as a seaman gunner or acting range taker third class. After that he might qualify via a gunnery school as gunnery lieutenant's writer, range taker second class or gun layer second class. As a leading seaman, he could go on to become a captain of gun second class, director layer second class or gun layer first class. After that he could qualify as gunner's mate, but only if he was passed for petty officer.[26]

Anti-submarine training languished after the war, split between the torpedo and the signal branches, until 1925, when the captain of the school at Portland suggested that 'the A/S Service has now grown out of the experimental and pioneer stages into a fully fledged and vigorous youth'. He advocated a separate branch on a par with gunnery and torpedo, on the grounds that 'this Science of Subaqueous Sound is vast, and demands special and thorough attention'.[27] Training was duly set up at Portland, where the navy already had substantial facilities, and there were both sheltered and open waters nearby for training and experiments. The demands of the branch were quite small, only six men for each asdic-equipped destroyer or sloop, so that a three-watch system could be maintained with two men always on duty. Even so, it was always difficult to recruit adequately. Very little was said about it in the boys' training schools, though gunnery and torpedo instruction formed large parts of the syllabus. And when they got to sea the boys usually went to big ships, which had no asdic, and fell under the influence of gunnery and torpedo officers and petty officers. Portland was unpopular as a depot, being away from the livelier home ports and with poor rail communication. At the top level, the submarine detectors were paid slightly less than gunners and torpedomen, and they were only employed in small ships, destroyers and sloops, where men liable to seasickness would live very uncomfortably. But this was a positive advantage to John Whelan:

> Submarine detectors live in small ships. Thus, if I became an Asdic operator, the odds were heavily in favour of my staying in small ships for the rest of my naval service. I promptly volunteered – and was accepted.[28]

However, it was felt that the best men were being creamed off by the more traditional branches, leaving mostly failures for the anti-submarine branch. The Admiralty appealed for volunteers in 1928, 1930 and 1932, but the results were barely adequate, with no margins in either numbers or quality. By 1935 there were still only 352 men in the branch, a shortfall of 84; it was planned to increase it to 837 by 1940. Anti-submarine officers were well aware of the vital importance of good asdic operators, if no one else was:

> On the suspicion of an echo, he has to investigate and report. A constant state of concentration and alertness is required, and, in watches, has often to be maintained for days on end.
>
> Having reported his echo, and being ordered to hold it, the operator has to find the width of the target, determine whether it is opening or closing, and its change of bearing, and keep his Control Officer constantly informed of all he can deduce. He has also to classify the echo as a 'submarine' or 'non-sub'. With a 'cracking' echo, this is not too difficult for an intelligent man to do, but, as often happens, when echoes are faint and uncertain, it becomes a fine art.

A good operator, then, had to be 'a man of character, keenness and intelligence' rather than one of the dregs that were sometimes sent for training. The captain of HMS *Osprey*, the base at Portland, drafted a notice to put on the boards of training establishments.

> We nearly lost the last war because we had no suitable device for detecting and attacking submarines

We now have such a device and special ratings known as S/D Operators are trained to work it.

The S/D Operator carries out similar duties to the other seamen except that instead of being stationed at a gun or torpedo tube when at action he keeps watch in a Cabinet and operates a special listening device to search ahead of the ship for enemy submarines.

His job is a very responsible one as any submarine he fails to hear may slip through and sink a battleship.

S/D Operators do courses of instruction at Portland. Good men can go on to the higher ratings of S/S 1st Class and S/D Instructors.[29]

Within the seaman branch, there was a feeling that pure seamanship skills were being disregarded, as the only way forward was to qualify as a gunner or torpedoman:

It is recognised that there will be in the future as in the past certain men who will rise to the rank of Petty Officers without obtaining a higher non-substantive rating than Seaman Gunner or Seaman Torpedoman. Moreover there is a demand for such Petty Officers in the Service to fill such posts as Leading Hands of Shell Rooms, Magazines, Control, Boatswain's Mates and in charge of other isolated parties.[30]

In 1922 it was suggested that a new branch should be set up for quartermasters. One duty was to take the helm of the ship in action: 'The importance of good steering to good gunnery is generally admitted, but the degree to which the efficiency of the ship as a fighting unit depends on the manner in which she is conned and steered does not appear to be fully realised. An injudicious use of the helm, or bad station keeping, will create irregularities in the speed of the ship which will make it difficult for the ship's gunfire to be kept on for line ...' Steering should be 'recognised as being skilled work and duly paid as such ...' Quartermasters could also take charge of the ship's boats and assist the navigator with plotting duties. The old warrant rank of boatswain was dying out, and a new one of warrant quartermaster should be developed to replace it. Despite these compelling arguments, nothing was done. The powerful gunnery branch did not want the best men to be creamed off, while the navigation branch resented ratings taking any part in their craft.[31]

Photography was a more modern branch, though it remained very small. It was recognised that the camera could be used to assess the success of gunnery and other exercises, to record coastlines and shore features in the surveying branch, while the movie camera could help make what the officers called 'Mutt and Jeff' training films. Aerial photography, however was to remain the province of the RAF, which had a large and formally organized photographic branch. In contrast, the navy retained a small number of men and civilian women attached to HMS *Excellent* in Portsmouth Harbour but declined to set up a fully fledged non-substantive branch.

The domestic branch (including servants and cooks) was looked at by a committee in 1921. It found that, 'The branch has hitherto been regarded by the recruiting sergeants as one of extreme utility as into it they can place the rejected and as often as not, the undesirable candidate for other branches.' It recommended a warrant rank, which might cause some difficulties afloat if former servants found themselves messing with officers – so the rank was only to be used in shore training bases, where the education of domestics was to be increased in scope. It was suggested that marine servants should be replaced by properly trained stewards, but that was not achieved for some decades. The most important change was to transfer the bulk of the branch to continuous service for the first time, though the committee recommended that officers of commander's rank and above should be able to take their valets with them from ship to ship if they wished.[32] But the navy was not going solve its 'servant problem' easily, for the middle classes were beginning to move into the new 'servantless' homes in the suburbs, so the prospects for a man leaving the service, and the prestige of the servant generally, were in decline.

In 1931 a committee tried to reduce the ever-growing number of non-substantive badges worn by ratings, with limited success – a few of the stars worn with badges were abolished, but the system remained arcane to anyone but a specialist.[33] Even the simplest badge was important to a young sailor. When promoted to stoker first class, Sydney Greenwood was pleased: 'Proudly and joyously I unpicked the stitches from the propeller badges on my uniforms and overalls and sewed on replacement badges having a star above a propeller.' And later, 'I now felt entitled to appraise arrogantly the new-entries as they arrived in our block of buildings from their training quarters. I hoped they felt as inferior as I had a year earlier, and enjoyed watching them looking enviously at my badge.'[34]

## A Golden Age in the Mediterranean

Since there was no post-war alliance with France, the navy resumed its policy of keeping up a large Mediterranean Fleet: it regarded the area as a good one for fleet training in reasonably favourable weather. It was popular with the lower deck, providing congenial foreign travel in an age when very few working-class people had gone abroad except as emigrants. Some compared it with an expensive cruise: 'You travel by destroyer, not yacht; drink beer rather than champagne; eat sausages instead of caviar; wear bell-bottoms, not natty gents' suitings. But you will have spent a couple of years touring the Mediterranean, which is more than your home town neighbours will have done.' [35]

According to Stoker Sidney Greenwood,

To me it seemed that Gibraltar consisted on one main street, and that crowded with sailors of the Home and Mediterranean Fleets. Shops were stocked full of novelties from Europe and the East in readiness for this annual assault of the ships' companies. Ladies' orchestras belting out popular tunes drew men into the Trocadero and Universal bars. Beer sloshed about as we jostled to get a closer look at the attractive musicians.[36]

Malta was equally exciting, according to Stoker Greenwood:

As far as I could see, with my blinkered young eyes, Malta's main interest was a narrow street made up of steps leading from a main avenue down to the harbour. In the evening it was jammed full with white suited sailors and khaki uniformed marines who were popping in and out of doorways at the sides.

Each of the closely joined buildings was either a place of entertainment or some other facility for our benefit. Barbers' shops, bed-and-breakfast, fortune telling, all doing a roaring trade. Music filled the air. A dozen public house pianos mingled with the small bands from the bigger saloons with names such as Egyptian Queen and Silver Horse. Smells of lovely fatty fried food invaded the nostrils of sailors unused to rich living. Maltese men and girls found little resistance to their 'Come inside, Jack, very cheap'. As the evening progressed so did the noise and the odours. Men got drunk and there were brawls; but it was all kept in hand by naval patrols provided by the ships.[37]

Like many sailors, Fred Copeman also saw the seamier side of life in the ports:

Another memory of Malta is of the row of small, squalid buildings near Floriana on the way to Cite Victoria, in which the prostitutes are housed. Young and old, black and white, each has her own small quarters and – like the rest of the population – serves the Fleet. My first visit to a brothel was here. With a couple of chums I went ashore to have a drink. One thing led to another and we were soon induced to visit the brothel by one of the Maltese gharry drivers. At that time I was training for boxing and didn't like the idea, but still less liked to feel out of things. However, when we got to the place it was so filthy and squalid that I refused to go on – a bit of luck, for both my chums were in a rotten mess a few days later with gonorrhoea.[38]

## THE STATUS OF OFFICERS

Old-fashioned deference, and the idea that the upper classes were worthy of automatic respect, had largely disappeared during the war, but naval officers were not prepared to give up any of their old privileges. Moreover, schemes for the promotion of officers from the lower deck were much more restricted as the opportunities were diminished in a reduced fleet.

The officer corps was divided into factions, which did not make it any easier for the lower deck to respect it. The failure of Jutland remained an issue until both Jellicoe and Beatty died in 1936, and those who had fought in the battle tended to blame one or the other for the disappointing performance. Occasionally senior officers attracted unfavourable press attention by their behaviour. In 1927, Bernard Collard of the 'on the knee' incident, now a rear admiral, had an open dispute with his flag captain in the *Royal Oak*, Kenneth Dewar, involving Marine Bandmaster Barnacle. It resulted in a highly publicized court martial that did the navy no credit. AB Len Wincott wondered 'what further ridicule' the officers 'were prepared to inflict on the Royal Navy'.[39]

Officers received no training in leadership, and not all had natural skills. According to one officer, the system had limitations as well as strengths:

> For the most part what emerged was a definite breed of fit, tough, highly trained but sketchily educated professionals, ready for instant duty, for parades or tea parties, for catastrophes, for peace or war; confident leaders, alert seamen, fair administrators, poor delegators; officers of wide interests and narrow vision, strong on tactics, weak on strategy; an able, active, cheerful, monosyllabic elite.[40]

It was Dewar who proposed a change: 'Midshipmen should also be instructed in the technique of command. Instead of working out schoolboy sums under the naval instructor, they might study principles of command and organisation, typical defects such as over-centralisation, lack of co-ordination, secrecy mania, excessive paper work, etc., being illustrated by practical examples.'[41]

Officially there was a tendency to keep the officers and men as far apart as possible. In 1923 the Admiralty was made aware that 'a practice has arisen of dinners given to Naval officers by Clubs or Societies of Chief Petty Officers or other Naval Ratings under their orders'. This was contrary to King's Regulations, as no officer was 'to allow himself to be complimented by presents or any collective expression of opinion from Officers or Ships Companies'.[42]

## INVERGORDON

The world economic crisis had been developing since the Wall Street Crash of 1929. In the autumn of 1931 a new National – or coalition – government took power in Britain, determined to make severe cuts. The duty of finding the navy's contribution to this fell on a brand new Admiralty Board – the experienced secretary was on leave at the time, and the commander-in-chief of the Atlantic Fleet was ill. But even so, it showed spectacular incompetence in the way the cuts were carried out. In the first place, one shilling across the board was blatantly unfair – it would hardly affect an admiral at all but would take away a substantial part of the income of a seaman, stoker or Marine.

Whatever its reason for choosing an across-the-board cut, the Admiralty had touched a particularly raw nerve – one shilling a day was exactly a quarter of the basic pay of an able seaman on the 1919 rates, so it had a peculiar symbolism. In fact, the cut was hardly ever as stark as that since practically all of the 1919 men had at least one good conduct badge, and the great majority had some kind of non-substantive pay. Most of them would be over 25 and entitled to marriage allowance, and it was generally agreed that married men would be hit hardest by the cuts. But the four shilling rate had been defended over several series of cuts already, and its sanctity had even been promised in Parliament. The Admiralty itself conceded privately that the cut would be a serious breach of contract by a private employer, and only crown immunity made it legal. To the lower deck it was the last straw. If that could be taken away, which of the lower deck's few and hard-won privileges was safe?

To make matters worse, the Admiralty failed to ensure sure that the cuts were announced to the men openly and clearly. Instead the news leaked out, and, as the Atlantic Fleet left the home ports to sail north and carry out exercises at Invergordon on 8 September 1931, it was already the talk of the messdecks. The official announcement was made on the 10th, while the fleet was still at sea. When the six capital ships and attendant cruisers and destroyers anchored at Invergordon on Friday the 11th, the news was in the press but the seamen had not been told officially. When the men were allowed ashore on the Sunday they were able to buy newspapers, and their worst fears were confirmed. An Admiralty telegram that was supposed to break the news officially to the men lay unread on the desk of the C-in-C, Admiral Sir Michael Hodges, who was on sick leave.

From an Admiralty point of view, Invergordon was the worst possible place for the news to break. If the ships had still been at their home ports,

Two aspects of the new navy – submarines passing HMS *Dreadnought*, *c*.1910, as drawn by
W. L. Wyllie. (National Maritime Museum PW 1230)

Above: A group of naval police in 1901 – petty officers with a master at arms in the centre. From John Blake, *How Sailors Fight*, 1901.

Below: A trawler's crew *c*.1916, showing men who were not easily brought under traditional naval discipline. From E. Keble Chatterton, *The Auxiliary Patrol*, 1923.

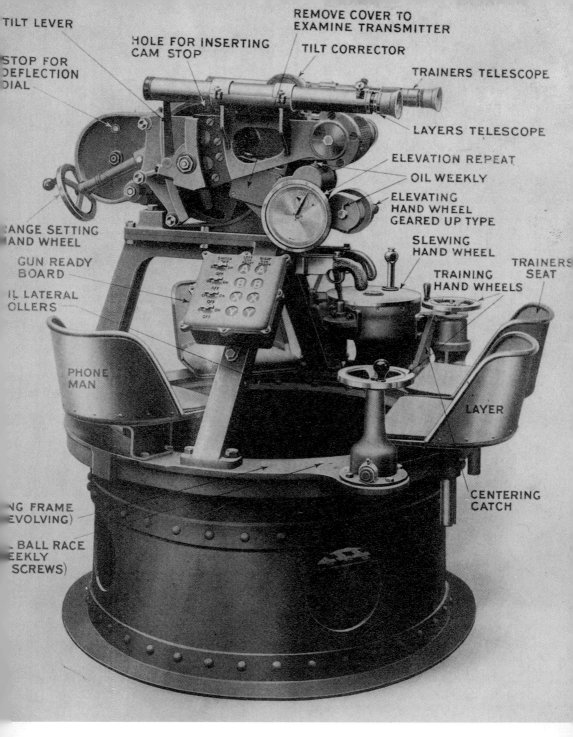

TILT LEVER

STOP FOR
DEFLECTION
DIAL

HOLE FOR INSERTING
CAM STOP

REMOVE COVER TO
EXAMINE TRANSMITTER

TILT CORRECTOR

TRAINERS TELESCOPE

LAYERS TELESCOPE

ELEVATION REPEAT

OIL WEEKLY

ELEVATING
HAND WHEEL
GEARED UP TYPE

RANGE SETTING
HAND WHEEL

GUN READY
BOARD

IL LATERAL
OLLERS

SLEWING
HAND WHEEL

TRAINERS
SEAT

TRAINING
HAND WHEELS

PHONE
MAN

LAYER

NG FRAME
EVOLVING)

BALL RACE
EEKLY
SCREWS)

CENTERING
CATCH

An early gun director, showing the seats and instruments used by the trainer, layer and the
phone man. Later directors also had seats for officers in charge.

**Above:** The Grand Fleet at sea, with the ships steaming in columns. (Imperial War Museum Q18121)

**Left:** Boy First Class Jack Cornwell, who won a posthumous VC by standing by his gun when fatally wounded at Jutland. (Imperial War Museum Q20883)

Using hydrophones on board the drifter *Thrive* as part of the Otranto Barrage in the Adriatic Sea in 1917. (Imperial War Museum Q63034)

**Above:** A naval airship, North Sea No. 4, showing the large crew needed to handle her on the ground. (Imperial War Museum Q27433)
**Below:** Sailors scrubbing the decks, *c.*1930. From *The Wonder Book of the Navy.*

Visitors on board ship looking at the guns. From *The Wonder Book of the Navy*.

DAILY HERALD, September 16, 1931.

**WANTED 100 Persons (either sex) who have the ambition to earn a nice sum in their spare time.**

Would you like some crisp £1 notes to spend just as you please? Then if you are enterprising, you can have the thing you so much want this very Christmas by selling Private Christmas Cards to your friends and acquaintances. This is the way. Address a postcard to us asking for one of the beautiful Sample Books. This book and full particulars will be sent you by return of post, quite free of charge. Remuneration most generous, and many valuable prizes in addition. Apply FIRTH GRAHAM AND CO., Ltd., Dept. F.51 Corporation St., Accrington.

# Daily Herald

No. 4863 • WEDNESDAY, SEPTEMBER 16, 1931 • ONE PENNY.

**Holbrook's** *Worcestershire* **Sauce** *the Sauce of appetite*

# ATLANTIC FLEET RECALLED—*Official*

CLEANING THE DECKS under the guns of H.M.S. Warspite, one of the big ships now lying at Invergordon.

## UNREST FOLLOWS PAY CUTS AMONG LOWER RATINGS

*Exercises Suspended Pending Admiralty Inquiry*

*Premier's Talks With Crew of Warship at Portsmouth*

REAR-ADMIRAL TOMKINSON

## SAILORS HOLD MASS MEETING ON SHORE

**THE Admiralty issued the following statement last evening:**

*"The Senior Officer, Atlantic Fleet, has reported that the promulgation of the reduced rates of naval pay has led to unrest amongst a proportion of the lower ratings.*

*"In consequence of this he has deemed it desirable to suspend the programme of exercises of the Fleet, and to recall the ships to harbour while investigations are being made into representations of the hardship occasioned by certain of the cuts in pay, in order that these may be reported to the consideration of the Board of Admiralty."*

Later, the Board of Admiralty issued another statement, as follows:—

*"Their lordships have approved of the exercises of the Atlantic Fleet being temporarily suspended whilst certain representations of hardship under new rates of pay are being investigated for the consideration of their lordships."*

Rear-Admiral Wilfred Tomkinson, C.B., M.V.O., is the senior officer mentioned. He commands in the absence on sick leave of Admiral Sir Michael Hodges, K.C.B., C.M.G., M.V.O.

### *AIR DASH TO LONDON*

At Invergordon, where ten ships of the Atlantic Fleet are lying, the men to-day await the return of an officer who flew to London yesterday.

He bore with him to the Admiralty full news of resolutions protesting against pay cuts passed at mass meetings of the Lower Deck held ashore.

At the famous Rosyth dockyard 375 men of the battleship Iron Duke presented a protest petition to their commander.

From Our Special Correspondent

ABERDEEN, Tuesday.

INVERGORDON to-night is as quiet as a village on the shore of a South Sea island.

All the ships of the fleet are lying peacefully at anchor in the bay, and there is no sign of trouble or disturbances.

Members of the local town council and municipal officials assure me that for two days there has been no difficulty with members of the crews.

PROTEST RESOLUTIONS

Meetings of the lower ratings were held ashore on Saturday and Sunday, at which resolutions were passed protesting against the cuts in pay and seeking their withdrawal.

**The Saturday meeting was very boisterous, for most of the sailors had been to Invergordon games, and attended the gathering in a lively mood.**

Extra pickets were brought on shore to prevent disturbance.

The Sunday meeting was an orderly and serious affair, at which speeches were delivered and questions asked and answered. There was no trouble with pickets or police.

Resolutions passed at the meeting were presented to the commanding officer with the request that they should be communicated to the Admiralty.

**I learn to-night that a high officer travelled by air to London to-day.**

The lower deck hopes that he will return to-morrow with a reply to their resolutions.

All shore leave was stopped yesterday and to-day, when Invergordon was surprised to find the Fleet had not sailed, nor a single bluejacket landed.

Meanwhile no hostility has developed between the men and the bulk of the officers, and the ships seem absolutely at peace.

Yesterday spectators on the shore observed crowds of men meeting on board various ships, from which sounds of cheering could be heard, followed by the singing of popular choruses.

**On one ship sailors were collected in groups on deck. A party gathered round a piano and held an informal concert.**

Another crowd indulged in an acrobatic performance, and this indicated that they were having time off from their usual duty.

### 375 SIGN PETITION

PROTEST BY IRON DUKE'S SEAMEN

From Our Special Correspondent

DUNFERMLINE, Tuesday.

Dissatisfaction has also arisen among the lower naval ratings at the Rosyth naval base, on the Firth of Forth.

A petition against the pay reductions was signed to-day by 375 seamen of the battleship Iron Duke, and presented to the Commander, Captain E. G. Boyle, V.C.

He explained that the cuts were not made at the direct command of the Admiralty, but in accordance with the Government's economy policy.

It is expected that the protest will be sent to the Admiralty.

Protests are also possible from the destroyer crews.

### SAVING ON SHELLS

ECONOMY MANŒUVRES PLANNED

The training period of the Atlantic Fleet exercises is considered the most important event of the naval year.

Economy, however, was to be enforced throughout this year's exercises.

**Every effort was being made to cruise at speeds most economical for oil consumption, and gunnery practice was to be curtailed to save on the enormous expense incurred each time a shell is fired.**

The Moray Firth, where these sea "battles" with gunfire, smoke screens and all the elaborate and expensive paraphernalia of modern war, takes place, is ideal for the purpose.

Desolate and wide, it is hardly used by normal shipping.

**Admiral Sir Michael Hodges, the Commander-in-Chief of the Atlantic Fleet, who flies his flag in Nelson, is in hospital at Gosport, recovering from a severe attack of pleurisy.**

Rear-Admiral Tomkinson, who took command in his stead, flies his flag in Hood, which is the largest man-o'-war in the world.

(Continued on Page Two, Col. Four.)

### *Where the Ships Are*

**UNITS of the Atlantic Fleet, now at Invergordon, Cromarty Firth, comprise the battleships**

**Nelson, Rodney, Warspite, Valiant, Malaya.**

**The battle-cruisers Nelson and Rodney,**

**and the cruisers Norfolk, York, Dorsetshire.**

**Destroyers and submarine flotillas, also belonging to the Atlantic Fleet, are at Rosyth, Firth of Forth.**

## *SNOWDEN HINTS AT ELECTION*

### SUGGESTS IT MAY COME ABOUT IN FEW WEEKS

**MR. SNOWDEN, in the House of Commons last night, hinted at the possibility of a General Election within the next few weeks.**

**"During the last few days," he said, "I have been able for the first time to study in the House the faces of my late associates. I have admired the way they have cheered to keep their spirits up.**

**"I have admired those who have done that, knowing that only a few weeks possibly remain before the place which now knows them will know them no more."**

THE only motion on the House of Lords' paper for Thursday is for the adjournment.

To-day Lord Melchett will put down a motion to the effect that "This House approves the action of the Government with setting up a Committee of the Cabinet to inquire into the question of methods of balancing the exchange trade."

His real purpose in putting down this motion is to get a house before which he can demand that there shall be no immediate election—no election in fact until after the Budget of 1932 has been passed.

The "Daily Herald's" disclosure yesterday of the Tory scheme to force a snap General Election on October 15 created a sensation at Westminster.

Tories who had hoped to catch the Labour Party napping were angered at the disclosure, which put Labour on its mettle throughout the constituencies.

A very prominent Tory M.P. closely in the confidence of the Cabinet, when asked yesterday if the General Election would take place in November, replied: "It must be earlier than that—some time in October."

During the day Lord Stonehaven, Chairman of the Conservative Party Organisation, met London M.P.s and candidates, and warned them to get ready for a General Election at any time after the new register comes in force on October 15.

There is strong opposition in the City and especially on the part of the Bank of England to the proposals of the Tory Party organisers for an early election (writes our City Editor).

All the influence of the Bank of England will be used to obtain an agreement to keep the present Government in office till next year.

CONVERSION LOAN PROSPECTS

The City considers it especially necessary that there should not be an election before the end of October, as plans will be ready for launching the Five per Cent. War Loan Conversion scheme by the middle of that month.

Accompanying the conversion offer there will probably be an issue of a new loan offering interest of either four or 4½ per cent., and issued at a slight discount, to raise funds for repaying foreign holders of five per cent. War Loan who are not prepared to convert into new stock.

The banks and the big insurance companies are holding funds ready to subscribe for this new loan.

An immediate election would upset all the plan for war loan conversion and might also, in the opinion of the Bank of England, lead to another crisis in sterling.

POLICE RESENTMENT

Mr. J. H. Hayes, M.P., yesterday said there was considerable feeling and resentment in the police force concerning the proposed cuts.

"Not only," said Mr. Hayes, "is their opposition to the amount of the cuts, but to the methods employed to bring them about.

"Although put forward as emergency measures, the Government proposals have about them the atmosphere of permanency.

"The wholesale revision of expressed and implied standards—some even laid down by Statute—has done much to destroy the belief that the Government would honour its contractual obligation to its employees.

"This has been made perfectly clear by members of the Force at the many meetings which have been held all around London and in the provinces where the machinery of negotiation has been roughly and ruthlessly swept aside."

HOOVER'S NEW DEBT MOVE

President Hoover has been recommended to extend immediately the one-year moratorium on war debts and reparations to three or five years.

It is believed, cables the New York correspondent of the "Daily Herald," that the suggestion of a further war debts moratorium was put to Mr. Hoover at a dinner at the White House attended by Governor Eugene Meyer and twelve business men and bankers who compose the Federal Reserve Board's Advisory Council.

The invitation to them was interpreted as eagerness on Mr. Hoover's part to stimulate business developments and to obtain ideas to relieve the crisis.

He sounded the bankers on the necessity of liberalising credits for the benefit of both domestic and foreign interests.

Mr. Snowden stated in the Commons yesterday that he was inquiring into the Lord Nelson pension and similar payments.

### *Premier Talks to Lower Deck Men*

**THE "Daily Herald" learns that the Prime Minister was among men of the Navy at the week-end when he visited Portsmouth to see the Schneider Trophy race.**

**He embarked with the First Lord of the Admiralty, Sir A. Chamberlain, on the destroyer Winchester, and at Spithead transferred to the aircraft carrier Courageous, the only big ship of the Atlantic Fleet at Portsmouth.**

**Mr. MacDonald talked to some of the lower deck men on the question of cuts in pay.**

**He explained to them the financial position of the country, and asked them to pass on to their shipmates what he had told them.**

**The men thanked him afterwards for their friendly talk.**

### RATHER WARM

(SEE PAGE THREE)



MISS SLADE

## TRUTH ABOUT MISS SLADE

### LIFE DEVOTED TO INDIA

### LUXURY RENOUNCED

**"I have come to London to strive my utmost to find points of agreement," declared Mr. Gandhi yesterday in putting before the Round-Table delegates the claims of the All-India Congress (as reported on Page Four).**

**Congress, he said, was intent on complete independence. He contemplated a partnership of two absolute peoples "held, not by force, but by the silken cord of love."**

**Mr. Gandhi (says the Central News) will visit Manchester on Friday week.**

By Our Special Representative

A TALL, slight woman, wearing Indian costume but unmistakably British, who is now to be seen sometimes moving among the costermongers' barrows and entering the little shops in the streets of Bow, is the centre of as much interest and curiosity, almost, as Mahatma Gandhi himself.

She is Miss Madeleine Slade, daughter of the late Admiral Sir Edmond Slade.

She renounced a life of ease and elegance in London to become a disciple of the Mahatma, and she has followed him through good and evil report for the past six years.

**Women write to her, begging for advice;**

**Poor people send her their blessings [illegible] doors of Kingsley Hall asking for a message from her to the United States.**

She, meanwhile, has probably slipped out by a side door to buy a cabbage or some fruit for the frugal meals of Mr. Gandhi's little party.

Four people at Kingsley Hall have constituted themselves into a personal suite for the Mahatma.

They are his son (Mr. Devidas Gandhi), his secretary (Mr. Desai), Mr.

(Continued on Page Two, Col. One.)

### *£500 A WEEK FILM ACTOR*

*RECORD SALARY FOR MR. LESLIE HOWARD*

From Our Film Correspondent

Mr. Leslie Howard, the young English actor, who played here in Tallulah Bankhead's "Her Cardboard Lover," has come over from Hollywood to play in a British film at a salary of £500 per week.

This is a record salary for a film actor in this country.

Mr. Howard has the leading part in the Paramount Company's new picture, "The Head Waiter," now starting at their Elstree studios, under the Austrian director, Mr. Alexander Korda.

Another American company, Warner Brothers, have engaged Mr. John Longden, Mr. Ben Field, Miss Florence Desmond and Miss Pat Paterson, for "Murder on the Second Floor," their first British film, now started at the Teddington studios.

Two leading young West-End actresses, Miss Gillian Lind and Miss Jane Welsh, are playing with Mr. Gordon Harker and Mr. Arthur Wontner, in "Jack o' Lantern" at the Twickenham studios. F. L. M.

£423,000 SCHEME SHELVED

Norwich City Council yesterday decided by 30 votes to 26 to postpone the proposed construction of a north-south road through the city at a cost of £423,890. The scheme was sanctioned two months ago.



The Invergordon Mutiny as reported by the *Daily Herald* on 16 September 1931. (CPL) any revolt would have been fragmented, and perhaps it would have been moderated by the men's families. At Invergordon, on the other hand, a large group of ships was massed together in a port where there was little for the lower deck to do ashore except play football and drink. Men from different ships began to gather in the naval canteen, and feelings were running high – it was noticed that the three-badge men, by definition on the 1919 scale of pay, were the most vociferous, and some of them climbed on to tables to make speeches. Inter-ship rivalry, encouraged by the navy for centuries as a way of team building and getting the best out of the men, now began to backfire as the crews of one ship accused another of being too 'yellow' to do anything. Able Seaman Len Wincott of the cruiser *Norfolk*, relatively young at 24, began to emerge as one of the leaders. The officer from the battleship *Warspite* who was in charge of the naval patrol sensed that something was happening and asked for extra men; but very few could be found aboard the ship. By the end of Sunday, a consensus had arisen in the canteen that on Tuesday, when the ships were due to sail, the crews would refuse to weigh anchor.

On Monday morning the acting commander of the fleet, Rear Admiral Wilfred Tomkinson, sent a signal to the Admiralty:

Important. There was a slight disturbance in the Royal Naval canteen at Invergordon yesterday Sunday evening caused by one or two ratings endeavouring to address those present on the subject of reduction in pay. I attach no importance to the incident from a general disciplinary point of view but it is possible it may be reported in an exaggerated form by the press. Matter is still being investigated.[43]

That afternoon the men were given leave again, and unusually large numbers went ashore, although there was little to do in Invergordon. Normally they should have been from alternate watches, and not the same men who had taken part in the Sunday meetings, though some may have changed with their opposite numbers in the other watch. According to a seaman in *Valiant*:

We decided to – well, more or less down tools, go on strike, that's what we called it. The spokesmen said that we ought to show our disapproval of

289

what was going to happen and the only way to show that disapproval was to just stop work. They stood up ... I think there was two or three men spoke. I can't say who they were because they were from other ships. There was nobody from our ship. People had removed their cap ribbons, so we're not supposed to know ... There was so many of us we could hardly move. We had a show of hands, what we should do, and it was agreed we should down tools.

Then we heard a banging at the door. Someone looked out of the window and said, 'It's the Officer of the Patrol.' We'd got the door on a latch so that he couldn't push it in if he wanted to.[44]

The intruder was Lieutenant Robert Elkins of *Valiant*, who had been sent a message about the meeting in the canteen. He was let in and spoke to the men:

After a short while I was able to make my voice heard, and everybody in the Canteen listened quietly while I told them that I would stay in the canteen until I was satisfied that what was being discussed was not to the prejudice of discipline. When I stopped speaking the Cat-Calls and shouts continued, although I was not jostled. I heard one man behind me say, 'That stops the meeting', and I hoped it had.[45]

Someone threw a glass at Elkins, who was pushed out of the door by a scrum of seamen. Patrols were increased yet again, and officers observed that the men in town were reluctant to salute them. As the men got on board the boats to get back to their ships, some called out, 'Don't forget. Six o'clock tomorrow.' The officers had a deep sense of foreboding, but Tomkinson still did nothing. Perhaps he was out of his depth, perhaps he hoped that it would all blow over if the men were not provoked.

Tuesday morning came, bringing great tension among both officers and men. The crew of the battlecruiser *Repulse*, the first to sail and the nearest to the harbour entrance, had only been together a few weeks and had no collective solidarity. At 6.30 her anchor was raised and she duly sailed out of the harbor. But things were very different in the other capital ships. *Valiant* was due to sail next, but in her and *Rodney* the petty officers had neglected to rouse the men from their hammocks. In *Nelson* the stokers passed through the seamen's messdeck and invited them to a meeting on the forecastle. And in 'the mighty *Hood*', the pride of the Royal Navy, Stoker Hargreaves was on the way to his duty:

> I was stopped from going down the boiler room. I was stopped by a big stoker. He said 'get back' and I said 'No!' and he said 'Won't you? and I looked at him and that was it. The ship had been taken over, otherwise he wouldn't have dared say it.[46]

The crews assembled on decks and cheered from one ship to another, as well as using flashing light signals.

> Everybody cheered, and you was trying to spell out the name of the nearest ship, which for us was *Rodney*. R-O-D-N-E-Y RODNEY! ARE YOU WITH US? And you'd get the answer back. And the next ship down the line would cheer. A tremendous cheer from each ship.

By 9 o'clock, even Admiral Tomkinson had to accept that the situation was serious. He telegraphed the Admiralty, cancelled the exercise and recalled the ships, including *Repulse,* that were outside the harbour.

Different ships reacted differently during the mutiny. In general captains were remote figures, and some of them did not handle the situation well when they addressed the crew. It is probably not true that one of them said, 'We all have to tighten our belts. I myself have just written to my wife telling her to dismiss one of the maids.' But others were little better. When Captain Custance of the cruiser *York* told the men to have their wives take in washing, an angry rating called out, 'You fat bastard! How would you like your old woman to crash out the dirties?'[47]

In many ships it was the commander, the second-in-command who worked daily with the men, who was the most influential figure. In *Nelson* the popular Commander 'Lou' Lake won them over and maintained order:

> 'I don't blame you chaps for what you're doing.' These were his actual first words. Of course everybody cheered. Cheering died down. He said, 'But I'd ask you fellers to remember that there are officers in this fleet who have

had their salary docked every year ... Now those of you who are suffering as a result of this, I want you to write it down on a piece of paper, don't give it to anybody. I shall leave my cabin window open and just drop it through, so I don't know who it is. I want to collect all these together so I've got something to show how much you are suffering.'[48]

As a result, the crew of the *Nelson* remained well-disciplined and maintained naval routine. It was different in her sister ship *Rodney*, where the men treated it as a well-earned holiday:

We spent the rest of the day till dinner time on the upper deck, joining in with the lads, cheering the ships in the Fleet. We came down to dinner, and then in the afternoon volunteers were called for; the baker needed flour and asked for volunteers to go to the stores, and the galley wanted meat, so volunteers were called for to bring up meat from the cold store. They were never short of volunteers.

They were playing the piano, a bit of a sing-song, they played the 'Red Flag' very often. Leaders stood up on the forecastle with some of the crew around, giving morale-boosting speeches. 'Stick together – we don't want this pay cut – if we all stick together they're bound to give in eventually.'[49]

In *Norfolk*, Wincott and his committee organized the work of the ship, but 'links between the officers and men were severed' – though in no case was any violence threatened against the officers. The men were always keen to state their basic loyalty to the crown and the navy, and it was Wincott and George Hill, the commander's writer of *Norfolk*, who drew up what became the main statement of the men's position:

We, the loyal subjects of H M the King, do hereby represent to My Lords Commissioners of the Admiralty our representations to implore them to amend the drastic cuts in pay that have been inflicted upon the lowest paid man of the lower deck. It is evident to all concerned that this cut is the forerunner of tragedy, misery and immorality among the families of the lower deck, and unless we can be guaranteed a written statement from the Admiralty, confirmed by Parliament, stating that our pay will be revised, we are still to remain as one unit, refusing to serve under the new rate of pay.

292

Hill added another sentence of his own to moderate the statement – 'Men are quite willing to accept a cut which they, the men, consider to be fair and just.'[50] Copies were circulated to other ships, and to the press.

The affair at Invergordon differed from other mutinies in that it was quickly reported in the newspapers, for there was no means of censorship in peacetime. At first the coverage was low key, and the men were incensed when they read in the papers the Admiralty statement that 'the reduced rates of pay has led to unrest among a proportion of the lower ratings'.[51] But the world press was soon on to a mutiny that paralysed the main striking force of the Royal Navy, still the greatest and most prestigious force in the world and the guardian of a great empire. Moreover there was the possibility that it might spread elsewhere, and the *New York Times* reported, 'There is fear among Government officials tonight that the trouble will spread to the army and the police forces, which were also subject to very heavy cuts.' The pound fell sharply on the exchanges, and the government was forced to abandon the gold standard, the centrepiece of its economic policy.

The admirals considered the possibility of using force against the men, but that was fraught with danger. The captain of marines of the cruiser *Adventure* tried it on a small scale, but the ratings overheard his preparations and battened themselves down. The more sensitive Captain Dibden realized that 'clearing the decks would have been a bloodthirsty job' and backed down. The Admiralty conceived another plan, to order the ships to sail to their home ports. This divided the men, and there was fierce debate in some ships about whether to obey the order. In *Adventure,* 'They were all discussing this now in the recreation room. The discussion was "shall we or shan't we." The people that lived in Devonport or Plymouth were all for it – they were going home. But the foreigners, like the Welshmen or the Irishmen, or the Scotsmen, who didn't care two hoots, they wasn't concerned.'[52] There were fist-fights in *Norfolk* before it was agreed to sail. The men of *Repulse, York* and *Rodney,* on the other hand, saw the return to the home ports as a definite victory. All the ships raised their anchors, sometimes with the officers doing most of the work, and steamed out of Invergordon on the evening of Wednesday 16th after two days of mutiny. The admiral broke regulations to get the ships to their home ports faster, and all had arrived by Saturday, giving the crews weekend leave. They found an atmosphere of suspicion and espionage in the ports, where the government feared a full-scale rising.

## AFTER INVERGORDON

In November 1931 the Admiralty had an order read out to all ships' companies. It agreed that 'no disciplinary action should be taken' after Invergordon, even if 'this insubordinate behaviour' was 'inexcusable'. It was grateful that 'in the whole of the rest of the Navy, the ships' companies acted, at a very critical time, in accordance with the high traditions of the service'. The affair had 'done grave injury to the prestige of the Navy and the Country', and they were confident that every officer and man would 'do his utmost to restore the proud position the Royal Navy has always held in the eyes of the world'.[53]

But the mutiny had shaken the establishment, and the cuts were indeed revised so that no man had his wages reduced by more than ten per cent. No formal punishments were handed out, and both sides tended to avoid the word 'mutiny', but 24 men, including Len Wincott and Fred Copeman of *Norfolk*, were dismissed from the navy – 'services no longer required' – into the harsh economic climate of the 1930s. Both joined the Communist party. Wincott went to live in the Soviet Union, where eleven years in Stalin's labour camps did not shake his faith. Copeman led the British Battalion of the International Brigades in the Spanish Civil War but eventually renounced Communism.

The mutiny was clearly about money, but it was difficult to ignore a number of underlying factors. Many officers were convinced that the loyalty of the lower deck could not have been lost so easily if outside forces were not at work, and the fact that Wincott and Copeman became Communists seemed to reinforce this. Lieutenant Commander Kenneth Edwards produced a book with chapter heading such as 'The beginnings of outside propaganda', 'The growth of socialist influences' and 'The birth of the Sailors' Soviet' to put forward this theory.[54] But, as with previous mutinies, the actual evidence of conspiracy was very scant and more moderate officers were aware that the navy needed to look more closely at its own practices to prevent a repetition. Captain Francis Pridham advised his fellow officers, 'there is a great danger that many misconceptions may remain in officers' minds if they are not warned that this book, whose author had <u>not</u> had access to full and reliable information, contains many half-truths, and mis-statements. It is certainly a pity it was ever published.'[55]

The Admiralty sent the popular and outspoken Admiral Sir John Kelly to investigate the fundamental causes of the grievances. He was aware of the faults of many of the officers, and listed intoxication, 'failure to attend to the wants and grievances of the men' and 'rowdy parties in Officers' Messes which, if imitated on the lower deck, would not fail to be immediately suppressed, and would probably result in disciplinary action … Supper parties or "Egg and Spoon Parties" on board ship late at night … usually following a dance on shore'. Len Wincott was witness to one kind of 'high jinks':

One night we had a remarkable spectacle of two officers, each wearing nothing more than a tie, swimming to the ship, whilst on the forecastle of the accompanying motorboat two women and some other officers screamed with hysterical laughter and shouted lurid observations to be heard all over Hong Kong harbor. Their innocent evening frolics ended up with one of the women quite drunk, literally riding totally naked up and down the officers' passage way on a bicycle, met at either end with officers with fire hoses. Of course all the mess had to be cleaned up by the seamen.[56]

Officers who behaved in this way would never earn the description 'He's a proper gent, he is' from the lower deck.[57] More formally, Kelly concluded that, 'the sole reasons for the discontent which led to the failure of discipline in the Atlantic Fleet were the size and inequitability of the cuts of pay, which, in some cases, were considered not only to be unfair, but to mean actual starvation for wives and families.'

Complaints about the quality of the petty officers were raised yet again. In the economic climate of the times there was a strong tendency for men to stay in the security of the navy as long as possible, even if they did not love the service or prosper in it, which meant an increase in the unambitious, slightly subversive but highly-skilled 'three-badge AB' – a man who had stayed out of trouble for at least thirteen years of service with good conduct, but had not risen beyond able seaman. One officer remarked on

(a)   The tendency of the senior Able Seamen to hinder and undermine the authority of the young Petty Officers.

(b)   The greater susceptibility of the senior Able Seamen to subversive influences from outside sources through:–

(c)   His tendency to become stale and 'fed-up' with the Service, either through lack of ambition, or failure to have been advanced to a Higher Rating, and the danger of retaining an experienced man in a position of no authority or responsibility.[58]

Admiral Kelly felt that many of these men were a liability, and suggested that

the policy for the future should be to reduce very largely the proportion of senior Able Seamen in the service, and I see no reason why any but a negligible number should be allowed to re-engage for pension. Exceptions might be made in favour of high Non-Substantive ratings on account of the expense of training them, but even these, if worth their salt, should at least have reached the Rating of Leading Seaman.[59]

Another proposal was that sail training should be reintroduced to increase the skill of the men and the authority of the petty officers. This had gone through the stages of approval when Ernle Chatfield became First Sea Lord in 1933, and he was horrified:

It was pleasant to read that [a] number of officers had volunteered to serve in these ships … Most of them had only yachting experience. Were these officers considered competent to take a 1,000 ton barque to sea; denied weather reports, to forecast the weather from the clouds, to judge which tack to be on after sunset, to estimate the probability of squalls, or whether the wind might veer or back, rise or fall, on which safety at night must depend? The men (183 would be required) would necessarily be equally inexperienced. How were soft-footed sailors to climb the ratlines and hold on to the foot-ropes?

I felt the whole proposal was playing with fire; and a disaster, such as happened to training ships even in the old days of sail, and of which we had seen a painful example in the past year, would be only too probable.[60]

But in fact very few reforms were carried out as a direct result of Invergordon, partly because the world situation soon changed.

## THE THREAT OF WAR

The navy was still looking for other ways to make cuts in its personnel budget in the early 1930s, and in November 1931 it allowed some relaxation in the regulations for discharge by purchase in 'specially deserving cases' where documentary evidence could be produced.[61] But the need for a strong navy slowly became more apparent. When Japan invaded Manchuria in 1931, that seemed far away. When Adolf Hitler came to power in Germany early in 1933, pledged to renounce the Versailles Treaty, the Nazis were principally concerned with domestic policy for their first three years. Meanwhile, Benito Mussolini was claiming that the Mediterranean was Italy's *Mare Nostrum*, which implicitly opposed Britain's policy of a strong fleet and several bases there.

The Spanish Civil War broke out in 1936, and it caused direct naval involvement. Britain maintained a policy of 'non-intervention' between the Republicans (backed by the Soviet Union and the International Brigades, including Fred Copeman) and the insurgent Nationalists, who were supported by Fascist Italy and Nazi Germany. The British seamen, according to most of the evidence, inclined towards the Nationalists, but only because they were horrified by 'red' atrocities early in the war. But there is evidence that seamen despised the bombast of Mussolini's regime in Italy:

'Listen, chum. Ever since we let Musso shove us around as though we was a lot of blinkin' pansies, Hitler's been fancying 'is chances. If Nelson was alive e'd 've kicked Mussolini's backside all round this bloody pond. He released the stranger's arm and waved a hand towards the Mediterranean. 'Italian lake, my fanny!'

Although he did so more strongly than most, Dusty was voicing the feelings of most lower deck sailors, who loathed Mussolini long before British civilians were officially authorised to do so. It was a matter of pride, not politics.[62]

The Royal Navy protected British trade around Spain, swept mines and evacuated refugees, which proved the most popular activity. John Whelan was in the destroyer *Fame* on her fourth rescue mission to Santander and was moved by the occasion:

It was the middle of the forenoon watch when they came on board: mostly old people with a sprinkling of young women. Some of the latter were extremely attractive, laughing and singing as the ship moved from the harbour. The old people, however, stared shorewards in silence, choked with a grief that was too profound and bitter for words or tears.

Clear of the harbour we increased speed, and the singing stopped with the first shuddering crash of the sea against the ship's hull. Soon the girls

Spanish refugees entertained by sailors on board a British warship.

were a ghastly sight, yellow and green showing through their powder, giving their lipsticked, mascaraed faces the macabre unreality of circus clowns in a bad dream. They moaned and whined piteously, and were sick where they stood and sat. Fame pushed forcefully through the Bay of Biscay.[63]

And from the big ships, the Coombes brothers in *Hood* witnessed what became a celebrated incident involving a merchant ship trying to break the Nationalist blockade:

What the government was playing at was unknown to us but one thing that stuck out like a sore thumb was that Non Intervention had a lot of meanings depending on which side you were on, as we saw Spud Jones, the blockade runner of Girl Pat fame had been helped to make a run into territorial waters by the *Hood*. He was heading for Bilbao with an old coaster when he was stopped by one of Franco's heavy cruisers who trained their guns on him and threatened to shoot if he went inside the 3 mile limit. We trained all our bigger guns on the cruiser and Spud Jones, with a heavy pall of smoke training him, set off for the port, the cruiser smartly trained her guns fore and aft and set off ...[64]

## THE FLEET AIR ARM

By an agreement of 1924, the Fleet Air Arm, as the naval wing of the RAF was now called, would have a high proportion of naval officer pilots, and all the observers would be naval officers, for the navy rightly distrusted the RAF's approach to navigation. Skilled servicing crews would be provided by the RAF. For a time, therefore, the flying service was almost peripheral to the lower deck of the navy. It would provide seamen, gunners and all the necessary crew of aircraft carriers but would only come into contact with the aircraft themselves as relatively menial members of handling parties on the decks. A carrier had about twenty or thirty ratings assigned to this duty. Well in advance of any planned flying, they would get the aircraft out of the hangars and on to the lifts, under the command of a petty officer and a flight deck officer provided by the RAF. As their aircraft returned, they had the job of grabbing the wingtips of each to bring it under control, which was essential before arrester wires were fitted to the decks. There was no specific non-substantive rating for them and they were drawn from different branches. Stoker Bill Collier thought his work on *Glorious* was 'the best job I ever had in the Navy. Coming up from the bowels of the ship into the sun and fresh air was like a holiday.'[65] Control of the Fleet Air Arm caused intense infighting in Whitehall for more than fifteen years, but on the decks of the carriers relations between the services were reasonably cordial.

In 1925 the navy began to train telegraphists to operate the radio sets in aircraft as well as the Lewis machine-guns. They wore the badge of an aeroplane and were rated as telegraphist air gunners, with two shillings extra per day while on flying duties. From 1935, as demand increased, they were recruited from other branches besides the telegraphists, so they were known as air gunners. At the same time, a new rating of observer's mate was introduced, to make up for the shortage of officers applying for the job.[66]

By 1935 the navy was finding it difficult to persuade enough officers to train as pilots. It wanted to boost the numbers by training selected ratings. The RAF objected to this (though it used sergeant-pilots itself), and the breach between the services widened. Then, in 1937, it was agreed that naval aviation should be completely under the control of the navy, though the RAF would remain responsible for shore-based maritime aircraft. This meant that the navy would have to find large numbers of skilled men to service the aircraft; in the short term it could use personnel seconded from the RAF. The new trade of aircraft artificer was created, and the first three-year course for apprentices began at RAF Halton in 1938. But the policies of the two services soon diverged, and the navy set up its own course at Lympne in Kent. This was clearly not an instant solution, and the navy had to find a more immediate source of slightly less skilled men in the meantime. The first courses for air fitters (airframe) and (engine) were set up at RAF Halton in September 1938. Like artificers, they wore the fore-and-aft rig like artificers and were promoted to leading rate six months after qualifying. At the lowest level were air mechanics, who did an eighteen-week course and continued to wear square rig. Meanwhile the first non-commissioned pilots, selected mainly from the seaman, signal and telegraphist branches, began their year's training in March 1938. When trained they were rated as petty officers.

## THE EXPANSION PROGRAMME

With the growing threat of a European war, the navy began to expand again. From a low point of £90 million in 1933–4, the Naval Estimates rose to £119 million in 1938–9, and personnel rose from 89,863 to 118,167 men. The policy of closing training bases was thrown into reverse: by 1934 the Admiralty was considering the possibility of a new one and debated the advantages of Rosyth in Scotland and Trevol in Cornwall. The latter area was a fertile naval recruiting ground, and men from the home port at Plymouth could fit in easily as instructors. Scotland was a 'doubtful field of recruiting' (though it might also attract boys from the North of England), and service on shore there was not popular, so it would not be easy to persuade instructors to volunteer. On the other hand, there was an excellent site already owned by the navy with good water supply and access to the River Forth.[67] In 1935 a training school was set up in the old detention quarters at Plymouth with a view to transferring it to the barracks as soon as possible. It revived the name of *Impregnable*. A fourth establishment at Rosyth was authorized in 1936, and initially this was to be in the liner *Majestic* (the ex-German *Bismarck*) moored alongside in the dockyard basin and renamed *Caledonia* after the ship that closed in 1906. By 1938 the navy was training 2,100 boys at *Ganges*, 1,500 in *Caledonia*, 850 in *St Vincent* and 200 in *Impregnable,* a total of 4,650. This compared favourably with 1932, when less than a third of that number had been under training in *Ganges* and *St Vincent*.

Short or 'special' service had been used intermittently during the years of peace, and from 1934 the scheme was gradually expanded. According to the First Lord of the Admiralty, it had 'the advantages of enabling the necessary increase in Seaman to be achieved without undue strain on the existing Training Establishments, and of improving the proportion of Long-Service Able Seamen who can become Leading Seamen or Petty Officers. It has the further advantage of increasing our trained Reserves.'[68] In 1936 it was extended to allow boys aged between 16½ and 17½ to enter, filling the gap between boys and adults. By 1938 there were more than 8,000 men and boys undergoing initial training in one form or another, five times the number for 1932.[69]

Unemployment remained very high, despite the rearmament programme, with rates of 16% in 1935 and 14% in 1936. Even the industrial heartlands of the Midlands, the North of England and central Scotland were now producing their share of naval recruits despite the legacy of bitterness from the strikes of the previous decades. Between 1932 and 1935 the share of men from Liverpool, Manchester and Newcastle rose from 21.1% to 24%. The figure for Scotland was even more striking, from 5.4% to 9.9% of the total recruits entered. [70]

A crisis was already beginning to develop about the supply of senior ratings. The large numbers of men who had joined just before or during the First World War were reaching the end of their 22 years' service from 1935 onwards. Those who had joined before the reduction of pay in 1925 were at the end of the first twelve by 1937 and had the option to leave and enter an economy that was beginning to recover from depression. This coincided with the first sustained expansion for nearly twenty years and left a gap among the petty officers and chiefs. New officers joining HMS *Hood* in 1938 were warned, 'Do not expect too much of your Petty Officers. We cannot expect that their standard shall be a very level one; large numbers are being made up and many are of very limited experience.' 'Fast-tracking' promising men was not likely to succeed: 'It is well known that few men on the Lower Deck regard special promotion with any enthusiasm. Trade Unionism and an innate fidelity to their own kind limit their aim to one of general security, i. e. equal opportunity to rise steadily on a pay scale.' Nor was life easy for those promoted, and officers were warned, 'the young Petty Officers and Leading Seamen have a difficult job. They find themselves in charge of men older than themselves (to whom the young seamen defer) and some of these will endeavour to trip them up.'[71] By May 1939 the Portsmouth division roster was almost dry, with very few men eligible for promotion to leading seaman – 141 men were fully qualified on paper but not recommended by their captains; another 165 lacked sea experience; and 20 more had not passed the education test.[72] The situation could only get worse, as a much greater expansion would take place in the war that was now looming.

## THE COMING OF WAR

By 1939 war seemed ever more likely, and the government planned to introduce conscription for the first time in peace. It was mostly intended to boost the army, by taking on young men at the age of eighteen for six months' training followed by a period in the reserves.[73] At first the Admiralty was divided about how to react to this scheme. It might have been possible to restrict it to seafarers of the merchant navy and fishing fleet, or keep the numbers as small as possible and rely on existing resources. The First Lord of the Admiralty, however, decided that, 'we should aim at keeping our reserves on the high side, that we should endeavour to provide a course of training which would appeal to the trainees, and generally that our object should be to make the new reserve as useful and popular as possible.'[74] Men would be enrolled in the newly created Royal Naval Special Reserve. Twelve thousand men were to be called out in August and September 1939. The journalist John Gritten was one of them and arrived at HMS *Drake*:

> Once the 500 were assembled on the parade ground an officer prefaced his welcoming remarks by calling us 'Gentlemen of the Navy' without any manifest irony. Whether this was his own inspiration or a greeting hit upon in the course of lengthy discussion on how to deal with this influx of birds of six months' passage, it was certainly the last time we would be so addressed in the next few years. We were segregated in a different barrack block from the young lads who had recently joined, intending to make the Navy their full-time career. I suspect they were treated rather differently from us.[75]

This was soon overtaken by events.

# CONCLUSION

One does not have to read this book for very long to realize that some complaints about the lower deck are perennial – for example, that petty officers are closer to the lower deck than they are to their officers or are too absorbed in their technical skills to pay any attention to discipline; that seamen are brave and patriotic in action but feckless when left to their own devices. Perhaps the most recurrent of all is that seamen are not what they used to be. What do the stories of Sam Noble, James Woods, 'Clinker Knocker', John Whelan, and many others tell us about naval history and the modern navy? All of them are unusual in that they published books about their experiences, and some of them were better educated than the average sailor. But all of them, in their own way, tend to confirm another eternal truth. Unless something is badly wrong, a sailor is unconditionally loyal to his messmates, his ship and his country. His officers have to earn that loyalty, and they are not always successful.

Naval officers, like those of other services, tend to believe that they alone create the ethos and skills of the rank and file by means of training and discipline. This is rarely as true as they would like to think, for the culture of the lower deck has always tended to promote fearlessness and applaud real, valuable skills. If it were not so, it would be far harder to motivate seamen in action. Inexperienced officers have always relied on petty officers, and that has probably not changed much through the ages. Moreover, it is often the seaman who has to take the initiative in identifying the enemy with eye, or asdic, and in attacking him with gun or guided missile. Of course, there have always been negative aspects to lower deck culture. His constant swearing is a matter of taste, though only a minority would object to it nowadays. His aggressive style of messdeck conversation, once understood, is as legitimate a way of expressing feelings as any other. His tendency to violence against shipmates, other crews or the public, however, is harder to excuse. Other things being equal, the seaman is generous and even sentimental.

The sailor's life is full of paradoxes, and this was never more so than in the late nineteenth and early twentieth centuries. He cultivated a free and easy image but afloat he lived in a tightly controlled society. He was noted for his daring and adventurousness, but unlike most people of the period he had guaranteed employment with a pension at the end. He lived in an all-male society in his ship – unlike the sailors of Nelson's day, he was not allowed to bring women on board, and the Women's Royal Naval Service made only a fleeting appearance during the First World War. Yet he adopted feminine customs on his messdeck, learning to cook and sew in an age when gender differences were more rigid than today. But if homosexuality was present on the messdecks, it was talked and written about less than at any other time, because it was illegal and because of the prudish nature of the age.

Despite his highly controlled environment, the sailor developed his own very strong culture. He continued to develop his own vocabulary of slang, alongside the technical and official terms that were necessary for naval life. He evaded the rigid regulations his officers tried to impose on him, for example in the matter of uniform, and often he prevailed in the end. Nevertheless, he became an increasingly military figure in the later nineteenth century, adopting uniform after his fashion and learning how to salute his officers properly, as well as taking part in many shore expeditions. Culturally he became almost completely different from the merchant seaman for the first time, with the adoption of boy entry, continuous service and uniform.

Unless he was creating trouble on the streets of a dockyard town, the sailor was a popular public figure, more so than at any other time before or later. His face appeared on cigarette packets from 1888. Yet the individual sailor was not tested to the full, and it was not an age in which he enjoyed much initiative. True, he might show individual heroism in shore parties, and the gunlayer was a key figure in the early twentieth century. But when war came in 1914, the shore party was largely extinct and the gunlayer was rapidly being superseded by director firing. A large proportion of the navy was concentrated in the tightly organised Grand Fleet, which saw only one full-scale battle, at Jutland. It is significant that the best-known hero, Jack Cornwell, was awarded the Victoria Cross for the passive role of staying at his post. The sailor was brave, and he faced sudden and often unexpected death – armour plate more than a foot thick was not always enough to keep out enemy shells or torpedoes. But for most of the war his main enemy was boredom. After the war the sailor suffered from governments that cut expenditure with half-baked schemes. To stop this, he had to revive the ancient tradition of mutiny.

Twenty years of peace gave the navy a breathing-space between two great conflicts, but, like British society as a whole, it had failed to carry out social reform. Starved of funds, it had used what money it had to build more ships, unlike the United States Navy, which did much to improve the conditions of its men. The gap between officers and ratings was as wide as ever, and it was still difficult for a rating to get a commission. Nothing had been done to reform the boys' training ships, which were increasingly out of step with society. Long service was valued too highly, and the three-badge AB was not always a positive force. The navy was still failing to attract the growing middle class into its ranks, and it had done little to improve family welfare. All these issues would need attention eventually, but for the moment the navy was about to be locked in a life-or-death struggle in which it would rely more than ever on the loyalty, skill and determination of the lower deck.

# THE GUNNERY BRANCH
## c.1930

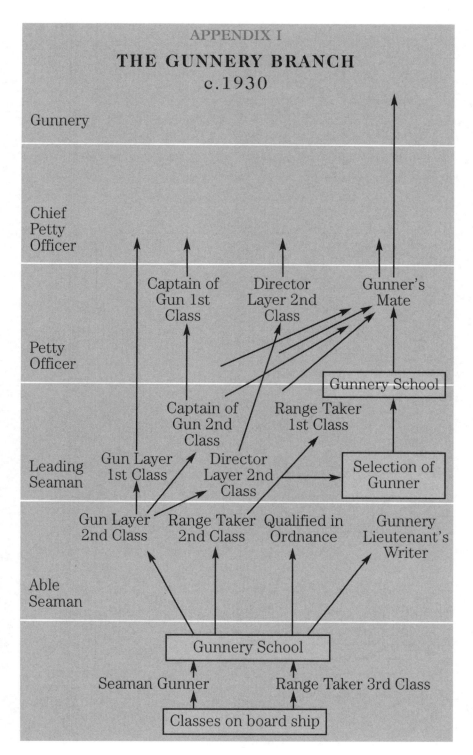

Gunnery

Chief
Petty
Officer

Captain of
Gun 1st
Class

Director
Layer 2nd
Class

Gunner's
Mate

Petty
Officer

Captain of
Gun 2nd
Class

Range Taker
1st Class

Gunnery School

Leading
Seaman

Gun Layer
1st Class

Director
Layer 2nd
Class

Selection of
Gunner

Gun Layer
2nd Class

Range Taker
2nd Class

Qualified in
Ordnance

Gunnery
Lieutenant's
Writer

Able
Seaman

Gunnery School

Seaman Gunner

Range Taker 3rd Class

Classes on board ship

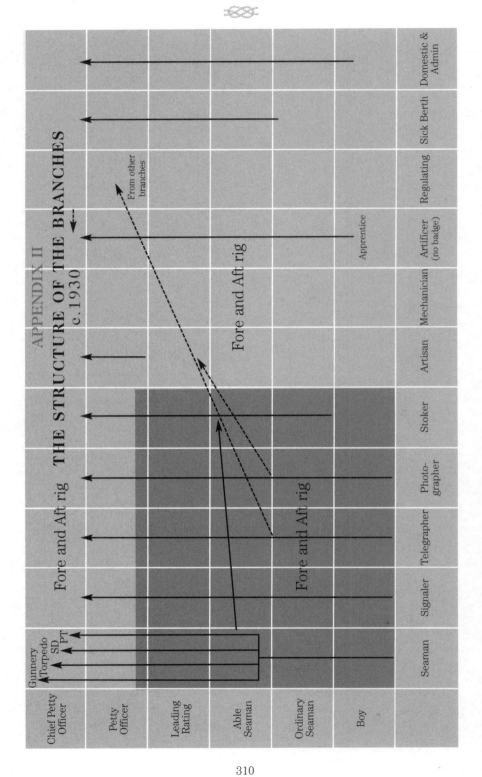

APPENDIX II

THE STRUCTURE OF THE BRANCHES
c.1930

# TRACING NAVAL RATINGS

As always, sailors are among the most interesting of subjects for research. They travelled the world when most people had rarely gone beyond their own towns and villages and had never been abroad, they witnessed some of the great events of history, and came home with a fund of stories and souvenirs. The great majority of those who served in the Royal Navy were, of course, ratings rather than officers.

In many ways the period from 1853 to 1923 is the ideal one for tracing individual naval ratings. With the coming of continuous service in 1853, a central record was kept of the men, so it is no longer necessary to know the names of the ships they served in before starting. After 1923 the position becomes more difficult again, as personnel records have not been released yet and are only accessible to those who can prove they are close relatives of the people concerned. It is always worth remembering that the records were kept for the use of the officials concerned and not for the modern researcher.

An understanding of the administrative system is necessary to get the best out of any records. The vast majority of the records concerned are held in the National Archives at Kew. The golden rule for all research is to look at the printed sources first, in this case the latest edition of Bruno Pappalardo's *Tracing Your Naval Ancestors*, published by the National Archives in 2003. This can be supplemented by Randolph Cock and N. A. M. Rodger's *A Guide to the Naval Records in the National Archives of the UK* (London, 2006) which is mainly about records to be found in non-naval collections. Today it is equally essential to check what is available electronically, which of course changes from year to year, and no guide can be completely definitive in this respect.

Other useful sources for manuscripts are the National Maritime Museum at Greenwich, which has diaries of various sailors and order books and watch and quarter bills for a small number of individual ships. The Royal Naval Museum at Portsmouth (now part of the National Museum of the Royal Navy) has a smaller but more focused collection. Large selections of printed books are available in the naval history section of the Central Library at Portsmouth, and a similar section in the Plymouth Local and Naval History Library. The Imperial War Museum collects the papers and memoirs of individuals in both World Wars, as well as conducting oral history. Even if one's subject is not represented in any of these collections (which is likely in the vast majority of cases), it is worth looking to see if there is anyone who served in the same ship or fleet and might give an indication of the atmosphere on board, the duties carried out and so on. The entries are catalogued in some detail, and it is often possible to trace comments on shipboard life, medicine, action and so on by searching the indexes.

It is also essential to look at any family records that might be available, especially service certificates, letters and so on. A photograph will probably show the subject's ship on his cap tally and his rating at the time, as indicated by substantive and non-substantive badges and good conduct stripes. It might also be possible to find out something about the campaigns he served in as indicated by his medals, though the Naval General Service medal might be awarded for many different campaigns up to 1913.

## SERVICE RECORDS

The service records of ratings are the key to research into any individual, and their use can be divided into four periods. From 1853 to 1872, each continuous service rating's service was recorded in the continuous service engagement books, in ADM 139. Numbers up to 40,000 were issued from 1853 to 1858; then the series started again with 'A' added after the number. From 1859 another series was started with 'B' after the number, so when finding the man's continuous service number it is important to note whether there is an 'A' or 'B' after it. To find the continuous service number, look in Adm 139/1019–1027, which can be downloaded free of charge from the National Archives website. Again the amount of information varies with the period. Up to 1862 it gives the man's name, ledger number and the page number where he can be found. After that (in Adm 139/1021–1026) it gives the name, date of birth and continuous service number of the man, the name of the ship in which he signed the engagement, and any previous ships or former continuous service numbers. The last volume in this series, Adm 139/1027, gives lists of men who entered before 1873, arranged by official number from 40,101 onwards. Having found the official number, it is possible to look up the man's service record in Adm 139/1–1018.

Most of this is unnecessary today, as the individual seamen's records between 1853 and 1923 are available online at moderate cost. Thus it is quite easy to find out that John Early was born in Manchester on 2 February 1852 and baptized in St Wilfrid's Catholic Church three weeks later. He grew up with brown hair and grey eyes with fair complexion and had reached a height of 5 feet 3½ inches when he signed on for ten years' adult service at the Liverpool recruiting station, HMS *Donegal,* on 25 September 1867. His mother Mary countersigned the form, and he attested that he had 'never been an inmate of a reformatory' and was not indentured as an apprentice. The surgeons agreed that he was 'a well grown, stout lad; of perfectly sound and health[y] constitution, free from all physical malformation, and intelligent ...' so he duly became a boy second class in the Royal Navy.[1]

The records are more extensive on a man's shipboard service in later years. Alfred James Meredith was born in Bristol on 16 October 1884 and worked as a labourer until he entered the navy on 11 January 1900. He was 5 feet 2 inches tall but grew four inches by the age of eighteen, with brown hair, grey eyes and a fresh complexion. He trained in HMS *Impregnable* and *Lion* then went to sea in the battleship *Albion.* He was rated ordinary seaman on his birthday in 1902 to begin his twelve years of service, then able seaman a year later. He served in several ships and had two periods of training as a torpedoman in HMS *Defiance,* with occasional periods in HMS *Vivid,* the naval barracks at Devonport. His conduct was always rated as 'VG', and he wore two good conduct badges, but he did not rise to leading seaman before he was invalided out with heart disease in

1914.[2] George Henry Robertson had already served an apprenticeship as a carpenter before he signed on as a shipwright in 1895 at the age of 21. He spent a few months in *Vivid* before joining the armoured cruiser *Orlando* as part of the carpenter's crew. He was rated shipwright in 1900 and leading shipwright three years later, earning two badges before his engagement ended in 1907.[3] Charles William Conway of Kensington, London, was a grocer's assistant until he joined for 'Hostilities Only' in August 1917, not long after his eighteenth birthday. He was attached to HMS *Pembroke*, the Chatham Barracks, until he was sent to the old battleship *Hannibal* in April 1918. He was demobilized in September 1919 with a war gratuity.[4]

The digital project is continually being augmented, and it is likely that many more records will be added in future years, so it is essential to check the National Archives website, which is very accessible. Documents that are not digitized can be ordered in their entirety, though it is far more expensive unless one knows exactly which pages are needed.

## OTHER DOCUMENTS

The term 'muster book' was no longer used to record the men on board an individual ship. Instead, they were recorded in record and establishment books from 1853 to 1879 in Adm 115. The 1090 volumes are arranged by ship's name and date, and include the man's pay book number, whether in continuous service, details of birth, rating, badges, date of entry, name of last ship and discharge to another ship. The continuous service number is also given where applicable. These were succeeded by the ships' ledgers of 1872–84 (Adm 117), which are arranged alphabetically by name of ship. They do not record the place and date of birth but give 'the full pay and allowance of every officer, man and boy on board, and all necessary particulars as to victualling'. Those between 1878 and 1909 were destroyed by enemy action in 1941.

Census returns were collected for individual ships in 1861, 1871, 1881 and 1901. They are filed under the name of the ship. Most of them are available by subscription from ancestry.co.uk. They usually give the man's rank or rating, married status, date of birth and birthplace. Those for 1891 were not gathered separately but can be found under the registration district in which the ship was stationed and do not have a surname index.

Court martial returns are among the more specialized forms of records, though of course only a tiny proportion of ratings are likely to feature in them, either as accused or witnesses. Medical records for selected ships are to be found in the Adm 101 series, in the form of journals kept by surgeons. They, of course, give accounts of seamen who were under treatment, sometimes in considerable detail. For example, in 1925 AB William Totten, a former coal miner, was noticed for his 'peculiarity of manner'. His letter to his MP about conditions in the navy was returned via the Admiralty. He believed his petty officers had a 'down' on him, and he was transferred to work in the sick bay where he 'did his work well and seemed and said he was quite happy' until he refused to obey orders and was absent from his duty.[5]

Often the surgeon made detailed comments on the service of the ship and  the condition of the crew in the 'General Remarks' section. For example, the surgeon of HMS *Colombo* in 1925 tells us that accommodation was good in all the messes, except that the marines had to live in excessive heat over the forward engine room. The crew still had a daily issue of lime juice. Surgeon John Mullan described the voyages of his ship in 1873:

> The early part of January saw HMS *Magpie* on her way from Zanzibar to Bombay to complete stores and make good defects. This necessitated a sojourn there of nearly two months. Towards the end of February we started for the Persian gulf, passed 17 days at Muscat in March, visited Bushire in April and then proceeded to Bahrein [sic] where we remained until summoned by the admiral in May 23, to join the squadron at Zanzibar collected there to force the Sultan into compliance with the proposals made to him by Sir Bartlet Frere for the suppression of slavery ...[6]

He also gives us some detail on the running of the ship. The men did not 'chew [tobacco] nor smoke unreasonably', and ill health was mainly attributable to their sleeping between decks rather than in the open in hot weather. On exercise drills, Mullan noted that, 'It is a very remarkable fact that men are always in the best spirits after a hardship. They get up the fiddlers and music, singing and dancing enliven the forecastle; whereas when they [have] little or nothing to do for some days they are dull and silent at night.' Probably this is why 'in the Persian Gulf the Captain commenced a system of drill which contributed greatly to maintain a *mensem sanam in corpore sane*, judging from the jollity on the forecastle in the evening and the small sick list.' The men were encouraged to bathe when there was no danger from sharks.

But most records after about 1925 are closed for normal inspection.

## THE HISTORY OF THE SHIP

It is not difficult to trace the history of an individual ship while the rating was serving on her. It is necessary to make sure that something described as 'HMS' was a real ship – these are listed in J. J. College's *Ships of the Royal Navy*, which was most recently updated in 2010. Shore bases are to be found in Ben Warlow's *Shore Establishments of the Royal Navy*, the most recent edition being published in 2000. For an actual ship, the first place to look is the microfilm index in the National Maritime Museum, which will give an outline history, including captains, stations and notable actions. The Adm 8 series in the National Archives gives the station of each individual ship on a monthly basis up to 1909. Adm 12 consists of indexes to letters, including those from and about individual ships, largely about administrative matters.

Log books are available for most ships of the period, but they are not easy to use. They give information on the ports visited and men under punishment, but they are mostly filled with navigational data that is little use to the researcher, and they rarely give any indication of the purpose of the voyage. Captain's letters to the Admiralty rarely mention individual ratings, but they often give some detail of the ship's services. They can be found in the Admiralty 1 series from 1/5608 in 1851, listed under the initial letter of the captain's name. In 1870, for example, the paddle sloop *Antelope* sailed around the Greek Islands for a purpose that was almost the reverse of gunboat diplomacy and was described by the consul carried on board:

I called in HMS *Antelope*, at all of the islands of the Sporades for the purpose of informing their inhabitants that there was no truth whatever in the reports transmitted to them from London, that a British fleet with British commissioners on board was about to visit the Sporades for the purpose of redressing certain complaints they had against their own government, a belief which had already brought about some implications. The islands which I was bound to visit were thirteen in number, and considering the advanced season of the year, I trust that you will admit that I have not uselessly detained the Antelope, having performed the voyage in less than three weeks, out of which, bad weather detained us at Patmos during 5 days.[7]

Admiral's letters start from 1/5602 in 1850. They tend to give an overview of the campaign and list the ships that moved together as part of the fleet. Also they often include letters from captains on detached service for forwarding to the Admiralty. They are filed under the station of the admiral concerned, i.e., Mediterranean, Pacific, and so on.

The official histories of the navy in the First World War were written by Sir Julian Corbett and Henry Newbolt, and were published in five volumes from 1920 to 1931. The papers from which they were researched were often taken out of the normal archive series and collected in ADM 137. In addition, there were staff histories created by the Naval Historical Branch for internal use and largely unpublished up until now (though many of the Second World War ones are now being published). An interesting one is the anti-submarine campaign, 1914–17; unfortunately the next war interrupted the work of the historians before they got to the most interesting period, the second U-boat campaign in 1917–18.

Commission books were often compiled by officers and crew and these were printed for individual ships around 1900. Most were published by Gale & Polden in Portsmouth, and often edited by Lionel Yexley. They are particularly common for cruises to exotic places such as the Caribbean and China. They sometimes give the names of individuals, though mostly officers or members of sporting teams. Indeed, sport and tourism take up the majority of the space, and they generally say little about the daily life of the ship – ordinary routine, relations between groups and individuals, and so on. A large selection is available in the National Maritime Museum, the Royal Naval Museum and Portsmouth Central Library.

Victorian seamen often spent a large amount of time in landing parties, and it is not often possible to trace exactly who took part in them. Otherwise, it is usually safe to assume that the subject took a full part in the normal life of the ship, according to his branch and rating, and I hope that the present work will give some idea of what was involved in that, or provide the basis for further research.

Several officers also wrote on what they expected from their ratings and their ideas on how to lead and manage them. These include the works by James, O'Conor and Liardet cited in the Bibliography.

# GLOSSARY

Note that the meaning given is the one in use at the time, which is not necessarily the same as the modern meaning.

*Able Seaman.* A highly skilled seamen with several years of experience

*Admiralty.* The government body that administered the navy, headed by the Board of Admiralty

*Aft.* Towards the stern in a ship; by association, the seamen who lived there

*Artificer.* A highly skilled man, originally in the engine room, rated as chief petty officer when fully qualified

*Artisan.* A skilled man in a trade that can be learned ashore, for example a plumber or painter, usually rated as a petty officer

*'Aristocracy of labour'.* Well-paid craftsmen who could separate themselves from the rest of the working class

*Asdic.* Echo-sounding equipment used to detect submarines underwater

*Badge.* Specifically, a good conduct badge or chevron

*Ballot.* Drawing lots, especially to select men for compulsory service in the militia

*Barbette.* An armoured area covering the magazines and the passages to them

*Battlecruiser.* A type of large warship, a compromise between battleship and heavy cruiser

*Battleship.* The largest class of warship, successor to the ship of the line

*Before the Mast.* The state of being a common seaman rather than an officer

*Berth, Birth.* The position of a ship at anchor, or a man's sleeping accommodation, or the space for a mess between two guns

*Boat.* A small craft usually with open decks; a ship's boat is one that belongs to the ship and can be hoisted on board or towed behind

*Boatswain.* One of the standing officers of a ship, in charge of boats and rigging as well as the organization and discipline of the crew

*Bounty.* Money paid to men on volunteering for the navy

*Bowsprit.* A mast-like structure extending diagonally forward from the bow, used to support square sails below it or triangular sails above

*Brig.* A two-masted vessel, square rigged on both masts

*Broadside.* The guns on one side of a ship, not counting those firing forward or aft, or the shot produced by firing them all at once

*Bulkhead.* A vertical division in a ship, often dividing it into watertight compartments

*Cable.* The very thick rope or chain attached to an anchor

*Calibre.* The size of a piece of ordnance, usually measured by the internal diameter of the barrel, or by the weight of solid iron ball

*Cannon.* A general term for a large gun

*Capstan.* A device for allowing large numbers of men to operate on a particular rope, especially an anchor cable

*Captain of Gun.* A seaman appointed to a particular gun. He was unpaid, though he might also hold the rating of quarter gunner, etc.

*Captain of Mast, etc.* The leader of a group of seaman in a part of the ship, e.g., foremast, forecastle, waist, etc.

*Captain.* A naval rank, equivalent to a colonel in the army. Also a courtesy title for the commanding officer of any ship, especially naval

*Carpenter.* A warrant officer appointed to maintain the hull, masts, etc., of a ship

*Chief petty officer.* The most senior rating

*Chief stoker.* Originally, a highly skilled man in the engine room; from 1885, a man who had risen through the ranks of the stokers

*Civil Service Commission.* A body that examines candidates for the civil service and other government appointments

*Coal Trimmer.* A man who shovels coal from the bunkers towards the stokers

*Coastguard.* In the late nineteenth century, a body of ex-naval men who assisted the Customs and carried out other duties such as rescue

*Commander.* The naval rank below captain; an officer in charge of a small warship, a sloop or smaller, or the second-in-command of a large warship

*Commission* 1. The certificate held by an officer to establish his rank. 2. A period of service for a specific warship

*Common Sailor or Seaman.* This term is often used to distinguish the non-officers; 'common' as 'ordinary' would imply a more specific rating

*Continuous service.* Signing on in the navy for ten or twelve years

*Corporal.* In the navy, an assistant to the master at arms, a ship's policeman

*Coxswain.* A petty officer who steers a ship's boat and leads its crew, often under the charge of a midshipmen; the senior rating in a small warship such as a destroyer or submarine

*Craft union.* A trade union dedicated to protecting the interests of men in a particular trade

*Crew.* As well as the ratings of an individual ship, it can mean a particular group, e.g., carpenter's crew, gunner's crew

*Cruiser.* A large warship, next in size below a battleship

*Crusher.* Lower deck term for a ship's corporal

*Depth-charge.* A charge of explosive that can be set to explode at a certain depth for attacking a submarine

*Destroyer.* Shortened form of 'torpedo boat destroyer'

*Detention.* A form of confinement with rigorous training, which did not carry the stigma of normal imprisonment

*Dhow.* A small Arab sailing craft

*Director.* An erection high up in a ship from which the guns are directed

*Disrated.* Reduced in rate

*Division.* A group of the crew under a lieutenant for disciplinary, health and welfare purposes

*Dreadnought.* A battleship (not necessarily British) that followed the principles of HMS *Dreadnought* of 1906

*Drifter.* A small fishing boat

*Drill ship.* An old, static warship used for training naval reserves

*Engagement.* The period for which a seaman signs on

*ERA.* Engine room artificer

*Fathom.* Six feet, mainly used in the measurement of depth of water

*Flagship.* A ship carrying an admiral and therefore flying his flag

*Fleet Air Arm.* Originally a part of the RAF, the force that operated aircraft from ships; it was fully navalized from 1937, though officially the navy preferred the term 'naval aviation' for a time

*Fleet.* Either the navy as a whole, or a large body of major warships made up of several squadrons

*Flogging round the fleet.* An obsolete punishment in which a man received several hundred lashes, with some being administered opposite each of the ships in the anchorage

*Fore and Aft Rig. 1.* Cutters, schooners, etc., in which the sails run fore and aft in their neutral position. *2.* The dress of the seamen who were not in square rig, with peaked cap and collar and tie.

*Forward.* The fore part of the ship, or moving towards it

*Frock coat.* A formal jacket, usually worn by those in authority

*Frock.* The seaman's main upper garment in the late nineteenth century

*From the shore.* From outside the navy

*Galley.* The cooking facility in a ship

*Gatling.* An early machine-gun

*General Messing.* The system by which the whole crew of a ship is fed centrally

*Good conduct badge.* A chevron awarded to a seaman after a specific period of good conduct

*Grog.* Originally rum diluted with two parts water; later any alcoholic drink issued to the crew

*Guardship.* A static ship, partly manned but ready to be fitted out at short notice

*Gunboat.* A small warship, often built around a single gun

*Gundeck.* A deck bearing guns, especially the lower gundeck in a ship of the line

*Gunlayer.* The rating who aims the gun

*Gunner.* A warrant officer in charge of the maintenance of the guns, carriages, ammunition, etc.

*Gunport.* A square hole in the side of the ship to allow a gun to fire through it, usually closed by a lid when not in use

*Gunroom.* Space aft on the lower deck, used by midshipmen, etc., in a ship of the line, and the equivalent of wardroom for officers in a frigate

*Hard-lying money.* Extra money paid as compensation for living in difficult conditions

*Hawse.* The fore part of a ship's bow, where the anchor cables come out through the hawse holes; also refers to the situation of a ship at anchor, e.g., 'a clear hawse' means the cables are not fouled

*Heel.* The lean of a ship to one side or the other, usually caused by the wind; unlike a list, it is considered normal and is not a subject of concern

*Helmsman.* The man who actually steers the ship, as distinct from the officer of the watch or quartermaster who supervises him

*Home port.* The three home ports to which warships were attached were Chatham, Portsmouth and Plymouth; these became manning divisions late in the nineteenth century

*Hulk.* An old ship that no longer puts to sea, used as a depot ship or for other purposes

*Hydraulic power.* Uses the pressure of water to move cranes, gun turrets, etc.

*Hydrophone.* A listening device to detect submarines underwater, from their own noise

*Immobile.* Wrens who continued to live at home

*Impressment.* The practice of pressing seamen into the Royal Navy

*Instructor.* A highly qualified man, in the gunnery or torpedo branches, for example; he did not necessarily spend a large part of his time in instruction

*Ironclad.* Originally a ship with a wooden hull encased in iron; later a ship built entirely of iron or steel

*Keel.* The straight, square section timber that is the lowest part of the ship and forms its backbone

*Killick.* A small anchor, hence a leading seaman, who had an anchor as his badge

*Landsman.* An unskilled adult who helps with the sailing of the ship; abolished in 1853

*Larboard.* The left-hand side when facing the bows of the ship; also one of the watches in a two-watch system

*Lead.* A lead weight attached to a long line, used to measure the depth of water

*Leading Seaman.* Originally a skilled man, an able seaman; later a man with some authority over the junior members of the crew but with little legal power to back it

*Leading Stoker.* Originally the equivalent of a petty officer; from 1908 the equivalent of a leading seaman

*Leadsman.* A man skilled in casting the lead to find the depth of water

*Leeward.* The side of a ship, etc., away from the wind

*Lieutenant.* The most junior grade of commissioned officer. Originally the captain's deputy, later an officer who took charge of a watch and a division of the ship's company

*Lock.* A device fitted to the rear of a gun to produce a spark to fire it

*Marconi.* An early radio set

*Marine.* A soldier recruited with a view to service at sea

*Master at Arms.* The most senior petty officer in a ship, the chief of the ship's police

*Mate.* A petty officer and assistant to a warrant officer, e.g., master's mate, gunner's mate; from 1912 a man selected from the lower deck for training as a commissioned officer

*Mechanician.* A man trained as a skilled engineer, selected from the stokers

*Merchantman.* A merchant ship

*Mess.* A group of seamen who get together for meals and recreation, and the table at which they eat

*Midshipman.* A trainee officer

*Midships.* The centre part of a ship, either in the fore and aft direction, or athwartships; to put the helm amidships, to have the rudder in the neutral position

*Militia.* Usually an army force, part-time in peacetime but mobilized for home service in war; in 1939, militiamen were six-month conscripts, including some naval men

*Muster Book.* An official document listing the crew of the ship with certain details of age, joining the ship, payment, etc.

*Mutiny.* Deliberate disobedience of orders, either by a small group or a mass movement

*Naval Lords.* Another term for the Sea Lords who were members of the Board of Admiralty

*Navigation Acts.* Acts that largely restricted British trade to British ships, finally repealed in 1848

*Navy List.* A publication that listed all the ships in the fleet, and officers in order of seniority; it often contained information on the latest regulations

*Non-substantive rating.* A seaman's status in a skill such as gunnery, largely independent of his 'substantive' rating as a leading seaman, petty officer, etc.

*Nucleus crew.* A skeleton crew to keep the ship in order and make it ready for service if called upon

*Oilskin.* A waterproof coat

*Ordinary Seaman.* A man with approximately two to seven years at sea, less skilled than an able seaman

*Ordinary.* Ships kept in reserve in the home ports; such ships would be 'laid up in ordinary'

*Penny.* A unit of currency, a twelfth of a shilling and equivalent to 0.4 of a decimal penny

*Pensioner.* Originally a retired or disabled seaman in receipt of a pension from Greenwich Hospital, or living there; later a man who had served time in the navy to qualify for a pension, usually after 22 years' service or at the age of 40

*Petty Officer.* An officer without a commission, the equivalent of a non-commissioned officer in the army; became more of a permanent rank in the latter part of the nineteenth century

*Pilot.* A mariner with local knowledge to guide a ship into or out of a specific port, or through a particular area

*Plain sail.* The normal amount of sail in medium winds, without the studding sails, which were only used in very light winds

*Point.* A division of the compass, one 1/32 of the full circle, or 11¼ degrees

*Poop.* A short deck above the quarterdeck in a ship of the line or other large ship, covering the captain's cabin

*Port division.* After 1893 the port to which each seaman is allocated

*Pound.* The basic unit of British currency, consisting of 20 shillings or 240 pence. Also a measure of weight, especially of the ball fired by a gun, equal to 0.454 kilogrammes

*Predreadnought.* A battleship whose design pre-dated that of HMS *Dreadnought* of 1905–6

*Press Gang.* A group of men under a commissioned officer to press men into the navy, either afloat or ashore

*Press Warrant.* The document, signed by the Lords of the Admiralty, that gives an officer authority to press men into the navy

*Press.* To force seamen to serve in the Royal Navy

*Prize Money.* The money raised by selling a captured enemy merchant ship or warship and dividing the proceeds between officers and crew

*Purser.* The supply officer of a ship

*Puttees.* Strips of cloth wound round soldiers' lower legs, like bandages

*Quarter bill.* The list of the crew and their positions for fighting or battle practice

*Quarter gunner.* A petty officer, part of the gunner's crew under the gunner's mate

*Quarterdeck.* The deck above the upper gundeck, running about half the length at the same level as the forecastle, and used mainly by the officers; hence also the officers of a ship

*Quartermaster.* A petty officer who supervises the helmsmen and carries out other seamanlike tasks

*Quarters.* The men's positions in action, hence 'beat to quarters'

*Rate, Rating.* As applied to a seaman, his rating in a particular level of skill as a seaman; also a man holding a rating, i.e., a member of the lower deck

*Rear.* The rearmost part of a squadron in line of battle, hence rear admiral

*Reefer jacket.* A close-fitting jacket originally worn by midshipmen and later by petty officers and artificers

*Reform Bill.* The bill that, when passed, extended the voting franchise for the United Kingdom Parliament in 1832

*Registry of Seamen.* A failed attempt of 1835 to collect information on seamen so that they could be called up for the navy if required

*Rendezvous.* A public house or other building hired for use as a traditional recruiting station

*Roster.* The system by which seamen were promoted according to their place on a roster in the home port concerned

*Royal Fleet Reserve.* Seamen who had already served with the fleet, who kept up some training and were liable to recall

*Royal Naval Air Service.* The navy's flying arm until it was merged into the Royal Air Force in 1918

*Royal Naval Coast Volunteers.* A body of reserve seamen who could be called on to serve no more than 600 miles from the coast

*Royal Naval Division.* A body of sailors and marines that served in the land battles of the Western Front, 1914–18

*Royal Naval Reserve.* Professional merchant officers and seamen who trained with the Royal Navy and could be called on to serve in wartime

*Royal Naval Volunteer Reserve.* Amateurs who did some part-time training as seamen

*Sea Lords.* Naval officers serving on the Board of Admiralty; the First Sea Lord (not to be confused with the First Lord of the Admiralty who was usually a civilian politician) was the professional head of the navy; the Second Sea Lord was usually the head of naval personnel

*Seaman-gunner.* A seaman with extra training in gunnery either at sea or in one of the gunnery schools

*Sennet.* A form of straw used for hats

*Sepoy.* An Indian native serving as a soldier under British command

*Shilling.* A twentieth of a pound, consisting of twelve pennies

*Ship of the Line.* A ship that was large enough to stand in the line of battle, with at least two complete decks of guns

*Slops.* Clothes issued or sold to the crew by the purser

*Small-arms.* Firearms that could be carried by hand, e.g., pistols, muskets and rifles

*Special entry.* A scheme by which midshipmen began their training at eighteen rather than thirteen

*Special service.* Short service for ratings, usually involving a period with the fleet and with the reserves, adding up to twelve years in total

*Squadron.* A group of warships smaller than a fleet, usually ten or less

*Square Rig. 1.* A rig in which the sails are hung from yards and are at right-angles to the direction of movement of the ship when in their neutral position. *2.* The dress of the ordinary seaman, so called because of its square collar

*Starboard.* The right-hand side of a ship, looking forward; also one of the watches in a two-watch system

*Station Bill.* The list of each man's position during various manoeuvres

*Station.* The position of an individual man for various activities, e.g., in battle, tacking, raising anchor, etc.

*Stern.* The rear part of a ship

*Steward.* A servant in the wardroom or captain's cabin, or the purser's assistant

*Stoker mechanic.* A stoker who had learned something of the use of tools, etc.

*Stoker.* A man employed to shovel coal into a furnace and tend the water in a boiler; later a semi-skilled engineer

*Stone frigate.* A naval shore base

*Stonnicky* (various spellings). A rope used by instructors in training schools to chastise boys

*Substantive rating.* A man's rating as able seamen, leading seaman, petty officer, etc.

*Tender.* A small ship or boat that is attached to a large one

*Three badge AB.* A long-service seaman who has not been promoted beyond able seaman

*Three-Decker.* A ship with three complete decks of guns

*Tons.* In a merchant ship, the measurement of the capacity of a ship; in a warship, the result of a standard calculation that gives an approximate comparison between one ship and another; it is not the same as her actual displacement

*Torpedo boat destroyer.* A vessel designed to fight off enemy torpedo boats and to launch attacks of its own; destroyers eventually took on many other duties

*Torpedo boat.* A boat designed to launch one or more torpedoes

*Torpedo.* A self-propelled weapon designed to strike an enemy ship underwater

*Tower Hill.* The base for the press gang in London

*Transport.* Usually a hired merchant vessel to carry troops and naval and military supplies

*Trawler.* The largest type of fishing boat

*Triple expansion engine.* An engine that uses the power of high-pressure steam in several cylinders in succession, giving much greater efficiency

*Turbine engine.* An engine in which steam turns a series of blades

*Two-Decker.* A warship with at least two complete decks of guns, independent of those mounted in the forecastle, quarterdeck. etc.

*Unrestricted (submarine) warfare.* Sinking of merchant ships without warning

*Van.* The leading part of a squadron, theoretically commanded by a vice admiral; also a room for commissioned and certain warrant officers

*Warrant Officer.* An officer appointed by warrant rather than commission

*Watch Bill.* A list of the men in watches on a particular ship

*Watch.* A period of two or four hours during which particular seamen are on duty; or a group of seamen who form a watch

*Waterline.* The line on a ship's hull at the level of the water when she is afloat; or a horizontal line used to assess the streamlining of the underwater hull

*Weigh.* To raise an anchor

*Wet dock.* A dock used for loading or retaining ships, with the water kept at a constant level

*Whitehead torpedo.* The type of torpedo that became standard in the latter part of the nineteenth century

*Wireless telegraphist.* A radio operator, skilled in Morse code

*Women's Royal Naval Service, WRNS or Wrens.* Women recruited from 1917 for non-seagoing duties with the navy

*Yeoman of signals.* A petty officer in the signals branch

*Yeoman.* Originally a trusted man of junior petty officer status

# NOTES

## Introduction

1   Snow, C. P., *The Masters*,
    1951
2   Jolly, p 273

## 1. The Beginning of Change 1850–56

1   1852 Report, p 9 para 1
2   Manning the Navy. Copies
    of Extracts 'of the Report
    and Appendix of the
    Committee of 1852 on
    Manning the Navy',
    reprinted 1859, p 132
3   Report of the
    Commissioners appointed
    to enquire into the best
    means of Manning the
    Navy, 1859, p 261, para
    4892
4   H. Y. Moffat, *From Ship's
    Boy to Skipper*, Paisley,
    1909, p 25–6
5   1859 Report, p 203, para
    3439
6   1852 Report, p 9 para 13
7   John [Hodgkinson], *A
    Sailor Boy's Logbook,
    from Portsmouth to the
    Peiho*, p 4
8   1852 report, **p 8, 2**
9   Hodgkinson, op cit, pp 9–
    12
10  Ibid, pp 12–7
11  Basil Hall, *Fragments of
    Voyages and Travels*,
    London, 1860, p 230
12  1852 Report, p 61
13  Ibid, p 51, para 13; p 52,
    para 16
14  Ibid, p 130
15  Admiralty Circular No 121,
    14 June 1853, in 1859
    Report, p 433
16  Hodgkinson, op cit, pp

243–4
17  1852 Report, pp 23, para 6
18  Ibid, p 15
19  Ibid, pp 36–7, para 2
20  Ibid, p 37, table
21  1859 Report, pp 401–5
22  Ibid, pp 405–7
23  Circular no 121, op cit, p
    438
24  Admiralty Circular No 167,
    24 November 1854, in
    1859 Report, p 449
25  Circular No 121, 14 June
    1853, in ibid, p 438
26  1859 Report, pp 201–2,
    para 3403
27  Ibid, p 202, paras 3426–7
28  Ibid, p 62, para 804
29  *United Services
    Magazine*, May 1859
30  1859 Report, p 7, para 4
31  Ibid, p 119, para 2088
32  Ibid, para 2099
33  British Library Additional
    Manuscripts 49586, f 95
34  1859 Report, p 262, para
    4927
35  Ibid, p viii, para 16
36  John G. Wells, *Whaley, the
    Story of HMS Excellent*,
    Portsmouth, 1980, p 6
37  1852 Report, p 27, 5
38  Ibid, p 27, para 7
39  National Archives, Adm
    1/6495
40  Admiralty Circular No 67,
    19 June 1857, in 1859
    Report; 1858, Circular No
    167
41  Lord C. E. Paget,
    *Autobiography and
    Journals*, London, 1896,
    pp 78–9
42  Michael Lewis, *The Navy
    in Transition*, London,

1965, p 186
43  Ibid, p 187
44  *The Times*, quoted in Basil
    Greenhill and Ann Giffard,
    *The British Assault on
    Finland, 1854–55*,
    London, 1988, p 113
45  Greenhill and Gifford, op
    cit, p 116
46  Williams, Noël, *Admiral
    Sir Charles Napier*,
    London, 1867, pp 262–3
47  Henry Baynham, *Before
    the Mast*, London, 1972, p
    118
48  Ibid, p 119
49  Victoriacross.org website
50  The Victoria Cross Society
    website: Harry Willey, *The
    True Story of James
    Gorman, VC*

## 2. The Dominance of Steam 1856–60

1   *Hansard*, vol 136, col 1478
2   Sir Howard Douglas, *A
    Treatise on Naval
    Gunnery*, 1860, p vii
3   Ibid, p x
4   Manning the Navy. Copies
    of Extracts 'of the Report
    and Appendix of the
    Committee of 1852 on
    Manning the Navy',
    reprinted 1859, p 15, para
    114
5   Douglas, op cit, p 81
6   Admiralty Circular No 263,
    in National Archives 7/890
7   1858 Report, p 44, para
    550; p 46, para 598
8   Ibid, p 127–8, para 2167
9   P. M. Rippon, *Evolution of
    Engineering in the Royal
    Navy*, vol 1, 1827–1939,

Tunbridge Wells, 1988, p
123

10  Douglas, op cit, p 81 *n*
11  1859 Report, p 17, paras
    184–6
12  Admiralty Circular No 173,
    in 1859 Report, p 450
13  Robert Murray,
    *Rudimentary Treatise on
    Marine Engines*, London,
    1852, p 44
14  Navy Records Society, Vol
    87, *The Naval Brigades
    in the Indian Mutiny*, ed.
    Robotham, 1947, p 149
15  Ibid, pp 282–3
16  Ibid, pp 86, 192
17  Ibid, pp 254–5, 163, 263
18  1859 Report, p 44, para
    528
19  Ibid, p xxvi
20  Ibid, p 69, para 981
21  Anon, *Instructions for the
    Exercise of the Great
    Guns*, London, 1858, pp
    126
22  Ibid, p 6
23  Reproduced in B. Lavery,
    *Empire of the Seas*,
    London, 2009, p 216
24  Amy Miller, *Dressed to Kill*,
    Greenwich, 2007, p 88
25  Sara Stevenson, *Hill and
    Adamson's The
    Fishermen and Women of
    the Firth of Forth*,
    (exhibition) Edinburgh,
    1991, p l 24
26  1859 Report, p 208, paras
    3607–8
27  Ibid, p 260–1, para 4882
28  National Archives, Adm
    1/5685
29  1859 Report, p 290, para
    5673
30  Ibid, p 199, paras 3358–9
31  Ibid, p 466
32  *Parliamentary Papers*,
    Session 3 Feb to 19 April
    1859, Vol VI
33  1859 Report, p 206, para
    3533
34  Navy Records Society, Vol
    118, The Manning of the
    Royal Navy, ed. J. S.
    Bromley, 1974, p 245
35  Ibid, pp 259–60
36  1859 Report, p 250, para
    4611
37  Ibid, p 278

38  Ibid, p 22 para 271
39  Ibid, p xii para 38
40  Navy Records Society, op
    cit, p xlvii
41  1859 Report, p 398
42  Ibid, p 45, para 567
43  Ibid, p xxvi
44  Navy Records Society, op
    cit, p 249, etc.
45  1859 Report, p 44, para
    529; p 45, para 569
46  John [Hodgkinson], *A
    Sailor Boy's Logbook,
    from Portsmouth to the
    Peiho*, p 244
47  Francis Liardet, *Friendly
    Hints to the Young Naval
    Lieutenant*, London, 1858,
    pp 46–7
48  Ibid, p 48–9
49  Hodgkinson, op cit, pp
    129, 202–4
50  National Archives, Adm
    1/5716
51  Navy Records Society, Vol
    147, The Milne Papers, vol
    1, ed. John Beeler, 2004, p
    279
52  National Archives, Adm
    1/5742
53  H. Y. Moffat, *From Ship's
    Boy to Skipper*, Paisley,
    1909, p 26
54  Liardet, op cit, p 10
55  1859 Report, p 69, para
    983
56  Hodgkinson, op cit, p 24
57  Ibid, p 39
58  Ibid, pp 24–5
59  Ibid, p 41
60  Liardet, op cit, p 93
61  Hodgkinson, op cit, p 111
62  Ibid, pp 200–1
63  Ibid, p 38
64  Liardet, op cit, pp 63–4
65  *Hansard*, Vol 152, col 890
66  National Archives, Adm
    1/5714
67  National Archives, Adm
    1/5716
68  *United Services
    Magazine*, June 1859, p
    172
69  Ibid, August 1859, p 596
70  National Archives, Adm
    1/5742
71  *United Services
    Magazine*, Aug 1859, p
    516

**3. The Age of Iron 1860–75**
1   See Lavery, Brian, *Royal
    Tars*, London, 2010, pp
    322–3
2   Report of the Commis-
    sioners appointed to
    enquire into the best means
    of Manning the Navy, 1859,
    p 159, para 2714
3   Manning the Navy. Copies
    of Extracts 'of the Report
    and Appendix of the
    Committee of 1852 on
    Manning the Navy',
    reprinted 1859, p 7, para
    5; p 9, para 6, para 5
4   1859 Report, p 6
5   Phillip Newell, *Greenwich
    Hospital, a Royal
    Foundation*, 1692–1983,
    Greenwich, 1984, p 176
6   1859 Report, p 163, para
    2825
7   National Archives, Adm
    1/6001
8   *Caledonia Journal*, 1938,
    p 24
9   National Archives, Adm
    1/6084
10  Henry Baynham, *Before
    the Mast*, London, 1972, p
    179
11  Ibid, p 180
12  S. Noble, *Sam Noble AB*,
    London, nd, p 21
13  National Archives, Adm
    1/5732
14  Henry D. Capper, *Aft from
    the Hawsehole*, London,
    1927, pp 8–9
15  Noble, op cit, p 126
16  National Archives, Adm
    1/5811
17  Noble, op cit, p 151
18  National Archives, Adm
    1/6742
19  Eugene, L. Rasor, *The
    problem of discipline in
    the mid-19th century
    Royal Navy*, 1972, thesis
    held in the National
    Maritime Museum, THS/5,
    p ???
20  National Archives, Adm
    1/5974
21  *Queen's Regulations and
    Admiralty Instructions*,
    1862, p 119
22  National Archives, Adm
    1/5742

23 National Archives, Adm 1/5833

24 Admiralty, *Rules and Regulations for Naval Prisons*, 1862, *passim*

25 National Archives, Adm 1/5783

26 National Archives, Adm 1/6159

27 National Archives, Adm 1/6061

28 *Queen's Regulations*, 1862, app 42

29 National Archives, Adm 1/5756

30 *Queen's Regulations*, 1862, p 82

31 Ibid,, pp 129–30

32 National Archives, Adm 1/5756

33 National Archives, Adm 1/6921, paras 1572, 1477

34 Ibid, para 1553

35 Ibid, paras 1403, 1420, 1444, p 13

36 Lionel Yexley, *The Inner Life of the Navy*, London, 1908, pp 7, 57–8, 124, 127, 207

37 National Archives, Adm 1/6921, para 1478

38 *Queen's Regulations*, 1862, p 85, para 22

39 National Archives, Adm 1/6388, paras 4698 *ff*

40 Ibid, paras 2762–85

41 *Navy List*, 1869, pp 422–3

42 National Archives, Adm 1/6407

43 National Archives, Adm 1/6388

44 National Archives, Adm 1/6388, para 86

45 National Archives, Adm 1/6921, paras 5673–74

46 Ibid, para 4678

47 National Archives, Adm 1/6157

48 National Archives, Adm 1/6921, p 28

49 National Archives, Adm 1/6921

50 Inner Life, op cit, pp 90–1

51 National Maritime Museum manuscripts, MSS/73/069

52 Royal Naval Museum ms no 93/967

53 Mariners Mirror 1976 pp 287–9

54 Yexley, op cit, p 172

55 Ibid, p 185

56 National Maritime Museum, JOD/71

57 John Winton, *Hurrah for the Life of a Sailor*, London, 1977, p 198

58 Ibid, p 197

59 James Graham Goodenough, *Journal ... With a Memoir, by his Widow*, London, 1876, p 77

60 Baynham, op cit, pp 219–27

61 G. A. Ballard, *The Black Battlefleet*, Lymington, 1980, p 24

62 Ibid, p 65

63 Ibid, p 102

64 Ibid, p 205

65 *The Navy and Army Illustrated*, 1 October, 1897

66 Post Office, *Hampshire Trades Directory*, 1847, p 1164

67 Capper, op cit, pp ix–x

68 Guy Fleming, *Plymouth's Past*, Plymouth, 1980, plate 3.6

69 Bryan Joyce, *The Chatham Scandal*, Rochester, 1999, p 28

70 S. D. Scammell, *Chatham Long Ago and Now*, London, 1903, pp 67–8

**4 Stability and Technology 1875–89**

1 National Archives, Adm 116/29

2 S. Noble, *Sam Noble AB*, London, nd, p 2

3 Lionel Yexley, *The Inner Life of the Navy*, London, 1908, p 3

4 National Archives, Adm 116/29

5 National Archives, Adm 1/6472

6 Navy Records Society, Vol 131, *British Naval Documents 1204–1960*, ed. Hattendorf *et al*, 1993, p 732

7 Naval Estimates in *Brassey's Naval Annual*, 1887, p 531

8 *Caledonia Journal*, p 23

9 National Archives, Adm 116/29

10 National Archives, Adm 1/6084

11 *Caledonia Journal*, p 24

12 Yexley, op cit, p 21

13 National Archives, Adm 1/6047

14 National Archives, Adm 1/6921, p 18

15 National Archives, Adm 1/6921, para 1450

16 National Archives, Adm 1/6061

17 National Archives, Adm 1/6872

18 Henry Baynham, *Before the Mast*, London, 1972, p 172

19 Ibid, p 180

20 Phillis Cunnington and Anne Beck, *Children's Costume in England 1300–1900*, London, 1965

21 National Archives, Adm 116/320

22 National Archives, Adm 1/6921, p 11

23 Ibid, pp 10–11

24 Ibid, p 7

25 Yexley, op cit, p 117

26 Ibid, pp 117–19

27 Baynham, op cit, p 231

28 Yexley, op cit, p 196

29 Arthur Hezlet, *The Electron and Sea Power*, London, 1975, p 12

30 National Archives, Adm 1/6681

31 Ibid

32 National Archives, Adm 189/5

33 Yexley, op cit, p 141

34 National Maritime Museum JOD/71

35 National Archives, Adm 116/23

36 National Archives, Adm 1/6921, p 52

37 Ibid.

38 Ibid, p 31

39 National Archives, Adm 1/6923

40 Admiralty Circular No 64, 27 Sept 1873

41 National Archives, Adm 116/1245

42 National Archives, Adm 1/6921, p 27

43 National Archives, Adm 1/7025

44 National Archives, Adm 1/6921, pp 12, 39

45 Ibid, paras 1543, 1506, 1507

46 National Maritime Museum, JOD/71

47 G. A. Ballard, *The Black Battlefleet*, Lymington, 1980, p 231

48 National Archives, Adm 1/6405

49 Noble, op cit, p 72

50 Ibid, p 75

51 Agnes Weston, *My Life among the Bluejackets*, London, 1909, p 289

52 Ibid, p 109

53 S. D. Scammell, *Chatham Long Ago and Now*, London, 1903

54 Bryan Joyce, *The Chatham Scandal*, Rochester, 1999, pp 227–8

55 Chris Robinson and Jane Slavin, *Union Street*, Plymouth, 2000

56 47 & 48 Victoria, cap 46, Adm 1/6746

**5. The Age of Expansion 1889–1904**

1 Mitchell and P. Deane, *Abstract of British Historical Statistics*, Cambridge, 1962, p 344

2 W. J. Gordon, *A Chat about the Navy*, London, 1891, p 14

3 *Brassey's Naval Annual*, 1896, p 402

4 Henry Baynham, *Men from the Dreadnoughts*, London, 1976, p 74

5 *Brassey's Naval Annual*, 1891, p 372

6 Ibid, 1897, p 394

7 Baynham, op cit, p 63

8 Ibid, pp 60–1

9 National Archives, Adm 116/320

10 Baynham, op cit, p 145

11 Ibid, p 146

12 *Brassey's Naval Annual*, 1903, p 438

13 Quoted in Lionel Yexley, *The Inner Life of the Navy*, London, 1908, p 70

14 John G. Wells, *Whaley, the Story of HMS Excellent*, Portsmouth, 1980, p 48

15 Peter Padfield, *Guns at Sea*, London, 1973, p 214

16 National Archives, Adm 1/7732

17 Yexley, op cit, 158–60

18 National Archives, Adm 1/6084

19 Admiralty, *Manual of Seamanship*, Vol 1, 1908, p 4

20 National Archives, Adm 116/976, app VIII, p 65

21 National Archives, Adm 1/7070

22 National Archives, Adm 1/7594

23 Navy Records Society, Vol 145, *The Maritime Blockade of Germany in the Great War*, ed John D. Grainger, 2006, pp 412–13

24 National Archives, Adm 1/7054

25 National Archives, Adm 1/7208B

26 National Archives, Adm 1/6921, pp 42–4

27 National Archives, Adm 116/938

28 National Archives, Adm 116/1245

29 Statement of the First Lord of the Admiralty, 1894–5, in *Brassey's Naval Annual*, 1894, p 430

30 Admiralty Circular No 6906

31 National Archives, Adm 1/8272

32 Wells, π , *passim*

33 *The Navy and Army Illustrated*, 6 August 1897

34 National Archives, Adm 116/725

35 *Brassey's Naval Annual*, 1891, p 367

36 *Hampshire Telegraph*, 3 October 1903

37 Baynham, op cit, p 98

38 Admiralty Circular No 364, 1889, in Adm 7/941

39 National Archives, Adm 7/941

40 National Archives, Adm 116/1009, p 7

41 W. M. James, *New Battleship Organisations*, Portsmouth, 1916, figs 21, 22

42 D. J. Lyon, *The First Destroyers*, London, 1996,

p 106

43 D. K. Brown, *Warrior to Dreadnought*, London, 1997, p 139

44 Lyon, op cit, p 107

45 Jon Sumida, *In Defence of Naval Supremacy*, London, 1988, p 352

46 National archives, Adm 1/7877

47 National Archives, Adm 1/7594

48 *Brassey's Naval Annual*, 1904, p 418

49 Ibid, 1912, pp 432–3

50 Baynham, op cit, p 54

51 T. T. Jeans, *Naval Brigades in the South African War*, London, 1901, pp 222–4

52 Ibid, p 4

53 Ibid, p 95

54 Ibid, p 75

55 Ibid, p 176

56 Crowe, HMS *Terrible*, London, 1903, pp 108, 360–3

57 P. M. Scott, *Fifty Years in the Royal Navy*, London, 1919, p 133

58 Frederick A. Sharf and Peter Harrington, *China 1900: the Eyewitnesses Speak*, London, 2000, p 112

59 Ibid, pp 45, 108, 119–20, 123

60 Adm 1/8273, *Preliminary Report of the Committee on Commissions of HM Ships*, 1912, p 8

61 *Brassey's Naval Annual*, 1905 pp 455, 456, 458–9

62 Ibid, 1913, p 424

63 Ibid, 1905, pp 460–1

64 National Archives, Adm 1/8272

65 James, op cit, p viii

**6. The Road to War 1904–14**

1 *Brassey's Naval Annual*, 1905, p 404

2 *Hansard*, 16 March 1903, col 866

3 Henry Baynham, *Men from the Dreadnoughts*, London, 1976, p 65

4 Ibid, p 88

5 'Clinker Knocker', *'Aye, Aye, Sir'*, London, 1938,

78

6   Sidney Knock, *Clear Lower Deck*, London, 1932, pp 43–4

7   National Archives, Adm 116/976, para 104

8   Navy Records Society, Vol 106, *The Papers of Admiral Sir John Fisher*, ed. P. K. Kemp, vol 2, 1964, p 121

9   Admiralty, *Stokers Manual*, 1901, revised 1912, p 121

10  National Archives, Adm 116/976

11  National Archives, Adm 1/8273

12  National Archives, Adm 116/3151

13  National Archives, Adm 116/1014

14  NRS Fisher op cit, vol 2, pp 119–22

15  National Archives, Adm 1/8331

16  National Archives, Adm 7/941

17  National Archives, Adm 116/976, evidence, para 127

18  National Archives, Adm 116/976, para 127

19  National Archives, Adm 116/976, p 56

20  National Archives, Adm 116/320

21  Navy Records Society, op cit, vol 2, pp 127–8

22  National Archives, Adm 116/1009

23  Knock, op cit, p 55

24  National Archives, Adm 116/1009

25  National Archives, Adm 1/7940

26  Baynham, op cit, pp 126–7

27  Ibid, pp 144–5

28  National Archives, Adm 116/1014

29  National Archives, Adm 7/904, Circular No 100

30  National Archives, Adm 1/8368/35

31  National Archives, Adm 182/1, no 245

32  Lionel Yexley, *Our Fighting Sea Men*, London, 1911, pp 261–5

33  Ibid, p 263

34  National Archives, Adm 116/1202

35  National Archives, Adm 116/1202

36  Yexley, op cit, p 270*n*

37  Sir William James, *The Sky was Always Blue*, London, 1951, p 77

38  Ibid, p 79

39  'Clinker Knocker', op cit, p 109

40  Ibid, pp 191–3

41  National Archives, Adm 116/1182

42  National Archives, Adm 1/7396

43  Baynham, op cit, p 109

44  National Archives, Adm 1/7396

45  Navy Records Society, Vol 142, *The Submarine Service 1900–1918*, ed. Nicholas Lambert, 2001, p 150

46  Ibid, p 135

47  Julian Thompson, *The Imperial War Museum Book of the War at Sea, 1914–1918*, London, 2005, p 40

48  Anthony Carew, *The Lower Deck of the Royal Navy, 1900–1939*, Manchester, 1981, p 15

49  National Archives, Adm 116/1182

50  Quoted in Carew, op cit, pp 68–9

51  William O'Byrne, *A Naval Biographical Dictionary*, London, 1849, reprinted 1990, vol 1, p 616

52  Thompson, op cit, p 28

53  Lionel Yexley, *The Inner Life of the Navy*, London, 1908, p 288

54  Henry D. Capper, *Aft from the Hawsehole*, London, 1927, p 21

55  Men from the Dreadnoughts, op cit, p 128

56  Naval Review, 1913, p 159

57  'Clinker Knocker', op cit, p 196

58  Baynham, op cit, p 129

59  *Brassey's Naval Annual*, 1913, p 430

60  Carew, op cit, pp 207–10

61  Yexley, op cit, pp 330–9

62  National Archives, Adm 1/7880

63  Carew, op cit, pp 70–1

**7. Stalemate at Sea 1914–16**

1   Imperial War Museum documents, W. A. Jenkins, 03/14/1

2   National Archives, Adm 116/1313

3   'Clinker Knocker', *'Aye, Aye, Sir'*, London, 1938, p 133

4   Imperial War Museum documents, E. F. Locke, 95/23/1

5   'Clinker Knocker', op cit, pp 133–5, 139

6   Ibid, p 142

7   Henry Baynham, *Men from the Dreadnoughts*, London, 1976, p 214

8   Alexander Scrimgeour, *Scrimgeour's Small Scribbling Diary*, London, 2008, p 32

9   Baynham, op cit, pp 215–16

10  Julian Thompson, *The Imperial War Museum Book of the War at Sea, 1914–1918*, London, 2005, p 75

11  Navy Records Society, Vol 128, *The Beatty Papers*, vol 1, ed B. McL. Ranft, 1989, pp 139, 141

12  Imperial War Museum documents, Misc 240, item 3394

13  M. Brown and P. Meehan, *Scapa Flow*, London 1968, p 59

14  Ibid, p 86

15  Ibid, p 26

16  Stephen King-Hall, *My Naval Life*, London, 1952, pp 112, 114

17  Brown and Meehan, op cit, p 70

18  Baynham, op cit, pp 217–18

19  Max Arthur, *Lost Voices of the Royal Navy*, London, 2005, p 67

20  A. Trystram Edwards, *Three Rows of Tape*, London, 1929, pp 49–50

21  Imperial War Museum documents, W. T. C.

Hawkes, 85/25/1

22 Thompson, op cit, pp 110–11

23 Max Arthur, *The True Glory*, London, 1996, p 108

24 Ibid, p 110

25 Ibid, p 113

26 Ibid, p 113

27 Admiralty War Order No 487, 1914

28 National Archives, Adm 182/5, *passim*

29 Navy Records Society, op cit, pp 249, 260–1

30 National Archives, Adm 1/8149/12A

31 Stan Smith, *Sea of Memories*, Tunbridge Wells, 1985, pp 9–13

32 Randolph S. Churchill, ed., *Winston S. Churchill: Companion*, 1969, vol 2, part 3, p 1870

33 Lord Wester Wemyss, *Life and Papers*, London, 1935, p 184

34 National Archives, Adm 1/8395/335

35 National Archives, Adm 182/5, No 536

36 National Archives, Adm 1/8396/349

37 National Archives, Adm 116/1685

38 James Graham, Sixth Duke of Montrose, *My Ditty Box*, London, 1952, pp 168–70

39 National Archives, Adm 1/8149/12A

40 National Archives, Adm 1/8391/280

41 National Archives, Adm 1/8149/12A

42 *Brassey's Naval Annual*, 195, p 135

43 Imperial War Museum documents, F. W. Turpin 91/11/1

44 Imperial War Museum documents, W. Wise 92/13/1

45 A. Trystram Edwards, op cit, p 4

46 National Archives, Adm 1/8149/12A

47 'Clinker Knocker', op cit, pp 123, 111

48 National Archives, Adm

1/6501/229

49 'Clinker Knocker', op cit p 206

50 Ibid,, pp 204–6

51 E. W. Bush, *Gallipoli*, London, 1975, pp 58–60

52 Thompson, op cit, p 230

53 Victoriacross.org website

54 Bush, op cit, pp 98–101

55 Baynham, op cit, p 231

56 Thompson, op cit, pp 251–2

57 Bush, op cit, p 277

58 Imperial War Museum documents, F. W. Turpin 91/11/1

59 Imperial War Museum documents, J. E. Attrill 87/20/1

**8. Jutland and After**

1 Julian Thompson, *The Imperial War Museum Book of the War at Sea, 1914–1918*, London, 2005, pp 300–1

2 Navy Records Society, Vol 153, Miscellany, vol 7, ed. Duffy and Rose, p 401

3 Navy Records Society, Vol 128, *The Beatty Papers*, vol 1., ed. B. McL. Ranft, 1989, pp 356–7

4 Henry Baynham, Men from the Dreadnoughts, London, 1976, p 245

5 Ibid, p 236

6 Ibid, pp 237–8

7 Stan Smith, *Sea of Memories*, Tunbridge Wells, 1985, p 21

8 M. Brown and P. Meehan, *Scapa Flow*, London, 1968, p 101

9 Stan Smith, op cit, pp 24–6

10 Thompson, op cit, pp 201–3

11 'Clinker Knocker', *'Aye, Aye, Sir'*, London, 1938, p 216

12 Imperial War Museum manuscripts, 95/23/1

13 Imperial War Museum manuscripts, 131/106

14 J. P. W. Mallallieu, *Very Ordinary Seaman*, London, 1944, p 51

15 Thompson, op cit, p 33

16 Ibid, p 33

17 Ibid, pp 39–40

18 Navy Records Society, Vol 142, *The Submarine Service 1900–1918*, ed. Nicholas Lambert, 2001, p 269

19 *The Accident to 'K13'*, Address to the Greenock Association of Engineers and Shipbuilders, 4 March 1919

20 Quoted in Don Everitt, *K-Boats*, reprinted Shrewsbury. 1999, p 3

21 Navy Records Society, op cit, 340–1

22 *Brassey's Naval Annual*, 1919, pp 215, 225

23 Henry Allingham, *Kitchener's Last Volunteer*, Edinburgh and London, 2009, p 69

24 National Archives, Adm 1/8378/122

25 National Archives, Air 10/263, *Notes on Rigging for Air Mechanics*, 1918, pp 1, 37–9

26 Allingham, op cit, pp 73–4

27 Ibid, pp 78–9

28 Ibid, pp 79–80

29 F. Snowden Gamble, *The Story of a North Sea Air Station*, London, 1967, p 203

30 Allingham, op cit, pp 81–2

31 C. G. Jefford, *Observers and Navigators*, Shrewsbury, 2001, p 26*n*

32 Bruce Robertson, *Air Aces of the 1914–1918 War*, Letchworth, 1959, p 46

33 Jefford, op cit, p 24

34 Ibid, p 69

35 Patrick Abbot, *The British Airship at War*, Lavenham, 1989, *passim*

36 National Archives, Adm 131/106

37 Max Arthur, *Lost Voices of the Royal Navy*, London, 2005, p 92

38 National Archives, Adm 131/106

39 National Archives, Adm 186/415

40 National Archives, Adm 131/106

41 Arthur, op cit, p 96

42 Gamble, op cit, p 357

43 Ibid, p 357

44 Allingham, op cit, p 113
45 Brassey, *The Naval Annual*, 1919, pp 224–5
46 Ursula Stuart Mason, *The Wrens, 1917–77*, Reading, 1977, pp 43, 44
47 Imperial War Museum manuscripts, 03/14/1
48 Navy Records Society, Vol. 131, *British Naval Documents 1204–1960*, ed. Hattendorf et al., 1993, p 92
49 Anthony Carew, *The Lower Deck of the Royal Navy, 1900–1939*, Manchester, 1981, p 211
50 National Archives, Adm 1/8511/18
51 Ibid
52 Imperial War Museum manuscripts, 91/11/1
53 Imperial War Museum manuscripts, 87/20/1

**9. The Aftermath of War 1919–25**

1 *Brasseys Naval and Shipping Annual*, 1919, pp 14–17
2 National Archives, Adm 156/157
3 Geoffrey Bennett, *Cowan's War*, London 1964, p 202
4 Henry Baynham, *Men from the Dreadnoughts*, London, 1976, p 253
5 Anthony Carew, *The Lower Deck of the Royal Navy*, Manchester, 1981, p 112
6 Baynham, op cit, p 254
7 Ibid, pp 250–1
8 Max Arthur, *The True Glory: The Royal Navy 1914–1939*, London, 1996, pp 165–8
9 National Archives, Adm 116/1728
10 Carew, op cit, p 114
11 Admiralty Fleet Order 3657, 1920
12 Len Wincott, *Invergordon Mutineer*, London, 1974, pp 72–3
13 *Brassey's Naval Annual*, 1920, p 28
14 National Archives, Adm 1/8796/201
15 National Archives, Adm

116/3175
16 'Clinker Knocker', *'Aye, Aye, Sir'*, London, 1938, p 275
17 Ibid, pp 276–7
18 National Archives, Adm 156/157
19 National Archives, Adm 116/2439, 1/8697/70
20 National Archives, Adm 167/95
21 *Brassey's Naval Annual*, 1921, pp 28–29
22 National Archives, Adm 116/2109
23 National Archives, Adm 116/2381
24 National Archives, Adm 116/2109
25 Alan Ereira, *The Invergordon Mutiny*, London, 1981, p 12
26 Ibid, p 11
27 National Archives, Adm 116/2893
28 Imperial War Museum documents, J. F. Clark, 93/26/1
29 National Archives, Adm 156/157
30 Admiralty Fleet Order 2853/23
31 National Archives, Adm 116/2561
32 National Archives, Adm 1/22608
33 National Archives, Adm 116/2109
34 *Brassey's Naval Annual*, 1926, p 12
35 National Archives, Adm 116/3058

**10 Crisis and Revival 1915–39**

1 Adm 116/2456
2 National Archives, Adm 116/2748
3 Max Arthur, *Lost Voices of the Royal Navy*, London, 2005, p 298
4 National Archives, Adm 116/3337
5 Len Wincott, *Invergordon Mutineer*, London, 1974, p 16
6 Fred Copeman, *Reason in Revolt*, London, 1948, p 24
7 John Whelan, *Home is the Sailor*, London, 1957, pp

6–7
8 Ibid, p 7
9 Copeman op cit, p 25
10 Leonard Charles Williams, *Gone a Long Journey*, Havant, 2002, p 27
11 Copeman, op cit, p 25
12 Whelan, op cit, p 8
13 National Archives, Adm ED 12/245
14 Wincott, op cit, p 20
15 Williams, op cit, pp 61–2
16 D. A. Rayner, *Escort*, London, 1955, p 21
17 Imperial War Museum documents, Coombes, 91/7/1
18 C. R. Benstead, *HMS Rodney at Sea*, London, 1932, p 2
19 Whelan, op cit, p 38
20 National Archives, Adm 116/2109
21 Williams, op cit, p 72
22 Copeman, op cit, p 34
23 Whelan, op cit, p 33
24 Wincott, op cit, pp 61–2
25 National Archives, Adm 116/1821
26 BR 224, *Gunnery Pocket Book*, 1932
27 National Archives, Adm 116/2410
28 Whelan, op cit, p 55
29 National Archives, Adm 1/8371/212
30 National Archives, Adm 116/1843a
31 National Archives, Adm 116/1840
32 National Archives, Adm 116/1840
33 National Archives, Adm 1/8747/106
34 Sidney Greenwood, *Stoker Greenwood's Navy*, Tunridge Wells, 1983, pp 28, 31
35 Whelan, op cit, p 55
36 Greenwood, op cit, p 33
37 Ibid, p 34
38 Copeman, op cit, pp 27–8
39 Wincott, op cit, p 153
40 Charles Owen, *No More Heroes*, London, 1975, p 131
41 K. G. B. Dewar, *The Navy from Within*, London, 1939, p 357
42 Admiralty Fleet Order 1922/2697

43  Quoted in Alan Ereira, *The Invergordon Mutiny*, London, 1981, p 61
44  Ibid, pp 68–9
45  National Maritime Museum ELK/2
46  Ereira, op cit, p 86
47  Ibid, p 65
48  Ibid p 97
49  Ibid p 101
50  Ibid, p 103
51  S. W. Roskill, *Naval Policy Between the Wars*, vol II, London, 1976, p 107
52  Ibid, p 128
53  National Archives, Adm 178/111
54  Kenneth Edwards, *The Mutiny at Invergordon*, London, 1937, p xi–xv
55  National Archives, Adm 178/133
56  Wincott, op cit, p 68
57  National Maritime Museum KEL/109
58  National Archives, Adm 116/2893
59  National Archives, Adm 178/111
60  Ernle Chatfield, *It Might Happen Again*, London, 1947, p 57
61  Admiralty Fleet Order 2794/31
62  Whelan, op cit, p 92
63  Ibid, pp 75–6
64  Imperial War Museum documents, Coombes, 91/7/1
65  John Winton, *Carrier Glorious*, London, 1999, p 53
66  G. Jefford, *Observers and Navigators,* Shrewsbury, 2001, pp 124–5
67  National Archives, Adm 116/3337
68  *Brassey's Naval Annual*, 1934, p 198
69  *Brassey's Naval Annual*, 1938, p 139
70  National Archives, Adm 116/3337
71  National Archives, Adm Adm 1/15676
72  National Archives, Adm Adm 1/10930
73  G. Granville Slack and M. M. Wells, *Liability for National Service*, second edition, London, 1943, p 6
74  National Archives, Adm 167/103
75  John Gritten, *Full Circle*, Dunfermline, 2003, p 29

**Tracing Naval Ratings**
1  National Archives, ADM 139/828
2  National Archives, ADM 188/362
3  National Archives, ADM 188/514
4  National Archives, ADM 188/800
5  National Archives, ADM 101/510
6  National Archives, ADM 101/189
7  National Archives, ADM 1/6146

# BIBLIOGRAPHY

### GENERAL HISTORY
Hoppen, K. Theodore, *The Mid-Victorian Generation, 1846–1886*, Oxford, 1998
Mitchell, B. R., and P. Deane, *Abstract of British Historical Statistics*, Cambridge, 1962
Mowat, C. L., *Britain Between the Wars*, Cambridge, 1968
Taylor, A. J. P., *English History, 1914–1945*, Oxford, 1992

### NAVAL HISTORY
Bell, C. M., and Elleman, B. A., *Naval Mutinies of the Twentieth Century*, London, 2003
Campbell, A. B., *Customs and Traditions of the Royal Navy*, 1956
Halpern, Paul G., *A Naval History of World War I*, London, 1994
Lewis, Michael, *The Navy in Transition*, London, 1965
Newell, Phillip, *Greenwich Hospital, a Royal Foundation, 1692–1983*, Greenwich, 1984
Roskill, S, W., *Naval Policy Between the Wars*, vol. II, London, 1976
Sumida, Jon, *In Defence of Naval Supremacy*, London, 1988
Warlow, Ben, *Shore Establishments of the Royal Navy*, Liskeard, 1992
Wells, John G., *Whaley, the Story of HMS* Excellent, Portsmouth, 1980

### CONTEMPORARY WORKS ON THE NAVY
Blake, John, *How Sailors Fight*, London, 1901
Golding, Harry, *The Wonder Book of the Navy*, London, *c*.1928
Gordon, W. J., *A Chat about the Navy*, London, 1891

### LOWER DECK HISTORY
Baynham, Henry, *Before the Mast*, London, 1972
— *Men from the Dreadnoughts*, London, 1976
Carew, Anthony, *The Lower Deck of the Royal Navy, 1900–1939*, Manchester, 1981
Ereira, Alan, *The Invergordon Mutiny*, London, 1981
McKee, Christopher, *Sober Men and True*, Harvard, 2002
Rasor, Eugene, L., *The problem of discipline in the mid-19th century Royal Navy*, 1972; thesis held in National Maritime Museum, THS/5
Winton, John, *Hurrah for the Life of a Sailor*, London, 1977
Yexley, Lionel, *The Inner Life of the Navy*, London, 1908
— *Our Fighting Sea Men*, London, 1911

## OFFICIAL REPORTS

Manning the Navy. Copies of Extracts 'of the Report and Appendix of the Committee of 1852 on Manning the Navy', reprinted 1859
Report of the Commissioners appointed to enquire into the best means of Manning the Navy, 1859

## RATINGS' BIOGRAPHIES

COLLECTED:
Arthur, Max, *Lost Voices of the Royal Navy*, London, 2005

INDIVIDUAL:
Allingham, Henry, *Kitchener's Last Volunteer*, Edinburgh and London, 2009
Capper, Henry D., *Aft from the Hawsehole*, London, 1927
Copeman, Fred, *Reason in Revolt*, London, 1948
Edwards, A. Trystram, *Three Rows of Tape*, London, 1929
'Clinker Knocker', *'Aye, Aye, Sir'*, London, 1938
Crowe, George, *The Commission of HMS Terrible*, London, 1903
Greenwood, Sidney, *Stoker Greenwood's Navy*, Tunbridge Wells, 1983
Gritten, John, *Full Circle*, Dunfermline, 2003
[Hodgkinson], John, *A Sailor Boy's Logbook, from Portsmouth to the Peiho*
Knock, Sidney, *Clear Lower Deck*, London, 1932
Moffat, H. Y., *From Ship's Boy to Skipper*, Paisley, 1909
Noble, S., *Sam Noble AB*, London, nd
Whelan, John, *Home is the Sailor*, London, 1957
Williams, Leonard Charles, *Gone a Long Journey*, Havant, 2002
Wincott, Len, *Invergordon Mutineer*, London, 1974

## OTHER BIOGRAPHIES

Ernle, Chatfield, *It Might Happen Again*, London, 1947
Dewar, K. G. B., *The Navy from Within*, London, 1939
Goodenough, James Graham, *Journal ... With a Memoir, by his Widow*, London, 1876
Hall, Basil, *Fragments of Voyages and Travels*, London, 1860
James, William, *The Sky was Always Blue*, London, 1951
Owen, Charles, *No More Heroes*, London, 1975
Paget, Lord C. E., *Autobiography and Journals*, London, 1896
Scott, P. M., *Fifty Years in the Royal Navy*, London, 1919
Weston, Agnes, *My Life Among the Bluejackets*, London, 1909

## SHIPS

Ballard, G. A., *The Black Battlefleet*, Lymington, 1980
Benstead, C. R., *HMS Rodney at Sea*, London, 1932
Brown, D. K., *Before the Ironclad*, London, 1990
— *Warrior to Dreadnought*, London, 1997
— *Nelson to Vanguard*, London, 2000
College, J. M., *Ships of the Royal Navy*, Newton Abbot, 1969
Gardiner, Robert, ed., *Conway's All the World's Fighting Ships, 1860–1905*, London, 1979
— *Conway's All the World's Fighting Ships, 1906–1921*, London, 1985

— *Conway's All the World's Fighting Ships, 1922–1946,* London, 1980

— and Brown, D. K., eds., *The Eclipse of the Big Gun,* London, 1992

Gardiner, R., and Lambert, J., eds., *Steam, Steel and Shellfire,* London, 1992

Lyon, D. J., *The First Destroyers,* London, 1996

Winton, John, *Carrier Glorious,* London, 1999

## NAVY RECORDS SOCIETY

Vol. 106, *The Papers of Admiral Sir John Fisher,* ed. P. K. Kemp, vol. 2, 1964

Vol. 118, *The Manning of the Royal Navy,* ed. J. S. Bromley, 1974

Vol. 128, *The Beatty Papers,* vol 1., ed. B. McL. Ranft, 1989

Vol. 131, *British Naval Documents 1204–1960,* ed. Hattendorf et al., 1993

Vol. 142, *The Submarine Service 1900–1918,* ed. Nicholas Lambert, 2001

Vol. 145, *The Maritime Blockade of Germany in the Great War,* ed. John D. Grainger, 2006

Vol. 147, *The Milne Papers,* vol. 1, ed. John Beeler, 2004

## TECHNICAL AND SPECIALIST SUBJECTS

Abbot, Patrick, *The British Airship at War,* Lavenham, 1989

Anon, *Instructions for the Exercise of the Great Guns,* London, 1858

Cronin, Dick, *Royal Navy Shipboard Aircraft Development 1912–1931,* Tonbridge, 1990

Cunnington, Phillis, and Anne Beck, *Children's Costume in England 1300–1900,* London, 1965

Douglas, Sir Howard, *A Treatise on Naval Gunnery,* 1860

Gamble, F. Snowden, *The Story of a North Sea Air Station,* London, 1967

Hackman, Willem, *Seek and Strike,* London, 1984

Hezlet, Arthur, *The Electron and Sea Power,* London, 1975

Jefford, G., *Observers and Navigators,* Shrewsbury, 2001

Mason, Ursula Stuart, *The Wrens,* 1917–77, Reading, 1977

Miller, Amy, *Dressed to Kill,* Greenwich, 2007

Murray, Robert, *Rudimentary Treatise on Marine Engines,* London, 1852

Padfield, Peter, *Guns at Sea,* London, 1973

Rippon, P. M., *Evolution of Engineering in the Royal Navy,* vol. 1, 1827–1939, Tunbridge Wells, 1988

Slack, G. Granville, and M. M. Wells, *Liability for National Service,* second edition, London, 1943

Thetford, Owen, *British Naval Aircraft since 1912,* London, 1991

## OPERATIONS

Bennett, Geoffrey, *Cowan's War,* London 1964

— *The Battle of Jutland,* London, 1964

Bridgland, Tony, *Field Gun Jack Versus the Boers,* Barnsley, 1998

Bush, E. W., *Gallipoli,* London, 1975

Greenhill, Basil, and Ann Giffard, *The British Assault on Finland 1854–55,* London, 1988

Hore, Peter, *Seapower Ashore,* London, 2001

Jeans, T. T., *Naval Brigades in the South African War,* London, 1901

Thompson, Julian, *The Imperial War Museum Book of the War at Sea, 1914–1918,* London, 2005

## LOCAL HISTORY

Marinell, Ash, *This Noble Harbour, A History of the Cromarty Firth*, Invergordon, 1991

Brown, M., and P. Meehan, *Scapa Flow*, London, 1968

Elliot, Peter, *The Cross and the Ensign, a Naval History of Malta*, Cambridge, 1908

Fleming, Guy, *Plymouth's Past*, 1980

Hewison, W. S., *This Great Harbour – Scapa Flow*, Stromness, 1985

Joyce, Bryan, *The Chatham Scandal*, Rochester, 1999

Scammell, S. D., *Chatham Long Ago and Now*, London, 1903

Robinson, Chris, and Jane Slavin, *Union Street*, Plymouth, 2000

## OFFICIAL AND OTHER HANDBOOKS

Admiralty, *Gunnery Pocket Book*, 1938

— *Manual for Officers' Stewards*, 1932

— *Manual of Seamanship*, 2 vols., 1908

— *Manual of Seamanship*, 2 vols., 1932

— *The Stokers Manual*, 1912

James, W. M., *New Battleship Organisations*, Portsmouth, 1916

Liardet, Francis, *Friendly Hints to the Young Naval Lieutenant*, London, 1858

National Archives, *Brinestain and Biscuit*, 2006

O'Conor, Rory, *Running a Big Ship*, Portsmouth, 1937

Sturdee, B. V., *Five Minutes to One Bell*, London, c 1916

## ARCHIVES

The most important primary sources for official policy on the lower deck are, of course, in the National Archives at Kew. They are rather weak for the 1850s, when few records were retained, and most of the information from that period comes from the reports of 1852 and 1858–9. After that there is a great wealth of material in the Adm 1 series, in letters to the Admiralty. These are filed under 'from Admiralty', as if that body was writing to itself. They contain papers on many subjects but include most of the reports that form the basis of any study of this period. They are indexed under Adm 12, but the index gives little indication of the value or extent of an individual paper, so it is often just as easy to go straight to the documents. After about 1900 the papers are to be found in files on individual subjects, either in Adm 1 or Adm 116. Much information is also to be found in Admiralty circulars, which are filed under the Adm 7 series.

The Imperial War Museum has many valuable personal accounts of naval service, which are discussed in 'Tracing Naval Ratings' on page 312. The National Maritime Museum at Greenwich has the best collection of maritime books in the country, as well as a few personal papers of ratings, the papers of admirals such as Beatty and Kelly, microfilm copies of many official papers and useful aids such as short histories of individual ships. Ship's plans are to be found in the appropriate department at Woolwich and often give information on the living arrangements on board. Winston Churchill's papers in Churchill College, Cambridge, contain some papers from his period as First Lord of the Admiralty.

## PERIODICALS

*Brassey's Naval Annual*, from 1886; *Brasseys Naval and Shipping Annual* from 1921

*Caledonia Journal, c.*1938, in the National Maritime Museum

*Naval Review*, 1913 to date, written and produced for naval officers

*The Navy and Army Illustrated*, 1890s

*United Services Magazine*

*Mariners Mirror*, 1911 to date

*Navy List*

*Warship*

# INDEX